HESBAN

Series Editors

Lawrence T. Geraty
Øystein Sakala LaBianca

ANDREWS UNIVERSITY PRESS  BERRIEN SPRINGS, MICHIGAN

in cooperation with the

INSTITUTE OF ARCHAEOLOGY
ANDREWS UNIVERSITY

SEDENTARIZATION AND NOMADIZATION:

FOOD SYSTEM CYCLES AT HESBAN AND VICINITY IN TRANSJORDAN

by

Øystein Sakala LaBianca
(Andrews University)

Managing Editor
Lori A. Haynes

Assistant Editors
Lorita E. Hubbard
Leona G. Running

Technical Assistants
James K. Brower
Oscar Canale
Larry W. Coyle
Tung Isaiah Duong
Sandra L. Penley
Eric Shults
Toni Stemple

HESBAN 1

Published with the financial assistance of the
National Endowment for the Humanities
and Andrews University.

A joint publication
       of the
Institute of Archaeology
       and
Andrews University Press
Berrien Springs, MI 49104

96 95 94 93 92 91 90   7 6 5 4 3 2 1

ISBN 0-943872-00-6
Library of Congress catalog card number 89-082543

To the People of the Hashemite Kingdom of Jordan

Table of Contents

Translated by Adnan Hadidi

List of Figures

List of Plates

List of Tables

Preface

Because 1990 is the centenary of the first stratigraphic excavation in Palestine—that of Sir Flinders Petrie at Tell el-Hesi—it is appropriate to recall his admonition when embarking on the publication of archaeological field data:

> The record should be presented finally in an intelligible form. To empty the contents of notebooks on a reader's head is not publishing. A mass of statements which have no point, and do not appear to lead to any conclusion or generalization, cannot be regarded as an efficient publication. The meaning of each fact should be made apparent, and the relative importance of the details should be kept in view, so as to present the conclusions as a picture, in which each touch is in its proper place, and where each point adds to the whole without being disproportionately treated (*Methods and Aims*, pp. 50-51).

This volume has taken to heart that advice as it deals with the results of a decade of fieldwork followed by another decade of analysis having to do with another Levantine site, that of Tell Hesban. This multiperiod site is located southwest of Amman in the zone of transition between the Ammonite hill country (north) and the Madaba Plains (south), and the Jordan Valley (west) and Transjordanian Plateau (east). Though it began humbly as a traditional effort to correlate archaeology and the Bible, it rapidly developed into a genuinely multidisciplinary project that attempted to utilize all the scholarly and scientific resources at its disposal. If there is one thing that the Heshbon Expedition (and its successor, the Madaba Plains Project) has striven for, it is to integrate, to fit together into a coherent whole, its diverse data.

First of all, this was done in the field with each successive season attracting more and varied specialists whose individual contributions yielded a more comprehensive whole. This was followed by prompt publication of preliminary reports by these specialists in one comprehensive volume within a year or two of each digging season.

But integration really got underway with the final publication project. It soon became apparent that to achieve the integration desired, the data had to be standardized in a way that had not yet taken place. Computerization of all field data was the only answer. Fortunately, the expertise for this enormous task lay with my graduate students, especially Larry Mitchel, Jim Brower, and Bjørnar Storfjell, along with my "post-docs" Larry Herr and Sten LaBianca. This effort required many discussions of theory and strategy which eventually bore the fruitage of a body of comparable data. This data became the basis for all subsequent reports.

The Heshbon Expedition next became the first archaeological project, in the context of the American Schools of Oriental Research, at least, to involve a comprehensive array of specialists for the same project at an all-day symposium (1977 Annual Meeting of ASOR, San Francisco). The next year, in 1978, the National Endowment for the Humanities sponsored an authors' symposium at Andrews University in Michigan where more than a score of author specialists from around the world joined in face-to-face dialogue on the data they were attempting to interpret. These author symposia have continued, usually on a smaller scale, each year, often in connection with the annual meeting mentioned above, as well as at the annual meetings of the Middle East Studies Association and the Archaeological Institute of America. These symposia allowed Hesban authors to dialog with the widest possible spectrum of interested scholars.

No single scholar has attempted to summarize insights gained from all this integrative work until this volume, hence the logic of placing it first in the series of final reports on the excavations that took place between 1968 and 1978 at Tell Hesban in Jordan. In fact, its key contribution to the entire publication project is the conceptual framework for integration that it presents, namely the food system concept along with the related concepts of intensification and abatement, sedentarization and nomadization. Though these concepts have grown out of the integrative activities mentioned above, they are primarily the contribution of the author who has drawn together a thesis for this volume from ten lines of information, namely archaeological

xv

stratum descriptions, pottery readings, registered small finds, animal bones, carbonized seeds, archaeological survey findings, ecological survey findings, ethnoarchaeological findings, explorers' accounts, and other secondary sources.

Øystein LaBianca joined the Heshbon Expedition during its second season (1971) and from then on has been, in many ways, the primary goad to integration and synthesis. This has been due not only to his training in anthropology which has equipped him for this study, but to his naturally creative and questioning mind. The debt owed to him by the Heshbon Expedition and its successor, the Madaba Plains Project, is immense. Sir Flinders Petrie would surely approve of his work as that of a kindred spirit. It is a pleasure and an honor, then, to have Professor LaBianca's revised doctoral dissertation serve as the introductory volume, in this centenary year, of the ambitious final publication series for the Heshbon Expedition. For a fuller description of this 14-volume series, see Appendix B in this volume.

It remains to thank all of those visionary, patient, and generous souls who made the excavation, subsequent analysis, and publication happen. The names of most of these individuals will be found in Appendix C in this volume and so will not be repeated here. We must give special credit to the Heshbon Expedition's primary institutional sponsor, however, namely Andrews University in Berrien Springs, Michigan. Through the years it has provided logistical and financial support out of proportion to the means available to a small church-sponsored university. This is due entirely to the good offices of at least the following administrators: Presidents Richard Hammill, Joseph Smoot, and Richard Lesher; Provost Roy Graham; Vice President Arthur Coetzee; Seminary Deans Siegfried H. Horn, Thomas Blincoe, and Gerhard Hasel; College of Arts and Sciences Deans Dwain Ford and Merlene Ogden; Andrews University Press Directors Robert Firth and Delmer Davis; and after I left Andrews University, Institute of Archaeology Directors William Shea, Bjørnar Storfjell, and Randall Younker.

In Jordan, the project has always had the full and enthusiastic support of the Royal Family (particularly H.R.H. Crown Prince Hassan and Prince Raad Zeid Hussein) and the Department of Antiquities (through Director Generals Awni Dajani, Mikhael Jmei'an, Mansour Bataineh, Yacoub Oweis, and Adnan Hadidi). The Nabulsi family,

primary land owners at Hesban, were always eager to facilitate our work as were individuals at the U.S. Embassy (particularly Ambassador Thomas R. Pickering and Richard Undeland from the USIS). While both in Jordan and in the United States, it has always had the endorsement and support of the American Schools of Oriental Research through Presidents G. Ernest Wright, Philip J. King, and James A. Sauer. In addition to a helpful series of ACOR directors and staff, we owe a special debt of gratitude to the recognition and encouragement of William Dever, Chairman of ASOR's Committee on Archaeological Policy.

Obviously, none of this work could have been done without the hospitable and gracious people of the Hashemite Kingdom of Jordan themselves. This volume's attention to food systems has helped to bring the daily lives of these very people and their predecessors into clearer view; it is therefore with gratitude and admiration that the volume is dedicated to them. In this connection, we are pleased to include a summary of the volume's contents in Arabic. This has been prepared with the kind assistance of Dr. Adnan Hadidi, formerly, as mentioned above, Director General of the Department of Antiquities of Jordan, and presently of the Department of Archaeology at the University of Jordan.

Finally, absolutely essential to the realization of this entire publication project has been the unswerving commitment of Lori Haynes, as managing editor, to editing, typesetting, and layout of every page that has made up the text of this volume and the others in this series. Without her keen attention to detail and her patient prodding of authors, editors, and technical staff, none of these volumes would have reached you the reader.

As one associated with the project from the beginning, in the field as director, and stateside as organizer, fund raiser, and editor for thirteen years while I taught at Andrews University, it is my hope that this series, in general, and this introductory volume, in particular, may prove of lasting value as archaeologists, anthropologists, and historians of the ancient Near East move into the second century of stratigraphic excavations in Palestine.

Lawrence T. Geraty
Atlantic Union College
South Lancaster, Massachusetts
July 1, 1990

Foreword

Behind the publication of this book lies a dream inspired by the "new archaeology" revolution. Were it not for this, the work which has gone into this study would probably not have been commenced, especially as five book-length preliminary reports were published about Tell Hesban throughout the '70s. In the present climate of criticism and re-evaluation of this revolution, it seems appropriate to say something about how it influenced fieldwork at Tell Hesban during the early '70s and catalyzed the research and writing of this volume.

How, then, did the "message" of the new archaeology begin to nudge a team whose original mission was to explore the connection between a Transjordanian tell and biblical narratives dealing with the conquest of Canaan by ancient Hebrews? More precisely, how did the quest for new evidence with which to join the debate about the historical date of the biblical Exodus get upstaged by the agenda of the new archaeology? As I see it, it was an unforeseen consequence of the expedition's directors', namely Siegfied H. Horn and Lawrence T. Geraty, openness to experimentation with certain of the scientific fieldwork procedures of this new approach. This, in turn, eventually necessitated deliberate engagement with the theoretical issues of the new archaeology.

Certainly Roger Boraas, the expedition's chief archaeologist during all five seasons of fieldwork, deserves credit, along with others, for insisting that scientific excavation procedures be followed in how the tell itself was dug. Thus, it was he who had the most influence in making sure that a pattern was set in which no shortcuts were taken in reaching the layers crucial to answering the historical questions pertaining to the Bible. To the consternation of many who had come to learn of the biblical periods, he insisted on the Islamic and Greco-Roman layers being unearthed with the same meticulous scientific rigor as the biblically significant ones which lay below. As a result, a multiperiod body of archaeological information spanning three and a half millennia began to accumulate which

had no readily discernable relevance to the original historical question which had focused the team's attention on this site.

To the emphasis on meticulous scientific excavation provided by Boraas, Geraty, director of the 1974 and 1976 seasons of fieldwork, added the new archaeology's emphasis on specialists' participation. In doing so, he had been encouraged by many individuals, including Horn, who had directed the 1968, 1971, and 1973 campaigns. Indeed, even during the first three campaigns, Horn had provided for the participation of a geologist, namely Reuben Bullard, and a person to work with bones full-time, namely Robert Little and, subsequently, myself. Geraty, however, greatly expanded the multidisciplinary scope of the project.

As I, being a team specialist, and other core staff struggled to see how the fieldwork and findings of these various specialists were relevant to the original concern of the project, engagement with the theoretical issues of the new archaeology revolution gradually began. In particular, its message about the importance of a systems perspective for making sense out of the archaeological record was beginning to take hold. An important source of encouragement to me personally during these crucial years was Larry Geraty, whose timely and positive reinforcement of these efforts played a crucial role in helping me to keep going.

One of the consequences of my own engagement with the new archaeology was that as I was becoming aware how of our project could benefit from this new approach, I was also coming to see some of its limitations. For example, neither the various adaptivist perspectives which seemed to reign supreme among the new archaeologists, nor their revamped hypothesis regarding the origins of domestication, urbanization, and civilizations seemed directly applicable to our situation. On the one hand, the long-term cultural changes which had occurred at Tell Hesban seemed somehow to include factors beyond those which the various cultural ecological, and adaptivist approaches assigned decisive roles. On the other hand, since Tell

Hesban began occupation long after animals had been domesticated and cities and civilizations had been invented, the theories which were being advanced with regard to their origins could not readily be brought to the rescue either.

It was this dilemma which gave rise to the quest described in this volume: to formulate a systems perspective by means of which the archaeological record from Tell Hesban could be grasped as a whole. The outcome is the food system perspective which, along with the related concepts of intensification and abatement, sedentarization and nomadization, have enabled the fitting together of the multiperiod, multidisciplinary body of data from Tell Hesban. The extent to which I have succeeded in offering a systemic picture of changes over time at Hesban and vicinity in the light of these concepts is a measure of the influence of the new archaeology revolution on this project.

Ironically, as this volume goes to press, the very foundations of the new archaeology revolution are being shaken by critics, most notably the post-processualists! To begin with, these critics are concerned about the implicit functionalist assumptions which they say are common in most anthropological systems perspectives, for such assumptions have tended to shut the door to anthropological understanding of long-term cultural changes. They are also concerned about reductionistic, even monocausal explanations to which many systemic approaches ultimately lead when it comes to dealing with the causes of culture changes. Finally, they warn against the tendency of systems approaches to lose sight of the individual human being, to forget about the complex, social contexts within which individual human lives are lived.

These are concerns to which I feel I need to reply briefly in this Foreword. To begin with, I believe that the food system perspective, as operationalized here, opens rather than shuts the door to understanding long-term cultural changes. The reason is that it has been intimately linked to the concepts of intensification and abatement, sedentarization and nomadization. Together these concepts have greatly facilitated our efforts to grasp the dynamic, long-term changes which have taken place at Hesban and vicinity. I believe this claim is borne out by the discussion in this volume of long-term changes in Hesban's food system.

To the degree that a deliberate attempt is made in this volume to isolate the causes responsible for changes over time in the structure of Hesban's food system, I believe it is one that avoids the reductionism warned against by the post-processualists. This is not to say that the full complexity of these causes have been adequately dealt with, for this is far from the case, but rather to point out that systemic approaches do not always have to lead to reductionistic explanations. Again, the reader will have to judge for her/himself.

The criticism that systemic approaches tend to lose sight of the complex, social contexts within which individual human lives are lived is a concern which I believe is valid with respect to this particular study. I see no problem, however, with incorporating this concern into future food systems research projects of the sort carried out here. Indeed, I believe that this perspective can shed significant light on the work worlds and social worlds of men and women, of adults and children, and of rich and poor. This is because, more than any other domain of human instrumental or symbolic action, the quest for food is likely to involve both genders, all ages, and all classes of society.

Perhaps to the disappointment of some, this volume does not specifically address the question of the significance of the Heshbon Expedition for understanding the Exodus narratives in the Bible. This question is one which we plan to take up in a separate volume in this series tentatively entitled *Hesban and Biblical History*. Suffice it to say here, however, that in hindsight, we have no regrets about having sought to grasp and interpret the archaeological record of Tell Hesban and vicinity as a whole. We believe that had we recoiled from this challenge, had we not allowed our concerns to widen beyond the original quest for biblical Heshbon, we would perhaps have saved ourselves a lot of work (there are ten more volumes that have still to be published in the 14-volume final report series), but we would have done the archaeology of Jordan a great disservice.

Over the years of research and writing which have preceded the publication of this volume, a large number of individuals have been helpful. To begin with, I got my start at Andrews University thanks to Robert M. Little, the anthropology instructor who placed that first fateful animal bone fragment in my hand while I was still an undergraduate. On the basis of his recommendation, I was invited to join the Heshbon Expedition. Thus I became acquainted with Siegfried Horn, Lawrence

Geraty, and Roger Boraas, all of whom have facilitated, in innumerable ways, my progress along the way toward completion of the present study. Others belonging to the Andrews community who have assisted me with this project include Glenn Bowen, James Brower, Arthur Coetzee, Richard Davidson, Shirley Finneman, Robert Firth, Marc Gutekunst, Larry Herr, Jennifer Higgins, John Lindquist, Joan Milliken, Larry Mitchel, Duane McBride, Merlene Ogden, Paul Perkins, Ronald Russell, Richard Schwarz, Bill Shea, Joseph Smoot, Bjørnar Storfjell, Patsy Tyner, Douglas Waterhouse, and Randy Younker.

It has been my privilege as well to become acquainted with a number of Jordanians whose help I have deeply appreciated. For example, the kind attention to my needs provided by Adnan Hadidi, when he was Director-General of the Department of Antiquities of Jordan, and his staff, helped make possible the successful completion of the ethnoarchaeological fieldwork which I did in connection with this research during 1980-1981. Other Jordanians whose assistance I would like to acknowledge are Diab Abu Assef (taxi-driver), Bishara Aziz (S.D.A. Orphanage, Amman), Ghazi Bisheh (Department of Antiquities), Issa Ghishan and family (our hosts in Madaba), Samir Ghishan (Ministry of Agriculture), Yousef Hamarneh (Natural Resources Authority), Shogi Kerachi (Ministry of Agriculture), Osame B. Nbhan (University of Jordan Library), Helmi Musa (Palestinian farmer), and Mohammad Said (Hesban resident and university student).

Several individuals who have done ethnographic research in Jordan have helped me as well. These include Richard Antoun (University of New York-Binghamton), Ricardo Bocco (University of Rome), Linda Layne (Princeton University), Norman Lewis (England), Alison McQuitty (British Institute in Amman), Seteny Shami (Yarmouk University) and Ken Russell (ACOR).

Crucial to this research have been individuals from the American Center for Oriental Research (ACOR) in Amman and its parent organization, the American Schools of Oriental Research (ASOR). In Amman, James Sauer and David McCreery, ACOR's Directors over the period of this research, facilitated our progress by their advice and support in innumerable ways. Others in the ACOR-ASOR network who have helped and encouraged along the way include Denis Baly

(Kenyon College), Ted Banning (University of Toronto), Patricia Crawford (Boston University), William Dever (University of Arizona), James Flanagan (Case Western Reserve University), Michael and Nethery Fuller (University of Washington-St. Louis), Joseph Green (Oriental Institute, University of Chicago), Robert Gordon (ACOR), David Hopkins (Wesley Theological Seminary), John Holladay (University of Toronto), Gary Rollefson (USC-San Diego), and Scott Rollston (ACOR and University of Chicago).

Another community of scholars with which I have been involved in connection with this research is that of zooarchaeologists, or individuals who specialize in the study of animal bones from archaeological sites. I shall never forget the graciousness of Johannes Lepiksaar of the Museum of Natural History in Gothenburg, and his wife Nina, who received me that summer in 1971, a complete stranger to them, and my suitcase full of bones. They welcomed me into their home as if I had been their son. Other zooarchaeologists with whom I have had the opportunity to work include Joachim Boessneck and Angela von den Driesch of the Institute of Palaeoanatomy, University of Munich. Thanks to their cooperation an authoritative analysis has been completed of the animal bones from Tell Hesban. Their long over-due volume will be published later.

Also very influential in the development of this research was the 1972-1973 school year which I spent at Harvard University as a special student. Although my primary reason for spending a year there was to study zooarchaeology with Richard Meadow and Barbara Lawrence, the class which I took from Ruth Tringham in archaeological method and theory played a pivotal role in introducing me to the "new archaeology."

Many individuals have read and offered comments on specific chapters of this volume. Chapters One and Two, which set forth the theoretical framework of this research, benefitted greatly from the critical comments of Robert Hunt and Judith Zeitlin of Brandeis University, for they persisted in challenging me to articulate clearly how this perspective could help in making sense out of the data from Tell Hesban and vicinity. Others at Brandeis who encouraged me as I was working on the dissertation from which this volume has come include Dan Boneh, Miriam Chernoff, Helen Codere, George Cowgill, David Kaplan, Robert

Manners, Emanuel Marx, Robert Zeitlin, and Charles Ziegler.

Chapter Three, dealing with changes in the project area food system in the recent past, was read and commented upon by Raouf Sa'd Abujaber (Amman).

Richard Meadows (Harvard) and Judith Zeitlin (Brandeis) offered many helpful suggestions on Chapters Four through Seven.

Lawrence Geraty (Atlantic Union College), Larry Herr (Canadian Union College), Siegfried Horn (Andrews), Patrick McGovern (University of Pennsylvania), Bill Shea (Andrews), Lawrence Stager (Harvard), and Randy Younker (Andrews) had valuable comments to offer on Chapter Five which deals with the Iron Age Millennium.

Chapter Six, which deals with the Greco-Roman Millennium, was read and commented upon by Glenn Bowersock (Princeton Institute for Advanced Study), Philip Mayerson (New York University), and Thomas Parker (University of North Carolina).

Chapter Seven, which deals with the Islamic Centuries, was read and commented upon by Ghazi Bisheh (Department of Antiquities), Bert de Vries (ACOR), Fred Donner (University of Chicago), Robert Schick (ACOR) and Safwan Tell (University of Jordan).

While all of them can take credit for having helped to make the chapters they read more persuasive and accurate, none are to be blamed for the weaknesses that still remain in them.

Finally, with the tasks of editing and preparing this volume for the printers I have benefitted greatly from the assistance of Lori Haynes of the Institute of Archaeology at Andrews. Others who have helped with some of these tasks include Oscar Canale, Isaiah Duong, Lorita Hubbard, Sandra Penley, Eric Shultz, and Toni Stemple, all workers at the Institute of Archaeology.

Throughout nearly all of the years that I have pursued this research, my wife, Asta Sakala LaBianca, has believed in me and patiently waited to see this volume completed. For her support, and for the patience of our three sons, Erik, Aren, and Ivan, I shall never quite be able to thank them.

The various sources of financial assistance which have made this undertaking possible must also be mentioned. Specifically, I am indebted to the American Schools of Oriental Research for travel and research grants, including the Albright Fellowship which enabled us to spend six months in Jordan during 1980-1981. Funding for some of this research was also provided by Brandeis University in the form of a Sacchar Fellowship, by the National Endowment for the Humanities in the form of a stipend, and by Andrews University in the form of summers off for research and writing.

Øystein Sakala LaBianca
Institute of Archaeology
Andrews University
March 1990

Chapter One

INTRODUCTION TO THE
FOOD SYSTEM CONCEPT
AND THE HESHBON EXPEDITION

Chapter One

Introduction to the Food System Concept and the Heshbon Expedition

The Problem

The phenomena that this study is concerned with are the archaeological residues encountered in the Hesban region in Transjordan which bear witness to four millennia of changing configurations of human occupation and livelihood. Over the centuries since the dawn of history in this region, the residues of sedentary inhabitants, such as the ruins of farmsteads, villages, and towns, have been laid down in alternating sequence with the residues of nonsedentary, migratory peoples, such as the scattered remains of ancient campsites, storage depots, and burial sites. Sedentary occupation, therefore, has been a transient phenomenon in this region rather than an unabated development.

Simply stated, the primary purpose of this investigation is to reconstruct and analyze various diachronic and synchronic dimensions of these long-term changes in human occupation and livelihood going back to about 1500 B.C. or to the Late Bronze Age. What were the extent and nature of the sedentary occupation at various points in time? What were the extent and nature of the migratory populations at various points in time? To what extent were their modes of livelihood intermeshed with those of the sedentary populations? What were the forces which account for the growth and decline of sedentary occupation? Who were the peoples involved in the successive dramas which have taken place on this stage?

As will be explained in greater detail further on, a three-tiered scaffolding had to be set up in order to come to grips with these questions. Given the diverse and fragmentary nature of the archaeological information upon which our quest for answers had to rely, some way had to be found whereby these many different lines of evidence could be integrated and pieced together into a dynamic whole. The first tier of this scaffolding, therefore, is the concept of the *food system* which is introduced in the present chapter. This concept, along with the related concepts of food system *intensification* and *abatement*, enabled the sort of integrative fitting together of the disparate pieces of archaeological and historical information upon which we had to rely in the present study.

The second tier of this scaffolding involved ascertaining, in a general way, certain salient characteristics of Middle Eastern food systems. To this end, a review was undertaken of pertinent secondary sources which resulted in the delineation of a number of environmental and sociocultural factors which appear to have played a role in determining food system conditions throughout past millennia in this region. A crucial assumption as far as the present investigation is concerned was confirmed as a result of this review. This was the assumption that in the Middle East, temporal changes in food systems involving intensification and abatement have traditionally manifested themselves in the processes of *sedentarization* and *nomadization*.

The third tier which had to be erected in order to provide an adequate foundation for answering the aforementioned questions involved ascertaining the salient features of the present-day food system of central Transjordan. To this end, an investigation was carried out of the changes in food system conditions which have occurred over the past century and a half in the vicinity of Hesban. The insights gained from this undertaking proved to be absolutely essential in guiding the process of reconstructing and fitting together the disparate lines of archaeological information on which this study of long-term changes in the food system of this locality have had to rely. The project area with which this research has been concerned, along with the types of residues of ancient patterns of occupation and livelihood upon which this analysis is based, are briefly described toward the end of the present chapter and are discussed in greater detail in chapters three and four.

The Roots of the Food System Concept

As an explicit theoretical construct within the field of anthropology, the concept of the food system, as defined further on, represents a convergence of many formerly disparate approaches to the subject of food within anthropology. Indeed, a review of anthropological approaches to matters related to the quest for food inescapably leads to encounters with some of the most prominent theoretical orientations within French, British, and American anthropology. A brief review of some of the most influential of these is offered next in order to acknowledge the diversity of perspectives and approaches which, in a general way, constitute the theoretical underpinnings of the food system concept.

British and French Approaches

In the second chapter of his book, *Cooking, Cuisine and Class*, Jack Goody (1982) offers a succinct overview of British and French approaches to the anthropological study of food. His review is divided into five sections: precursors, functional approaches, structural approaches, cultural approaches, and historical approaches ("changing worlds"). Between these approaches Goody attempts merely to "make a conjunction," believing that "shifts of the kind from functionalism to structural functionalism can hardly be said to reorganize a body of theory and data in the way that Kuhn (1962) suggested for the natural sciences" (1982: 39).

Among the precursors Goody names Sir James Frazer (1890), Ernest Crawley (1927), and W. Robertson Smith (1889). These 19th-century investigators were interested largely in practices dealing with religious aspects of the process of consumption such as taboos, sacrifice, and communion (Goody 1982: 10). These authors were searching for a rational explanation for these ritual and supernatural aspects of consumption in the light of evolutionary theory. In isolating "certain

widespread features of human behavior," these investigators "set the terms" of subsequent inquiry of cultural aspects of food and eating.

The contribution of the functionalist approach was to focus attention on the social function of food (Goody 1982: 13). Radcliffe-Brown (1922: 227), for example, noted that among the Andaman Islanders, the "social value" of food was inculcated in the young by means of initiation ceremonies involving prohibitions of relished foods from which they were later released. Such observations led him to conclude that the getting of food is "by far the most important social activity" among these islanders, because it is around food that "the social sentiments are most frequently called into action" (*cf.* Firth 1964).

In the works of other functionalists such as Malinowski (1935), and especially that of Audrey Richards (1939), the quest for food is seen as a principal agent in fostering cooperation and as the "chief determinant of human relationships, initially within the family, but later in wider social groups, the village, age-grade, or political states" (Richards 1939: ix; Goody 1982: 15). In Richards' pivotal study, *Land, Labour and Diet in Northern Rhodesia* (1939), for example, patterns of consumption are placed "firmly and more specifically in the context of the whole process of productive activity" (Goody 1982: 16). Thus her book includes treatment of such topics as the organization of labor in relation to notions of time, techniques for producing and preparing food, and the "cultural determinants of food and feeding" (Richards 1939: 405).

While Goody (1982: 17) acknowledges the larger purpose behind Levi-Strauss' structuralist approach to food preparation and eating manners, namely "to look at the structure of human thought itself, even of the human mind," he is critical of Levi-Strauss' tendency

> to spirit away the more concrete aspects of human life, even food, sex and sacrifice, by locating their interpretation only at the deeper level, which is largely a matter of privileging the symbolic at the expense of the more immediately communicable dimensions of social action (Goody 1982: 25).

Furthermore, in emphasizing binary oppositions in the tradition of structural linguistics, such as that between the "raw" and the "cooked," Levi-Strauss' analysis not only abstracts arbitrarily the symbolic aspects of culinary activity from other related activities, such as the "relation between consumption, production and the social economic order," it simultaneously "defines biological factors out of the explanation of social action" (Goody 1982: 25).

This tendency to neglect or even deny the role of biological and material factors is also evident in the cultural approaches of Mary Douglas (1966, 1971; Douglas and Isherwood 1979) and, especially, Marshall Sahlins (1976). Douglas' investigations focus, for example, primarily on such cultural aspects of food getting as the symbolic meaning of the meal. Her approach "is strongly reminiscent of Radcliffe-Brown's attempt to extract meaning by examining similar *ritual* acts in dissimilar social contexts" (Goody 1982: 31). Rather than contributing a broadly unifying framework to the anthropological analysis of food, therefore, both structuralist and cultural approaches have tended to restrict the analytic field within which behaviors related to the quest for food are examined.

Goody's review of British and French social anthropologists' approaches to the study of food concludes by noting that the dimension that all of them "play down is time—and to a lesser degree space" (1982: 33). The focus on the meaning of activities related to the preparation and consumption of food in specific cultural contexts "has tended to push aside studies of long-term change" (1982: 37). This limited focus has also tended to obscure the fact that changes in patterns of consumption, particularly in complex societies, occur as the result, not only of local changes in production and distribution, but of changes in world-wide patterns of production and exchange. Thus, "the meaning of sugar for the Lancashire mill worker is not determined in the metropolitan heartland alone. It is embedded in a world economy" (Goody 1982: 37).

Goody's own work, *Cooking, Cuisine and Class* (1982), is offered as a beginning remedy to this situation. He suggests a framework which emphasizes the "conjunction" between the various aspects of the quest for food isolated for study by investigators such as those whom he reviews. Specifically, he proposes to examine the "four main areas" of the "process of providing and transforming food," namely that of "growing, allocating, cooking and eating, which represent the phases of production, distribution, preparation and consumption" (1982: 37). These four phases, in turn, have their respective loci in which they occur, namely farm, granary/market, kitchen, and table. To these he adds an

often forgotten fifth phase, that of clearing up or disposal, which occurs in the scullery.

In attempting to account for why a differentiated haute cuisine has not emerged in Africa, as it has in other parts of the world, Goody adopts the sort of comparative historical approach pioneered by Marc Bloch, Lucien Febvre, and Ferdinand Braudel, members of the so-called French Annals School of social history. Goody (1982: 38), by trying

> to link the nature of different cuisines to the ways in which food is produced, and to relate the system of agricultural production to the subcultures and social strata that are differentiated by their styles of life,

makes apparent the conjunctions which link the various phases of the quest for food into one complex unity. His work, therefore, represents the current state of the art of European and British contributions toward the development of a broadly integrative concept for thinking about food.

American Approaches

In contrast to the emphasis on symbolic interpretations of food preparation and consumption which has occupied British and French anthropologists for more than half a century, American anthropologists have tended to focus their research on economic and ecological aspects of food production and distribution. As Hatch (1973) has noted, the path followed by American anthropologists was one which Franz Boas, the father of American anthropology, had implicitly approved, despite his anti-theoretical and anti-materialistic biases.

While rejecting environmentalism, Boas espoused possibilism, the idea that the historical development of cultures is restricted by the limits set by environmental conditions. Wrote Boas (1940: 265-266):

> The lack of vegetable products in the Arctic, the absence of stone in extended parts of South America, the dearth of water in the desert, to mention only a few outstanding facts, limit the activities of man in definite ways.

Furthermore, in the Boasian view, the implicit assumption was made that

> when environmental factors pass beyond the thresholds established by man's material needs—when the climate is too cold for human survival, or when the local flora and fauna do not provide adequate sustenance for a given population

density–cultural adjustments must take place (Hatch 1973: 232).

It was during the 1930s and 1940s, as American anthropologists sought to rise above the theoretical limitations of Boasian historical particularism, that a solid foundation was laid for the growth of economic, subsistence, and ecological studies in American anthropology (Hatch 1973). This foundation was provided, in particular, by Leslie White (1943, 1947) and Julian Steward (1936, 1937, 1955). While there were many potential directions for American anthropologists to follow, including those pursued by British and French anthropologists, the nascent materialism in Boas' writings–i.e. his implicit assumption that those institutions which were rooted in the physical world through the life-sustaining needs of the members of society were somehow immune to the vicissitudes of history–appears to have been a deciding factor in accounting for the widespread acceptance of White's, and in particular, Steward's theoretical proposals among American anthropologists (Hatch 1973).

Julian Steward's (1955) cultural ecology went beyond the possibilism of Boas in that it involved an attempt to classify cultures according to the salient features of their technoeconomic core. In particular, his work aimed at elucidating how different ways of exploiting the environment, or how different types of subsistence activities and economic arrangements, created similar or differing institutions. For example, societies which came to depend on irrigation could, according to Steward, be expected to possess certain parallel features when it came to how they were organized sociopolitically. Whereas such irrigation civilizations were thought of as representing a certain cultural type with respect to their socioeconomic cores, those societies which depended on hunting-gathering were thought of as representing another, and so on.

While it might be concluded from these examples that Steward's views had their basis in some kind of doctrinal materialist position (cf. Harris 1968), this appears not to have been the case. Indeed, as Bennett (1976: 214) has noted, a balance or interplay between "the role of the environment as a facilitating factor–permitting choice–and its role as a limiting factor–constraining choice," is implicit in much of Steward's work. While he "felt that the core caused other features of culture," he also believed that "these same features shaped the core at some past time" (Bennett 1976: 214). It is

this implicit notion of systemic feedback which has made Steward's work foundational for much of the subsequent work being carried out in the name of cultural ecology by anthropologists over the past three decades.

One of the earliest American anthropologists to be concerned with such systemic feedback relationships was Clifford Geertz (1963). In his book, *Agricultural Involution*, for example, he advances an explicitly ecosystemic approach which emphasizes the interdependence of the physical environment and human institutions. By means of their food production activities, humans either disrupt balanced environments, help to maintain them, or even help to create new balanced environments (cf. Bennett 1976: 166; Hardesty 1977: 14-15).

An even more explicit attempt by an anthropologist to operationalize the idea of ecosystemic feedback is Rappaport's (1967) analysis of warfare and territorial expansion among the Tsembaga Maring peoples of New Guinea. In this study it is asserted that ecological control is ultimately maintained by means of a cycle of rituals. Ritual, writes Rappaport (1967: 28-29),

> helps to maintain an undergraded environment, limits fighting to frequencies which do not endanger the existence of the regional population, adjusts man-land ratios, facilitates trade, distributes local surpluses of pigs throughout the regional population in the form of pork, and assures people of high-quality protein when they are most in need of it.

Although both of these approaches involve the use of the ecosystem concept, they differ considerably in how they use it. For example, for Geertz the concept is at best a kind of metaphor which has been invoked in order to emphasize the complex interdependence which exists between human activities and their environments. In Rappaport's case, by contrast, the concept has been operationalized with far greater attention to analogies between human and biological systems. In other words, to a much greater degree than Geertz, Rappaport seems to assume that human social systems are analogous to biological systems, and hence, that they are stable, self-regulating systems which function at a level of organization largely beyond human awareness and control (cf. Bennett 1976: 182-193).

It is when it comes to reckoning with the role of human control and self-conscious awareness that adaptivist anthropology represents an advance over formulations such as these. To the concern with systemic feedback between environments and human institutions manifest in Geertz's and Rappaport's cultural ecosystemicism, adaptivist anthropologists have added the dimension of human decision-making and choice. Rather than assuming that human social systems operate at a level of organization largely beyond human awareness, adaptivists acknowledge the fact that humans make explicit choices, some of which may be good and some of which may be bad in terms of their consequences for the maintenance of a balanced environment (*cf.* Bennett 1976: 166).

An example of a society in which interrelationship between environment and humans is clearly mediated by a conscious effort to resist using the most efficient means of exploiting the physical environment and to limit consumption are the Amish communities of North America (Stoltzfus 1973). Another would be the Hutterites, whose sectarian beliefs form the foundation for numerous self-imposed controls over their use of the physical environment (*cf.* Hostetler and Huntington 1980).

To a significant degree, the adaptive dynamics approach represents a synthesis of the concerns of American cultural ecologists and British social anthropologists. This is true, at least, to the extent that adaptivist anthropologists have added to the traditional preoccupation of cultural ecologists with settlement patterns and subsistence techniques numerous dimensions relating to the social environments within which human choices are made, many of which have been the traditional preoccupations of British social anthropologists. Specifically, their focus on adaptive behavioral processes has led them to incorporate in their analysis of systemic feedback loops dimensions such as ideology, attitudes, politics, and social reciprocities (Newman 1970; Thompson 1972; Stini 1975; Vayda and McCay 1975; Yellen and Lee 1976; Haas and Harrison 1977; Hardesty 1977; Thomas, Winterhalder, and McRae 1979; Bartlett 1980; Rappaport 1968, 1971, 1977; Ortner 1983).

This trend is clearly apparent in the rapidly developing field of nutritional anthropology, a specialization into which a number of adaptivist anthropologists have recently been moving (Haas and Harrison 1977; Benham 1981; Messer 1984). For example, a recent review of anthropological perspectives on food, completed by Messer (1984), details the ways in which anthropologists, in their

search for factors that govern food choices, have been concerned with a wide range of biological and cultural factors influencing adaptive behavioral processes in humans. These include how sensory judgments and preferences such as taste, smell, texture, and color affect selection of foods; how foods are classified by various cultures for purposes of symbolic representation of their edible and health environments; how foods and their manner of preparation have been utilized to express social relations; how foods and foodways function in the maintenance of ethnic identity; how economic factors limit the extent to which people can satisfy their taste choices; and how styles of cooking and eating are shaped by traditional nutritional wisdom.

Perhaps one of the most significant developments which have taken place as a result of Julian Steward's work is that his cultural ecological perspective set in motion a gradual rapprochement of the concerns of American ethnographers with those of prehistoric archaeologists. Particularly catalytic, in this regard, was the Stewardian focus on subsistence-settlement systems. This focus stimulated increasing coordination between investigators studying the present and those studying the past in so far as both were interested in fundamentally the same problem, namely in arriving at typologies of technoeconomic cores. Furthermore, as the orientation of American ethnographers shifted in the direction of adaptive behavioral processes, so did the orientation of prehistorians. This was in particular the case with the new archaeologists (*cf.* Binford 1962, 1964, 1965, 1983; Adams 1965, 1966, 1978; Adams and Nissen 1972; Flannery 1967, 1972, 1976; Flannery *et al.* 1967; Deetz 1967, 1972; Trigger 1968, 1971; Angel 1972; Leone 1972; Redman 1973, 1976, 1978; Sterud, Straus, and Abramovitz 1980; Sabloff 1981; Orme 1981; Butzer 1982). A good example is Flannery's (1972) attempt to identify specific behavioral mechanisms whereby cultural evolution proceeded in Mesopotamia. In this study what is emphasized is the adaptivist's concern with cultural processes rather than the Stewardian focus on cultural types.

Approaches From Other Disciplines

Because of the centrality of food to the human experience, it is hard to think of an academic discipline which, in one way or another, has not had something to offer in the way of a perspective on either its production, distribution, preparation, consumption, or disposal. Any attempt, therefore, to identify tentacles of the food system concept emerging from other disciplines can at best be a highly selective undertaking. Offered here, therefore, is a brief overview of selected perspectives from disciplines other than anthropology which have been influential in the present formulation of the food system concept.

A wide range of disciplinary perspectives dealing with how people and other living organisms utilize natural resources for the purpose of food procurement depend upon concepts developed in biological ecology. Examples would include such concepts as ecosystem, food chain, and food web (Boughey 1973; Cox and Atkins 1979; Clapham 1981). The ecosystem concept, for example, emphasizes the complex unity which ultimately accounts for the systematic interactions between various abiotic and biotic components of terrestrial ecosystems. These interactions are the result of solar energy flowing through biogeochemical cycles, including the carbon, nitrogen, phosphorus, and hydrologic cycles.

The idea of the food chain is one approach to describing the flow of energy through living organisms. Green plants are the primary producers upon whose tissue various kinds of herbivores, collectively called primary consumers, feed. Carnivores, in turn, consume the animal tissue of herbivores and other carnivores, thus establishing various trophic or feeding relationships in the system. These trophic levels, it is suggested, constitute links in a chain of feeding relationships (Boughey 1973: 121-131).

A more complex model of the pathways for energy flow through living organisms is the food web concept. While the food chain concept may be adequate to describe ecosystems with very few species, the food web concept has been advanced as a means to think about feeding relationships involving a number of species on each trophic level—some species eating both herbivores and other carnivores and others being omnivorous (Boughey 1973: 132-141).

Mention needs also to be made of the detritus food chain, whereby "dead plant and animal matter accumulates and is gradually broken down by detritus feeding animals and decomposers" (Cox and Atkins 1979: 42). Of the total energy which flows through an entire ecosystem, about half of it flows through the former, and about half of it flows through the latter of these two chains.

Agroecosystems, or ecosystems managed by human beings, differ from natural ecosystems in that they concentrate energy flow through a particular group of plant and animal species desirable to the human managers. Smith and Hill (1975) have shown that natural and agricultural ecosystems form a continuum. To distinguish natural from manipulated ecosystems, these investigators used species diversity and the intensity of human intervention (management) as the basis for constructing the continuum shown in fig. 1.1, which illustrates the relationship between natural versus managed ecosystems. While the scheme portrayed in this figure applies in a general way to agroecosystems, it should perhaps be noted that there are some types of managed ecosystems which it does not reckon with. An example would be the highly diverse, little managed, mixed-crop swidden systems found in the tropics.

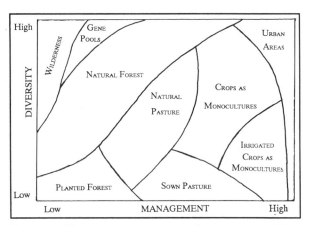

Fig. 1.1   Natural versus managed ecosystems (after Smith and Hill 1975)

The principle of energy flow through ecosystems has been applied by Duckham and Masefield (1971: 9) to the analysis of the relative efficiency of various farming food chains. They distinguish four chains: tillage crops—people (A); tillage crops—livestock—people (B); grassland—ruminants—people (C); tillage crops and grassland—ruminants—people (D). Overall Chain A is the most efficient, followed by Chains C and D. The least efficient is Chain B (Duckham and Masefield 1971: 9).

The arena in which the concerns of anthropologists most clearly overlap with those of investigators from disciplines such as economics and agricultural science involves attempts to identify the factors which cooperate in determining the form and intensity of a particular agroeconomic or farming system. Duckham and Masefield (1971: 97), for example, have identified nine independent variables or locating factors which cooperate in determining the form and intensity of actual farm enterprises. These include climate, landform, operational facilities (such as farm buildings, farm tools and equipment), agrarian, social, and economic infrastructures, price conditions, market conditions, and feasible species. A similarly broad scheme of factors has been suggested by Gilbert, Norman, and Winch (1980: 6-10), although their "farming systems approach" emphasizes to a greater degree the pivotal role of the farmer as a rational, maximizing strategist at the center of farming system interactions.

The significance of these ecological and agronomic perspectives for the present investigation is twofold. To begin with, they remind us of the fact that anthropological perspectives represent only a portion of the range of possible perspectives from which to begin an analysis such as is being pursued here. More important, perhaps, the fact that each of the approaches referred to above is founded upon the same fundamental assumption that most of the anthropological perspectives mentioned in the preceding sections are founded upon—namely the assumption that the quest for food by all forms of life involves systemic interactions of various kinds—is suggestive of the paradigmatic status of the systems perspective when it comes to investigations of the topic of food procurement by natural and social scientists.

Definitions, Scope, and Parameters of the Food System

Toward a Definition of the Food System Concept

Despite the vast amount of research and writing which has been done on the general topic of food, no widely-held consensus appears to exist regarding which term should be used in referring to the range of phenomena having to do with the quest for food. Depending on the interests and disciplinary orientations of different investigators, a wide range of terms are used to delimit the field of study. For example, in the literature cited above,

> a food system is a complex unity consisting of all of the purposive, patterned (institutionalized), and interconnected activities carried out by a group of individuals in order to procure, process, distribute, prepare or consume food, and dispose of food remains

terms like subsistence activities, agriculture, farming systems, agroecosystems, cultural ecology, foodways, cuisine, and diet have all been used to delimit different and overlapping aspects of the field of study which deals with the quest for food.

Conspicuously infrequent in the literature reviewed thus far by this investigator are references to the notion of the food system. Significantly, however, where the term is encountered, it is in studies where the complex unity which exists between production, processing, distribution, preparation, and consumption is either explicitly or implicitly acknowledged (Steinhart and Steinhart 1975; Bodley 1976: 95; Pimentel and Pimentel 1979: 8; Pelto and Pelto 1983; Messer 1984: 205; Goode, Theophano, and Curtis 1985; Khare and Rao 1986). In common as well in these analyses, therefore, is a systems perspective emphasizing the common purpose and interconnectedness of the many diverse parts of the system.

Even harder to come by than the term itself, are explicit definitions of the food system concept. As noted, the authors cited in the previous paragraph all assume a common implicit meaning of the term. Central to this investigation, however, has been the following definition: *a food system is a complex unity consisting of all of the purposive, patterned (institutionalized), and interconnected activities carried out by a group of individuals in order to procure, process, distribute, prepare or consume food, and dispose of food remains.* This formulation incorporates into an earlier definition proposed by Dyson-Hudson and Dyson-Hudson (1970: 92-123) the five phases of the process of providing food discussed by Goody (1982: 37) and others (Pimentel and Pimentel 1979; Messer 1984).

There are a number of reasons why the food system concept is preferable to the many other terms which have been utilized in delimiting the broad field of study having to do with people's quest for food. Particularly when the meanings of

The food system concept . . .

- includes all institutions and processes providing and transforming foodstuffs;

- focuses on daily activities;

- examines interaction between populations and their environments;

- avoids the sedentary bias;

- focuses on hunting and gathering;

- focuses on feeding relationships; and

- provides a framework using varied lines of research.

terms such as those mentioned above are kept in mind do their limitations become apparent. On the one hand, to most people the terms agriculture and farming suggest enterprises having to do with the production of food on cultivated fields by sedentary farmers. Thus they tend to exclude from consideration the livelihoods of nomadic pastoralists, hunters, and gatherers. On the other hand, terms like foodways, cuisine, and diet bring to mind practices having to do with the preparation and consumption of food. The term subsistence has become very closely associated with subsistence farmers—people who produce food primarily for their own consumption rather than for the market. Thus, in various ways, these alternatives fail to focus analysis on the complex unity or, as Goody (1982) would say, the conjunctions between the various parts of the whole system, including (as mentioned above) the production, processing, distribution, preparation, consumption, and disposal of food.

The Scope of the Food System Concept

The suitability of the food system concept as a vehicle for integrating different aspects of the quest for food needs to be further explained. Among the reasons for why the concept has been employed in this investigation are the following.

First, as already noted, what recommends the food system concept over any other concept now in use for systematically thinking about people's life-maintenance activities is that it brings together conceptually all of the diverse institutions and processes involved in providing and transforming foodstuffs into nutriment for human beings. Examples of such institutions and processes would be those which regulate how access to land and water resources is allocated, how labor is organized, how the means of production are controlled, how food products are distributed, how land and labor disputes are settled, which animals and foods are clean and which are unclean, how and what plants and animals are produced (landuse conditions), how and where people settle or migrate on the land (settlement conditions), how and what facilities, tools and equipment are produced or imported (operational conditions), how and what foods are eaten (dietary conditions), and so on.

Second, the food system concept provides a framework for analyzing the majority of the daily activities carried out by the majority of the people living in the world today and having lived in earlier times. Representing a fundamental concern of all human populations throughout all historical and prehistorical times, this concept offers an important linkage point between the present and the past. This continuity with the past is particularly in evidence when it comes to traditions governing how food is prepared and eaten, for, as Braudel (1967) has noted, such traditions belong among history's deepest and slowest moving undercurrents. A food system perspective, therefore, provides a theoretical rationale for the study of present-day practices as a means to gain insights for use in interpreting the historical and archaeological record.

Third, a food system perspective directs attention, on the one hand, to the interaction between populations and their local environments or habitats insofar as the latter are exploited for the purposes of gathering or producing food. On the other hand, it also directs attention to interactions between populations located in outlying geographical regions insofar as these are involved in competition over land resources and exchanges of food surpluses, technological know-how, and production resources.

Fourth, as noted earlier, the food system concept avoids the sedentary bias which often results from conceptualizations based on the term agriculture. To most Europeans and North Americans, except perhaps those who are experts in the field of agricultural development, agriculture implies village-based farming. In the case of the Middle East, however, village-based farming is only part of the whole picture, the other part being the food production activities of nomadic pastoralists, such as the Bedouins of the Arabian desert. In the food system notion we have a concept which lends itself equally well to the analysis of the food production activities of both village farmers and Bedouins. Furthermore, as defined above, this concept reaches beyond what happens in the fields to the infrastructure which lies behind what happens there—*i.e.* to all those political, economic, social, religious, educational, and technological arrangements which are supportive of particular strategies of procuring food.

Fifth, the food system concept, in contrast to the food production concept, makes important consideration also of hunting and gathering as components of the food system. In the case of both villagers and nomadic pastoralists, hunting and gathering have traditionally played a much greater role than has hitherto generally been acknowledged. Furthermore, hunting and gathering were, for the greater part of prehistory, the primary means of obtaining food.

Sixth, the food system concept—in so far as it is rooted in ecological theory—provides a framework for consideration of the larger web of feeding relationships in which humans play just one part. For example, the wildlife encountered in villages and towns, as well as in archaeological excavations in the form of animal remains, can in most cases be readily accounted for when the feeding habits of the particular species represented are taken into consideration. In the case of animals such as dogs, cats, certain species of rodents and reptiles, their entire lives are lived out within the confines of human settlement. When they die, therefore, their remains represent a natural *thanatocoenosis*—an assemblage of organisms or their parts existing together in death as they had in life. Other species, in turn, are civilization followers—animals that belong either to cereal or grassland ecosystems, or scavengers feeding upon the organic wastes which abound in and around human settlements. Thus the large majority of animals found in association with human populations can be accounted for

when considered in the light of the theoretical underpinnings of the food system concept.

Seventh, the food system concept has proven itself capable of dismantling the arbitrary disciplinary walls which have tended to frustrate attempts at fitting together the results of such varied lines of research as epigraphy, ethnoarchaeology, ethnohistory, stratigraphy, ceramic analysis, metallurgy, faunal analysis, palaeobotany, numismatics, surface survey, geology, hydrology, pedology, human osteology, taphonomy, and so on. To the extent that each of these and other lines of research illuminate individual food system components, or their dynamic interrelationships, they may be drawn upon. Indeed, once explicitly promoted as a vehicle for integrating various lines of research, various members of a multidisciplinary team of investigators are in a much better position to offer suggestions as to the pertinence of their results to understanding the food system. Without such a concept, their results will, understandably, be offered as contributions to a particular discipline rather than as contributions toward the solution of problems requiring multidisciplinary cooperation.

Parameters of the Food System Concept

In order to operationalize research concerned with food systems it is necessary to analytically isolate parameters of such systems which are capable of being investigated empirically. While the idea of the food system itself is a theoretical abstraction—a sort of heuristic device for thinking about the complex unity of parts and processes of which food systems are made up—it is possible to draw up a large number of observable phenomena which would constitute empirical referents of food systems. Many of these have been suggested in the foregoing section.

For reasons which will be stated in greater detail in Chapter Four, this study focuses attention on five broad parameters of the food system: *environmental conditions, settlement conditions, landuse conditions, operational conditions,* and *dietary conditions.* The primary reason for the selection of these five parameters is that all five are more or less directly traceable archaeologically. Changes in environmental conditions, for example, can be traced through analysis of plant and animal remains; changes in settlement conditions can be traced through analysis of the locations of ruins of villages, campsites, and buildings; changes in land-use conditions can be traced through analysis of plant and animal remains, terrace walls, and soil conditions; changes in operational conditions can be traced through analysis of the remains of agricultural tools and facilities such as storage installations, water management installations, food processing installations, and so on; and finally, dietary conditions can be traced through analysis of plant and animal remains as well as human skeletal remains. The sufficiency of these five parameters with respect to providing data about food systems is indicated by the fact that together they embrace the majority of the locating factors which, according to Duckham and Masefield (1971: 97), cooperate in determining the form and intensity of particular food systems (see above, p. 9).

While the reconstruction of past states of the food system is made possible by focusing on these five parameters, reconstruction of recent changes in the state of such systems is equally possible and, indeed, desirable. It is desirable because through investigation of present conditions of the food system, as apprehended by means of these five parameters, what many of the important parts of the system are and how they interact with one another

can be observed directly. Because such present-day conditions are so much more readily available to empirical investigation than are past conditions of the food system, they offer archaeologists and historians a base line against which to compare and contrast conditions in the past. This investigation illustrates this point by including a chapter (Three) which provides base line information about a food system (that of present-day Hesban and vicinity) which then is also traced archaeologically.

The Dynamics of Food System Transitions

Towards a Balanced Conception of Food System Changes

Food systems are dynamic, constantly changing configurations, oscillating in their degree of intensity. This point can be illustrated with reference to the above-mentioned five parameters of the food system. Thus, environmental conditions may oscillate between states involving high species diversity and the dominance of wild plants and animals and states involving low species diversity and the dominance of cultivated plants and domesticated animals (*cf.* Smith and Hill 1975). Settlement conditions may oscillate between states involving migratory groups of hunter-gatherers occupying the land in low population densities and states involving urban-dominated settled farmers occupying the land in high population densities (*cf.* Murdock 1965). Landuse conditions may oscillate between states involving low amounts of human intervention and management, such as in the case of hunting and gathering, and states involving high amounts of human intervention and management, such as in the case of farmers engaged in specialized production of selected field crops, tree crops, or animals (*cf.* Boserup 1965). Facilities conditions may oscillate between states involving a few readily transportable facilities such as tents, storage skins, and light arms for protection and hunting and states involving massive public works such as regional water management systems, terraces, public granaries and fortifications (*cf.* Barth 1973; LaBianca 1984). Finally, dietary conditions may oscillate between states involving consumption primarily of locally available raw or unprocessed foods in season and states involving consumption of a wide variety of imported, preserved, or processed foods (*cf.* Goody 1982; LaBianca 1984).

Parameters of food system conditions

environmental: plant and animal remains;

settlement: ruins of villages, campsites, and buildings;

landuse: plant and animal remains, water and soil management works, and settlement conditions;

operational: food storage, water management, and food processing installations, market places, road remains; and

dietary: plant and animal remains, human skeletal remains and food residues on pottery.

Definitions of intensification and abatement

intensification: when, within a given locality, there is a measurable *increase* in the totality of energy expended on producing and transforming foodstuffs into nutriments for humans and their animals

abatement: when, within a given locality, there is a measurable *decrease* in the totality of energy expended on producing and transforming foodstuffs into nutriments for humans and their animals

When the anthropological literature is canvassed for theoretical frameworks dealing with how and why food systems change, a striking imbalance is encountered. While one can find hundreds of articles and books which in some way or another offer insights pertinent to understanding how and why food systems intensify, explicit theoretical frameworks for dealing with the opposite process, how and why food systems decrease in intensity, are far less common. Indeed, it appears that when anthropologists are concerned with change, it inevitably turns out to be a concern with notions of progress and increase of some kind or another. Thus, some of the most familiar concepts in the anthropological literature are usually tied somehow to notions of development and progress. A quick scanning of word indices of some general works on anthropology helps to make this point. While concepts like evolution, domestication, sedentarization, specialization, stratification, maximization, urbanization, industrialization, and modernization recur as constructs around which a body of literature has emerged within the field of anthropology today, it is hard to even come up with the antonyms to these concepts, let alone a body of literature concerned with their opposites.

In order to remedy this imbalance, we have introduced elsewhere (LaBianca 1986) the concept of abatement as a term to refer to the process whereby food systems decrease in intensity. The specific sense in which this concept is used is as an antonym to the concept of intensification. Since, according to Webster's Third New International Dictionary there is no such word as dis-intensifica-tion, the word abatement comes the closest to expressing the opposite of intensification. According to the same dictionary *abatement* means "to reduce or lessen in degree or intensity" and suggested synonyms include "diminish" and "decrease."

One general dimension along which temporal transitions in food system intensities can be conceptualized is that of the amount of energy expended in the process of providing and transforming food. Thus, as noted earlier, by means of human manipulation and management of natural resources, energy in the form of water, mineral, plant, animal, and human resources is harnessed to serve culturally prescribed ends. For the purposes of this investigation, therefore, what is meant by the word *transition* is a passage or movement from one state to another with respect to amounts of energy expended. We shall assume furthermore, that the greater the amount of human manipulation and management of natural resources for the purpose of providing and transforming food, the greater the amount of energy expended and, therefore, the more intense the food system. The lower the amount of human manipulation and management, the lower the amount of energy expended and the less intense the food system.

Correlates of Food System Intensification

As already noted, a great amount has already been written about how and why food systems intensify. Anthropological research concerned with this problem can be grouped into four general categories. First, there are the studies of the origins of domesticated plants (Halbaek 1959a; Renfrew 1973; Ford 1979; Wing and Brown 1979) and animals (Angress and Reed 1962; Bokonyi 1971; Olsen 1971; Clutton-Brock and Uerpmann 1974; Flannery 1974; Meadow and Zeder 1978; Lyman 1982; Reed 1983). Second, there are those dealing with the origins and development of agricultural communities (Halbaek 1959b; Braidwood 1964: 112-135; Ucko and Dimbleby 1969; Flannery 1970, 1974, 1982; Sahlins 1972; MacNeish 1974; Butzer 1976; Cohen 1977; Redman 1978; Rhindos 1980; Binford 1983: 195-213; Hassan 1983). Third, there are those which deal more broadly with the role of agricultural intensification in accounting for the rise of cities and civilization generally (Clark 1962: 76-98; Adams 1965, 1966, 1974, 1978, 1981; Flannery 1972; Cowgill 1975a, 1975b; Cohen and Service

1978; Wenke 1981; Goody 1982). And fourth, there are those which focus more narrowly on the nature of agricultural intensification as a problem in and of itself (Geertz 1963; Boserup 1965, 1983; Spooner 1972; Cowgill 1975a, 1975b; J. W. Bennett 1976; Barlett 1980; Green 1980; Pelto and Pelto 1983; Dow 1985). To each of these categories dozens of additional references could be added.

In this overview of correlates of food system intensification we shall limit ourselves to consideration of seven correlates, namely innovation, population growth, new opportunities, centralization due to cost of transport, craft specialization, state

---

Intensification has been linked to . . .

- innovation
- population growth
- new opportunities
- centralization
- craft specialization
- state formation and bureaucratization
- delocalization of diet

---

formation and bureaucratization, and delocalization of diet. Represented among these seven correlates are proposals not only regarding the manner in which food systems intensify, but also regarding why they intensify in the first place. Since each of these correlates have been discussed in much greater detail elsewhere by the individuals cited below, we offer here a mere orientation to each.

Innovation

Taking issue with those who would argue that humans are basically uninventive and complacent creatures, H. G. Barnett (1953) has argued that the innovative process is "the basis of culture change." According to Barnett, innovation involves a process of synthesis and recombination in order to manipulate and transform resources to meet culturally prescribed ends. He notes, for example, the variety of specialized tools and implements developed by the Eskimos, such as bow drills, shoe cleats, snow goggles, needles, buoys, seal lures and detectors, sledge runners, blood stoppers, skewers, whale harpoons, bird arrows, bows, fishhooks, snow houses, skin boats or kayaks, and their "tough,

warm, and well-tailored skin clothing." Tools and implements such as these have made the Eskimos "admirably adapted to their habitat" and testify to "achievements of real insight and skill" among traditional peoples (Barnett 1953: 23-24, 237-238).

While the occurrence of the innovative process is indisputable, why it occurs and how it contributes to food system intensification is problematic. As already noted, many anthropologists disagree with Barnett's assumption that the innovative process is inescapable in humans—a voluntaristic impulse which continuously leads to new inventions and culture change. Furthermore, as Bennett (1976: 253) has noted, the rationality assumption which is implicit in Barnett's view of the innovative process "is no guarantee of survival-oriented outcomes. The 'right' choice based on abundant information may be the 'wrong' choice from the standpoint of ecologically adaptive consequences if the ends sought were destructive or exploitative." Thus, although the innovative process is an important one to reckon with in accounting for either food system intensification or abatement, its function and outcome are probably best understood in relation to other cooperative mechanisms, including the following ones.

Population Growth

Another proposal regarding why food systems intensify claims that it is a consequence of population growth. Proposed in 1965 by the Danish geographer Esther Boserup in *The Conditions of Agricultural Growth* (1965), this model is based on the assumption that population growth, due to natural birth rates or immigration, creates the conditions which lead to agricultural development. As population pressure on resources intensifies, people are forced to change their methods of food procurement so that a greater population density can be supported on a given hectare of land. In order to do this, populations usually increase the amount of labor expended per hectare by shortening fallow periods and increasing the frequency of cropping. Thus although the amount of food produced may diminish in relation to the amount of labor expended, intensification continues as long as the need to feed more people keeps growing. According to this proposal, therefore, it is population pressure which creates the conditions which lead to innovation and adoption of improved methods of food procurement, not the other way around.

The population pressure hypothesis has found a number of influential advocates within the camp of adaptivist anthropology (Binford 1968: 332; Flannery 1969: 80; Harner 1970: 69; Smith and Young 1972: 33; Spooner 1972; Cohen 1977). It has not, however, been unanimously accepted. A widely cited critique of this hypothesis is Cowgill (1975a, 1975b). He (1975a: 513) draws attention to the tendency of most adherents of the population pressure hypothesis to view population growth rates as "relatively inelastic, that is, relatively unresponsive to moderate changes in other variables." By taking population growth more or less for granted, they tend to overlook the fact that preindustrial population rates "have been very elastic, and very responsive to a host of still poorly understood factors." Consequently, "why some societies, and not others, embark on episodes of population growth remains a fundamental problem, and growth, just as much as decrease, needs to be explained" (Cowgill 1975a: 514).

New Opportunities

To understand why developmental episodes occur when and where they do, Cowgill (1975a) calls attention to the role of economic and institutional factors in either encouraging or discouraging it. Noting that the Industrial Revolution was spurred, not by European overpopulation, but by the sense of new opportunities which followed in the wake of the age of discovery and exploration, Cowgill favors taking into consideration basic motivational factors in accounting for the behavior of populations. When people perceive that a certain change may be to their advantage, and the economic and institutional possibilities exist to act on this perception, chances are that a change will be made, regardless of population pressure. Thus,

> asking whether population growth is *the* independent or *the* dependent variable is an inept question, and we should think of population variables as members of sets of variables, including technological and environmental variables and political, economic, and other institutions, which are all concomitantly interacting with one another (Cowgill 1975a: 516-517).

Centralization Due to Cost of Transport

In addition to the incentives for change created by a sense of new opportunities, locational factors may play a role as well in accounting for food system intensification. Thus, von Thünen (1930) noted

already in the previous century that the cost of transport will in certain locations lead to concentration of agricultural production near major centers. This tendency may be reinforced by other factors such as

> greater accessibility of the nonagricultural goods and services which are provided by the center, importance of the center as a place one must visit for various business or political transactions and participation in important rituals, or simply the greater excitement and variety of the center (Cowgill 1975b: 517-518).

By means of this process, population densities as well as food production intensities will tend to be relatively high in the vicinity of such centers, "while at the same time more remote regions may be actually losing population, and land that is potentially quite productive may be going out of use" (Cowgill 1975a: 518).

Craft Specialization

The existence of a correlation between the division of labor into nonagricultural craft specialties (such as pottery making, weaving, basketry, and metalwork) and agricultural intensity is an empirical phenomenon which has been known for some time already (Hobhouse, Wheeler, and Ginsberg 1914; Gouldner and Peterson 1962; Murdock and Provost 1973; Childe 1946; Smith 1976; Fried 1967; and Service 1975). Recently Dow (1985), by means of computer-assisted regression analysis of a worldwide sample of 131 pre-industrial societies, has provided support for the hypothesis of reciprocal effects between these two variables. More specifically, he reports that "the reciprocal effects display a marked asymmetry in magnitudes" involving a stronger effect from labor specialization to the agricultural intensity variable than vice versa (Dow 1985: 150). Thus, the process of food system intensification seems to occur simultaneously with growth in nonagricultural craft specialization, the latter having an important role to play in promoting growth in the former.

State Formation and Bureaucratization

A well-documented phenomenon in the anthropological literature is the co-occurrence of state-level political systems and high-intensity food systems (Adams 1966; Flannery 1972; Sanders 1973; Bodley 1976: 109-110; Hunt and Hunt 1976; Wenke 1981; Hassan 1983). This literature offers ample empirical evidence for the reciprocal nature of the processes involved in the intensification of food systems and the development of state-level political systems and bureaucracies. On the one hand, state-level political systems and bureaucracies play an important role in developing and maintaining the socioeconomic infrastructure which is needed to support high intensity agriculture. Functions typically provided for by this infrastructure include formalized systems of land tenure and conflict resolution; protection against predatory populations; region-wide water management facilities and organizations; facilities for marketing, transporting, and storing produce; and centers of worship for the agricultural population. The bureaucrats, of course, are "those officers who are in the chain of command between the policy-makers and those who actually do the production work" (Hunt 1985). The farmers, on the other hand, are depended upon not merely to supply themselves with food, but also to produce a sufficient surplus to feed the state-level infrastructure personnel, craft specialists, and other specialized groups that usually exist within state-level societies.

Delocalization of Diet

The term *delocalization* has recently been suggested to describe the process whereby "food varieties, production methods, and consumption patterns are disseminated throughout the world in an ever-increasing and intensifying network of socioeconomic and political interdependency" (Pelto and Pelto 1983: 507). Three principal processes are involved in delocalization: first, "world-wide dissemination of domesticated plant and animal varieties"; second, "the rise of increasingly complex, international food distribution networks, and the growth of food-processing industries"; and third, "the migration of people from rural to urban centers, and from one continent to another . . . with a resulting exchange of culinary and dietary techniques and preferences" (Pelto and Pelto 1983: 508-509).

While delocalization is a process which has been ongoing since antiquity, its rate has accelerated markedly in the past two and a half centuries. As it has progressed, it has resulted in decreased local autonomy of food supplies and increased sensitivity of local regions to world-wide fluctuations in supply and demand. While local abatements in delocalization have no doubt occurred in certain isolated regions of the world at certain times and places in history, delocalization rep-

resents a "unidirectional tendency in human history" (Pelto and Pelto 1983: 510) which has contributed to increasingly widespread occurrences of high intensity food systems. Consequently, low intensity, autonomous, subsistence-based food systems are today practically extinct.

Correlates of Food System Abatement

The absence of a commonly agreed upon term among anthropologists and other social scientists for referring to the abatement process makes it difficult to ascertain the full extent of previous work on this topic. No doubt, as future research becomes more focused and cumulative, past contributions to this line of research will gradually come to light. Meanwhile, it seems appropriate to begin by recalling some of the social science disciplines in which the problem of abatement has been addressed, if only to emphasize that this is by no means a novel subject.

To begin with, it can be noted that among historians the subject of abatement, as it pertains to nations and empires, has received considerable attention. The classic work on this subject by an historian is, of course, Gibbon's (n.d.) *The Decline and Fall of the Roman Empire*. Since this classic appeared, literally dozens of historical works have been published which have utilized the first five words of Gibbon's title. A theme which is frequently encountered in these works is that abatement is the result of character weaknesses and shortsightedness on the part of rulers and other powerful people and organizations. This theme is, of course, at least as ancient as the Greek tragedies of the 4th and 5th centuries B.C. Historians, however, tend not to be concerned specifically with food system abatements.

The subject of abatement has also had a long and venerable following within the discipline of economics. Indeed, ever since Malthus' (1914) classic, the field of economics has had the distinction of being known as "the dismal science" because of its practitioners' frequent predictions of doom and gloom. The Malthusian doctrine that population tends to increase at a faster rate than its means of subsistence and that this inevitably results in degradation and poverty of the lower classes must certainly be ranked among the earliest and most influential theoretical propositions pertaining to the general subject of abatement. Recently, as noted earlier, this doctrine has been challenged by Boserup (1965) whose thesis that population growth leads to agricultural intensification and economic specialization has spawned much recent research and writing in the field of anthropology (Spooner 1972; Cowgill 1975a; Cohen 1977).

Also from the field of geography have come proposals which must be reckoned with in an overview of social science research on the problem of abatement. Specific mention can be made of Ellsworth Huntington's influential, but today largely discredited notions regarding climatic change and the destiny of nations. As Chappell (1970: 358) explains,

> Huntington speculated that pulsations of climate had served as a driving force in the history of Eurasia, impelling nomadic invaders to overrun the civilized nations that surrounded them whenever the climatic cycle neared a trough of aridity.

This conclusion led Huntington (1907: 385) to write in the *Pulse of Asia* that

> With every throb of the climatic pulse which we have felt in Central Asia, the center of civilization has moved this way or that. Each throb has sent pain and decay to the lands whose day was done, life and vigor to those whose day was yet to be.

The controversy which has surrounded Huntington's thesis within the field of geography has been reviewed by Chappell (1970).

In the past two decades sociologists working within the framework of world system theory have focused attention on the economic imbalances which have led to the stagnation and demise experienced by certain third world peoples. According to Wallerstein (1974), one of the leading proponents of this approach, since the beginning of colonial times the industrialized nations of the world have taken advantage of the cheap labor and natural resources of "third world" countries in order to stimulate continuous growth within their own economies. The demonstrable inability of the underdeveloped countries to catch up with the economies of the developed nations is attributed to the process of underdevelopment. In essence, this process has involved the capitalist or core nations having introduced and maintained scarcity producing mechanisms in the world's peripheral or poor nations. Thus, rather than experiencing the same process of development which occurred in the west, these local food systems have, so to speak, been set on a path of abatement leading to food

shortages, famines, and general cultural degradation (*cf.* Frank 1966; Franke and Chasin 1980; Lappe and Collins 1985).

Despite the absence of any widely-accepted concept in the anthropological lexicon for dealing with the problem of abatement, isolated studies do exist in both Old and New World archaeological literature which offer a starting point for theory building with regard to food system abatements. As I have discussed elsewhere (LaBianca 1986) a well-known example from the Old World would be

---

Abatement has been linked to . . .

- accumulating hazards
- lost opportunities
- hyperintegration
- myopic policies
- underdevelopment
- food shortages and epidemics

Adams' study of the collapse of the Sassanian canal network which integrated the flooding cycles of both the Euphrates and Tigris rivers to support intensive hydraulic agriculture in the Mesopotamian floodplain between A.D. 226 and 637 (Adams 1978). In the New World, Upham's study of the pre-Columbian abandonment of sedentary agriculture in favor of seasonal subsistence strategies by Pueblo groups in the American southwest represents another example (Upham 1984).

As a further step toward developing a framework for analyzing the problem of abatement, particularly as it pertains to food system transitions, we shall next distinguish analytically between several different correlates of abatement. Specifically, we shall introduce accumulating hazards, lost opportunities, hyperintegration, myopic policies, underdevelopment, and food shortages and epidemics as examples of such correlates. I have discussed each of these in greater detail elsewhere (LaBianca 1986).

Accumulating Hazards

All over the world, people's quest for food brings them into dynamic interactions with a wide variety of extreme events or hazards such as droughts, floods, earthquakes, and epidemics. A useful framework for analyzing how people manage the risks involved in occupying a particular place with respect to such hazards has recently been proposed by Burton, Kates, and White (1978: 19). Their approach involves examining three elements in the situation, including how people recognize and describe a hazard, how they deal with it, and how they choose among the various possible actions that seem to them available (Burton *et al.* 1978: 19). The cumulative hazardousness of a place can be determined by ascertaining the probability of various extreme events occurring over a given period of time (Burton *et al.* 1978: 28). As a general rule, the more hazardous a particular location is, the more difficult it is to intensify as far as the food system is concerned.

Lost Opportunities

The role of new or lost opportunities in accounting for population and landuse dynamics is another important matter to consider in accounting for food system abatements. As noted earlier, Cowgill (1975a, 1975b) has argued that population growth is "a human possibility which is encouraged by certain institutional, as well as technological or environmental circumstances, but equally may be *discouraged* by other circumstances" (Cowgill 1975a: 516). Locational factors, such as availability of transport and proximity to major regional centers, play a crucial role as well in food system abatements. The growth of such centers

> can encourage local population concentrations, so that population density may be relatively high and agricultural intensification relatively great in the vicinity of major centers, while at the same time more remote regions may be actually losing population, and land that is potentially quite productive may be going out of use (Cowgill 1975a: 518).

Hyperintegration

A condition which may lead to the abatement of very intense food systems is *hyperintegration* or *hypercoherence*. This condition results when, in a highly centralized system, the autonomy of the various smaller subsystems is completely broken down (Flannery 1972: 421). Hyperintegration is one among several cultural pathologies identified by Rappaport (1969) which can lead to destabilization of high intensity systems. According to Flannery (1972: 420) hypercoherence may have

contributed to abatements in both the Mesopotamian and the Mayan context. In both cases "marriage alliances between the ruling families of formerly hostile states" so strengthened "communication and influence between them" as to have destroyed "the natural buffering" which "insulated one from the upheavals in another." In the period which comes before the collapse of the Classic Maya, this condition appears to be reflected in the settlement pattern which reached, during this time, its nearest resemblance to the hexagonal spacing of sites which is characteristic of highly interdependent patterns of alliances and trade.

Myopic Policies

Myopic or shortsighted policies prevail where the long-term consequences of particular policies and technologies are ignored for the sake of short-term gain or preservation of the status quo. Thus, in Mesopotamia, in order to overcome uncertainty over future water supplies, excessive watering whenever canal levels allowed led to exacerbation of the problem of salinization, and eventually to abatement of the food system. In the Mayan context, the policies which encouraged intensification in the direction of terrace-and-field agriculture also appear to have led to subjugation of the peasants for the sake of more intensive agricultural output. The long-term consequence of this development was that it produced the discontent which led ultimately to abatement of the food system (*cf.* Hamblin and Pitcher 1980).

Underdevelopment

The possibility that some food systems may take a downward turn as a result of meddling by outsiders in the affairs of indigenous populations has, as we have noted earlier, received considerable attention recently by sociologists. Lappe and Collins, for example, have argued that colonialism actively prevented certain indigenous populations from remaining self-sufficient in their quest for food. By means of the process of underdevelopment, colonial powers

> forced peasants to replace food crops with cash crops that were then expropriated at very low prices; took over the best agricultural land for export crop plantations and then forced the most able-bodied workers to leave the village fields to work as slaves or for very low wages on plantations; encouraged a dependence on imported food; (and) blocked native peasant cash crop

production from competing with cash crops produced by settlers or foreign firms (Lappe and Collins 1985: 210; *cf.* Lappe and Collins 1977).

While in some cases such colonial interventions stimulated an upward turn in the intensity of food production, as in the case of South Africa, in many other instances, such as in the Sahel region of West Africa, the introduction of more intensive forms of cultivation by colonial powers eventually resulted in ecological destruction, food shortages, and degradation of certain formerly productive regions (Franke and Chasin 1980).

Wallerstein's (1974; *cf.* Chirot and Hall 1982; Ragin and Chirot 1984) scheme for understanding the global relations which lead to underdevelopment and dependency was briefly noted beforehand. According to his model, what accounts for the success of entrepreneurs from the industrialized West is the fact that they have been able to take advantage of global inequalities without becoming subject to political pressures toward redistribution. By exploiting new opportunities in regions beyond the boundaries of their native countries they have been able to escape the strains toward redistribution which operate within their own societies (see Ragin and Chirot 1984).

Food Shortages and Epidemics

As correlates of abatement, food shortages and mass infections are appropriately discussed last in this line-up of mechanisms. The reason for this is that one or the other or both usually occur as the consequence of the above correlates—cumulative hazardousness, lost opportunities, hyperintegration, myopic policies, and underdevelopment. Furthermore, the unabating threat of food shortages may actually make food system intensification harder to achieve in certain regions, thus exerting a kind of downward pull in the direction of self-sufficiency and resiliency. The reasons for this have been illuminated by recent investigations of social responses to food shortages and epidemics.

To begin with, Dirks (1980: 31) has noted that how people respond to food shortages and famine is "remarkably uniform cross-culturally." Reviewing a wide range of studies of famished communities, he has shown that the changes which take place in human interaction patterns as food shortages worsen correspond to the triphasic pattern of Selye's (1956) general adaptation syndrome. Thus, like the human body's response to stress, popula-

tions respond to nutritional stressors by an initial *alarm phase* involving system-wide hyperactivation; this is followed by an energy-conserving *resistance phase*, which in the end is followed by an *exhaustion phase* during which a last all-out effort to survive is followed by death.

When the behaviors which characterize each of these phases are examined, insight is gained into a number of processes which play a role in abating food system intensity levels. For example, the alarm phase is manifest by speculative hoarding, emigration, increased hostility, and political unrest. Indeed "rebellion and revolution are more likely to occur during the first phase of famine than later" (Dirks 1980: 27). The next phase, resistance, begins when "hyperactivity gives way to hypoactivity." There is a "general depression in the frequency of interaction, particularly mating behavior, greeting behavior, play, and fighting." Social life becomes progressively atomistic and there is increasing economy of action. There is also a tendency for

the division of labor to collapse as everyone turn(s) attention to the quest for food . . . As obtaining food from familiar sources becomes more and more difficult, efforts to procure nourishment expand into previously unexploited niches, competition intensifies, and agonistic encounters increase (Dirks 1980: 27-30).

This situation, in turn, necessitates greater concern with the protection of food stores and gardens. Thus people begin to take turns day and night looking after their food supply.

Whereas families usually remain together during the resistance phase, they collapse during the exhaustion phase: "Reciprocity eventually constricts to a point at which the family ceases to function as a redistributive, protective entity and individuals begin to fend exclusively for themselves" (Dirks 1980: 30). Turnbull's (1972) controversial report on the Ik of East Africa is a classic example of the behavior which characterizes the exhaustion phase.

Particularly in the world's dry regions, the threat of famine has played a crucial role in shaping the structural arrangements which govern traditional food procurement strategies (Kates, Johnson, and Haring 1977; Marx 1977; Burton *et al.* 1978; Colson 1979; Franke and Chasin 1980; Campbell 1984). In such regions there is a constant pull in the direction of self-sufficiency which is realized through resilient food strategies emphasizing diversification rather than specialization. This pull toward self-reliance is obviously a crucial factor to be reckoned with in accounting for periodic abatements in food system intensities.

That a synergistic relationship exists between famines and epidemics is a "recurrent theme in human history" (Taylor 1983). What accounts for this synergism is, of course, the fact that prolonged periods of nutritional stress gradually weaken the effectiveness of the body's ability to overcome or contain the constant invasion of biological and physical pathogens into the system (Cassel 1974). While individuals and populations are capable of a certain amount of physiological adaptation to such stress (Stini 1973), when the limits of such adaptation are reached the physical organism is overcome by disease and eventually dies.

There can be little doubt that epidemics, by affecting the labor pool of local food systems, have contributed significantly to abatement processes in different times and places. Large scale die-offs have repeatedly affected Old World populations (McNeill 1976; Dols 1977) and have played a pivotal role in the history of the New World as well (Cook 1973; Joralemon 1982). Indeed, it has been argued that what subdued the native Indians of America in the face of European expansion was

---

Stability and resilience

stable systems: absorb *as few* disturbances as possible and return *rapidly* to equilibrium.

resilient systems: absorb *large amounts* of disturbances and return *more slowly* to equilibrium.

---

not the superior methods of warfare of the latter, but the mortality which resulted from the diseases transmitted to the Indians by the European invaders (Crosby 1972).

Another way in which infectious microparasites may impact the labor pool of local food systems is by setting in motion various cycles of migrations. McNeill (1979) has noted, for example, that urban centers must maintain a constant inflow of persons from rural communities in order to make up for the excessive die-offs which result from the greater ease with which diseases develop and spread when

large numbers of people live so close together. He also notes that isolated communities on the periphery of such centers are more vulnerable to the new diseases incubated in urban centers because they have less opportunity to develop immunities to them. Throughout the history of the Old World, this situation, he argues, has tended to set in motion two flows of people—

> one toward the center, where endemic high mortality rates maintained what we might think of as a zone of demographic "low pressure" inviting in-migration, and the second towards the periphery, where epidemic die-offs produced sporadic zones of demographic "low pressure" that also invited in-migration (McNeill 1979: 96).

Stability and Resilience

Viewed from a temporal perspective, food systems can be expected to oscillate up and down in intensity, depending on the actions of mechanisms such as those mentioned above. This, it turns out, is a temporal characteristic of all living systems as has been noted by Holling (1973) and Winterhalder (1978). In a widely-cited article, for example, Holling (1973) employed the concepts of stability and resilience to describe the two alternative responses of living systems to perturbations. On the one hand, a system might respond to perturbations by fluctuating within certain ranges, and yet may return by more or less regular oscillations to an equilibrium. Because such systems are capable of absorbing large amounts of perturbations, they are said to be resilient. On the other hand, a system might respond to perturbations by returning as rapidly as possible, and with the least fluctuations, to equilibrium. Because such systems absorb fewer disturbances and are more rapid in returning to equilibrium they are said to be stable. Stable systems, consequently, are more likely than resilient ones "to shift into another domain" or to go into extinction (Holling 1973; Winterhalder 1978: 52).

Holling's proposals have been adopted by Adams (1978) to distinguish between the adaptive strategies of two competing social elements in ancient Mesopotamian society: those of the urban elites and those of the farmers and herdsmen on whom the "urban edifice of power, privilege, tradition, and ceremony ultimately depend" (Adams 1978: 333). On the one hand, he sees the urban elites of the Third Dynasty of Ur (3rd millennium B.C.) and the later Sassanian dynasty (A.D. 226-

637) as the protagonists of stability. As noted earlier, their state ideologies "assumed the convergence of everyone's interest on a single, maximizing approach" emphasizing short-term maximization of benefits by and for urban elites. In the long-run, however their strategies produced an unstable mixture of concerns and goals that tended to preclude the development of plans and institutions to promote continuity and survival.

On the other hand, the alternative to the centralizing propensities of the urban elites is furnished by the survival strategies emphasized by the primary producers, in particular the tribally organized, seminomadic elements of ancient Mesopotamian society. Their emphasis on "mobility, military prowess, and the maintenance of a spectrum of subsistence options that balanced herding with limited cultivation" assured survival, if not comparable stability or prosperity. In the long term, therefore, it is this element in ancient Mesopotamian society which has persisted between the short-term "peaks of dynastic consolidation."

Building on the insights of Holling (1973) and Adams (1978), Stuart and Gauthier (1981), and Upham (1984) have offered another pair of metaphors for use in differentiating between strategies of survival and strategies of maximization. Distinguishing between strategies of power and strategies of efficiency, they note that, on the one hand, cultural systems create a power drive—they pump up, so to speak—"when they increase rates of population growth, rates of production, or rates of energy expenditure" (Stuart and Gauthier 1981: 10). Such systems also burn out.

On the other hand, efficient systems are "rather the opposite, so that energy in and energy out are more nearly equal, and the efficiency drive is characterized by decreased rates of population growth, production or energy expenditure" (Stuart and Gauthier 1981: 10). Given these two opposing strategies, most food systems could be located somewhere along an axis with hunter-gatherers at the efficient end and United States agribusiness at the power end. While efficient strategies tend to be areally extensive and to involve the use of population-regulating mechanisms such as infanticide, postpartum sexual taboos, population budding, etc., to ensure a balance between population size and available resources, power strategies tend to lead to areally intensive landuse, population growth, intensive resource procurement, social stratification,

productive specialization, elite political organizations, extensive local and regional exchange, and social, economic, and political alliances (Upham 1984: 236-237).

The Heshbon Expedition

The Expedition's Name

Throughout the entire period of fieldwork in Jordan, the campaigns at Tell Hesban and vicinity were carried out under the name of *Heshbon Expedition*. The reference to "Heshbon" rather than "Hesban" in this name reflects the original reason for initiating fieldwork, namely to advance our understanding of various biblical events linked to this site, known in the Old Testament as Heshbon. As will be explained below and in Chapter Four, the decision to use "Hesban" instead of "Heshbon" in the present context is a consequence of the broadening of the expedition's goals over the period of fieldwork and beyond. In the following brief overview of the history of the expedition, however, we shall use its original name.

Autobiographical Background

This investigation of food system cycles in Transjordan began in the autumn of 1969 while I was an undergraduate student in the Behavioral Sciences Department at Andrews University. By invitation from Robert Little, Instructor in General Anthropology, I was given the opportunity to assist with cleaning and identifying animal bones recovered from the first season of excavations at Tell Hesban, which had taken place during the summer of 1968. My involvement with animal bones was greatly accelerated during the summer of 1971, when I was asked to take Mr. Little's place as faunal analyst during the second campaign at Tell Hesban. I continued as the Heshbon Expedition's "bone man" during all of its subsequent campaigns.

This involvement with animal bones during each of the four field seasons of the Heshbon Expedition was fortuitous in that it led to a personal quest to justify time and energy thus spent (LaBianca 1986). Since animal bones were not normally collected by biblical archaeologists at this stage in the development of the discipline, it was also unclear to many fellow staff members why time and money should be spent on bone work and other pursuits which I insisted on being allowed to carry out, such as collecting skeletal remains of recently butchered or killed animals, making ethnographic observations of present-day animal husbandry and butchering practices, and collecting samples of present-day wild plants and cultigens. Were it not for the willingness and encouragement of the leadership (identified below) of the expedition to let such nontraditional inquiries proceed, this research would have been aborted a long time ago.

Ready answers to why "bone work" should be carried out at a historical site like Tell Hesban were not forthcoming from the writings of anthropological archaeologists either, for nearly all of their published research at that time dealt with prehistoric sites where the problem of domestication of animals and plants provided an obvious justification for saving and studying their remains. However, from Tell Hesban little could be learned about the domestication process of animals like sheep, goats, and cattle, for all of them had been domesticated long before the Early Iron Age, the earliest stratum at this site. Add to this the fact that the excavations yielded thousands of bone fragments per week, and one can appreciate the traditional biblical archaeologist's solution to how to deal with animal bones, which was simply to throw them away.

Added impetus to the quest for a theoretical framework for justifying these new lines of inquiry emerged during the years immediately following the last major field season at Tell Hesban in 1976. This impetus was provided by the leaders' desire to publish a final report on the findings of the Heshbon Expedition. Since it was deemed necessary to go beyond the sort of descriptive accounts which had been published in the preliminary reports about the project, the need for a theoretical framework for integrating the wide range of specialist reports and stratigraphic analysis was seen to be urgent. This research must also be viewed, therefore, as an initial endeavor to meet this challenge by attempting to show that temporal transitions reflected in the animal bone assemblage, in survey results, in stratigraphic results, and in specialists' accounts of identified objects, etc., represent food system transitions involving the processes of intensification and abatement.

It is because of its comprehensiveness, involving the dimensions of procurement, distribution, preparation, consumption, and disposal of food, and be-

cause of its diachronic scope, involving the processes of intensification and abatement, that the food system framework was found to be the most helpful to carrying out the challenge presented by the findings from Tell Hesban and vicinity. Not only did these findings include material traces pertaining to each of these various aspects of the quest for food, the findings spanned a period of time reaching more than 3,000 years into the past, hence the need for a diachronic frame of reference. Furthermore, as delineated in the previous sections, the food system framework represents, first of all, a heuristic device whereby the findings of investigators representing the entire gamut of scientific and humanistic disciplines concerned, implicitly or explicitly, with one or another aspect of food and its uses, could be integrated. Yet, while it is a comprehensive concept, and entails both a concern with systemic relationships in general and ecological interactions in particular, it is sufficiently focused in its explicit concern with food that it avoids many of the ambiguities and/or causal presuppositions which ultimately ruled out, for the purposes of the present inquiry, wholesale adoption of one or another of the frameworks referred to in the above section dealing with the roots of the food system concept. Instead, by means of synthesis and recombination of various aspects of these previous proposals, the food system framework discussed above was arrived at.

The Campaigns

Ever since Seetzen's visit in 1805 to a site which the local Arabs called Hesban or Hisban (both spellings occur in 19th-century travelers' accounts), explorers and biblical scholars have returned to this prominent mound along the edge of the Transjordanian highland (see fig. 1.2). One after another, after seeing the site, they have accepted this as the location of biblical Heshbon. According to various Old Testament accounts (Num 21; Josh 13) Heshbon was the capital of Sihon, king of the Amorites (cf. Horn 1982). When the Israelites arrived from Egypt they were denied permission to travel through Sihon's kingdom. A war ensued which the Israelites won. According to these same accounts, the town of Heshbon, as well as its surrounding territories were thereafter settled by "the children of Reuben" (Num 21:21-26, 34; 32:37; Josh 13:15, 17).

Fig. 1.2   Map of Palestine showing location of project area

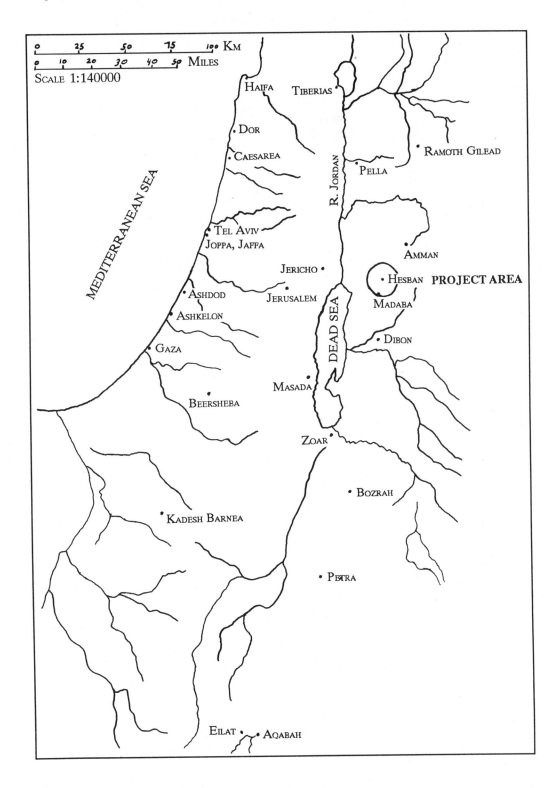

To find support for a hypothesized 15th century B.C. date for these events was one of the original purposes of the Heshbon Expedition. Another purpose was to illuminate subsequent biblical and historical events involving this site. To this end three eight-week campaigns were organized and carried out during the summers of 1968, 1971, 1973. These three campaigns were led by Siegfried H. Horn (pl. 1.1), then Professor of Archaeology and History of Antiquity at Andrews University in Michigan. His chief archaeologist was Professor Roger S. Boraas of Upsala College in East Orange, New Jersey. Their international team consisted of a staff of 42 members in 1968, 51 in 1971, and 59 in 1973. In addition, several dozen local villagers were hired each season as workmen.

Two additional campaigns were subsequently organized and led by Lawrence T. Geraty, Professor Horn's successor at the Theological Seminary at Andrews University. His chief archaeologist was again Professor Boraas and his international team consisted of 75 members in 1974 and 100 in 1976. In addition, about 150 villagers participated as workmen. In 1978, a sixth campaign was organized by John I. Lawlor of the Baptist Bible College at Clark's Summit, Pennsylvania. His chief archaeologist was Larry G. Herr, then a graduate student in the Department of Near Eastern Languages and Literatures at Harvard University. This sixth campaign consisted of a staff of about 20 persons, plus a few workmen. Except for the report on the carbonized seeds, the findings of the 1978 campaign have not been available for inclusion in this investigation.

Over the years that archaeological excavations and surveys were carried out at Tell Hesban and vicinity, the conceptualization of the goals of the expedition evolved substantially. To the initial concern with the chronology and biblical significance of a single site were added broader concerns pertaining to the regional environment and nature of cultural change and continuity in this region. Particularly under the leadership of Professor Geraty, multidisciplinary concerns were given a high priority, a fact which is reflected in the expansion of ethnographic and ecological inquiries during the '74 and '76 campaigns.

Extensive preliminary reports were published at the end of each campaign (Boraas and Horn 1969, 1973, 1975; Boraas and Geraty 1976, 1978). The marked increase in specialists' contributions included in the fourth and fifth campaigns' reports attest to the high priority given to anthropological concerns during these seasons. A number of accounts of these expeditions have been published elsewhere as well, including many popularized accounts (cf. Appendix A).

Ten Lines of Information:
A Challenge of Integration

As indicated earlier, the present investigation includes among its objectives to propose and test a single framework for fitting together the many different lines of information which are represented in the diverse findings of the Heshbon Expedition. For the sake of this initial introduction to the empirical context (more will be said in Chapter Four), reference will here be made to ten different lines of research or categories of information with which the present study has been concerned.

Archaeological Stratum Descriptions

Excavations at Tell Hesban were carried out in accordance with the standard procedures of tell archaeology in Palestine during the late '60s and early '70s. Specifically, squares measuring approximately 7 m x 7 m were laid out in sectors of the tell deemed suitable for uncovering such things as the remains of principal public buildings, fortification walls, and domestic housing areas. In all, 34 squares were excavated on the tell itself over the five principal seasons. Upon completion, these squares varied in depth between one and eight meters. Distinguishable by means of careful attention to soil layers in each square, and to their relationships to those in other squares, were a total of 19 stratigraphic horizons, the earliest one being Iron I or ca. 1200 B.C. (cf. fig. 4.1). In addition to these results, 41 "test trenches" were dug in various locations beyond the main part of the tell, and over 40 tombs and caves were entered. Examined here are the excavators' published and to-be-published accounts of what was found in these various undertakings insofar as they contained information having a bearing upon the subject of the quest for food by the tell's ancient inhabitants.

Pottery Readings

In order to establish the temporal context of the excavated materials, the ubiquitous presence of broken pieces of pottery was relied upon as a pri-

Plate 1.1   Siegfried H. Horn, Heshbon Expedition organizer and director '68, '71, and '73 campaigns

Plate 1.2   Prince Raad Zeid Hussein, royal patron of the Heshbon Expedition, excavating at Hesban

mary basis for assigning dates. Although other clues to the temporal context of finds were also relied upon, such as stratigraphic relationships, architectural features, and other datable small finds such as coins or inscribed objects, field readings of pottery fragments from each provenience unit were the most consistently relied upon data for dating purposes. Field readings of the pottery during the second through fifth campaigns were provided by James Sauer (Lugenbeal and Sauer 1972), the expedition's principal ceramicist. To the extent that every provenience unit was assigned a date on the basis of its pottery contents, the present investigation has relied on this line of information for the purposes of dating.

Registered Small Finds

For purposes of identification, analysis and preservation, the approximately 2,800 small finds unearthed during the five principal seasons, such as coins, bronze, iron, or bone implements, jewelry pieces, grinding stones, whole or restorable pieces of pottery, and so on, were processed separately by the expedition's object registrar, namely Siegfried H. Horn. A computer listing of these finds according to stratum of origin, as well as manuscripts dealing with these small finds by Wade Kotter (stone objects), Elizabeth Platt (jewelry), and B. London (metals), represent another line of information examined in this study.

Animal Bones

During the five principal campaigns of the Heshbon Expedition, over 100,000 animal bone fragments were recovered, the vast majority of which belonged to animals such as camel, horse, donkey, cattle, sheep, goats, pigs, and poultry. Over 800 fish bones were also included, along with varying quantities of wild mammal and bird remains. Animal bones were collected from day one at Tell Hesban, thanks to the efforts of Siegfried H. Horn and Robert M. Little (*cf.* Little 1969). As noted above, the bone work was continued during subsequent seasons by the writer (LaBianca 1973, 1978a, 1978b; LaBianca and LaBianca 1975, 1976), who invited Joachim Boessneck and Angela von den Driesch to carry out the final analysis of the bone material from the five principal campaigns. As a result of their efforts during a three-week marathon bone analysis session in Amman in 1976 (La-Bianca 1978a, 1978b), they and their associates at

> **Ten lines of information**
>
> - Archaeological Stratum Descriptions
> - Pottery Readings
> - Registered Small Finds
> - Animal Bones
> - Carbonized Seeds
> - Archaeological Survey Findings
> - Ecological Survey Findings
> - Ethnoarchaeological Findings
> - Explorer's Accounts
> - Secondary Sources

the University of Munich have completed several reports on the bone finds, some of which have been published and others await publication in the near future. All of these reports have been utilized in the course of this investigation (Boessneck and von den Driesch 1978a, 1981; von den Driesch and Boessneck forthcoming; Lepiksaar forthcoming; Lindner 1979; Weiler 1981) In addition, extensive use has been made of various computer summarizations of the 1976 campaign's bones.

Carbonized Seeds

Flotation of samples of ash and soil encountered in selected findspots from Tell Hesban was begun during the fourth season of excavations in 1974. Identification of the carbonized seeds thus recovered was carried out by Robert Stewart in cooperation with Patricia Crawford (Crawford, LaBianca, and Stewart 1976). Flotation sampling was continued during the 1976 campaign by Patricia Crawford. The samples from the 1976 campaign, as well as those from the 1978 campaign, were identified and studied by Dennis R. Gilliland (1986). Although the quantity of carbonized seeds and other palaeobotanical remains which were collected at Tell Hesban was small, an effort is made in this investigation to reckon with what was found.

Archaeological Survey Findings

Initiated in 1973, the first archaeological survey carried out in connection with the Heshbon Expedition had as its objective "to trace the Roman road from Livias (modern Tell er-Rameh) in the Jordan Valley to Esbus (the Greek-Latin designation for Biblical Heshbon)" (Waterhouse and Ibach 1975: 217). During the subsequent fourth and fifth campaigns, the survey initiated in 1973 was expanded to encompass the entire region within an approximately 10-km radius of Tell Hesban (Ibach 1976, 1978, 1987). The purpose of this expanded survey was to look for and map as many archaeological sites as could be found within this 10-km territory. The total number of sites recorded by the survey team after three summers' work was 155. Extensive use has been made of the findings of this survey in the present study, particularly of the descriptions of the individual sites offered in Ibach's (1987) report on the survey.

Ecological Survey Findings

The first survey of an aspect of the ecology of Hesban and vicinity to be carried out in connection with the Heshbon Expedition was Reuben G. Bullard's study of geological processes and features of the Hesban region during the summer of 1971 (Bullard 1972). In 1973, taphonomic surveys in and around the village of Hesban were initiated in order to illuminate the process whereby butchered or killed animals were preserved for the archaeological record (LaBianca and LaBianca 1975). Such studies were continued during the subsequent field seasons (LaBianca 1978a, 1980). The collection of samples of the local flora was begun in 1974 (Crawford and LaBianca 1976) and continued during the 1976 season (Crawford 1986). Field observations of present-day wild birds and mammals were carried out during the 1976 campaign by Merling Alomia (1978) and Joachim Boessneck and Angela von den Driesch (1978a). Climatological measurements were begun at Tell Hesban during the 1976 campaign as well (Ferguson and Hudson 1986). More recently, in the summer of 1979, studies of the ecology of the entire territory within a 10-km radius of Tell Hesban were carried out by Larry Lacelle, who produced reports on the geology, hydrology, and plant ecology of this territory (Lacelle 1986a, 1986b, 1986c). The findings reported by these various investigators is another line of information utilized in the present study.

Ethnoarchaeological Findings

The first ethnoarchaeological inquiries initiated in connection with the Heshbon Expedition were begun in 1973 and were concerned with patterns of animal exploitation observable in the village of Hesban (LaBianca and LaBianca 1975, 1976). During the 1974 and 1976 campaigns, such inquiries were broadened to include a generalized ethnographic study of the villagers of Hesban (LaBianca 1974, 1978a). These inquires served to heighten awareness of the links between present-day daily life activities and those of previous centuries. From this insight emerged the plans for the region-wide ethnoarchaeological work carried out between October 1980 and March 1981 (LaBianca 1984). It was as a result of this last inquiry that the significance of the food system concept as a vehicle for integrating the different lines of information discussed above emerged (LaBianca 1984).

Explorers' Accounts

In order to supplement the information provided by villagers regarding changes in the local food system over the past two centuries, the eyewitness accounts of travelers and explorers who visited Hesban and vicinity in the previous century and the early part of the present century have been extensively utilized. Their accounts and illustrations have also been referred to as a source of information about sites and ruins from earlier centuries.

Secondary Sources

Finally, numerous secondary sources dealing with Hesban's wider sociopolitical context, or ancient literary references to the site or its surrounding region, have been referred to throughout this study. Several of these were studies carried out specifically on behalf of the Heshbon Expedition by graduate students and core staff members.

The Project Area

Throughout this study reference will frequently be made to the Hesban project area or simply the project area (fig. 1.2). What is meant by this is the region within a radius of approximately 10-km of Tell Hesban. As noted above, this region was initially delimited for study by the archaeological survey team (Ibach 1976). Not only were archaeological sites recorded by this team within this region, it is also the region within which the ecological survey was carried out and 31 villages and towns were visited in the course of the ethnoarchaeological investigation completed in 1980-81 (LaBianca 1984).

> Four topographical units of project area
>
> **western descent:** slopes and valleys in the western half
>
> **plateau ridge:** highland strip running north-south along the center
>
> **northern hills:** hilly region in the north-eastern quadrant
>
> **eastern plain:** gently rolling plain in the southeastern quadrant

Included within this project area are four principal topographical units, namely *western descent, plateau ridge, northern hills,* and *eastern plain* (see fig. 1.3). The significant extent of ecological diversity which characterizes these units has contributed to considerable adaptive diversity in regards to human livelihoods within the project area as a whole. The ecological attributes and relationships between these four units, as well as the range of human adaptive diversity within the project area, will be discussed in greater detail in Chapter Three.

The 10-km limit within which the archaeological survey team carried out their work was chosen because it was practical and in part because of the influence of the work of Vita-Finzi (1978) on the expedition's leadership (Boraas personal communication). In the hilly region to the east of the ridge there were roads running along this 10-km perimeter which facilitated access to sites along the ridge, on the eastern plain, and in the northern hills. In the western descent, the Wadi Hesban with its tributaries was largely contained within the western half of this project area. These wadis passed through terrain which included valleys and springs in the vicinity of which signs of human settlement could reasonably be expected. Thus, the 10-km limit seemed to present a practical perimeter within which to carry out the archaeological survey, given its goals, its staffing, and the time available to do the work.

The ecological and ethnoarchaeological surveys were restricted to approximately the same territory as the archaeological survey in order to permit comparisons within a singular unit of present-day landuse and settlement patterns with those of previous centuries. For reasons discussed earlier, it was intended that present conditions would have provided a base line against which to compare livelihood conditions in the past.

Overview of Subsequent Chapters

Chapter Two provides a general background to the phenomena of sedentarization and nomadization in the Middle East. Whereas sedentarization is shown to be associated with the process of food system intensification, nomadization is linked to the process of food system abatement. As a foundation for understanding why and how these processes have operated, this chapter focuses attention on how the physical environment has contributed to the development and coexistence in this part of the world of a range of alternative food procurement strategies. Discussed with reference to this environmental situation are three structural mechanisms, namely tribal organization, political allegiance, and shared ideals, whereby Middle Eastern peoples are able to maintain a considerable degree of social fluidity as a means to cope with the natural hazards ubiquitous throughout their environment.

Chapter Three describes the process of intensification which took place within the project area over the past two centuries. Specifically examined are the interrelated changes which took place in environmental conditions, settlement conditions, landuse conditions, operational conditions, and dietary conditions. On the basis of this analysis, it is proposed that three different configurations of locally-prevailing food systems may be distinguished, including transhumant pastoralism, village cereal farming, and urban-oriented intensive agriculture. These configurations, in turn, provide a heuristic device for generating hypotheses, interpreting, and integrating the diverse lines of archaeological information which form the basis for the reconstructions of ancient food system changes which are offered in chapters five, six, and seven.

Chapter Four discusses in greater detail nature and limitations of the archaeological information available from Tell Hesban and the project area. It also details the type of analysis forming the basis for reconstructions of the local food system during the various historical epochs included in this investigation. To this end an overview of previous

Fig. 1.3   Four topographical subregions of project area

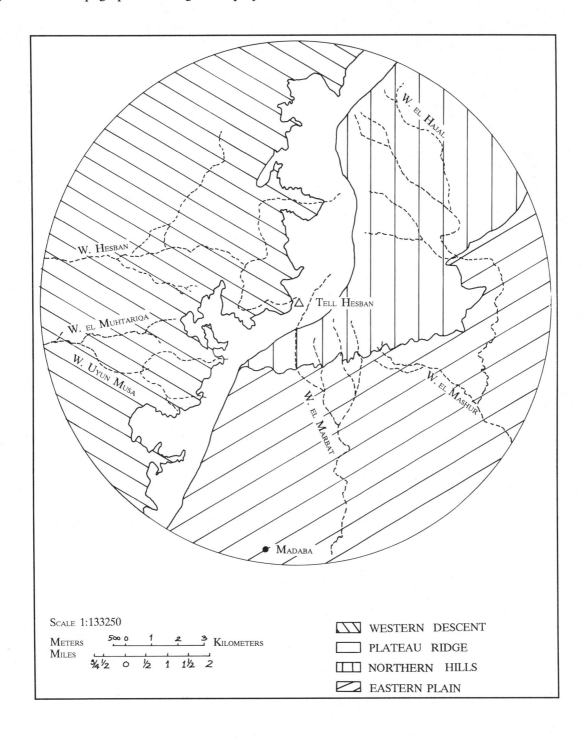

archaeological research in Transjordan is included, along with a discussion of how archaeological information generated by the Heshbon Expedition was converted into data about food system conditions. This information, in turn, enabled the formulation of proposals regarding food system configurations integrating the various lines of evidence from the various historical periods investigated here.

Chapters five, six, and seven present reconstructions of the interrelated changes in environmental, settlement, landuse, operational, and dietary conditions which occurred within the project area during the Iron Age (Chapter Five), the Greco-Roman period (Chapter Six) and the Islamic period (Chapter Seven) respectively. Evidence is presented which points to significant movement back and forth between periods of high and low intensity food systems in this region over the millennia in question.

Chapter Eight examines the food system transitions which took place within the project area in light of the intensification and abatement mechanisms presented in Chapter One. Certain features of the food system of Central Jordan, including suggestions regarding the reasons for the temporal variability in the intensity of the food system, are discussed. Also noted are the limitations of the present study and problems requiring further study.

Chapter Two

SEDENTARIZATION AND NOMADIZATION

Chapter Two

Sedentarization and Nomadization

Introduction

In this chapter an overview is presented, based on a survey of pertinent secondary sources, of certain of the salient features of Middle Eastern food systems. In particular, this review will be concerned with the temporal dynamics of food systems in this region. Are long-term changes in patterns of human livelihoods such as have been documented in Jordan phenomena which have been documented in other parts of the Middle East? What are the physical features of the Middle Eastern environment which must be reckoned with in accounting for such long-term changes? What are some of the social structural features of Middle Eastern societies which must be reckoned with in accounting for them?

It will be suggested in this chapter that the phenomena of food system intensification and abatement are ubiquitous throughout the Middle East and that they are manifest in the processes of sedentarization and nomadization which have occurred since antiquity in this region. Although a great deal more will be said about these processes further on, it may briefly be stated here that sedentarization is the process whereby a group of people gradually adopts a sedentary mode of existence. And nomadization is the process whereby a group of people gradually adopts a nomadic mode of existence. Whereas sedentarization usually involves food system intensification, nomadization usually involves food system abatement. In order to explain how these processes operate, this chapter begins by examining the influence of various physical factors on the quest for food in the Middle East. This is followed by a discussion of certain structural mechanisms whereby people in this region have adapted to continuously changing config-

urations of settlement and livelihood. Finally, particular regions of the Middle East are examined where long-term shifts in food system intensities have been documented.

As indicated, the geopolitical region with which this chapter deals is the Middle East as a whole. Leaving the discussion of precisely how to define this region to others (Coon 1958: 1-3; Fisher 1971: 1-3; Beaumont, Blake, and Wagstaff 1976: 1-3; English 1977: 164-173; Eickelman 1981: 1-6), the concern here is primarily with the territory which traditionally has been referred to as the Ancient Near East and which today is sometimes called the Central Middle East. Today, this territory includes the countries of Egypt, Cyprus, Israel, Lebanon, Syria, Jordan, Iraq, Saudi Arabia, the two Yemens, Bahrain, Qatar, Oman, the United Arab Emirates, Kuwait, Iran, and Turkey (see fig. 2.1).

Sedentarization: adopting a sedentary mode of existence usually involving food system *intensification*.

Nomadization: adopting a nomadic mode of existence usually involving food system *abatement*.

The Central Middle East has coherence as a unit of analysis for several reasons noted by Bates and Rassam (1983: x). First, this is the *cradle of civilization* where urban life and state forms of political organization arose along the great river banks of the Nile in Egypt, and the Tigris and Euphrates in Mesopotamia. Second, for at least 4,000 years, the peoples and cultures of this region have been politically and economically integrated in constantly changing configurations of power, influence, and economic exchange. Third, this is where the three great monotheistic faiths of Judaism, Christianity, and Islam were born. And fourth, more recently, it is within this region that the great cities and centers of power of the Islamic empires were located (Bates and Rassam 1983: xi).

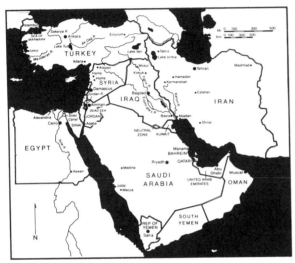

Fig. 2.1   The Central Middle East (after Bates and Rassam 1983)

Physical Influences on Middle East Food Systems

The Influence of Climate and Geology

According to Fisher (1971: 3), the single most characteristic feature of the Middle East as a natural region is its summer droughts. Not only does this feature set it apart from its neighbors, it also "induces highly distinctive and particular human responses and activities." Because the Middle East is located between two of the hottest regions in the world, namely the Sahara and northwest India, yet at the same time it is a part of the continent of Asia where some of the coldest temperatures on earth may develop, it is a region which experiences extremes in climatic conditions. Thus, while westerly winds originating in Siberia and Europe bring rain between October and May and sometimes freezing temperatures in January and February, winds originating on the African continent and in India bring hot, dry weather and water loss through evaporation in the summer months of June through September. Furthermore, since the winter westerlies are extremely capricious, annual rainfall

varies greatly from year to year. If low amounts of rainfall are brought in two or more successive years, water shortages may continue through the winter months. In most rain-fed regions of the Middle East, such successive years of drought occur at least once in a period of ten years.

Coping with the annual summer droughts and with periodic successive years of water shortages is the fundamental challenge to which Middle Eastern food systems have had to respond. To a great extent, this challenge is modified by topography and proximity to rivers and coastal areas. To begin with, the geology of the Middle East consists of two contrasting landform systems (Bates and Rassam 1983: 4). On the one hand, there are the vast, arid, lowland areas of Mesopotamia, the Arabian Peninsula, and Egypt which are geologically stable. On the other hand, there are the geologically active mountain regions of Anatolia, Iran, Lebanon, and Palestine which receive and are capable of storing, by means of subterranean reservoirs and stream flows, comparatively greater quantities of rainfall. Except for along the well-watered banks of the Tigris and Euphrates in Mesopotamia and the Nile in Egypt, both of which are located in arid, lowland areas, human settlement and cultivation of food crops in the Middle East has been concentrated on the coastal plains, along the piedmonts, and in the valleys of these geologically active mountain and coastal regions. In the arid, desert regions, such as the Arabian Peninsula, human livelihood has traditionally been very sparse and tied to the husbandry of animals adapted to dry regions, such as the camel and to a lesser extent sheep, goats, and donkeys.

Another important characteristic of the Middle East is that the desert and the sown are usually not far apart. This is particularly true in the Fertile Crescent, the famous grassland steppe which includes the Mesopotamian lowland, mountains, valleys, and plains of the eastern Mediterranean, and Egypt. An important consequence of this situation is that food procurement strategies which emphasize mobility by means of drought-resistant herds of animals have traditionally existed side-by-side in this region with those emphasizing varying degrees of stationary existence by means of either irrigation or dryland cultivation techniques (Kates, Johnson, and Haring 1977). Particularly prone to oscillations due to alternating movements in the direction of either stationary cultivation or migratory herding of animals are the fringes of the cultivated areas which border on the desert. In regions where the risk of droughts is less severe, such oscillations tend to be less pronounced (Gulick 1971: 99).

The Influence of Topography and Hydrology

To account for the location and nature of methods of food procurement in the Middle East, close attention must be paid to the influence of topographical and hydrological factors. In this regard, an examination of the relationship between these factors and the occurrence of irrigation agriculture, dry-farming techniques, and pastoralism is useful.

Irrigation along Riverine Lowlands and Piedmonts

Irrigation agriculture which relies on annual flooding cycles of rivers can be found in the major riverine lowlands of the Middle East (Beaumont et al. 1976: 168-171; Kates et al. 1977: 273). Reference has already been made to the famous hydraulic civilizations of Egypt and Mesopotamia. While both of these stream regimes relied on the annual flooding of their rivers for water and silt-rich alluvium, in the Mesopotamian case an elaborate system of canals was maintained to smooth out flooding irregularities and to bring water to outlying areas beyond the streams' normal flooding area. Because of the regularity of the flooding cycle of the Nile in both time and quantity, such canal networks were much less important in Egyptian agriculture. In the case of the Orontes River in Syria, which has cut its course deep below the plain, containers set in enormous wooden wheels which are turned by the force of the stream have been in use since Roman times for lifting water to the surface. Horizontal transportation of the water to outlying fields is provided for by canals (Gulick 1971: 90).

In many locations throughout the Middle East the sloping water table which exists in piedmont regions has been intersected by gently sloping tunnels which transport groundwater to the arid alluvial plains below (Beaumont et al. 1976: 170; English 1977: 177). Such *horizontal well* systems are particularly well known in Iran where nearly half of the irrigated land is watered by this method. The Arabic term for this type of irrigation is *qanat*. Qanats can also be found along the dry, alluvial plains of the piedmont regions of Mesopotamia, the Levant, and Saudi Arabia (English 1977: 177).

Dry Farming in Mountain Valleys and Highlands

The most prevalent method of food production in the Middle East is dry farming, a technique well suited to the high degree of rainfall variability in the mountains and highlands (Beaumont et al. 1976: 165-167). Kates et al. (1977: 271-272) distinguish between two principal types of dry-farming techniques: *moisture maximization* within field systems and *mixed agropastoralism*. In the case of moisture-maximizing dry farming, an array of diverse techniques are used, including careful seasonal plantings of fast-maturing varieties, scattered plantings of drought-resistant crops, careful weeding and mulching practices, the use of moist bottomlands, and the construction of terraces, bunds, and dams to impound run-off water.

Such techniques were particularly highly developed among the Nabataean Arabs of southern Palestine (Glueck 1959; Morris 1961; Mayerson 1962; Evenari, Shanan, and Tadmor 1971; Beaumont et al. 1976: 168-169). A succinct account of their moisture maximizing methods has been offered by Morris (1961: 51-52):

Nabatean constructions started on the slopes of the hills where rainwater flowed down by way of tributary wadis (dry stream beds) into the broad main wadi in the valley. The watercourses of those of the feeder wadis which were not too narrow or steep were terraced by the construction of a series of stone shelves. Instead of rushing violently down, the floodwater became rainwater gently cascading down the step-like shelves, part of it sinking into the ground at each shelf, depositing in the process some of its soil and organic debris. Shrubs were often left to grow on these shelves to help slow the rush of water and hold plant debris to enrich the soil. The shrubs were of inedible varieties, so that cattle would not eat them. Each of these terraces in the tributary wadis, accumulating soil year after year, became a farming plot, primarily for growing field crops.

And what of the broad wadi in the valley below? It was converted into a series of terraces, but in a more elaborate manner. Its area was divided into level plots by stone walls and the walls of the central plots served to divert some water to higher plots along the sides. During a rainstorm, all of them became small ponds, so that the water was distributed uniformly. In wadis where erosion had cut channels so deep that control of water flow by these means was too difficult, the Nabatean engineer-farmers built a series of stout dams to raise its flow so that part of the water would spill over to terraces along the sides.

To divert water to still higher ground, they built stone conduits upstream from the dams.

Realizing that the slightest change in the dimensions or direction of the watercourse would throw the entire system out of gear, they built strong masonry walls along its entire length to fix its boundaries permanently. Among the other refinements in the system was a low stone wall along the higher slopes which acted as an "inclined collector," diverting runoff water from plots already well watered and conducting it to otherwise unreachable plots.

Less labor intensive than moisture-maximizing dry farming is mixed-agropastoral dry farming. Found throughout the semiarid plains and highland regions of the Middle East, this technique involves raising field crops such as wheat, barley, and lentils on the arable plains and raising sheep and goats on the stubble fields and on nearby mountain slopes and desert pastures. Mixed agropastoral farmers may further diversify their production strategy by raising peas, tomatoes, cucumbers, and melons in garden plots in the vicinity of their villages. Sometimes orchards are also found near settlements in which primarily olives and grapes, but also other fruits, such as apricots and figs, are produced. The many different ways in which these various enterprises are combined vary not only in accordance with local topographic and hydrologic conditions, but also in accordance with sociopolitical and economic circumstances (Gulick 1971: 89).

Transhumance

One way to summarize the diversity of animal-based food production strategies which prevail in the Middle East is to distinguish between two principal patterns of migration, namely, *transhumance* or *vertical migration* and *plains* or *horizontal migration* (Beaumont *et al.* 1976: 152-158; Bates and Rassam 1983: 110-112). Transhumance, which involves the seasonal movement of people and animals from lowland to highland environments in search of pasture, is an ancient phenomenon in the mountainous regions of the Middle East. Typically, transhumants specialize in sheep and goats which they move between winter pastures in the lowlands and summer pastures in the cooler highlands. Cattle are also sometimes herded, especially in some parts of the Taurus and Zagros mountains where the supply of water and pastures is more plentiful than in the mountainous regions further to the south. In many cases, transhumants occupy permanent homes and villages in the winter season, moving into tents only in the spring and summer in order to follow their flocks. Transhumants may also engage in the production of wheat and barley on the highlands and in the vicinity of springs and wadis on the mountain slopes. Examples of this kind of agropastoral transhumance existed in Transjordan in the beginning of the present century and throughout certain historical periods (Tristram 1873; Glubb 1938).

Horizontal Nomadism

In comparison with transhumants, pastoralists engaged in horizontal migrations typically have to move longer distances in search of water and pasture for their animals. Because of the longer distances involved, such groups tend to rely more heavily on the dromedary or the single-humped camel. To the camel nomads of the Arabian Peninsula and the Sahara, this animal serves as the principal provider of food, as a means of freight transport, and as a source of leather and wool (English 1977: 181). Because the camel can exist for almost a month in the wintertime without water, and can go for three to four days without food in the summer, it is admirably suited to life in the desert regions traversed by horizontal pastoralists. As in the case of transhumant pastoralists, the migration routes and patterns of livelihood of plains pastoralists vary from place to place depending on the prevailing hydrological and sociopolitical conditions.

Hunting, Gathering, and Fishing

Throughout the Middle East hunting of wild animals and birds and gathering of wild herbs, roots, and fruits is carried out by both cultivators and pastoralists as a complementary activity. Because of their wider movements, which enhance access, and the greater seasonal scarcity with which they have to cope, transhumants and particularly camel nomads have traditionally been more dependent on hunting and gathering as a source of food than have stationary farmers (Musil 1907). The latter, on the other hand, have traditionally been more likely to eat fish caught in nearby streams or along the coasts of the Mediterranean, the Red Sea, the Persian Gulf, or the Indian Ocean. Typically, fishing is a specialty of certain members of otherwise agricultural villages located along the coasts or nearby inland bodies of water such as the Sea of Galilee (Gulick 1971: 89).

Interdependence of Strategies

As will be explained in further detail below, none of these various types of food production strategies are carried out independently of each other. They occur in various associations throughout the region, and various configurations of symbiotic relationships can be found, particularly between pastoralists and cultivators. Furthermore, as a result of the side-by-side occurrence of sedentarization and nomadization, individual households gradually become more nomadic or more sedentary. Thus, as we shall see in Chapter Three, in the course of a century, tribes formerly engaged in horizontal camel pastoralism gradually shifted their emphasis to agropastoral transhumance, then to mixed agropastoralism, and finally, today, to commercial agribusiness. The structural conditions which make possible such transitions in mode of livelihood throughout the Middle East will be examined in closer detail below.

The Influence of Plants and Animals
on Human Mobility

The effect which the type of plants and animals produced by a given producer unit has upon the degree of mobility of the people involved has been noted by several researchers concerned with the Middle East. Least free to migrate, for example, are those farmers who specialize in the production of perennial crops such as fruit trees. Not only do such enterprises require year-round protection, they also require a great deal of tending. Furthermore, in order for farmers to even consider making the investment necessary to grow large quantities of fruit trees, they must be able to count on having continuous cultivation rights on the land they desire to develop. Thus, production of perennial crops is possible only when certain prerequisite social and political conditions exists which assure the farmer that continuous rights to a particular plot of land are likely in the foreseeable future.

Because vegetables were difficult to transport over long distances and almost impossible to preserve for any length of time during antiquity, they were grown in small quantities primarily for local consumption in season (Beaumont *et al.* 1976: 160-162). Production of field crops such as wheat and barley, therefore, had, and still have, many advantages over fruits and vegetables. To begin with, grains can readily be transported over long dis-

tances and can last for several years under appropriate conditions of storage. Furthermore, once a field has been sown, it requires very little tending under dry-farming conditions, and a crop usually matures within a period of four to five months. Field crops, therefore, can be grown even when no long-term guarantees of continuous cultivation rights are possible. Once a crop has been harvested, the field can either be planted again in a system of rotation, or the stubble fields may be used for grazing by pasture animals. Indeed, in the Middle East, field crops are usually always linked to livestock production of one kind or another (Gulick 1971: 89; Grigg 1974: 123).

Much less tied to a stationary mode of existence than are cultivators are those households which specialize in the production of pasture animals. Although pigs and cattle are sometimes herded in comparatively well-watered regions, the vast majority of migratory households specialize in either sheep and goats or camels. While sheep need to drink every two days when the vegetation is dry and desiccated, they can sometimes go without drinking for up to ten days when the vegetation is fresh and green (Beaumont *et al.* 1976: 154). Goats are hardier than sheep because of their ability to go without water for longer periods than sheep and because of their omnivorous diets. Goats are also much better climbers, which means that they can graze where other pasture animals cannot go. Also, goats "have a higher rate of reproduction than sheep and a lactation period which is 50 to 100 per cent greater than that of sheep" (Beaumont *et al.* 1976: 154).

The camel's ability to go without water for up to thirty days in the wintertime and for three to four days in the hot summer has already been noted. Able to subsist on parched grass and desiccated shrubs, it is able to survive under the least favorable of watering and pasturage conditions. While the donkey can subsist on a similarly deteriorated pasture, it needs to be watered at least every two days, which makes it much more restricting in terms of migration in desert regions (Beaumont *et al.* 1976: 154). The distance which a common baggage camel can cover in a day is about 15 to 20 miles (English 1977: 181).

In order to provide a minimal supply of food for a household or tent, it is estimated that its members would have to raise "between 25 and 60 sheep and goats and from 10 to 25 dromedaries"

(Beaumont *et al.* 1976: 154). In good years, herders tend to build up the numbers of animals in their herds as a hedge against bad years, when their numbers sometimes reach a critical low. Because the reproduction rate of dromedaries is rather slow, formalized raiding by one tribe of the camels of another was traditionally a widespread practice among the inhabitants of the desert regions of the Middle East (Sweet 1960).

The composition of herds is seldom made up of one single species, but is instead variously constituted, depending on the particular landscape and social conditions to which herding households must adapt. Indeed, herders may over time adjust their numbers of camels, donkeys, sheep, and goats in accordance with whether their migration routes are being expanded or constricted. Glubb (1938) noted, for example, with regards to the Beni Sakhr of Transjordan, that as they became more sedentary, they gradually reduced their numbers of camels in favor of more sheep and goats. Furthermore, as they became more stationary, they began to grow limited quantities of cereals on the grasslands which formerly had served as pastures for their camels. This led eventually to the addition of cattle to their livestock in order to provide traction power for their plows.

The Structural Foundations of Sedentarization and Nomadization

The Fluidity of Social Units in the Middle East

We have seen in the previous section that the annual summer drought is an environmental hazard in the countries of the Middle East to which a range of different adaptive responses have traditionally been possible, depending, in part, on regional variation in topographical and hydrological conditions. Despite the range of methods by which food has been produced in different regions, a certain underlying unity should be noted, however. To begin with, the quest for food—whether by means of raising crops or livestock or both, or whether by means of stationary or migratory patterns or both—has furnished a common goal and has structured the daily and yearly routines of the vast majority of the rural population since ancient times. To a considerable degree, the end result of this quest has been the production of certain widely consumed foodstuffs, the most important of

which are cereals, specifically wheat or barley, the staple items grown or acquired by nearly every household in the Middle East (May 1961: 345). The preference for sheep and goats' meat is also widespread throughout the region, although the supply in different regions varies to a greater extent than does the supply of cereals.

It was also suggested in the previous section that a certain amount of flexibility in regards to how these staple items are acquired by a particular household or community is not only possible, but often necessary. It was noted, for example, that producers may adjust their strategies of production either in the direction of increased cultivation or increased pastoralism. Thus, despite the frequently stated conception of the Middle East as a region occupied by distinct groups of nomadic, seminomadic or transhumant, and settled peoples, the point which needs to be emphasized is that when the livelihood patterns of the various groups in this region are considered over time, they will be found to be much more fluid than has been generally acknowledged by investigators whose temporal frame of reference has primarily been the present (Patai 1951; Awad 1970). In other words, rather than viewing these groups, who because of their different modes of production at a given point in time appear to be somehow distinct from each other, as having always been either nomads, seminomads, or settled villagers, the view advanced here is that nomad, seminomad, and settled are stations on a temporal continuum along which successive generations of households have moved back and forth over the centuries.

While the rate at which shifts along this continuum occurred in the past probably involved periods extending over several centuries (Glubb 1938), during the past one hundred years shifts in the direction of stationary existence in either villages, towns, or cities have been greatly accelerated throughout the Middle East. To a large degree, this is due to the rise of modern national states, which have encouraged, and in some cases forced, the process of sedentarization of nomadic and seminomadic groups (Marx 1967; Awad 1970; Bates and Rassam 1983).

In the following paragraphs several proposals are advanced regarding the structural foundations of Middle Eastern society. Specifically, attention will be focused on the mechanisms whereby the fluidity of social groups in this region is facilitated, namely tribal organization, political allegiance, and shared ideals.

Tribal Organization

Perhaps one of the best examples of mechanisms which make possible the fluidity of social units in the Middle East is that of tribal organization. Over the past two decades research has been accumulating which shows that tribal identity in the Middle East is a complex phenomenon involving ethnopolitical ideologies such as notions of patrilineal descent and segmentary lineage; administrative assumptions regarding corporate identity and fixed territorial boundaries; practical notions invoked in the settlement of disputes over pastures and other political claims, marriage strategies, and patronage; and finally, analytical conceptions held by anthropologists (Eickelman 1981: 88).

As a mechanism facilitative of social fluidity, native notions of tribal identity are important to consider. First, the notion of common descent through patrilineal blood lines must be understood for what it is, namely a metaphor for signifying notions of *closeness* (Bates and Rassam 1983: 261). Closeness "can develop through cooperation with nearby households, mutual herding arrangements, kinship and patronage relations, and other bonds of mutual interest" (Eickelman 1981: 93). In other words, while blood lines may be involved in many cases of tribal identity and closeness, they are by no means always involved. Thus, considerable flexibility exists when it comes to who may belong to a given tribe. "What counts," wrote Eickelman (1981: 93) "is who acts together in a sustained way on various ritual and political occasions."

The linkage between notions of tribal identity and the quest for food has been emphasized by Marx (1977). Given the ecology of the nomad's habitat, it is necessary for the survival of individuals and households that they maintain networks of institutionalized relationships. To belong to a particular tribe, therefore, is to belong to a social entity which has control over particular natural resources or *areas of subsistence*. These areas may or may not be used exclusively by members of the tribe, and certain parts of their territory may even be controlled by other tribes. By means of "multiple close-knit networks of relationships that are coextensive with the territory controlled by the tribesmen," households of a given tribe are pro-

vided with access to watering places and pastures and afforded security in the face of natural hazards and dangers presented by outsiders (Marx 1977: 343-344).

It is in their relationship with outsiders that members of a tribe tend to emphasize their corporateness as a single political unit. It is in such contexts, as well, that the role and function of the tribal chief or headman comes into focus (Barth 1961; Marx 1967, 1977; Eickelman 1981; Bates and Rassam 1983). Indeed, as Bates and Rassam (1983: 258) have emphasized, "what most distinguishes the Middle East politically is the persistence of tribalism coexisting with the state." One major reason for this coexistence is that the tribal form of political organization has traditionally represented more closely the local and regional interests of rural subsistence units against the exploitative designs and undertakings of urban populations and city elites (Bates and Rassam 1983: 266). Thus, by claiming common descent and rallying behind a paramount chief, tribesmen are able to enter into negotiations with representatives of the state as a singular corporate entity. Alternatively, they may join together in alliances structured by means of the principle of segmentary lineage, and go to war against the state. Such alliances are impermanent and ever-shifting, however, depending on the purposes to be achieved at a given point in time and space. Whether for purposes of negotiations with outside powers or outright war, tribal entities are, as Bates and Rassam (1983: 267) have noted, "almost naturally competitive with the state form of political organization."

Given the importance of tribes as, among other things, a type of lobbying group representing the interests of various rural subsistence units throughout the Middle East, it stands to reason that tribal forms of organization may be found among settled villagers as well as among transhumants and more nomadic groups. In other words, the presence of this form of organization among settled villagers may not necessarily be taken as a sign of their nomadic descent, as has been suggested by Patai (1970: 191). Instead, as Gulick (1971) has emphasized, farming and herding are symbiotically related *ecologies* between whom exist certain common forms of organization and beliefs, such as adherence to the practice of patrilineal descent. With specific reference to the *Arab Levant* Gulick (1971: 99-100) writes as follows:

Farming and herding are both very ancient in the area. They appear to have developed together symbiotically. In the well-watered hills, farming has tended always to predominate, with herding as a technical adjunct; whereas east of the Arab Levant, where farming is impossible because of the aridity, herding predominates. In the very irregularly bordered intermediate zone, social groups specializing in one or the other ecology have always interpenetrated each other, and, in addition, there has always been a tendency for individuals or groups to be "converted" from one ecology to the other. This conversion has been made possible by the fact that despite the negative stereotypes in terms of which farmers and herders view each other at any given time, their techniques are symbiotically related and furthermore they share certain non-ecological patterns, such as patrilineal kinship. Owing to the latter, farmers and erstwhile herders settling together in a new village—as has happened very frequently since 1800 in the desert fringe area—have few conceptual problems to overcome, at least in the matter of basic kinship organization and related phenomena. Knowing that given a unilineal principle of kinship organization a people can relatively easily organize kinship groups which range greatly in extensiveness depending on their needs, we do not need to rely on imputed nomadic origins to account for the presence of widely ramified kin groups or on imputed sedentary origins to account for more restricted ones. In the desert fringe area there are groups of villages, each of which is inhabited by a section of a recently nomadic tribe, so that the whole can indeed be regarded as a "tribal" group consisting of localized sedentary sections. But not all herders become sedentarized in this fashion, and similar "tribal" localizations occur in other areas, the Jabal Ansariyah, for example, whose people have been farmers for a very long time.

The flexibility of the unilineal principle of kinship organization in facilitating the conversion from herder to cultivator or vice versa has been noted by other investigators as well. For example, Swidler has noted that the conversion of nomads into cultivators gives rise to the localized descent group and the extended family in order to "provide stabilized access to cultivable tracts through tenancy contracts." Such agnatic lineages do not arise to the same extent in the nomad camp structure because, as was noted above, greater flexibility is required in order to extend the network of relationships necessary to survive as a migratory subsistence unit. The stationary villager, by contrast, does not require, to the same extent, the "structural capacity to expand

and contract in response to nomadic requirements" (Swidler 1973: 36).

The importance of tribal organizations among settled cultivators as a means to organize access to tracts of land and protect against predation by hostile villagers or nomads has been reported in several accounts of village life in the Middle East in the previous century. For example, Antoun (1972) discusses the existence, in the Ajlun district of Transjordan, of cooperative arrangements between several villages for the purposes of mutual defense against predation. Under the leadership of a headman or sheikh from the largest village a local army could be constituted which was made up of males drawn from the various agnatic lineages living in the region. Reports of the existence of similarly organized villages and district sheikhs elsewhere in Palestine during the Late Ottoman Period have also been discussed by Reilly (1981) and Zenner (1972).

In a study dealing with the rural population of Saudi Arabia, Cole (1973) has proposed that, rather than thinking of the nomadic groups of this region being somehow discrete and well-bounded units, they should be thought of as being *enmeshed* in a single system with the sedentary population. This enmeshment or integration is evident at three levels: at the village level where villagers interact mainly with nomads at the subtribal grouping of the lineage; at the tribal level where a nomadic tribe, as a grouping in itself, is involved in dealings with regional urban centers; and at the national level where the nomadic tribes provide the major military support of the nation-state.

Finally, Barth's (1961) observations concerning the conversion of certain nomadic members of the Basseri tribe to settled villagers and vice versa offers a further example of the fluidity of social units in the rural regions of the Middle East. On the one hand, when the wealth accumulated by a nomadic household through the sale of animals and other enterprises reaches a certain level, it becomes economically advantageous for them to settle and invest in other resources, such as land, rather than risk sudden loss and impoverishment by continuing to migrate. But when drought or other adverse conditions result in the failure of a herd to grow, certain of the nomadic households are sometimes forced out of necessity to settle. In either case, when it becomes economically feasible for them to do so, such households may again elect to convert back into being nomads. Indeed, in the case of some Basseri households this process of sedentarization and nomadization may be repeated several times in the course of a century.

Political Allegiance

While tribalism furnishes an organizational context for the conversion of nomads into sedentaries and vice versa, patterns of political allegiance structure obligations between various social units and the flow of material exchanges between them. To the extent that such patterns of political allegiance structure the options available to individual households with regard to opportunities and incentives for becoming more sedentary or more nomadic in their quest for food, they can be regarded as mechanisms which make possible the fluidity of social units in the Middle East.

Differing views have been offered regarding the extent to which nomadic populations have traditionally dominated sedentary agriculturalists in the Middle East. One side of this debate is advanced by Barth (1973) who has argued that the inherent tendency of pastoral production systems to grow at a greater natural rate than agricultural ones has given the nomad the advantage. Because saving and investment are "necessary under all circumstances," given the nature of the pastoralist enterprise, and furthermore, given that such investment is possible without the benefit of economic institutions that facilitate the conversion of herd capital into food, *pure* pastoral systems lead more quickly to the accumulation of surpluses and give rise faster to military superiority. According to Barth, then, the basic pattern of nomad-sedentary relations in the Middle East is the result of the *seesaw of power* between pastoralists on the one side, and urban elites on the other, in their competition over cultivators' loyalties and surpluses. Writes Barth:

> On the domestic level, within local areas, an income flow tends to be set up from agricultural units to pastoral units, sustaining a local dominance by the pastoralists. However, cities with their urban elites, controlling the state apparatus, also prey on the cultivating households, and they do so by very effective and stable force and control, making peasants of the cultivators and drawing a substantial tax flow from them. Through this there is a tendency for the peasant households to be ground down even further by debt burdens to middleman entrepreneurs.

> **In rural households the process of . . .**
>
> *sedentarization* tends to be directly promoted by the policies and actions of the state apparatus
>
> *nomadization* is a form of resistance, a sort of natural response by the rural population to the exploitative undertakings of urban elites

These state systems, however, have great difficulties controlling and dominating nomadic pastoralists, who may choose among several strategies in their accommodation to the state: submitting to it in return for peace, withdrawing and defending themselves from it to avoid the tax drain, or seeking control by attempting conquest of the whole state apparatus. But any rising local elite of pastoralists, no matter what policy they choose vis-a-vis the state, tends to be drawn into the wider system of stratification obtaining in the region as a whole, and therefore to embroil themselves in competition with urban elites—perhaps reversing income flows and dissipating advantages that have been won (1973: 17-18).

On the other side of the debate over the nature of patterns of domination and allegiance in the Middle East is Asad (1973), who argues, on the basis of historical material, that the pastoralists' advantages are not what they are purported to be by Barth, and that, in fact, sedentary domination of pastoralists is more the rule than the exception historically in the Middle East. Like Barth (1973), Cole (1973), and Swidler (1973), Asad starts with the assumption that in the Middle East, pastoralists and cultivators belong to a single economic system, but rather than isolating conceptually systems of production from systems of power, as does Barth (1973), Asad notes "the intrinsic connection between the exercise of coercive power and modes of generating surpluses" (Asad 1973: 72).

The important distinction to note in this regard is that between exploiters and exploited. Since, in general, agricultural populations are more easily exploitable than are pastoralists, the point which historical materials dealing with nomad-sedentary relations bear out, according to Asad, is that first, "pastoralists have been more successful at resisting than imposing structures of domination," and sec-

ond, that whenever pastoralists have actually succeeded in capturing the state apparatus by means
of which cultivators have been controlled, they did
so by abandoning their power base in pastoralism,
becoming instead town-based rulers themselves
with their own regular armies. In other words, over
the millennia of competition between urban elites
and pastoralists for the surpluses produced by
cultivators, power has been shifted back and forth
between sedentary urban elites and sedentary
tribesmen. Never, according to Asad, has the
power base shifted from cultivators to migratory
pastoralist tribesmen (Asad 1973: 72). This is because migratory tribesmen "cannot constitute a regular state army and remain pastoralists." Thus, he
concludes, "it makes little sense to generalize about
the military advantage of nomadic mobility over
sedentary immobility as such" (Asad 1973: 71).

The difference between Barth's and Asad's
views on patterns of political allegiance is clearly
one of emphasis. While Barth emphasizes the opportunities for domination which come to pastoralists because of the inherent tendency of their
enterprises to expand more rapidly than those of
cultivators, Asad is more concerned about the
capacities for exploitation and the exercise of coercive power of nomadic pastoralists *vis-a-vis* sedentary elites (*cf.* Rosenfeld 1965). By keeping in mind
Asad's point, we are helped to see that the relations between nomadic and sedentary populations
are generally less antagonistic and oppressive than
is often suggested. However, there is no fundamental difference between these two views over the
basic fact that cultivators are generally more easily
exploited than are pastoralists.

Given the greater capacity of state systems for
the exercise of coercive power, it stands to reason
that the process of sedentarization of rural households is one which tends to be directly promoted
by the policies and actions of the state apparatus.
In order to feed the growing numbers of bureaucrats, craftsmen, and other specialists tending to
congregate in towns and at the urban centers of
power, policies are formulated and actions are
taken by members of the ruling elite which gradually induce cultivators to produce and turn over
greater quantities of food surpluses. In contrast to
this, the process of nomadization of rural households is best understood as a form of resistance, a
sort of natural response by the rural population to
the exploitative undertakings of urban elites.

Rather than being a process that is deliberately instituted by pastoralists, it represents instead a form
of escape, a return to greater independence, and a
distancing on the part of some members of the
rural population from the cultural and economic
domination of urban elites.

Shared Ideals

To the mechanisms of tribal organization and
political allegiance may be added a third mechanism facilitative of social fluidity in the Middle East,
namely shared ideals. To begin with, it was noted
already that the ideal of tribal or kin-based social
organization is one which is shared by cultivators
and pastoralists alike throughout the Middle East.
Related to this ideal are a number of others, including, as Patai (1970: 192) has noted, "the principle of collective responsibility, which is expressed
in such institutions as the blood feud and raiding,
the inviolate laws of hospitality and sanctuary, and
the concepts of honor, name, and nobility." Significantly, while all of these ideals appear in their most
intensive form among the true nomads . . . they
successively lose their significance as one proceeds
across the range from the true nomads, through
the seminomads, to the semisedentary and the
completely sedentary cultivators.

In light of what was stated above regarding patterns of political domination in the Middle East, it
is significant that the tendency to idealize the nomadic way of life is one which can be found among
cultivators and nomads alike throughout the Middle East. This tendency stems not only from the
fact that among nomads, the ideals of egalitari-
anism, collective responsibility, hospitality, honor,
and nobility are more intense, as noted above, but
also from the traditional perception of the nomadic
way of life as being independent of and less affected by the cultural and economic domination of
urban elites. Thus, despite their collection of trib-
ute and their raiding of agricultural villagers, a perception of them as *brothers* has traditionally prevailed in the rural regions of the Middle East
(Eickelman 1981: 68).

Finally, the extent to which shared religious beliefs and practices may have facilitated social fluidity in the Middle East is a matter that should be
further investigated. While it is beyond the scope
of this research to do so, it might be noted that
after the rise of Islam, a "commonality of practice

and ritual" emerged throughout the Middle East which served to integrate and bind together the peoples of this region in a manner which may have previously never existed (Eickelman 1981: 204). Whether a similar integrative influence was exerted by earlier monotheisms of the region, Judaism and Christianity, is a question which no doubt others have asked, although perhaps not specifically with reference to the role of these religions in facilitating social fluidity as discussed here.

Documented Cases of Sedentarization and Nomadization

Rationale Behind Selection of Cases

Given what has been said above about the existence of mechanisms in Middle Eastern societies which facilitate, over the course of successive generations of households, transitions between nomadic and sedentary modes of livelihood, is there any evidence that such long-term shifts have actually occurred? In reply to this question, we shall focus attention on two well-documented accounts of long-term changes in settlement and landuse from two separate regions in the Middle East, namely the Mesopotamian floodplain (Adams 1978) and Cyrenaica in eastern Libya (Johnson 1973). The selection of these two cases provides us with examples of the processes of sedentarization and nomadization in a riverine lowland environment and a mountainous environment (Cyrenaica). In each instance, a variety of literary, environmental, and archaeological data have been utilized in order to provide a reconstruction of food system transitions which have occurred since prehistoric times in these respective regions. The disciplinary backgrounds of the authors are anthropology (Adams) and geography (Johnson).

While other works have been published which include examples of long-term transitions in Middle Eastern food systems, such as for example Huntington (1907), Reifenberg (1955), Sweet (1960), McNeill (1963), Hole, Flannery, and Neely (1969), Butzer (1976), Redman (1978), and Naveh and Dan (1973), the two works examined here are of particular interest because both regard the processes of sedentarization and nomadization as being central to understanding the cyclic rise and fall of high-intensity food systems within their respective regional contexts. Furthermore, the tempo-

ral frame of reference of both overlaps with that of the present study, namely the period of time between 1200 B.C. and the present.

The Mesopotamian Floodplain, Iraq

On the basis of archaeological surface reconnaissance along a section of the Euphrates floodplain in Iraq more than 175 km in length and more than 75 km in width, Robert Adams and colleagues (Adams 1965, 1974, 1978, 1981; Adams and Nissen 1972) have sought to document and understand the relationship between changing configurations of canal irrigation and social institutions. Their surveys have enabled them to conclude that floodwater management along the banks of the Euphrates became increasingly intensive after 4000 B.C. This gradual process of intensification was repeatedly interrupted by periods of abatement, however. To understand why this occurred, it is first necessary to take a closer look at the hydrological and topographical conditions which existed along this floodplain in antiquity.

Unlike the Tigris River, which flows with great force to the east of the Euphrates in a single entrenched bed, the Euphrates River is a slow-moving stream which flows in a meandering pattern forming multiple channels that separate and rejoin. As these streams overtop their banks during flooding season, sediments are deposited on the back slope of the banks, thus forming natural levees which are used for cultivation. To these natural canals, the ancients gradually added artificial ones which also overtopped their banks, thus producing additional levees and extending the cultivatable area. Between these levees, and in the back swamps which are formed as the floodwaters find their way to depressions located along both sides of the parent stream, are lands providing pasturage for large herds of sheep and goats in the spring.

Sedentarization and urbanization along the Euphrates during the 4th and 3rd millennia B.C. (the Uruk through Early Dynastic periods) began with the gradual establishment of farmsteads and villages along the Euphrates floodplain. As the number of such rural settlements increased, regionally differentiated hierarchies of towns, urban centers, and cities began to appear which gradually began to assume importance as centers of economic, political, and religious administration and control (Adams 1981: 60, 90). Toward the end of the 4th millennium (during the Early Dynastic I Period), however, a process of progressive abandonment of rural settlements occurred which involved drastic reductions in the number of farmsteads, villages, and towns, and a concentration of the population in an increasing number of larger urban centers. Along with this shift came increased concentration of settlements along a small number of major Euphrates channels at the expense of the earlier pattern which had involved cultivation along multiple, often meandering and isolated channels not clearly related to one another in a continuous network (Adams and Nissen 1972: 12).

This pattern of sedentarization, whereby "isolated pockets of landuse coalesced into larger agglomerations" around cities and military strong points is contrary to "the entire historic record of Mesopotamian settlement" which "makes clear that stable, centralized regimes promote dispersion of the agricultural population into the countryside, closer to the fields" (Adams 1981: 88). Why, then, did it happen in this manner in this period of urban origins? In Adams' (1981: 88) view, this pattern is attributable to the existence during this period of a "discontinuous fabric of administration." Instead of a centralized, region-wide, political regime having been established, and "in spite of considerable intercommunication and cultural homogeneity," the political structure "remained a patchwork of constituencies" (Adams 1981: 90). Not explicitly discussed with reference to this period of urban beginnings is the process of nomadization which undoubtedly occurred simultaneously with the flight of rural farmers to the cities during the Late Uruk through Early Dynastic I periods. That such a process occurred during these millennia can safely be assumed, for as Adams has pointed out, "pastoralism was intimately linked in many ways with sedentary and even urban pursuits" throughout "all periods" along the Mesopotamian floodplain. Indeed, "it repeatedly served as the indispensable source of ecological flexibility and resilience in the aftermath of natural or socially induced disasters" (Adams 1981: 11).

In contrast to the Uruk through Early Dynastic I periods, which had been an epoch of steady growth leading to an urban climax, the next two millennia, namely the 2nd and 1st which included the Early Dynastic II through Middle Babylonian periods, experienced no similar accumulative trends. Instead, what is revealed by the settlement pattern maps is an "ebb and flow of population into and away from outlying regions, expanding and contracting the nuclei of settlement and cultivation in response to fairly transitory political stimuli" (Adams 1981: 130). The political corollary of this situation was a cyclic process involving alternating tendencies in the direction of political centralization and fragmentation (Adams 1981: 133).

During this same period, the inhabitants of the floodplain undertook to dike, straighten, and deepen the major watercourses in order to "assure the passage into the cities of barges with bulk foodstuffs and other riverine commerce" (Adams 1981: 245). Widened was the area under cultivation along each of the major channels, especially in the vicinity of the major cities, while the smaller channels located in more outlying areas decreased in number. In harmony with the impressions provided by the settlement data and the political picture, the watercourse configuration which emerged during these millennia "was not for the most part a product of planned, systematic construction, but was instead an outgrowth of small-scale modifications and improvements" (Adams 1981: 245).

To account for the expanding and contracting of settlements during these millennia, Adams (1981: 136) draws attention, among other factors, to Rowton's (1976: 24-27) research which has posited the existence of a pastoral corridor to the north and east of the Mesopotamian floodplain. This corridor is believed to have served "repeatedly to channel new groupings of nomads and seminomads into close proximity and hostile interaction with the great urban centers." Given the "structural and ethnic continuum" which Adams (1981: 136) believes existed across the frontiers of cultivation, a process occurred during these millennia involving the "acculturation of particular groups proceeding backward and forward between nomadization and sedentarization according to circumstances" (Adams 1981: 136).

The process of nomadization which occurred during these millennia is further illuminated when attention is focused on the textile trade. Since textiles enabled "commercial relations with regions whose natural resources Mesopotamia altogether lacked," the pastoral sector of the regional economy may at certain times have been encouraged by urban elites connected with the central state leadership. But as the powers of the ruling dynasties would erode, the attachment of outlying semisedentary elements would have been the first to loosen. Their largely pastoral basis conferred mobility, and mobility in turn conferred a greater opportunity either to shift loyalties to rival powers or to withhold support and tend toward greater degrees of independence and autarchy.

Thus, the formation of "impressive royal herds carried within it the seeds of a far-reaching dissolution of the web of political and economic interrelationships, once the initial organizing impulse had run its course" (Adams 1981: 149).

Beginning in the latter half of the 1st millennium B.C., in the Neo-Babylonian Period, the cyclic pattern of ebb and flow which had prevailed for over two millennia gave way to a millennium of steady intensification of the food system and a *pumping up* of the urban superstructure to an unprecedented climax during the Sassanian Period in the middle of the 1st millennium A.D. (*ca.* A.D. 226-637). During this period of growth, "the peoples of the lower Mesopotamian plain were more or less firmly incorporated in larger, longer-lived, more heterogeneous empires than had existed previously" (Adams 1981: 175). Simultaneously, an "immense expansion of the cultivated area" took place "so that the total population of the alluvium was significantly larger." Indeed, at its peak, the Sassanian intensification effort led to "three to four times as large an area" being devoted to irrigation agriculture as during the earlier agrarian climax during the Third Dynasty of Ur in the 3rd millennium B.C. (Adams 1978: 332).

To support this build-up of population and urban superstructure, dramatic advances in floodwater management were required and successfully carried out. Not only was the network of artificial canals greatly expanded, but more effective water-lifting machinery to supplement gravity-flow canals was introduced on a large scale so that cultivation could be extended to the outermost limits of the floodplain (Adams 1981: 246). Furthermore, for the first time in history, the turbulent and deep-flowing waters of the Tigris were harnessed so that its flow could be channeled into the network of canals which by this time had expanded southward to its banks. Unlike, therefore, the small-scale modifications implemented during the earlier millennia, the "ambitiousness and complexity" of the Sassanian scheme "strongly suggests that components of the irrigation system were planned and constructed according to uniform standards by full-time specialized, technically very competent cadres" (Adams 1981: 246).

The collapse of the Sassanian maximization drive appears to have been caused by "an array of political, economic, and ecological factors." To begin with, the system of intersecting grids of canal levees tended to disrupt the natural surface drainage channels, thus hastening the rise of saline water. Additionally, the high degree of managerial competency and bureaucracy, which was needed in order to manage the flooding cycles of both the Tigris and the Euphrates rivers, served to increase the vulnerability of the entire system to potential destabilization due to managerial incompetence and power rivalries. This vulnerability was further heightened by the emphasis given to cereal cultivation at the expense of a more diversified, mixed agropastoral economy. Not only did this lead to an increased sense of futility and frustration for the peasants who were forced to cultivate lands which were at best marginally productive, it also led to diminished supplies of meat and dairy products due to insufficient quantities of pasture animals being produced. The culmination of these general conditions led to malnourishment of the peasant producers, weakened resistance to disease, and eventually, to massive die-offs from famine and plague at the end of the Sassanian Period (Adams 1978: 333; 1981: 200-214).

That nomadization remained an option for many of the rural households during this millennium of build-up and collapse is certain, although Adams is short on specifics. This he implicitly acknowledges, noting that the two-way street between nomads and sedentaries is one which has been "systematically underrepresented," not only by his own methods, but also generally by most other "spokesmen for urban institutions" (Adams 1978: 334). The picture which emerges from his discussion, nevertheless, is one of a gradual process of accumulative failures on the part of urban elites resulting in a continual loosing of the web of interdependencies whereupon the Sassanian urban superstructure had come to rest. Rather than having actively contributed to this failure, the process of nomadization must have occurred as a natural survival response by the tribally organized elements of the rural population to the increasingly intolerable conditions which accumulated in the hinterlands of the once powerful urban centers. Over the following centuries, this response became the prevailing one in the Mesopotamian floodplain until the advent of the modern era (Adams 1981: 175-228).

The popular tendency in the literature about the Middle East to represent the relationship between nomads and sedentaries as inevitably antagonistic does not receive support in Adams' work. Instead, throughout his analysis, Adams repeatedly reminds of the fluidity of social life in the rural hinterlands, emphasizing the back-and-forth movement of individuals and households between nomadic and sedentary pursuits. Indeed, as was noted earlier, during certain periods of agricultural intensification, the pastoral sector of the economy was actually encouraged because of what it could offer in the way of long-distance transportation and animal products.

The Green Mountain of Cyrenaica, Libya

From Adams' research, which, as we have seen, dealt with food system alterations in a lowland, riverine environment, we shall next turn to another investigation which also offers evidence for long-term shifts in patterns of settlement and landuse involving the processes of sedentarization and nomadization. In this case, however, a mountainous highland region furnishes the ecological backdrop. Specifically, the region dealt with in this piece of historical geographic research is to be found along the North African shoreline of the Mediterranean in eastern Libya. It is known locally as Jabal al-Akhdar, the Green Mountain of Cyrenaica. According to Johnson (1973: iii), the purpose of his inquiries in this region was to accomplish two goals: first, to study the changes which have occurred over the past two centuries in the livelihoods of the Bedouin of Cyrenaica; and second, to analyze the settlement history of the same area in the light of insights gained from learning about the contemporary population's experience.

Jutting northward into the Mediterranean, the Jabal al-Akhdar region consists of a series of ascending platforms or terraces running from the western coastline toward the east and rising to about 800 m above sea level. As a natural resource, this mountainous landscape stands out as being relatively well endowed for the purposes of both pastoral and agricultural pursuits when compared with the marginality of areas to the east, west and south. This is because, although rainfall is both seasonal and extremely variable from year to year, a variety of different ecological zones exists along the ascending platforms and escarpments, which provide a wide range of options when it comes to alternative strategies for obtaining food and managing the risks of drought and famine.

Traditionally, that for which every tribal group has striven in Jabal al-Akhdar is control over a north-south strip of territory assuring access to the full range of ecological zones available between the coast and "across the agricultural areas of the high plateau into the steppe and semi-desert grazing areas on the Saharan fringes" (Johnson 1973: 34). Because control over this entire range of resources is beyond what is possible for any one family or lineage segment, attachment to one of nine noble tribes is claimed by all families in order to justify "the practical realities of ownership of land and water resources." In the case of each of these tribal entities, common descent is claimed by its members from a fictitious legendary ancestor said to be the progenitor of each tribe. Furthermore, to each of these nine noble lineages belongs a genealogically inferior tribe whose members stand in a client relationship to their noble lineage masters.

Until about four decades ago, nearly all Cyrenaicans were nomads in the sense that

> they derived most of their livelihood from animals, shifted their animals about in response to seasonal variations in the location of pasture and water, and participated in a shared value system, myths, and tribal social structure (Johnson 1973: 40).

Yet, "with few exceptions," all practiced agriculture as well. The extent is a function of the types of animals they herded. For example, along the coast, where plant life is unsuitable for large herds of cattle, sheep, and camels, goats were raised in large numbers by the genealogically inferior client tribesmen. In the alluvial fans of wadis and in wadi bottoms where the soil was sufficiently moist and fertile, these tribesmen also planted barley after the first rains in the fall. A few cattle were also kept for milk and plowing purposes, thanks to the spring water available at the foot of the mountains. Further inland, along the terraces, sheep, goats, and cattle were raised by members of both inferior and noble tribes. The better soils and rainfall conditions which are in this region permitted cultivation of relatively large quantities of wheat and barley, especially on the upper terraces. In December, following the planting of cereals on the mountain terraces, households would typically split up, with some of the young men migrating southward into the desert fringes with their flocks of sheep and goats after the winter rains had brought fresh supplies of water and pasture. In the wadi beds along the border of the desert, many of these herders would engage in speculative sowing in hopes that they might reap a rich harvest of grains. Such speculative sowing was deemed worthy of the risk, for if rainfall was sufficient, a harvest five times more plentiful than on the terraces was sometimes obtained. In late spring, when the desert fringe became too dry, the herds would be brought back to the mountain terraces where, as summer progressed, they would become concentrated around the springs and cisterns upon which they depended for water. Following the harvest of grains on the terraces, the stubble fields became pastures for flocks (Johnson 1973: 50-59).

To the south of the mountain slopes, along the dip-slope which leads into the southern desert, households specializing in camel breeding could be found. Unlike their northern kinsmen, who produced camels mainly for the sake of baggage transport, these tribesmen raised them in order to live by their milk on their seasonal treks into the desert oasis in the interior of the desert. Sheep and goats were also produced by these households, but these animals were herded separately from the camels. While the goats were kept close by the tents so that they could furnish milk to the family households, the sheep were herded to wherever sufficient pasture and water could be found. Near the principal watering points, in the broad flat wadi beds, these same herders would sow grain in limited quantities as well. Thus, a rather complex pattern of oscillating movements out from and back to the family households was the typical pattern in this more arid region at the edge of the desert.

Finally, a small number of tribesmen lived exclusively by the camel and raised no grain of their own. With these nomads, while their families would camp near desert oases and other watering places, their camels, herded by young men, would migrate out into the arid steppe and desert fringes during the rainy season. In the dry season, the animals were herded on pastures closer to the wells and the family tents.

Despite this range of different herding lifestyles among the nomads of Jabal al-Akhdar, a great degree of sameness existed as well. No "absolute separation between the man who herds and the man who farms" prevailed. Instead, the combination of herding practices "blended imperceptibly into one another" and differences were "of degree rather than of kind" (Johnson 1973: 39). Unlike nomadic groups in other regions of the Middle East, dependence on a sedentary population was minimal in Cyrenaica, because nearly all families engaged in both cultivation and pastoralism, albeit the relative importance of one over the other varied considerably as we have seen.

In order to obtain access to certain specialized goods required by their lifestyle, such as teapots, sugar, salt, tea, weapons, etc., the nomads of Jabal al-Akhdar would rely on periodic markets which appeared in the nearby larger villages and towns in the summer months, when the nomads were prevented from making their desert excursions. These markets were invariably controlled by urban merchants or rural shopkeepers (Johnson 1973: 78). Operating outside the network of periodic markets, furthermore, were complex patterns of trade and debt relationships between tribesmen living in different ecological zones, who were tied to each other by means of kinship or tribal affiliation.

The fluctuating frontiers of settled agriculture, which historically have characterized Cyrenaica, are understandable in light of the preceding ecological model. Since the upland terraces are resources capable of supporting either sedentary farming or pastoralism, farmers and herders have, over the centuries, lived in varying degrees of competition with each other. Periodically, hostile interactions between these two competing elements have occurred. This has been due largely to the fact that during certain centuries, the areas of high agricultural potential, which the pastoralists need access to in order for their economies to function smoothly, have been denied them by sedentary rulers bent on intensifying sedentary exploitation of the land.

In his monograph, Johnson (1973) has utilized historical and archaeological sources in order to reconstruct the repetitive pattern of advance and retreat of the agricultural frontier since pre-Roman times. The process he describes begins with the gradual alienation by colonizers of the fertile agricultural areas of Cyrenaica from its native nomadic population, namely the Libyan Berbers, who practiced a type of mixed agropastoral way of life involving cereals and herds of sheep and goats. This process was set in motion first, by the colonization of Cyrenaica by Hellenistic and Greek settlers (between *ca.* 639 and 96 B.C.), then later by the Romans and the Byzantines (between *ca.* 96 B.C. and A.D. 642). The process reached its climax during the Roman Imperial Period, when large numbers of military veterans were settled in fortified farmsteads and villages; when an extensive road network was built which facilitated the movement of soldiers to rural destinations and foodstuffs to urban areas; and when a series of forts and garrisons (the Cyrenaican *Limes*) were constructed along the borders of the cultivatable land to protect it from nomadic incursions. Along with these protective measures, the Imperial Romans also greatly improved the supply of water by digging cisterns, wells, and aqueducts throughout the rural areas, as well as by their construction of agricultural terraces and check dams to capture more effectively the limited wadi run-off.

As efforts to tighten the frontier *limes* intensified throughout the 3rd century A.D., "the level of nomadic raids rose correspondingly and reached a crescendo of violence" around A.D. 400 (Johnson 1973: 135). These nomadic reactions coincided with internal decay of administrative and military powers in the sedentary areas, resulting in the growth throughout the 4th century of "a quasi-feudal system of illegal patrons for villages," who in return for village support assisted the local inhabitants in escaping the payment of taxes and in protecting against the depredations of the nomads (Johnson 1973: 136). Throughout the remainder of the Byzantine Period, arrangements such as these prevailed, resulting in the decline of the large imperial cities, and a flourishing of castles and fortified churches in the countryside (Johnson 1973: 141).

Crucial to the turn of fortune in favor of the nomads was the camel, which in this region appears first to have been introduced by the sedentary population for transportation purposes. Its gradual adoption by the nomads was inevitable, however, and immensely strengthened their efforts to regain control over the vital agricultural areas, which the Imperial Romans had succeeded in alienating from them almost completely. As the centralized government apparatus continued to weaken throughout the 5th and 6th centuries, the rate of nomadic incursions, aided by the camel, became more sustained. Gradually, the settled population was forced to come to terms with "their now militarily more powerful bedouin neighbors."

Writes Johnson (1973: 160-161) about the resulting process of nomadization:

> The relative richness of the Jabal al-Akhdar for a pastoral people, coupled with the mixed agricultural-animal economy of the local bedouin, made them relatively independent of sedentary and urban products. Finding little of profit to be derived from the settled population, the bedouin went their own way, gradually incorporating the rural farmers and the vast majority of the urban population into the nomadic tribal structure either as outright genealogical equals or as marabtin client lineages. For the sedentary population the change was not an impossible one; animals always had held an important place in their economic system, now it increasingly superseded agriculture as the focus of attention . . . An alteration of style as much as of substance, this process of gradual acculturation culminated in a nearly complete bedouinization of al-Jabal al-Akhdar and a return to the same pattern of land use in vogue when Battus led the first party of Greek colonists to Cyrene in 631 B.C.

The period which intervened between the decline of the Byzantine Empire and the Italian colonization of Libya in 1911 were centuries during which the nomadic lifestyle prevailed, despite attempts by the Ottoman Turks to assert control over the region. Because of the low pressure which they exerted on the agricultural lands during these intervening years, the Bedouin helped to preserve and, in some places, actually contributed to the restoration of the arboreal vegetation of the Green Mountain of Jabal al-Akhdar (Johnson 1973: 194). In their own way, they also contributed to the continuity between the Greco-Roman civilization by "retaining regularities that related intimately to the pre-existing settlement scheme" (Johnson 1973: 194). Thus, agricultural fields, though reduced in extent, continued to be utilized; classical road beds continued to function as footpaths and donkey trails; Roman cisterns and wells continued to be used as sources of water; and tombs were turned into sites for human habitation, animal shelters, or storage depots. Continuity with the past, therefore,

> was inescapable, but found its expression through the medium of a different culture. Shaped and adapted to fit the predilections of a pastoral mystique, firm ties to the area's classical heritage were nonetheless maintained (Johnson 1973: 197).

In the present century, large-scale nomadic settlement has progressed at an unprecedented rate. This process has involved several different configurations, including the spontaneous settlement of nomads in small genealogical clusters in the vicinity of water resources close to their traditional agricultural fields; settlement within their traditional tribal territories in abandoned farmhouses left by the Italian colonizers; planned government housing projects and rural-urban migration. With these changes have come a rapid decline in the dependence on camels, increased production of cereals and cash crops, and nonagricultural employment in local government agencies or industries. Because of their traditional value as a source of capital investment and formation in the nomadic community, "sheep continue today as the primary symbol of continuity and stability in a society undergoing massive change" (Johnson 1973: 212).

The Levant

That the processes of sedentarization and nomadization, which have contributed to the repetitive advance and retreat of the frontier of agricultural settlements in Mesopotamia and Cyrenaica, have also contributed to the rise and fall of agricultural settlements in the countries of Israel, Jordan, Lebanon, and Syria is certain. Indeed, numerous scholars have noted the oscillating pattern of on-again off-again sedentary life in many localities throughout the Levant, especially along the eastern desert borders. Among them are Rostovtzeff (1932), Glueck (1939), Kirk (1944), Lewis (1954), Reifenberg (1955), Parr (1975), Bowersock (1983), Cohen and Dever (1981), and many others. For various reasons, however, systematic research—conceived in a diachronic frame—concerned with the comparative study of the processes of sedentarization and nomadization in the Levant, has barely been begun. Focusing on the country of Jordan, the research which is reported in the subsequent chapters is offered as a beginning contribution to this neglected anthropological problem.

Chapter Three

THE HESBAN AREA FOOD SYSTEM
DURING THE RECENT PAST

Chapter Three

The Hesban Area Food System
During the Recent Past

Introduction

In this chapter changes which have taken place within the Hesban project area food system since the early part of the 19th century are examined. Specifically, I shall attempt to discover some of the ways in which the processes of sedentarization and nomadization within the project area might be linked to changes over the past century and a half in the five parameters of the food system discussed in Chapter One, namely, in environmental, settlement, landuse, operational, and dietary conditions. Some of the principal indicators by which food system transitions in this region may be traced archaeologically are noted.

To the extent that this chapter is concerned with discovering archaeological indicators of food system transitions, it may be regarded as a contribution to the field of ethnoarchaeology (Gould 1978; Watson 1980; Binford 1983). Over the past three decades, archaeologists' interest in contemporary peoples has increased markedly because of the many clues to how the archaeological record is formed which can be obtained from studying them. Specifically, ethnoarchaeologists study present-day cultures to see how patterns of daily life become transformed into an assemblage of fragmentary remains of the sort encountered by archaeologists in their excavations and surveys (cf. Hodder 1982; Schiffer 1976; Binford 1983). Such research has become important especially among prehistoric archaeologists working in the Middle East (Watson 1980; Hole 1978), although recently scholars dealing primarily with historical periods have also begun to make contributions to this field (Murray and Chang 1980).

It should perhaps be noted that an interest in the daily-life patterns of contemporary peoples of the Middle East is not a novel thing among Middle East scholars. Indeed, such interest goes back to the previous century to the days of the rediscovery of Palestine by Western intellectuals and adventurers. Literally thousands of books which offer a wealth of detailed information about the material life of nomads, villagers, and town people throughout the whole of the Middle East, especially people living in what was called the "lands of the Bible" or simply "the Holy Land," were published before the turn of the century. These books not only offer textual accounts, but many of them contain exquisite illustrations such as pencil drawings, sketches, and photographs.

These sources represent a virtual gold mine of information useful to ethnoarchaeologists, for they not only constitute a record of how things were before the full impact of Westernization in the Middle East, but also provide information enabling a reconstruction of the linkages between successive changes in social and cultural patterns and co-occurring changes in material conditions. This chapter attempts to do just that, with particular reference to sedentarization and nomadization, as revealed in changes in the five parameters of the food system mentioned above. It thus goes beyond much of what has been published so far in the name of ethnoarchaeology, in that eyewitness accounts from the 19th and early 20th centuries are relied upon for confirmation of recollections and explanations offered by my informants and for inferences and reconstructions based on my own observations and experiences within the project area. Thus the research reported here approaches, perhaps, what might be categorized as local history or ethnohistory.

The reasons why such an undertaking is worthwhile have already been alluded to in the

53

previous chapters. To begin with, as was pointed out in Chapter One, the quest for food represents one of the most fundamental activities of humans everywhere. In the Middle East, as seen in Chapter Two, the traditional food procurement strategies pursued have been shaped, to a considerable degree, by the opportunities and challenges presented by the natural environment. By learning about present-day attributes of the natural environment, and by examining various ways in which local inhabitants, over the past century and a half, have altered their strategies for exploiting it, insights may be gained that in turn may lead to better understanding of the fragmentary archaeological record. Rather than being pursued, however, merely for the sake of analogy of the past with the present—a common but sometimes questionable undertaking—this chapter about Hesban and vicinity since Late Ottoman times has been included for two simple reasons.

First, the recent past of the project area constitutes an era which is as deserving of scholarly attention as are earlier historical eras. Indeed, the recent past is the most accessible of the successive eras of which it constitutes the latest. This fact in itself justifies its study for the same reason that it makes sense to learn about the anatomy of living animals before trying to piece together ancient ones from their fragmentary skeletal remains, or to learn about the structure of living languages before trying to decode ancient ones. Thus, the recent past of the project area is that point in time about which there is the potential for learning and understanding the most. As one proceeds to interpret and piece together life in the distant past, knowledge of the recent past is an indispensable vehicle by means of which new and insightful hypotheses can be derived. Furthermore, knowledge of the recent past furnishes a benchmark in time with which to compare the constructs which are developed to represent the experience of peoples whose way of life we are seeking to reconstruct on the basis of the fragmentary archaeological and historical record.

Second, precisely because the recent past is the most accessible to scholarly investigation, it furnishes the best opportunity for becoming acquainted with the workings of the project area food system. In the present chapter, therefore, the processes involved in the transformation of

the local food system during the recent past from a low intensity to a high intensity one are investigated. Specifically sought have been archaeological indices of sedentarization and nomadization. Such indices were sought with reference to changes in the five parameters mentioned earlier. Also sought were insights on how changes in these five parameters were interrelated; for example, whether changes in landuse occurred at a slower or faster rate than changes in diet, or whether they occurred at the same rate.

> The recent past of the project area constitutes an era which is as deserving of scholarly attention as are earlier historical eras. Indeed, the recent past is the most accessible of the successive eras of which it constitutes the latest.

The organization of the present chapter is as follows: first, a brief introduction is provided as to how the recent past was investigated; second, a brief review is included of relevant research by other investigators dealing with the project area; third, the project area as a natural resource is introduced; fourth, panoramic images of the project area as it appeared from the summit of Tell Hesban in 1870, 1910, and 1970 are set forth on the basis of what the writer has learned about each of these points in time; fifth, how the population lived when transhumance prevailed (*ca.* A.D. 1800-1880), when village life prevailed (*ca.* A.D. 1880-1950) and when urban interests prevailed (*ca.* A.D. 1950-1980), is discussed; and sixth, on the basis of these findings three different configurations of the local food system are distinguished which summarize the salient features of the food system during the three different historical periods mentioned above.

Objectives and Procedures

As noted in Chapter One, studies of the recent past were already begun in connection with the Heshbon Expedition in 1973, when observations of present-day animal slaughtering processes were carried out to arrive at some possible explanations for the patterning which was apparent in the sheep and goat remains unearthed in the excavations (LaBianca and La-

Bianca 1975). During the subsequent field seasons of 1974 and 1976, ethnographic inquiries in the village of Hesban were escalated (pl. 3.2), thanks to the expedition leadership's willingness to permit volunteers to work in the village instead of on the tell. Assisted by two volunteers during the 1974 campaign (namely Shirley Finneman and Douglas Fuller), and by four volunteers during the 1976 campaign (namely Mary Ann Casebolt, Del Downing, Theresa Fuentes, and Asta Sakala LaBianca and their informant/translators, Samir Ghishan and Hannan Salem Hamarneh) the writer was able to gather information about a wide range of daily-life activities in the village of Hesban during these two eight-week campaigns. While some of this information has been distilled and summarized in two short published reports (LaBianca 1976 and 1978a), most of it remains undigested, except for what has been used for this chapter and Volume 4 of the Hesban final publication series.

It was the launching, in 1977, of the Hesban final publication project which provided the impetus to further ethnographic fieldwork in the project area (LaBianca 1977). At first, it was felt that such fieldwork should focus on husbandry practices by project area villagers (LaBianca 1978a). It soon became clear, however, that such a limited focus could not adequately bridge the increasingly apparent gap between the findings of other lines of research, such as the regional survey and the stratigraphic excavations. Thus, a more fundamental problem began to emerge as the need for integration of the bone finds with the rest of the expedition results became increasingly compelling. This problem was to ascertain the extent to which the variation over time in the intensity of sedentary occupation within the project area, the variation over time in the intensity of occupation at Tell Hesban itself, and the changes over time in the composition of the domestic animals, as seen in the bone remains from Tell Hesban, was attributable to some yet unidentified underlying organizing principle. It was the quest for an answer to this question which gave direction to the fieldwork activities which were carried out in Jordan between October 1, 1980 and March 10, 1981 by the writer and his family (LaBianca 1984). Funding for this research was provided by the American Schools of Oriental Research in the form of a W. F.

Albright Fellowship, by Brandeis University in the form of a Sacchar Fellowship, and by Andrews University in the form of a loan.

While our first three months in Jordan were spent in Amman at the Adventist Orphanage near the University of Jordan, the remainder of our stay was spent living in the home of Issa Ghishan, a long-time resident of Madaba. During our stay in Amman, my time was spent tracking down information about the project area available in the form of scholarly publications, government reports, development agency reports, and verbal accounts offered by a number of experts and other knowledgeable individuals with whom I came into contact. Before leaving Amman, a rudimentary notion of the food system concept discussed in Chapter One had emerged in my mind. I had also determined that what I needed to focus further research upon was the extent to which changes in environment, settlement, land-use, operational, and dietary conditions within the project area were functionally related and could be utilized independently as parameters of food system transitions. If functional interrelationships between these variables could be shown to exist on the basis of empirical data, then a logical case for the existence of an underlying organizing principle in the form of the food system could be advanced. It was in order to gather such empirical data *on the ground* that we moved to Madaba.

Madaba was the base from which we visited the 31 hamlets, villages, and towns located within a 10-km radius of Tell Hesban (fig. 3.1): Kefeir el Wakhyan, Al Loba, Qaryat el Mukheiyat, Uyun Musa, Kefeir Abu Sarbut, Kefeir Abu Khinan, El Jureina, Gharnata, El Aresh, Mushaqqar, Hesban, El Manshiya, El 'Al, Es Samik, El Mansura, El Rawda, Umm el Quttein, Naur, El Amiriyah, El Adissyah, Khirbet Abu Nukleh, Umm el Asakar, Umm el Basatin, Umm el Gabbya, Umm el Amad, Umm el Zeituna, Umm el Rummana, Manja, Hanina, Jalul, and Madaba. Our observations and interviews in these villages were guided by the use of an observation guide developed while still in Amman (LaBianca 1984). This guide (fig. 3.2) prompted us to make note of the topography of the village hinterland, landuse in the village and on its hinterlands, operational facilities in the village and in its hinterland, the village settlement pattern, and any ancient agricultural installations within the village or in its hinterland.

Plate 3.1   Lawrence T. Geraty, Heshbon Expedition director '74 and '76 campaigns, standing beside G. Ernest Wright, his former professor at Harvard, on the latter's visit to Hesban in 1974

Plate 3.2   Ethnography team at work: Asta Sakala LaBianca, author, Del Downing, Samir Ghishan, and Mary Ann Casebolt

Fig. 3.1   Project area villages *ca.* 1975

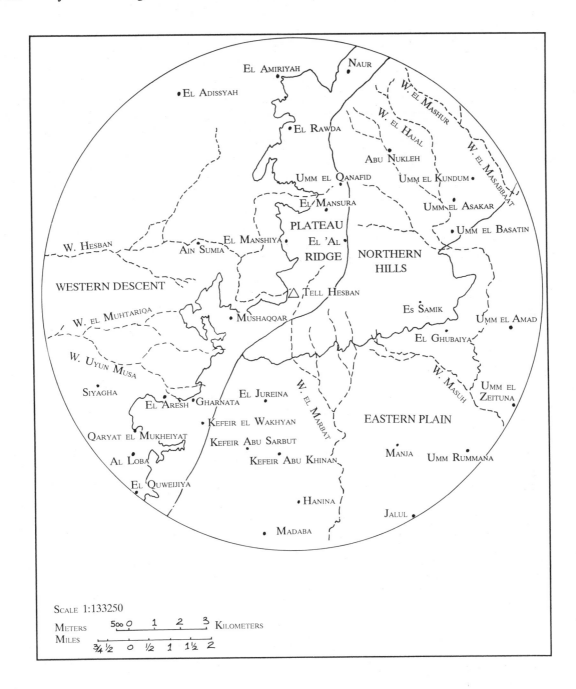

Fig. 3.2 Village food system survey observation guide

DATE _____

VILLAGE NAME _____   ROAD SIGN SPELLING _____

KM FROM MAIN ROAD _____   PANORAMIC APPEARANCE _____

CONDITION OF ACCESS ROAD _____   LOCATION ON MAP VERIFIED _____

A. TOPOGRAPHY
1. Slope—no slope, less than 20% slope, 20-40% slope, 40-60% slope, more than 60% slope
2. Ease of Cultivation—easy, medium, hard
3. Soil Depth—in meters of cultivatable soil
4. Soil Texture—heavy clay loam, calcium soil, light clay loam
5. Biochemical Status—high Ph, normal Ph, acid
6. Soil Stability—good, fair, poor
7. Vegetation—batha, garigue, woodland, forest

B. LANDUSE ON VILLAGE HINTERLAND
1. Tree Crops—olives, grapes, almonds, pears, apricots
2. Vegetable Crops—tomatoes, cucumbers, lentils, cauliflower, eggplant
3. Cash Crops—tobacco
4. Grain Crops—wheat, barley, millet, sorghum, maize
5. Pasture Animals—sheep, goats, local cattle, foreign cattle
6. Barnyard Animals—chicken, geese, turkeys, doves, rabbits, pigs

C. OPERATIONAL FACILITIES
1. Waterworks—reservoir, cisterns, aqueducts, water tanks, water-line hook-up, pumping stations, roof-collection facilities
2. Terracing Works—terraced wadis, terraced slopes, diversion dams, detention dams
3. Draft Power—camels, oxen, horses, mules, donkeys, tractors
4. Processing Works—olive presses, grape presses, mills, threshing grounds, combines
5. Fencing Works—stone fences, wire fences, mud fences, brush fences
6. Animal Shelters—caves, tents, old buildings, aluminum sheds
7. Storage Installations—silos, granaries, storage buildings, large jars
8. Transportation—pickup trucks, large trucks, horse-drawn carriages, camels, donkeys, private cars
9. Communication—paved roads, dirt roads, paths, radios, televisions, post offices

D. VILLAGE SETTLEMENT PATTERN
1. Fixity—degree to which community is migratory or sedentary
2. Compactness—dwellings clumped close together, dwellings strung out along roads, dwellings widely dispersed
3. Size—1-10 dwellings, 11-25 dwellings, 26-50 dwellings, 51-100 dwellings, more than 100 dwellings
4. Type of Dwellings—Neo-Roman stone houses, simple unpainted cement houses, elaborate painted cement houses, add-on cement houses, mud houses, tents, caves, shacks
5. Public Buildings—mosques, shops, schools, meeting halls, post office, suq, government office buildings
6. Ethnic Groups—Ajarmeh, Circasians, Palestinians, Thoabyya, Nabulsi, Sarabne, Belqawie, Keratchi, Azzizat, Maayeh

E. ARCHAEOLOGICAL REMAINS
1. Waterworks—reservoirs, cisterns, aqueducts, water-lifting works
2. Terracing Works—terraced wadis, terraced slopes, dams
3. Processing Works—wine presses, olive presses, mills
4. Fencing Works—stone fences, mud fences, large walls
5. Animal Shelters—caves, kraals, stables
6. Storage Installations—silos, granaries, storage buildings, jars
7. Communication—paved roads, communication towers
8. Domestic Dwellings—mud houses, stone houses, caves
9. Public Buildings—temples, churches, mosques, baths
10. Fortifications—large walls, guard towers
11. Pottery—Iron, Persian, Hellenistic, Nabatean, Roman, Byzantine, etc.
12. Bones—sheep or goat, cattle, equine, poultry, fish, etc.
13. Tombs—Islamic, Byzantine, Roman, Iron, Bronze

During our visits to most of these villages we were accompanied by an English-speaking local resident familiar with the terrain, the people, and local agricultural practices. The duration of our stay in each village ranged from half an hour in the case of some of the smaller hamlets to twenty or more hours (in the course of several different visits) in the case of some of the more important villages and towns, such as Hesban and Jalul. A considerable amount of time was also spent in interviews with a number of local residents obtaining oral accounts of the changes which have occurred in their lifetime within the project area and in obtaining population and production statistics for each of these settlements available from government district offices in Madaba, especially the Department of Agriculture Extension Office.

While all of the above activities were essential to the fulfillment of our research objectives in Jordan, what led to the deepest insights into the traditional way of life of people in this part of the world was our own experience in trying to meet the requirements of daily existence as a family. Despite our previous visits to Jordan and acquaintance with the experiences of others, we had really very little experiential understanding of how much time and effort goes into the quest for food when such modern conveniences as processed and prepared foods, refrigerators, and microwave ovens are not to be used. Though available for a price in Jordan, we had chosen to live without these conveniences.

When the lentils or rice you buy at the market need first to be sorted to get rid of small stones; when bread, milk, and produce must be bought daily from the shops for lack of refrigeration; when entrees must be made each day from scratch from seasonally available vegetables, nuts, and fruits (as we prepared only vegetarian meals for ourselves); when the laundry must be done by hand; and when all errands are to be made on foot (as we had no car available except during certain days when we conducted our village survey), the quest for food becomes an all-day undertaking rather than the quick stop in the kitchen or at McDonald's which it so easily can be for most of us in the West. Add to this the labor which was involved in traditional methods of producing food on the land in the first place, and one becomes readily convinced that for most

people involved in rural livelihoods, the activities involved in the production, distribution, preparation, and consumption of food accounts for the major portion of how they spend their day-time hours, what they work at and make, and with whom they interact on a daily basis. Thus, our own daily-life chores in Jordan provided a sort of existential validation and understanding of why a food-system perspective might prove to be a good starting point for studying the connections between innumerable daily-life activities and recurring themes in the material culture of peoples in this part of the world today and in the past.

A final procedure in the investigations concerned with the recent past involved locating and obtaining copies of as many as possible of the 19th and early 20th century sources dealing with Jordan and the project area. Although this research will continue for a long time, a good start was made, thanks to the holdings of a number of libraries in Amman and Jerusalem and in the United States, including the considerable holdings of the James White Library at Andrews University. As stated earlier, these literary sources have been utilized in supplementing and cross-checking the recollections of informants and in validating my own reconstructions of changes in the food system based on what I observed and heard in the course of carrying out the above fieldwork activities.

Previous Investigations in the Project Area

Of the hundreds of explorers and travelers who visited Palestine in the 19th century, at least a dozen of those who published accounts of their travels passed through the territory making up our project area. Probably the first of these was Ulrich Jacob Seetzen (1813), a German explorer who offered a brief account of the ruins of Hesban which he visited in 1806. Others who followed him to points within the project area included Charles Leonard Irby and James Mangles (1823), John Lewis Burckhardt (1822, 1831), J. S. Buckingham (1825; cf. pl. 3.3), Alexander Keith (1844), William F. Lynch (1849), Felicien de Saulcy (1853), Henry B. Tristram (1865, 1873, 1880), Captain R. E. Warren (1869), E. H. Palmer (1872), Henry C. Fish (1876), Selah Merrill (1877, 1881), Lieutenant H. H. Kitchener (1878), William M. Thomson (1880), Guy Le

Strange (1886), and Major Claude R. Conder (1889, 1891, 1892).

Plate 3.3 Portrait of James Silk Buckingham (after Ben-Arieh 1983)

While all of these visitors were ultimately interested in the antiquities of Jordan, particularly those related to biblical history, they were, to varying degrees, also interested in the contemporary conditions of the landscape and the people with whom they came into contact. This interest in the contemporary population stemmed partially from practical concerns and partially from an interest in contemporary Arab customs reminiscent of biblical stories. A good example of why an acquaintance with the contemporary inhabitants of the project area was of practical interest to the 19th century explorers is Tristram's experience in trying to visit biblical Heshbon and "the land of Moab," the region along the eastern highland of the Dead Sea. In his first attempt to do so, he employed Goblan, a sheikh of the Adwan tribe, as his guide. Upon reaching the borders of Moab, he discovered that his guide was unwilling to accompany him to points south of Hesban, for this was enemy territory under the control of

members of the Beni Sakhr tribe. In his second attempt to explore this territory he had learned his lesson, having sought out the services of a Beni Sakhr guide to accompany his team.

By far the two most outstanding accounts of sights, tribal life, and customs east of the Jordan during the latter part of the 19th century, are those published by Tristram (1873) and Conder (1889). Tristram's publications contain detailed descriptions of the landscape through which he traveled, and include extensive accounts of species of plants and animals found in a particular location, the way of life of native inhabitants encountered along the way, names of local personalities and tribes, and descriptions of ruins which include discussions of their ancient origins and significance, and their current state of preservation and use. Conder was even more meticulous in descriptions of ancient ruins and contemporary tribal relations and personalities, although his accounts are less concerned with the natural history of the terrain which he surveyed. Since both of these explorers included in their publications beautifully crafted drawings of much of what they saw, their works are indispensable to the student of the recent past east of the Jordan.

During the early decades of the present century reports by British military men and foreign service personnel also began to appear, some of which contain information dealing with the project area. Examples of such sources include the publications of Frederick G. Peake—also known as Peake Pasha—(1935), John B. Glubb (1938), Eliahu Epstein (1938, 1939), A. S. Kirkbride (1945), and G. F. Walpole (1948). To these can be added three important handbooks prepared by Baedeker (1876), Luke (1924), Luke and Keith-Roach (1930) and accounts by missionaries (Forder 1909), travelers (Bell 1927; Seabrook 1927), and explorers (Musil 1907, 1926, 1927, 1928; von Oppenheim 1943). Also noteworthy is A. Konikoff's (1943) economic survey of Palestine which was published by the Jewish Agency.

With the arrival of a central administration in Jordan in 1921, the collection and publication of statistical information by various government bureaucracies got underway. Particularly valuable for the present study are the census reports on agriculture prepared by the Department of Statistics since the early 1960s. Maps produced by many of the 19th century explorers, and by the

British and Jordanian governments, represent another important source of information utilized in this study.

Finally, during the past two decades a number of ethnographic inquiries have been completed which have been based on fieldwork either within the project area or involving ethnic groups represented within it. Specifically dealt with in these publications are the following project area ethnic groups: the Beni Sakhr of Manja and Jalul, the Arab Christians of Madaba, the Circassians of Naur, the Abujaber family of Yadoudeh, and the Ajarmeh clans of Hesban and its daughter villages. The first of these to be completed was one in which the "lore and customs of the Beni Sakhr tribe" were investigated in order to make possible a comparison "with those contained in the Book of Judges" in the Bible (Merry 1969). The object of this study was to gain further insight into the process of settlement of the Hebrews during the time of the Judges through comparison with the process of settlement of the contemporary Beni Sakhr tribes.

More recently, the process of sedentarization among the Beni Sakhr has also been studied by Hiatt (1984) and Bocco (1984a, 1984b, 1984c). In Hiatt's view, the process of sedentarization in Jordan is best understood as an adaptive response by camel nomads to the gradual efforts of the state to inhibit their movements, prevent them from raiding the settled population, and hire their sons for military service. Thus sedentarization is seen as a process of *encapsulation* of the nomadic groups within larger entities such as the state. Interestingly, while Hiatt has emphasized the state's role in encapsulating smaller groups without resorting to forced sedentarization policies, Boneh (1983), who has studied sedentarization of nomads in the Sinai, has emphasized the encapsulating efforts of the nomadic groups themselves in order to solidify the unity of the group in the face of forced sedentarization by the state.

The process of settlement of the town of Madaba has been briefly dealt with in two dissertations, one by Gubser (1973), the other by Allison (1977). While Gubser's research dealt primarily with sociopolitical changes in the Kerak region since the previous century, the fact that several families from Kerak fled to Madaba following a blood feud and became the first families

to settle there, is briefly dealt with in his book. A more in-depth and recent study of the Christian families of Madaba is found in Allison's (1977) dissertation, which dealt with "patrilateral parallel-cousin marriage with its related honor syndrome" among these families. Insofar as this study also includes a brief discussion of the history of the town and offers a general overview of the cultural patterns of its Arab Christian inhabitants, it represents a useful source of background information for the present investigation.

In addition to these studies of Beni Sakhr tribesmen and of the Christians of Madaba, mention must also be made of recent studies of a third ethnic group represented within the project area, namely the Circassians. Two studies of this important ethnic group are of interest to the present investigation—the first an article by Weightman (1970), and the second a doctoral dissertation by Shami (1984), herself a Circassian. Whereas Weightman's article is concerned with the rise of this ethnic minority to political power and influence in the country of Jordan as a whole, and the consequences of this for the Circassians as a group, Shami's research utilizes the experience of the Circassians as a people in an exploration of how the rise of the monarchy and clientelism in Jordan ultimately affected their solidarity as an ethnic minority. Her study concluded that, in contrast to the Bedouin of Jordan, whose patrilineal social structure was strengthened as a result of the clientelism of the monarchy, the Circassians, as a corporate ethnic group, were weakened because their traditional social structure "was one of mutually exclusive extended families, which did not provide a unified leadership for the Circassians as a whole" (Shami 1984: 138).

Another recent contribution to ethnographic literature of the project area is Abujaber's (1984) study of his own village, namely the village of Yadoudeh. Abujaber's research has focused on the role of his family in introducing modern agricultural techniques to Jordan. It traces the early 19th century roots of his family to the village of Nablus on the western side of the Jordan River, and describes the partnerships which were formed between his forefathers and the Beni Sakhr sheikhs for their mutual benefit. The careful attention to details of landuse and land tenure within a portion of the project area makes this an important source of background information for the present investigation.

Not dealt with in any of the above studies are the descendants of the Belqa tribes such as the Adwan and Ajarmeh. Ethnographic research concerned with the latter is restricted to what has been published by Peake (1958) and LaBianca (1976), whereas a limited amount of unpublished research is available about the former (Fikery 1979). Also missing are contributions dealing specifically with the settlement and integration of Palestinian refugees into the towns and villages of the project area. This process will be briefly discussed in the present chapter.

Finally, much in the way of general understanding of the social anthropology of Jordan can be learned from the publications of investigators dealing with other communities and tribes in Jordan. The pioneering studies of village communities in Jordan carried out by Lutfiyya (1966) in the village of Baytin, by Antoun (1968, 1972, 1979) in the village of Kufr al Ma, and by Gubser (1973) in the town and hinterland of Kerak form the foundation of modern community studies in Jordan. Modern anthropological studies dealing with the Bedouin of Jordan are now also beginning to accumulate. Among the current contributors to this literature are Lancaster (1981) who has been concentrating his research on the Rwala; Layne (1984) whose work has been among the Jordan Valley Bedouin; and Abu Jaber, Gharaibeh, Khasawneh, and Hill (1976) who have written about the Bedouin of Northeast Jordan. A number of books dealing with social, economic, and political conditions of the country of Jordan as a whole have also been published, mostly by individuals with political science backgrounds (Abidi 1965; Aruri 1972; Glubb 1938, 1948; Gubser 1973, 1983; Morris 1959; Nyrop *et al.* 1974; Patai 1958; Peake 1958; Shwadran 1959; Sinai and Pollack 1977; and Vatikiotis 1967). Of these works, the writer has only made use of those by Glubb, Gubser, Peake, and Vatikiotis.

A Varied Habitat

As mentioned briefly in Chapter One, the location of the Hesban project area is along the mountain plateau which rises to the east of the northern tip of the Dead Sea (pls. 3.4, 3.5). It is located almost exactly halfway between the Wadi Zerka (Jabbok) to the north and the Wadi Mujib (Arnon) to the south along the edge of the Madaba plateau. As a place for humans, plants, and animals to live, the Hesban project area is a varied habitat, offering a range of different local environments where food, shelter, and protection may be found by animals and peoples alike. What accounts for this environmental variability is that it straddles a territory containing the piedmont and foothills area which rises to the east of the hot Jordan River-Dead Sea lowlands; a sharply eastwardly ascending mountainous area containing numerous springs, perennial streams, and seasonally flooding wadis meandering through herbaceous valleys and escarpments; a hilly plateau area with fertile valleys and wadi bottoms which receives a relatively reliable supply of rainwater; and a gently sloping plain to the southeast of this hilly region containing shallow wadis and excellent agricultural soils.

Standing on the summit of Tell Hesban, *ca.* 895 m above sea level, one has a panoramic view of this varied habitat. To the north lie the northern hills, some of which seem to be gently rolling, others appearing as steep escarpments (pl. 3.6). To the west are slopes which descend gently at first, then more steeply down into the Jordan Valley (pl. 3.7). To the south and east lie the southern and eastern plains, which disappear in the horizon to the south (pl. 3.8) and in the desert to the east (pl. 3.9). Looking north and west, one notices small patches of cultivated land in the valleys and on the gentle slopes, and in the distance scrub and forest clinging to the bedrock which outcrops all over in these northern hills and western escarpments. Looking toward the plains to the south and east, one sees large expanses of cultivated fields interrupted only by a village settlement here and there and the modern road which comes from Naur and continues to Madaba.

As indicated in Chapter One, the Hesban project area has been divided, for analytical purposes, into four principal topographical subregions: *western descent, plateau ridge, northern hills,* and *eastern plain* (see fig 1.3). As we shall see next, these subregions are distinguishable along several dimensions, including elevational variability, temperatures, water availability, soils, plant, and animal life.

Plate 3.4   Aerial view of Tell Hesban 1979 (courtesy of Richard Cleave); view east

Plate 3.5   Aerial view of the Hesban region 1979 (courtesy of Richard Cleave); view east

Plate 3.6   Looking northward from Tell Hesban (1973)

Plate 3.7   Looking westward from Tell Hesban (1973)

Plate 3.8   Looking southeastward from Tell Hesban (1973)

Plate 3.9   Looking eastward from Tell Hesban (1973)

The most varied in terms of all of the above mentioned dimensions is the western descent. Because of extreme elevational differences, ranging between approximately 100 m and 800 m, temperatures along the lower elevations of this subregion run about four degrees higher than temperatures along its upper elevations. Thus in January, the mean daily temperatures run about 12° C in the lower piedmont area, compared with 8° C along the highland ridge. In July, the difference is 28° C versus 24° C. Rainfall is also uneven, the amount increasing as one ascends upward toward the ridge (figs. 3.3-3.5). Thus, in an average year, rainfall is less than 250 mm along the lower elevations and above 400 mm near the upper elevations. In a dry year, the upper elevations may receive less than 200 mm, and the lower ones less than 100 mm. In a wet year, the difference is between 600 mm in the upper elevations and 400 mm in the lower ones.

Streams and wadis in the western descent carry rain and spring waters to the Jordan River-Dead Sea basin below (fig. 3.6). Its principal wadis are the Wadi Hesban and its tributaries—among which are Wadi Majarr immediately adjacent to Tell Hesban—and the Wadi el Muhtariqa and its tributaries, among which is Wadi Uyun Musa which is located in the slopes below Mount Nebo. About a dozen springs were identified by Conder (1881) within this subregion, the most productive ones being the ones at Ain Hesban and at Uyun Musa. These springs owe their existence to underground aquifers replenished each winter by rainwater which has drained below the ground from surfaces higher up (see fig. 3.7).

In the valleys and wadis of the western descent Yellow Mediterranean Soils predominate (see fig. 3.8). Compared with the Red Mediterranean Soils found in the plains and hills above, these soils are less favorable for agriculture. Even so they are extensively used for both field crops and grazing; and in the vicinity of certain of the more productive wadis, irrigated agriculture is practiced. In eroded bedrock areas and along the steeper slopes of the western descent, Yellow Soils and young Regosolic Soils predominate. These soils have much lower ability to retain water than do typical Red or Yellow Mediterranean Soils. Their sandier texture and their high stone content render them unsuitable for most agricultural uses except extensive grazing.

The plants found in the western descent have been classified by Zohary (1962) as being transitional to the Mesopotamian Steppe Climax Vegetation Zone (Irano-Turanian Territory). Almost no arboreal climax exists, the predominant vegetation being herbaceous and dwarf shrub communities. A characteristic climax species is *Artemesia herba-alba,* a type of sage. As most of the hilltops and steep slopes are nearly barren, plant communities are mainly limited to wadi bottoms, shaded aspects, and localized areas receiving soil water seepage from higher up and from intermittent wadi drainage. Near springs such as those at Ain Hesban and Uyun Musa, however, vegetation is dense and lush and a wide variety of species of wild birds and animals may be found living nearby (*cf.* Tristram 1873: 348-350).

The plateau ridge, which runs along the center of the project area from north to south, and the northern hills which extend eastward from this ridge, have many common features. To begin with, this is a region of fertile valleys and hills, ranging in elevation between approximately 800 m and 960 m. In both subregions the mean daily temperatures are about the same, averaging 8° C in January, 16° in April, 24° in July, and 20° in October. Rainfall is also more plentiful than anywhere else within the project area, amounting to 400 mm in an average year, a minimum of 200 mm in a dry year and over 600 mm in a wet year (figs. 3.3-3.5). Along the southern half of the plateau ridge, these rainfall amounts are slightly lower and temperatures are slightly higher. In the vicinity of the village of El Rawda about six km north of Hesban are several springs which empty out into streams and valleys in the western descent (*cf.* fig. 3.7). Running eastward from the ridge are also a number of shallow and gently sloping wadis, including Wadi el Marbat which lies immediately to the east of Tell Hesban and transports rainwaters into the plains region to the southeast.

The soils which occur in the valleys and hillside slopes along the plateau ridge and northern hills have been classified as Red Mediterranean Soils (see fig. 3.8). The high clay content of these soils enhances their ability to infiltrate and retain water and nutrients for plant use. These characteristics, along with their favorable topography and low coarse fragment content, make them excellent for agricultural use. Although little of

Fig. 3.3 Rainfall distribution (in mm) in a normal year (after Agrar- und Hydrotechnik 1977)

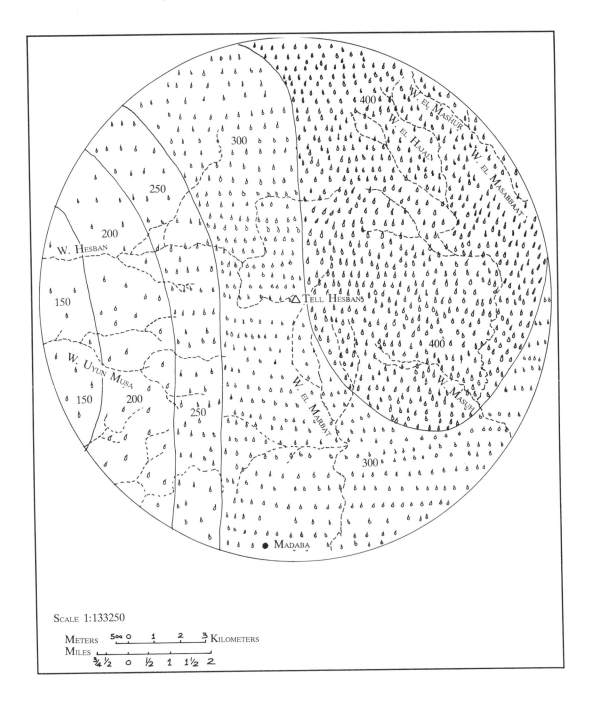

Fig. 3.4   Rainfall distribution (in mm) in a dry year (after Agrar- und Hydrotechnik 1977)

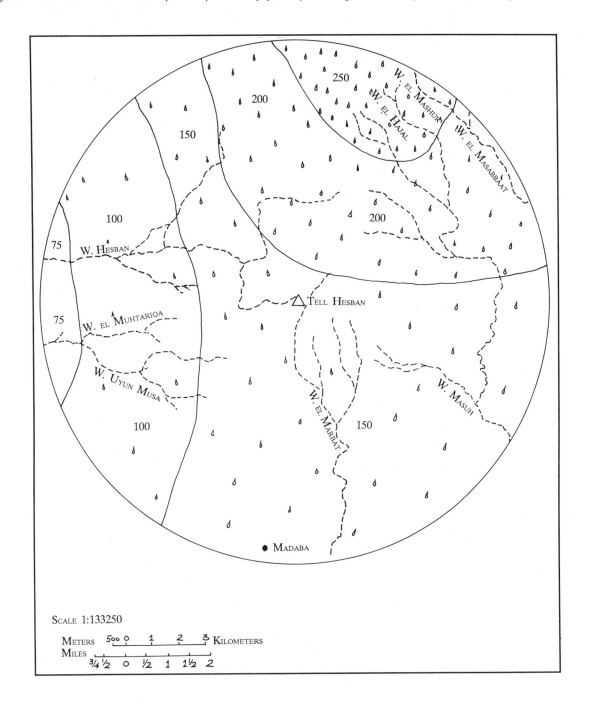

Fig. 3.5   Rainfall distribution (in mm) in a wet year (after Agrar- und Hydrotechnik 1977)

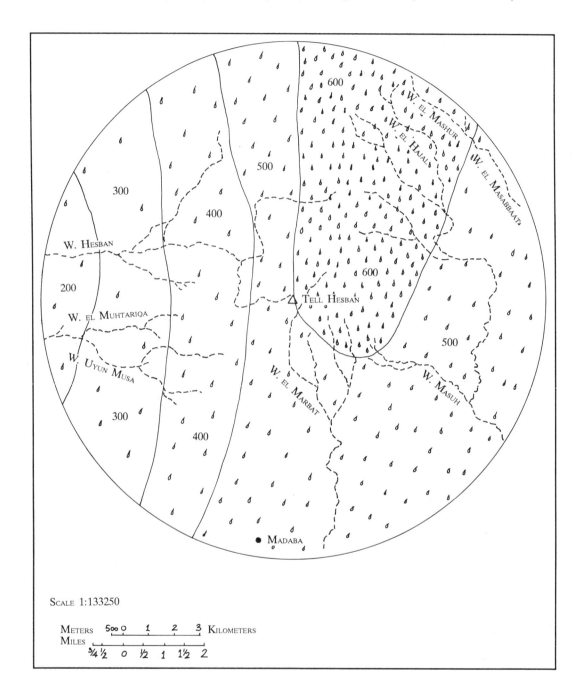

Fig. 3.6   Drainage basins and main river catchments (after Agrar- und Hydrotechnik 1977)

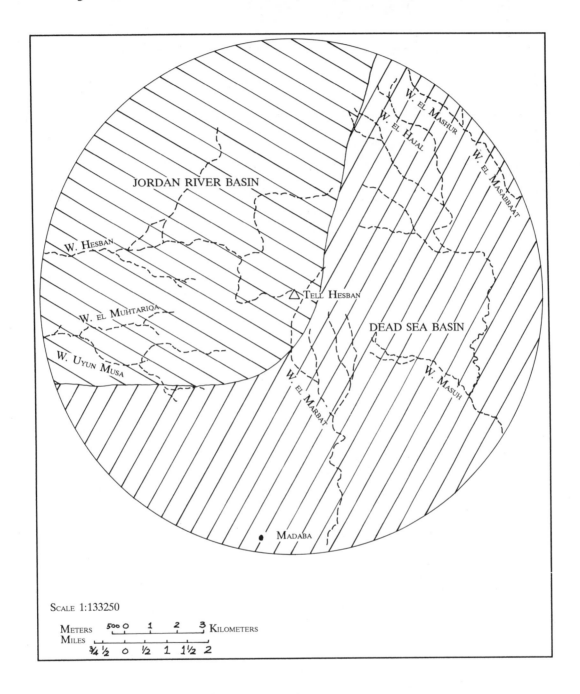

Fig. 3.7   Hydrogeological cross section (horizontal scale 1:250000; vertical scale 1:10000) running through project area (after Agrar- und Hydrotechnik 1977)

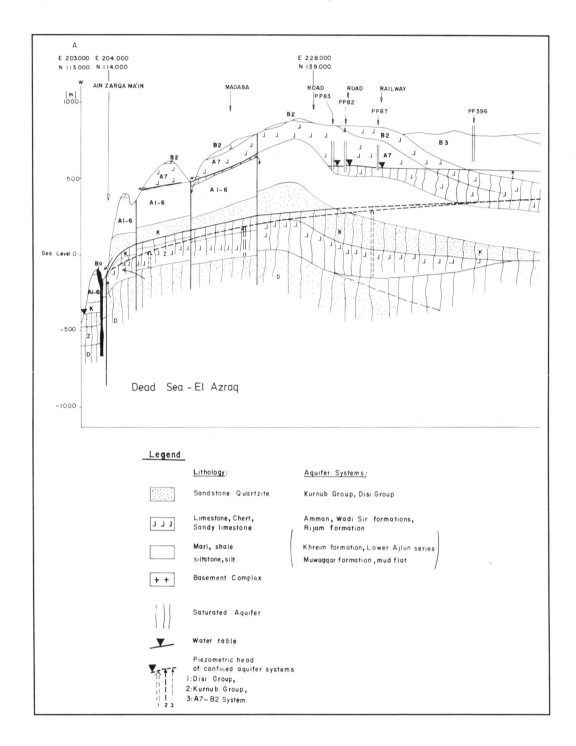

Fig. 3.8   Hydrological soil classification (after Agrar- und Hydrotechnik 1977)

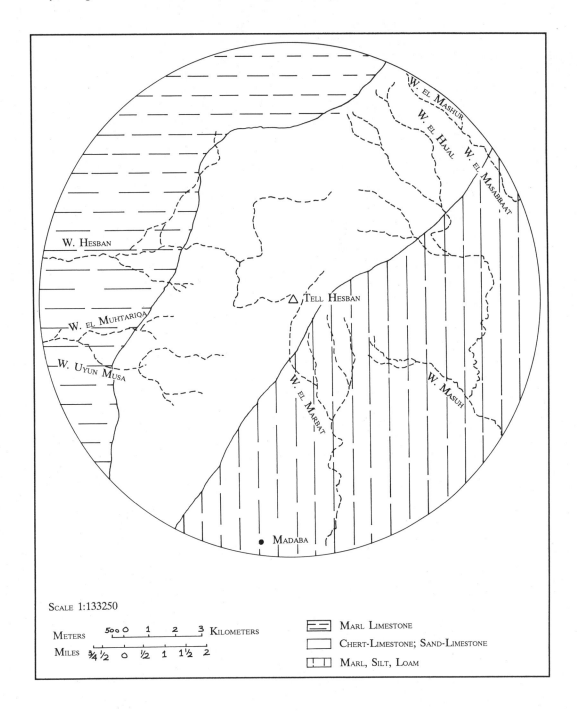

SCALE 1:133250

MARL LIMESTONE

CHERT-LIMESTONE; SAND-LIMESTONE

MARL, SILT, LOAM

the local natural flora can be found growing on these soils because of extensive cultivation and grazing, from a plant geographical standpoint these subregions have been classified as belonging primarily to the Mediterranean Territory (Zohary 1962: 52). This means that trees such as oak, pistachio, pine, and cypress once covered these hills and valleys, along with thick scrubby underbrush or maquis. In areas of rougher topography between fields, where vegetation disturbance is limited to grazing, thorny and unpalatable plants may be found which are evidence of the degraded state of the present flora. Afforestation on some of the hills attests, however, that this region is still capable of producing its original climax flora.

The fourth of the subregions into which we have divided the project area is the eastern plain. This territory reaches an elevation of about 850 m near the village of Es Samik at the southern edge of the northern hills subregion and descends gently to about 750 m in the vicinity of Umm el Rummana near the southeastern perimeter of the eastern plain. Whereas temperatures in this subregion are about the same as along the ridge, rainfall is generally somewhat less than along the ridge and in the northern hills and it tapers off considerably as one moves toward the eastern perimeter of the project area. In an average year rainfall in this region is between 300 mm and 400 mm. In a wet year it reaches over 500 mm whereas in a dry year it may reach only 150 mm. It is, of course, the eastern portion of this subregion which is the most at risk in terms of rainfall insufficiency. The wadis in this region are generally shallow, draining in an eastwardly direction (figs. 3.3-3.7).

Soils (fig. 3.8) and flora of the eastern plain are largely the same as those found along the plateau ridge and the northern hills, except that the somewhat drier conditions make this subregion a little more limiting in terms of what will grow, especially during dry years. On the other hand, because the topography is nearly level, the eastern plain is ideally suited for production of field crops such as wheat and barley. As grazing lands for herds of pasture animals, especially sheep and cattle, it is also ideally suited.

Except in the vicinity of Ain Hesban, Uyun Musa, and certain of the other perennial springs where certain exotic species of wild birds and other wildlife can still be observed (Boessneck and von den Driesch 1978a), the animals which still survive within the project area belong mostly to species which have learned to live in association with the human food system. For example, attracted to cereal fields are hares and field mice and their principal predators, the fox and weasel. Birds attracted to cereal fields include skylarks, wheat ears, partridges, blackbirds, and quails (Potts and Vickerman 1974: 107-197; cf. Devos 1969). Where herds of sheep or goats are pastured, their predators, such as wolves, cheetahs, leopards, and lions also used to roam; although today, with the possible exception of the wolf (Abujaber personal communication) these are no more to be seen. Birds of prey, such as hawks and falcons, are also rarely seen anymore.

Also important are those animals which feed on the carcasses and other organic material disposed of by people and beasts alike. Among those still found within the project area are hyenas, jackals, and several species of scavenging birds, including the Egyptian vulture and the griffin vulture. These birds can be observed awaiting their turn after the semiwild dogs and jackals have had their fill. Still other species feed on dung and other decaying materials, such as the hoopoe, a bird which feeds on small insects found in dunghills. The wild boar plays an important role in this natural sanitation system as well, although today its role has been significantly diminished.

While our focus here has been centered on the territory within a radius of 10 km of Tell Hesban, it is important to keep in mind that to the north, south, east and west of this particular area are territories which also at times have been utilized by peoples and animals occupying our project area. Indeed, for some of these people and animals, the project area has been but a convenient corridor through which they have passed on their migrations between the lowlands of the Ghor and destinations on the highlands to the east of the Dead Sea. The fact that the project area straddles the territory immediately to the northeast of the Dead Sea has meant that it has always been an important natural corridor for such through traffic. For such populations, still other alternatives than those described above have existed in the way of local environments, including, as we shall see later on, exploitation of the fertile foothills and lowlands along the Jordan River, and the desert regions to the south and east of the project area.

Finally, the disappearance of certain species of wild animals in Jordan, and the reduced numbers of others—especially grassland ruminants such as the gazelle and ibex and their predators, the cheetah and wolf—have been of concern to several naturalists who have studied the wildlife of Jordan (Mountfort 1964). It is fortunate that today, conservation efforts have gotten under way in Jordan which it is hoped will lead to improved conditions for still surviving species threatened with extinction.

Sights From Tell Hesban During the Decades of 1870, 1910, and 1970

Before discussing in greater detail changes which have taken place within the project area over the past two centuries, an initial idea of the sedentarization process, which occurred over this period, can be had from assuming the role of a visitor on top of Tell Hesban taking in the sights of the surrounding region at three successive points in time. Thanks to eyewitness accounts available from the previous century and the early part of the present century, and our own observations in the 1970s, a reconstruction of the panoramic sights visible from on top of Tell Hesban ca. 1870, 1910, and 1970 is both possible and instructive.

On the way up to the summit of Tell Hesban in a summer sometime in the 1870s, our visitor would have passed by numerous caves, a castle, and numerous ruined arches and buildings, many of which would have been temporarily occupied by families belonging to the Ajarmeh tribe at this time of the year. From the summit of Tell Hesban his eyes would next have been drawn to the eastern plain where lines of great black tents belonging to the Beni Sakhr tribesmen would have been visible for miles. Spreading across the plain would have been their large herds of camels. Turning his gaze westward, our visitor would have seen large flocks of sheep and goats grazing in the valleys and along the slopes of the Wadi Majarr. Their owners would have been members of the Belqa tribesmen whose tents would be visible on these slopes as well. Turning northward, an encampment of the Adwan tribesmen would have been seen, along with their flocks of cattle, sheep, and goats (Tristram 1873: 351).

Having taken in the situation of the living population, our visitor's gaze would next have been drawn to the extensive ruins of past inhabitants. The surface of Tell Hesban itself, along with the surrounding landscape, would have appeared to him as an outdoor museum with numerous half-standing buildings, ancient road beds, and, below his feet, innumerable remains of monumental buildings and pieces of pottery. To the west of the tell, straddling Wadi Majarr, he would have seen a large depression, the remains of a reservoir. Scattered along the hillside above this wadi he would have seen numerous caves, many of them having been closed off by a rude masonry wall containing a doorway. Another reservoir would have been discernible at the bottom of the tell to the west in Wadi el Marbat (Conder 1889: 104). Also clearly visible to him would have been the lines of parallel curbstones coming over the hill to the north from El 'Al and running past the tell toward Madaba. Scattered on many of the surrounding hills would have been more half-standing buildings and arches, as well as traces of footpaths and donkey trails crisscrossing the landscape.

While many of these same sights would still have been seen by our visitor on his summertime return to the summit of Tell Hesban sometime during the decade of 1910, some changes would also have been noticeable. Clumped together around the castle on the western shoulder of the tell he would have seen several fortified farmhouses built of anciently hewn stones. Around these he would have seen women and children going about their daily chores, and men, assisted by camels and donkeys, hauling bags of wheat to the makeshift granary in the castle. These would have been the descendants of the Ajarmeh and the Belqa tribesmen, these particular ones having abandoned their transhumant ways in favor of year-round settlement in their former summer quarters.

Looking beyond Hesban toward Mushaqqar and Madaba, he would have seen further evidence of permanently settled villages. Indeed, if his vision was good, he would have seen at Madaba the steeple of a newly erected Christian church, surrounded by a cluster of fortified farmhouses built on top of the ancient Byzantine ruins near the summit of this ancient city. In the fields surrounding these villages he would no doubt also have seen teams of oxen at work plowing up the fields which in former times had been devoted primarily to pasture. On the eastern horizon he would again have seen the lines of great Beni Sakhr tents, but this time their herds would have contained fewer camels. Instead, large numbers of sheep and goats would have been added to their flocks.

On his summertime return to the summit during the decade of 1970, our visitor, now over one hundred years old, would no doubt have been astounded by the changed sights before his eyes. The summit itself would have been markedly scarred, having been penetrated to bedrock by numerous archaeological excavation trenches. On most of the hills surrounding the tell he would have seen houses built of wrought iron and cement. Still there would have been many of the early fortified farmhouses, but many of the oldest of these now would have been converted to granaries or shelters for animals. To such uses many of the cave dwellings on the western slope of Wadi Majarr would also have been converted. Of the many half-standing ruins of buildings of which the earlier explorers spoke, hardly any would still be seen, except for the castle, which still stands. Most of these would either have been destroyed by villagers in search of building materials or they would have been incorporated into new buildings.

Other new sights in the village of Hesban would have been the numerous enclosed gardens; several large orchards containing rows of fruit trees surrounded by enclosure walls; the presence of several public buildings such as a school for boys and one for girls; parked and moving cars and trucks; TV antennas on the roofs of some houses; and, parked near the castle or in a nearby wheat field, a large wheat combine. Seen in large numbers everywhere in the village would have been chickens and doves, along with a few geese and turkeys. There would still have been the flocks of sheep and goats on the hills and in the stubble fields beyond the village, but these would have been much smaller in number than those kept by the present villagers' grandparents and their parents. A few heads of European-type cattle would also have been seen tethered near some of the village houses.

Looking southward toward Madaba, several large settlements would have come into view, including the greatly expanded villages of Mushaqqar, El Jureina, and Madaba. The latter would have appeared on the horizon as a large town, its houses sprawling in every direction out from the Christian center of the town. Along the skyline of Madaba would also have been seen numerous minarets, a testimony to the large influx of Muslims into the town, the majority of them Palestinian refugees. On the edges of the villages seen from on top of Tell Hesban, tents belonging to Palestinian refugees would also have been visible. These belonged to Palestinian families having taken up a migratory existence following their forced eviction from their former permanent homes on the other side of the Jordan.

Built along the track of the ancient Roman road, a paved highway connects Madaba, El Jureina, Hesban, El 'Al, Naur, and numerous other villages to each other and other points in Jordan. Along both sides of this highway the former cereal fields would still have been seen, although some of them would now have been in the process of being converted into irrigated vegetable fields and orchards. Almost absent altogether on the eastern horizon would have been the tents and flocks of camels and sheep and goats of the Beni Sakhr, most of their descendants having settled by this time.

In order to gain a deeper understanding of the changes which our three-time visitor to Tell Hesban would have observed, some of the salient characteristics of the project area food system during the decades leading up to A.D. 1880 (the Late Ottoman Period), A.D. 1950 (the Early Modern Period), and 1980 (the Modern Period) will be examined in greater detail. The first of these periods, the Late Ottoman, will be discussed first. Except for a brief introduction to the political conditions which prevailed during Late Ottoman times, attention will be focused primarily on those aspects of the local food system which, as was discussed in Chapter One, our ethnoarchaeological perspective gives priority to, namely the prevailing environmental, settlement, landuse, operational, and dietary conditions. Our purpose in the following section will be to identify those interrelated changes in material conditions which are indicative of changes in the local food system as a whole.

Plate 3.10   Habitation caves as seen from Tell Hesban; view west

Plate 3.11   Village of Hesban, 1971, note *qasr* in center; view east

When Transhumant Pastoralism Prevailed:
The Late Ottoman Period

Throughout the 19th century A.D., prior to *ca.* 1880, transhumant pastoralism prevailed within the project area. In other words, the large majority of its inhabitants were pastoralists migrating with their animals between the project area, which constituted their highland range, and lowland ranges in the Ghor, or in the interior of the Arabian desert. There were no towns or villages established within the project area before this date, although toward its end, a few campsites were gradually being converted into year-round settlements by the Ajarmeh and other Belqa tribes, and at Yadoudeh, a settlement *ca.* 2 km beyond the northeastern perimeter of the project area, the Abujabers had by this time begun a thriving farm in partnership with the Beni Sakhr sheikh (Abujaber 1984). The principal contemporary sources of information regarding the project area during this period utilized here include Burckhardt (1822), Warren (1869), Tristram (1865, 1873, 1880), Conder (1889, 1891, 1892), and Thomson (1880).

Throughout all of the 19th century, Transjordan belonged in a nominal sense to the Ottoman Empire, which had its seat of power in Constantinople (Istanbul). During the first half of that century Ottoman control over the Arab lands was minimal, except in principal cities, such as Damascus and Aleppo, where they maintained large military garrisons and staffs of civil officials (*cf.* Burckhardt 1822: 285-309; Glubb 1967: 107). During the latter half of the same century, however, reforms got under way in the Ottoman administration which led gradually to a greater Turkish presence throughout Syria and Palestine. Thus, Tristram (1873: 174) was favorably impressed with the improvements in public security and administration which the authorities had brought to Salt, a town 30 km north of Hesban, in the period between his two visits to that town (*ca.* 1863-1872). In the account of his second visit he comments, "Now that the Pasha of Damascus has placed a garrison there, the fellahin are better off, trade has quadrupled, and the country is as safe for Europeans as Western Palestine." Tristram (1873: 174) also indicates that a Turkish garrison was being set up in Kerak, a town *ca.* 70 km to the south of Hesban, around 1873. At the time of his visits these two towns were the only ones that existed in the whole territory east of the Jordan.

The environmental conditions which prevailed within the project area during the Late Ottoman Period were generally better than those which exist today. The best evidence for this is the fact that the plants and animals which were observed by visitors to points east of the Jordan, including the project area, were much more plentiful then than they are today. Because only a small portion of the arable land was actually tilled, and because the pressure from grazing animals was seasonally abated as the herds of sheep, goats, and camels were led in and out of the project area, there was less disturbance of both the natural flora and the natural fauna. Among the species of wild animals and birds observed by Tristram's (1873) party on the highland plateau in the vicinity of the project area (at places like M'Seitbeh, Umm Rasa, and Ziza) were the bubale or wild cow, oryx antelope, gazelle, wild cat, fox, jackal, wolf, cheetah, mole-rat, gerbille, Lammer-Geier or bearded vulture, griffin vulture, Egyptian vulture, spotted eagle, buzzard, kestrel, Lanner falcon, Sakk'r falcon, owl, eagle owl, raven, jackdaw, rock dove, partridge, Greek partridge, sand grouse, pintail duck, mallard duck, lark, calandra lark, crested lark, short-toed lark, and skylark. Today, most of these species have become rare or extinct in Jordan (Mountfort 1964).

In shifting our attention to the human occupants of the project area during the Late Ottoman Period (fig. 3.9), the first thing which needs to be emphasized is that throughout this entire period, a process of sedentarization of various tribes was continuously taking place. This meant that at any one point in time, a range of different food procurement strategies could be identified among local inhabitants, some tribes appearing to be more nomadic and some appearing to be more sedentary in their manner of living. This fact was well understood by Glubb (1938) whose many years among the Bedouin of Jordan, as leader of the Arab Legion, led him to caution against overly simplistic notions about how to distinguish the traditional way of life of the Bedouin from that of sedentaries. With great insight Glubb (1938: 448-449) explained as follows:

> We must first clear our minds somewhat as to the meaning we propose to give to the "Bed-

Fig. 3.9   Palestine in the Late Ottoman Period (after Conder 1891)

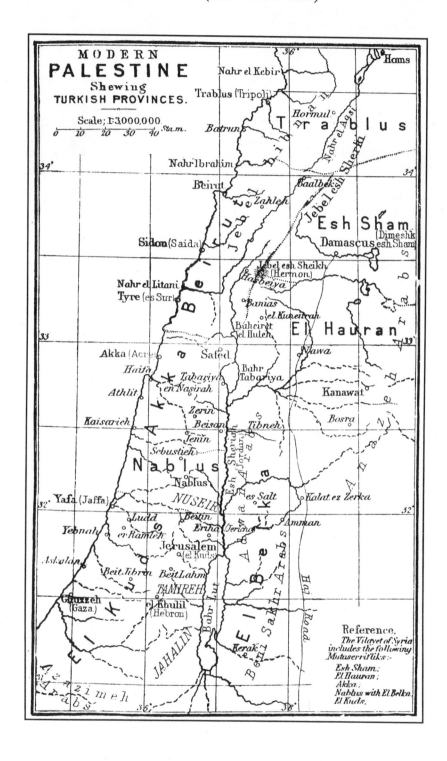

ouin." It is notorious that all the Northern Arab countries—Jordan, Syria, Palestine and Iraq—have for centuries past been recruited by nomadic tribes which have migrated from Central Arabia. These tribes at first continue their nomadic lives in the deserts bounding the cultivated area; they gradually reduce the distances of their annual migration, and increase the numbers of their sheep at the expense of the camels. Later they become interested in agriculture, abandon camels altogether and eventually become complete agriculturists; they retain their tents probably for a considerable time. The process of transformation of a pure nomadic camel tribe from Central Arabia into a group of agriculturalists still living in tents occupied in the past an average period of about three hundred years. But many such tribes continue to live in tents for several centuries longer. Indeed, the tribe itself and tribal organization usually disappear before the members abandon tents and take to stone villages.

Certain factors have made the last twenty years a period of exceptionally rapid change, not indeed in Trans-Jordan alone, but likewise in Asia, Europe and America. But the gradual transformation of camel nomads into sheep breeders, sheep breeders into tribal cultivators and tribal cultivators into non-tribal villagers has been going on for thousands of years. At all times, therefore, tribes have existed in Trans-Jordan in every stage of this metamorphosis, from the completely nomadic camel breeder to the completely sedentary cultivator. Indeed, the different sections and families of the same tribe may often be seen in different stages of sedentarization. To divide the inhabitants of Trans-Jordan into rigid groups of nomads, semi-nomads or settled is therefore difficult, for all these types of life shade off imperceptibly one into the other.

The settlement and landuse conditions which prevailed within the project area during the Late Ottoman Period are best understood as a local example of this process. Being the most recent tribe to enter Transjordan, the camel-breeding Beni Sakhr were the most nomadic, migrating between summer camps along the eastern plain of the project area and winter camps deep in the Arabian desert in the vicinity of the Wadi Sirhan (Hiatt 1984: 34). Conder (1892: 321) puts their numbers at 1,500 tents or about 7,500 persons. Having entered Transjordan before the Beni Sakhr, the sheep-breeding Adwan, along with their allies, migrated between campsites along the

Plate 3.12 Beni Sakhr sheikh (after Fish 1876)

plateau ridge and the western descent and their more permanent settlements in the Jordan Valley, where they were regarded as the ruling tribe. Allied to the Adwan were a number of even less nomadic sheep and cattle-breeding tribes, one of which was the Ajarmeh. Conder regarded this tribe, which sojourned primarily in the valleys of the western descent and around Hesban, as being the one with the most seniority in this part of Transjordan, and Tristram (1873) praised them for their proficiency as cultivators. Together, the Adwan and their allies numbered, according to Conder (1892: 321), "some 2,200 tents or 11,000 souls, giving a density of 10 persons per square mile, which appears to be a very probable result for such a district as that of the Belka."

The sociopolitical and territorial relationships which prevailed between the Adwan and Beni Sakhr tribal confederacies and their respective allies, and between the various subsections of each of these major tribal groups, have been discussed at some length by both Tristram (1873) and Conder (1892). Whereas the Adwan tribe had for centuries been the reigning tribe of the

Belqa (Tristram 1873), which at one time included the whole territory of the project area, they were considered "on their way down" by the time of Tristram's and Conder's visits, being gradually forced to retreat at the hands of the more powerful Beni Sakhr tribe from their former lands on the Madaba plateau into the western descent. Indeed, although Beni Sakhr territory was considered to be those lands which lay east of a line running between Yadoudeh, Es Samik, and Madaba or slightly to the east of the plateau ridge (Conder 1892: 315), they were known to cross over into Adwan territory in order to water their camels at the springs located along the plateau ridge and in the western descent (Conder 1892: 347). An indication of the enmity which prevailed between these two dominant tribes is provided by Captain Warren, who visited the project area in 1869. Having arrived at Es Samik where the border between these two tribes was located, he discovered that "the ground itself was black with fire, the hostile tribe (the Beni Sakhr) having burnt it when they left some weeks before, so that the Adwan might make no use of it" (Warren 1869: 291; cf. Tristram 1865: 541, 1873: 247; Thomson 1880: 629).

The particular arrangements whereby each of these pastoralist tribes went about providing for their grain requirements need to be explained further. While the Ajarmeh would themselves plant and harvest fields of wheat and barley in the fertile valleys of the western descent, the Adwan and the Beni Sakhr employed *fellahin* for this purpose—a socially inferior group of tribesmen whose livelihoods were closely tied in a servile relationship to specific Adwan and Beni Sakhr families (*cf.* Hiatt 1984: 129-131). Thus, in the Jordan Valley, members of the Ghawarneh tribe, or "Men of the Ghor," "rudely tilled" the soil for their Adwan masters (Conder 1892: 315), while on the eastern plain, members of the Abu Endi (or Abu Wandi) tribe produced wheat and barley for the Beni Sakhr (Tristram 1873: 316). In return for their services, these tribesmen received protection from their employers and assistance in obtaining the means of production—such as lands, tools, and shelters, assistance in finding wives for their sons, and the brideprice wherewith to seal their marriage arrangements.

Precise information about the quantity and types of animals raised by these different trans-

Plate 3.13 Adwan Sheikh Goblan (after Fish 1876)

humant groups is difficult to obtain. About the fact that the Beni Sakhr traditionally had raised primarily camels there is little dispute, although their *fellahin* apparently owned a number of oxen which they used for plowing (Tristram 1873: 333). An indication of the extent to which the Beni Sakhr were abandoning their traditional ways already during the Late Ottoman Period is provided by Tristram (1873: 238). He noted that each of their camps consisted of "on the average, twelve families, and each family averaging twenty camels and four hundred sheep and goats" (Tristram 1873: 238). It is doubtful, however, that this estimate applies across the board to all of the subsections and camps of the Beni Sakhr at the time of his visit; instead it must be regarded as applying to those families leading the way toward sedentarization. According to Kitchener (1878: 11) the Beni Sakhr were also noted for horse breeding and falconry. While camels were raised by the Adwan and their allies, they represented a relatively smaller proportion of their herds. As already indicated, these tribes were primarily sheep breeders, and among some, such as the Ajarmeh and the Ghawarneh, cattle were

Plate 3.14   Qasr at Seil Hesban belonging to Adwan sheikh

Plate 3.15   Qasr at Umm el Amad belonging to Beni Sakhr sheikh

also raised in considerable numbers because of their role as draft animals (Conder 1892: 347).

Although the various transhumant tribes of the project area were migratory to varying degrees, none of them were without certain nonmovable operational facilities. The most important of these were campsites, caves, watering sites, herding sites, storage sites, and burial sites. As a general rule, the less nomadic the household, the more extensive its nonmovable facilities. Thus, whereas most Beni Sakhr households dwelt year-round in tents, Ajarmeh families spent the cooler months of the year living in seasonal cave villages near their fields and herds (discussed further in Chapter Seven). As mentioned earlier, some of their caves were sealed off by masonry walls containing a doorway. Inside many of these could be found hearths above which a chimney was usually located. Such caves are particularly abundant in the traditional Ajarmeh territories (cf. pls. 3.16, 3,17). Even more permanently settled were the servile tribes of the Adwan and the Beni Sakhr, the Ghawarneh having dwelt in mud brick dwellings in the Ghor and the Abu Endi having occupied rudely constructed stone dwellings built on or near ancient ruins on the eastern plain where building materials were readily available.

Not surprisingly, a large number of campsites used seasonally by the various tribes tended to be located in the vicinity of tribally owned watering sites such as springs, streams, and anciently constructed cisterns or reservoirs. Thus, a favorite camping site of the Adwan was nearby the spring at Ain Hesban. At this site Thomson (1880: 666) reported seeing "the largest encampment of the Adwan tribe we have yet seen" (cf. Warren 1869: 286; Tristram 1873: 353). Frequently camped at Hesban were the Ajarmeh, partially because the site was honeycombed with anciently hewn cisterns. At Madaba and Ziza, where large reservoirs dating to Roman times were still capable of storing water, the Beni Sakhr could often be found watering their animals.

Another type of nonmovable agricultural facility used by the Late Ottoman Period Bedouin was herding sites. While in many instances these might simply have been ancient ruins or caves used as shelters or pens for herds of sheep or goats, they also included more elaborate walled enclosures used to separate selected groups of animals for various herd management purposes

(cf. Murray and Chang 1980). Conder (1889) noted the presence of a number of "goat folds" in his survey map. Tombs and caves filled with straw and dung, indicating that they had been used as animal pens, were also frequently encountered in our own survey.

One of the most intriguing aspects of the material life of the Bedouin of the Late Ottoman Period was the way in which their burial sites were used as inviolate places of equipment storage. Being only nominal Muslims and having retained aspects of their former ancestral religion (Conder 1892), including great respect for the deceased and a fear of violating another tribe's burial sites, they could safely deposit seasonally used tools and equipment inside the stone circles within which they buried their dead. Tristram (1865: 541) offers this account of a Beni Sakhr burial site located in the vicinity of El 'Al,

> Hard by was a rude enclosure of loosely-heaped stones, inside of which about fifty wooden plows were heaped—the graveyard being the depot for the agricultural implements of the tribe, during their absence for months in the interior.

Conder (1889) reported encountering several such sites as well. Also used for temporary storage of equipment were ancient tombs, caves, and ruins in the vicinity of tribal campsites. Grain was sometimes stored in plastered caves (Warren 1869: 287; Tristram 1865: 534).

The dietary conditions which prevailed throughout the Late Ottoman Period within the project area varied first of all in terms of how extensively cereals were used as a staple. As a general rule, the more nomadic the household, the lesser the contribution of cereals and legumes to the diet (cf. May 1961; Yacoub 1969). Although none of the tribes lived year-round without using cereals, those Beni Sakhr households which migrated for months at a time in the interior had to rely for their main source of nourishment on camel's, sheep, or goat's milk, supplemented by dried fruits, locusts, and a number of different edible plants and roots collected in the desert (cf. Burckhardt 1831: 238-242; Musil 1928: 86-114). Meat was eaten only on special occasions when hospitality or ceremonial requirements called for the slaughter of herd animals. Poultry or fish were normally not consumed, although game was a popular addition to the diet whenever available. Most common in this regard were gazelle and partridge, although a number of

Plate 3.16   Doorway (G.4:1) of Ajarmeh Cave G.4:2

Plate 3.17   Inside Ajarmeh Cave G.4:2

other species including the bubale, oryx, ibex, desert hare, coney, pigeon, rock dove, grouse, quail, and duck were also sometimes hunted and prepared for the platter (*cf.* Tristram 1880; Musil 1928: 20-43).

When Village Cereal Farming Prevailed: The Early Modern Period

Between the years 1880 and 1950 more than two dozen permanent villages came into existence within the project area as transhumant pastoralism gave way to cereal farming by a rapidly sedentarizing population. Because of the initial emphasis on field crops (see below), those portions of the project area which were the best suited to grain production, namely the eastern plains and the broad valleys of the northern hills and plateau ridge, were settled first. Although other crops, including legumes, vegetables, fruits, and nuts also gradually gained in significance, and while pastoral pursuits continued to be of importance, by far the most pervasive shift which occurred in landuse and settlement during this period was the conversion of pasture lands into cereal fields and the abandonment of annual migrations by the various local tribesmen in favor of permanent settlement in villages. Other than the recollections of the older members of the local population themselves, the contemporary published sources relied on here for information about this period in the history of the project area are records and accounts offered by Conder (1889), Forder (1909), Hoskins (1912), Glubb (1938), and Konikoff (1943).

The designation of this period as *Early Modern* can be justified on the grounds that modern technology and Western political and economic intervention played a major part in shaping the process of sedentarization which occurred during this period. First, between the years 1900 and 1910, the Hejaz railway, which had been conceived as a means to further strengthen the Turkish presence in the Arabian territories, was completed between Damascus and Kerak (Glubb 1967: 120). Second, the Emirate of Transjordan was born in 1921 out of the colonial aspirations of the British (Glubb 1967), and along with it came the Arab Legion as a powerful instrument of the state in pacifying the countryside and integrating the tribal entities of former times into the

newly established state government (Vatikiotis 1967: 5; Snow 1972: 22). Third, these events led to the establishment of the present central administration in Jordan along with which came the beginnings of a number of government bureaucracies and public education actively supportive and facilitative of modernization of the rural sector of the country.

As a result of the technological and political changes which took place in Jordan during the Early Modern Period, certain significant changes occurred in the natural environment of the country as a whole which are evident also within the project area. Perhaps the most devastating to Jordan's ecology was the large-scale cutting down of coniferous trees and forests, especially in northern Jordan, which accompanied the construction of the Hejaz railway. Additionally, as transhumance was abandoned in favor of settlement in villages and towns, the periodic abatement of grazing pressure on pastures which took place seasonally when transhumance prevailed, gradually became a thing of the past as flocks of sheep and goats owned by villagers were fed year-round on marginal local pastures. Furthermore, expansion of cultivation at the expense of pasture lands, which sometimes led to plowing of lands best left untouched by the plow, also had consequences for survival of native flora and fauna. Add to the above disturbances caused by increased collection of firewood by rapidly growing numbers of sedentaries and excessive hunting of favored species of birds and mammals, and it is clear why concern over the disappearance of wildlife in Jordan became a national issue by the end of the Early Modern Period, culminating in the establishment in 1966 of the Royal Society for the Conservation of Nature (R.S.C.N.).

At the time of Conder's survey in 1881, the extent to which the inhabitants of the project area had been settled is indicated by his observations upon visiting Naur, Mushaqqar, Umm el Qanafid, and Madaba. At Naur he noted that

half a dozen modern houses where corn is stored, and a little enclosed vegetable garden east of the spring is the property of (Adwan) Sheikh 'Aly Diab, under the care of a fugitive Arab from the Nejed (Conder 1889: 152).

whereas at Mushaqqar (Khirbet el Meshukkar) he found "modern huts of some fugitive Fellahin here settled. They cultivate a little corn and tobacco" (Conder 1889: 151). At Umm el Qanafid

Plate 3.18   Glubb Pasha (center) and King Abdullah (after Glubb 1967)

Plate 3.19   Soldiers of the Arab Legion mounted on thoroughbred Arab Horses (after Glubb 1967)

were "half a dozen modern houses on the Tell, and enclosures with drystone walls" (Conder 1889: 248).

At Madaba he noted "many caves, now inhabited by Christians from Kerak" (see pls. 3.20, 2.21). Having been "converted from the Greek to the Latin rite by the Jesuit missionaries" these inhabitants

> were settled at Madaba, under the leadership of these priests, in the spring of 1881. Some were yet in tents in the autumn of the same year, but were repairing cisterns, and preparing to build. They had constructed a sort of fort on the mound, called ed Deir, "the monastery," measuring about 80 paces (or 200 feet) square, and including graves, apparently of Arabs. The walls are drystone, carefully packed, and no doubt intended for protection (Conder 1889: 180; *cf.* Hoskins 1912: 349; Peake 1958: 177; Gubser 1973; Allison 1977: 28-30).

These are the only references to settled communities within the project area noted in Conder's report. In Tristram's (1873) account, no references are found indicating year-round habitation within the project area.

The resettlement of Madaba was a pivotal event in pushing forward the resettlement of other sites within the project area (pls. 3.22-24). One reason for this was that Madaba was settled by an estimated 2,000 experienced cultivators all at once (Allison 1977: 29). Having had to flee from their farmsteads at Kerak because of an escalating blood feud, the families involved had appealed to the Turkish administration for help in finding a new place to settle. Since their request to make their new homes at Madaba and to cultivate its fertile fields could only further Turkish attempts to gain control over the population of Jordan, it was granted. The transformation of Madaba which resulted has been succinctly portrayed by Hoskins (1912: 349-50), who visited Madaba sometime during the turn of the century. He writes:

> Twenty-five years ago Madaba was still a desert mound, lost in the Moab plateau. The Adwan Arabs, mentioned so often by travellers, pitched their tents and pastured their flocks about the mound and in the floor of the ancient pool, without knowing or caring that the ruins of a once flourishing city lay beneath their feet. But in 1880, some Christians from Kerak, weary of being trampled upon by the more powerful tribes and clans, in their never-ending blood feuds and pillage, resolved to quit that city and found a new colony about the mound of ancient Madaba.
>
> When the Kerak people settled on the mound, the Latins seized a most commanding site and built a modest church and school, which now boasts a small clock-tower. Other settlers came from the surrounding country, until there were several thousand people gathered together. Then the government, some fifteen years ago, made it a government center and built a small serai on the ruins of a church. The Greek orthodox people, in looking for a site, seized upon the ruins of an old basilica to the northwest of the mound, and here has been made the second great discovery beyond the Jordan (the Madaba mosaic map).

Significantly, all the villages which came into existence during the Early Modern Period were established on or near the ruins of an ancient settlement, most of which had been used as seasonal camps by the settlers during their days as transhumants. Not only were these sites strategically located in terms of access to cereal fields, they also contained reusable cisterns for collecting and storing water and ample supplies of anciently hewn stones for use as building materials. Thus, Conder (1889: 183) worried that "the ruins of Madaba are being much injured by the new Christian settlers who remove the stones to build walls before their caves." As the rebuilding of these villages progressed, these anciently hewn stones continued to be used to build the fortified dwellings which became the distinctive architectural style throughout the Early Modern Period.

As one would expect, the first families to settle permanently along with the Christians at Madaba were those belonging to the oldest tribes of the project area such as members of the various Belqa tribes. Of these, the Ajarmeh were among the first to settle when they began to live permanently at Mushaqqar as early as the Late Ottoman Period. As these earliest villages grew, they tended to spawn daughter villages. Thus, Mushaqqar spawned Hesban, and Hesban, spawned El Manshiya, El 'Al, and Es Samik—all of them originally inhabited by Ajarmeh families. In time, however, descendants of other tribal groups also became a part of these villages.

The continuing importance of tribal ideology throughout the Early Modern Period is evidenced by this tendency for new villages to be spawned along tribal lines. Not only did tribal ideology serve as a basis for allocating land to tribal sub-

Plate 3.20   Cave dwellings in Madaba (after Libbey and Hoskins 1905)

Plate 3.21   Cave dwellers west of Madaba (after Libbey and Hoskins 1905)

Plate 3.22   Madaba *ca.* 1909; view northeast (after Hoskins 1912)

Plate 3.23   Madaba *ca.* 1920; view south (Library of Congress Print Collection RPW 39764, LC-M32-1166)

Plate 3.24   Madaba *ca.* 1980 (courtesy of Erwin Syphers)

Plate 3.25   Abandoned Adwan houses in the Ghor

groups and families upon settlement so that those subgroups most closely related in the patrilineal idiom of the tribe often settled nearest each other (*cf.* Hiatt 1984: 26), it also served as a basis for unified military action by sedentaries against pillage by other tribes (*cf.* Antoun 1972: 16-18). Thus, especially in the interim period between the first village settlements and the rise of the nation-state, the tribal framework was facilitative of and reinforced by sedentarization.

On the basis of settlement data provided by Conder (1889), by a Hebrew map of Palestine from about 1924, and by the British Survey Engineer Map of 1953 (published in 1956), a rough idea of the rate at which villages were settled within the project area during the Early Modern Period can be gained (see figs. 3.10-3.12). As discussed earlier, at the time of Conder's survey in 1881 there were only four sites sufficiently settled to qualify as hamlets or beginning villages—namely Naur, Umm el Qanafid, Mushaqqar, and Madaba. By 1924, a total of 17 settlements were deemed worthy of inclusion on the map from that year. This figure rose to about 27 by the time the 1953 map was produced. Since the Survey Engineer Regiment Map (1956) includes dots representing the number and location of dwellings within each village, it is possible to estimate approximately the size of the population of the project area around 1950. Assuming that each dot represents about 6 persons per household (*cf.* Gulick 1971: 108), I arrive at a population estimate of approximately 13,000 individuals for the year 1953. This means that from the original settlement of about 2,000 persons in Madaba, the settled population increased at the rate of about 150 persons per year during the Early Modern Period. As noted earlier, most of this population growth took place in villages located near lands suited to the production of field crops, *i.e.*, on the edge of the fertile valleys of the plateau ridge, the northern hills and the eastern plain.

Although tonnage information regarding Early Modern Period increases in wheat and barley production have not been obtained for the project area, information for the country of Jordan as a whole during this period is available and offers an idea of the spectacular rate at which grain production was intensified. According to Konikoff (1943), the tonnage of wheat produced annually in Jordan jumped from 40,000 tons in 1927 to 168,000 in 1939. Between the same two dates, barley production jumped from 14,000 tons to 98,000. Since the Hesban region has historically been famous for its high quality wheat—indeed Irby and Mangles (1823: 473) and Tristram (1880: 492) wrote admiringly of its qualities—the rate at which its production was increased within the project area probably exceeded the national rate by a considerable margin.

The rise in wheat production was carried out by three principal means. First, as already mentioned, was expansion of cultivated land (*cf.* Glubb 1938: 451). Second was more frequent cropping of arable lands. Thus, in contrast to the Bedouin observed by Tristram (1873: 136) who would "take one crop and then leave the spot fallow for three or four years, while they scratch up the next patch," a rotation system was widely adopted during the Early Modern Period involving wheat or barley seeded in late fall and lentils, sesame, vetch, chickpeas, or sorghum seeded in early spring (Abujaber 1984). Third was the introduction of the tractor-powered plow, which greatly facilitated opening up formerly uncultivated lands at the fringes of the desert. The fact that the mechanical plow was first introduced to Jordan by cereal farmers cultivating on the fertile Madaba Plain is further evidence of the favorable conditions which exist there for its production (Glubb 1938: 451; Abujaber 1984).

The fact that intensification of food production in Jordan initially emphasized cereals rather than vegetables, vine, and tree fruits is a matter which requires a brief explanation, for although vegetables and fruits were produced during the Early Modern Period, it was on a relatively small scale and mostly for local consumption. One important reason for this pattern has to do with the state of security for sedentaries at the end of the 19th century. Because the threat of raids and pillage was a constant problem for these early settlers, crops requiring more than one growing season to bear fruit, such as vine and tree crops, were too risky to plant. Furthermore, cereals could be stored easier as a hedge against crop failure and surpluses were easier to transport over the long distances which had to be covered in order to be brought to urban markets (*cf.* Hunt 1985).

The changes which occurred in the composition of nonpoultry livestock as a result of seden-

Fig. 3.10   Project area villages *ca.* 1889

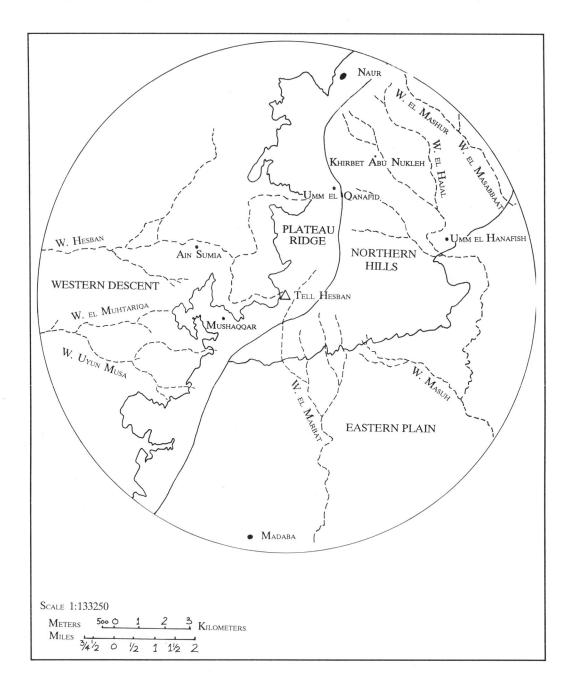

Fig. 3.11   Project area villages *ca.* 1924

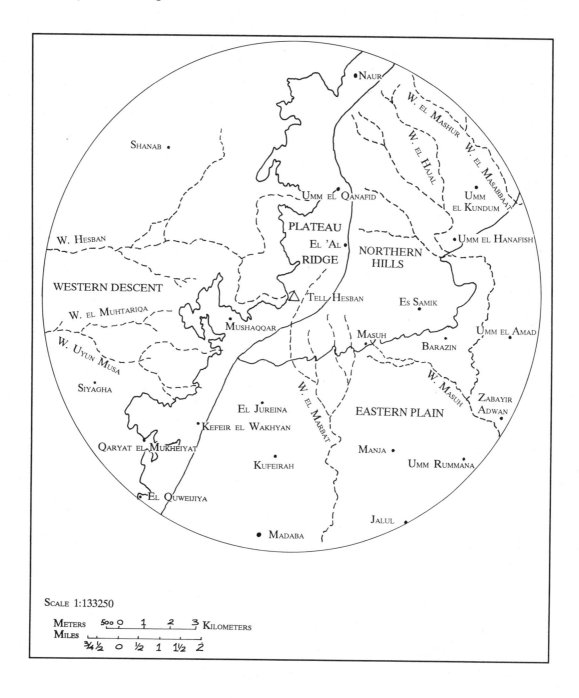

Fig. 3.12   Project area villages *ca.* 1953

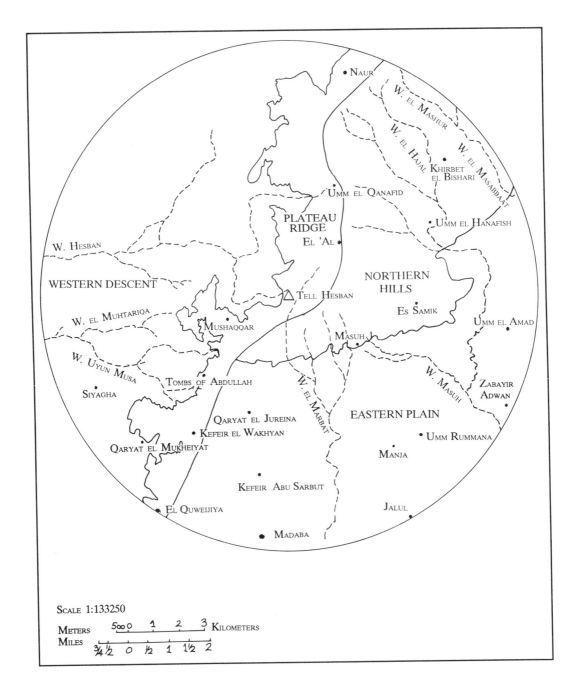

tarization are particularly noteworthy. Again, due to inadequate data for the project area, I must turn to data available for Jordan as a whole in order to gain an idea of what very likely happened on a smaller scale within the project area. Relying once more on Konikoff's (1943) figures for the years between 1927 and 1938, I note the following: a marked drop-off in the quantity of camels (from 13,800 to 4,700); a significant increase in the quantity of draft animals such as cattle (from 32,500 to 52,700) and donkeys (from 17,800 to 24,500); a slight decline in the quantity of sheep (from 220,900 to 200,400) and an appreciable increase in the quantity of goats (from 344,500 to 393,600). This latter change is readily accounted for by the fact that as more and more small livestock was being produced by sedentaries, and as more and more land was being put under cultivation, locally available pastures became increasingly sparse and marginal in quality. Under such conditions the goat, because of its hardier ways, became increasingly favored. Indeed, by 1938 goats came to outnumber sheep by 2:1. During this same period no appreciable changes occurred in the quantity of horses (from 5,000 to 5,500), although mules were decreased somewhat in numbers (2,400 to 1,500).

Another consequence of settlement which is worthy of notice was that poultry began to be produced in gradually increasing quantities. Thus, by 1938 the number of fowls and laying hens produced in Jordan had reached 45,200 and 271,000 respectively (Konikoff 1943: 53). The presence of poultry in the project area from the beginning of settlement is attested to by Forder's remarks upon being hosted as a guest in Madaba in 1891, for he comments that he was served "in usual Arab style . . . two baked fowls, boiled rice, and warm bread" (Forder 1909: 9). Because poultry require no pastures and are practically omnivorous in their eating habits, as sedentarization progressed they gradually came to be recognized as a practical alternative to sheep and goats' meat among villagers and townsmen alike.

In addition to the connection which has already been noted between the expansion of cereal farming, changes in the composition of livestock and the location of settlements on the edges of fertile valleys and plains on the plateau, a further connection appears to have existed between these developments and types of housing used. Of all of the operational facilities which became commonplace during the early decades of sedentary existence in Jordan, none are more characteristic of times of uncertain security than the fortified farm building. Architecturally such buildings are readily recognized, for most of them were built of anciently hewn stone; their roofs were held in place by one or more arches covered by mud-and-earth roofs laid down on top of wooden cross beams (pl. 3.26). Typically windows were either nonexistent or very small, being openings protected by bars of wrought iron. Inside, these buildings were partitioned by the two ends of the arches (pl. 3.27).

Granaries were often constructed between these arches on one or both sides of the room in order to assure protection of the grain. At night livestock would also be housed inside these dwellings for protection. Buildings of this type are particularly well-preserved in Madaba, Mushaqqar, and Jalul. Forder's (1909: 9) account of his visit to Madaba includes a description of one such building:

> Fifteen hours after leaving Jericho we reached Madaba, a large village on the plain. How thankful we were for the warm welcome given us by the chief of the place! He spread rugs and comforts on the floor for us, on which we lay, glad to stretch and rest our weary limbs. The house was just one large room; on each side were raised recesses, in which the family slept or stored their goods. Wide arches supported the roof, which was made of a thick layer of mud and earth held up by beams of wood (compare Buckingham 1825: 33-34 and Tristram 1865: 468).

The concern among pioneer settlers over mutual protection appears also to have led to a clumping together of fortified farm buildings inside a massive perimeter wall, as at Yadoudeh (pl. 3.28), or in a group around a central court as in the case of the *qasr* at Hesban. At Madaba they were positioned within close proximity of each other around a *monastery* which also served as a kind of fort (Conder 1889: 180). This latter arrangement stems, no doubt, from a pattern well-known to the early settlers of that town, most of whom came from Kerak, a town built around a massive Crusader castle. Interestingly, at Jalul, where certain Beni Sakhr tribesmen occupied fortified farm buildings even before the Early Modern Period, the dwellings were not similarly clumped together

Plate 3.26   Fortified farm building at Mushaqqar

Plate 3.27   Inside view of fortified farm building in Madaba

Plate 3.28   Yadoudeh, the Abujaber family farmstead

Plate 3.29   The Bisharat farmstead

for protection. Instead they were spread out over a larger area, having retained the appearance of a Bedouin encampment (*cf.* Hiatt 1984: 116).

Not only did these early cereal farmers cooperate in order to assure mutual protection against pillage, they also worked together in other ways, such as in the restoration of ancient water collection facilities such as cisterns and water channels, and in the rebuilding and replanting of anciently constructed terraces and floodwater control systems. Later on, as small garden plots and fruit trees were planted, perimeter walls had to be constructed as well to protect these crops from thieves and grazing animals. Such walls were usually made from boulders removed in the process of clearing and plowing. As already mentioned, livestock were kept inside their owners' fortified farm buildings at night, although caves continued to be used as well for this purpose.

Whereas during transhumant days, bread had typically been baked on a round concave metal platter over an open fire, upon settling in villages, people began to bake it in baking ovens called *tabuns* (*cf.* McQuitty 1984). These were made in different ways, some having been placed in the ground, others above the ground. Consisting of an enclosed heat chamber, *tabuns* permitted villagers to bake leavened bread which rises when placed inside the hot oven. By contrast, as transhumants they had to make do with thin sheets of flat unleavened bread called *shrack*, which is all that it was possible for them to make in the absence of any kind of enclosed oven. The making of *shrack* was by no means abandoned by most villagers, however, for, as we found at Hesban, it has continued to be a favorite type of bread among many of them right through to the present.

The emphasis on cereals and bread ovens during the Early Modern Period had a predictable effect on the diet which prevailed in that its most important ingredients were bread and gruel made from wheat or barley. Gradually, as sedentarization progressed, staple items common in the nomadic diet such as ghee and sour milk diminished in importance as legumes and fresh vegetables, especially tomatoes and cucumbers, gained in importance (*cf.* Yacoub 1969: 15-17). As orchards began to be planted locally, their fruits also gradually entered the diet in season. Particularly important in this regard were olives, for they

supplemented and gradually took the place of fat supplied by sheep and camels. As was noted earlier, sheep gradually diminished in quantity during the Early Modern Period because of the worsening of pasturage conditions. Also more common in the village diet were goats' milk and goats' meat, chicken and other poultry, but goats' meat as well. As in earlier times, sheep were slaughtered and eaten only on special occasions.

To a large degree, the shifts which occurred in dietary conditions during the Early Modern Period were due to changes in foods produced locally. These changes, in turn, were a consequence of the changes in landuse discussed earlier. Throughout most of this period, subsistence production was the rule for most farmers, cereals being the principal crop produced in sufficient quantities to generate a surplus. Of poultry, vegetables, and fruits very little remained for export to urban areas even as late as 1938 (Konikoff 1943). This emphasis on subsistence production represents, therefore, an important line of continuity between transhumance and village cereal farming which was not fully broken until the advent of intensive urban-oriented agriculture during the Modern Period.

When Urban-Oriented Farming Prevailed: The Modern Period

A turning point for agriculture in Jordan was the decade which began *ca.* 1950. During this decade the organizational center of gravity responsible for agricultural production in Jordan shifted from local villages to bureaucracies dominated by urban interests. Jordan's first Five-Year Plan was put into action, which meant that agricultural production goals for the country were being set in an explicit manner by the state. Along with this plan came a clear mandate for a number of government agencies, such as the Ministry of Agriculture, the Agricultural Credit Corporation, and the Ministry of Education to develop the infrastructure needed so that the plan's goals could be reached on the local village level (Aresvik 1976: 9). Furthermore, during this decade and those immediately before and after it, Palestinian refugees entered Jordan by the hundreds of thousands, resulting not only in increased pressure on village farmers to produce surpluses, but also in additional farm labor and new agricultural know-how. As a result of these and a number of related developments, the subsistence grain farming which had prevailed during the Early Modern Period in Jordan soon gave way to intensive, market-oriented production not only of cereals, but also of poultry and other livestock, and especially, of fruits and vegetables.

The influx of Palestinian refugees to East Jordan came in two waves, the first following the Palestine War of 1948 and the second after the Six-Day War in 1967. Of the first wave of refugees to territories controlled by the state of Jordan 318,686 ended up in East Jordan (as opposed to on the West Bank). To this number another 239,285 were added in the wake of the 1967 war, so that in December of 1972 the total number of registered refugees in East Jordan was 557,771 (Aresvik 1976: 9). Given a pre-war population for East Jordan of approximately 400,000, this means that the population more than doubled over the decade and a half following the war of 1948 (*cf.* Vatikiotis 1967: 9). Throughout the remainder of the 1970s to the present, the population of Jordan has continued to grow at a rapid rate because of the steady influx of Palestinian refugees and war-weary nationals from Lebanon.

The steady deterioration of the natural environment which had accompanied the process of sedentarization throughout the Early Modern Period has continued nearly unabated through the Modern Period. Of particular concern to government planners has been the heavy demand which the exploding population of the Modern Period has placed on already limited water supplies. This concern reached a high point in 1977 with the publication of a National Water Masterplan for the country of Jordan (Agrar- und Hydrotechnik 1977). Unlike the heavily populated Late Roman and Byzantine periods in Jordan, when the supply of water was increased largely through collection of rainwater in cisterns and reservoirs before it drained underground, the present population—including the population of the project area—has resorted to pumping up underground waters at a rate never before equaled in history (see Chapter Six). In certain areas, especially in the vicinity of heavily settled areas such as Amman, such pumping has exceeded the rate at which some underground water reservoirs have been able to recharge, a situation which has further heightened

concern over the long-term future of Jordan's water supply. It is to the credit of government planners that a comprehensive approach has been adopted in dealing with this problem, as is evidenced by the National Water Plan. It is encouraging also to see the growing emphasis which is being given to reforestation, the tangible results of which are readily apparent within the project area to those of us who have been returning on a regular basis to Jordan over the past two decades.

Between the end of the Early Modern Period, or *ca.* 1953, and *ca.* 1975, at least nine additional villages came into existence within the project area (fig. 3.1). During this period population growth was particularly heavy in the towns of Madaba and Naur, and in villages located along the plateau ridge and the western descent. On the basis of village data gathered in 1975 by CARE-Jordan, and the sources described earlier with reference to Early Modern Period population statistics, a more precise idea can be gained of the demographic shifts which took place within the project area during the first 25 years of the Modern Period.

For example, the population of Madaba jumped from an estimated population of about 8,000 in 1953 to more than 25,000 by 1975. Naur increased in size from an estimated population of about 2,000 in 1953 to more than 5,000 in 1975. This means that in Madaba, about 790 persons were added each year between 1953 and 1975. For Naur, this figure would be about 129 persons per year. For the other villages of the project area combined, the rate of accession of new members was about 634 persons per year, 381 or 60% being added to existing or new villages along the plateau ridge or the western descent. Thus, the combined population growth for the project area as a whole during the first 25 years of the Modern Period was from an estimated population of 13,000 in 1953 to about 42,000 by 1975 (see fig. 3.13).

The significantly higher rise in population numbers which occurred in the towns of Madaba and Naur and in villages along the plateau ridge and western descent is a phenomenon which can be explained in light of the livelihoods with which the Palestinian newcomers were most familiar. To begin with, unlike the native population of East Jordan, whose emphasis had traditionally been on

Fig. 3.13 Population density (inhabitants per mi²) *ca.* 1975 (after Agrar- und Hydrotechnik 1977)

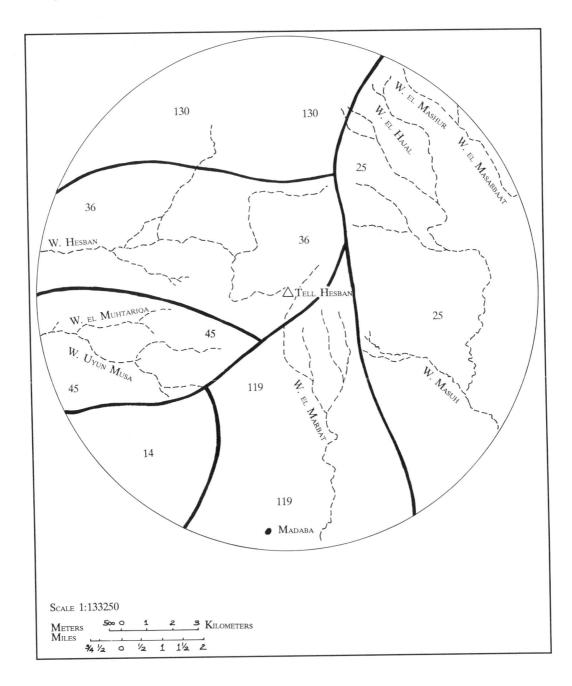

Fig. 3.14   Current administrative units (after Agrar- und Hydrotechnik 1977)

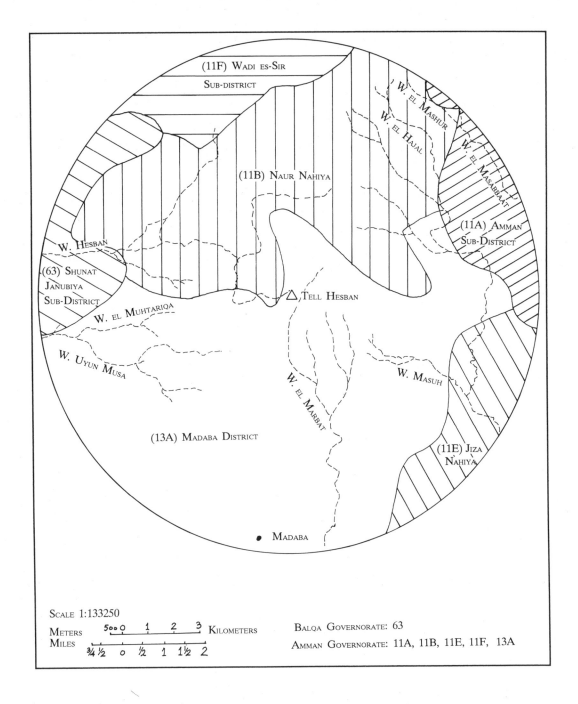

subsistence herding and cereal farming, these Palestinian newcomers were experienced orchardists and gardeners. They were also experienced wage laborers, having become increasingly dependent upon it in response to expanding opportunities created by the Public Works Department of Mandate Palestine during the 1930s and 1940s (Rosenfeld 1958; Taqqu 1979). Given their arrival at a time when opportunities for public service jobs were expanding in Jordan, especially in urban areas, but also in district headquarters like Madaba and Naur (see fig. 3.14), it can be seen why the influx of Palestinians into these towns was much more massive than it was into the smaller villages. Significantly, however, where Palestinians did settle in smaller villages, it tended to be in places where their know-how as growers of vegetables and fruits could be put to the best advantage, namely in locations along the plateau ridge and the western descent. Thus a direct link can be noted between the rise in population numbers in these villages and the rise in more labor-intensive forms of agriculture within the project area.

Another phenomenon which is particularly noteworthy in regards to the movement of Palestinians into East Jordan was that as large numbers of them were forced to abandon their sedentary existence in villages on the West Bank and elsewhere in territories under Israeli control, they turned to living in burlap tents and to herding of flocks of sheep and goats as a means to survive with their families during their sojourn. During the '60s and early '70s large numbers of such nomadized Palestinian families, surrounded by their flocks of sheep and goats, could be seen living in their tents on the edges of villages and towns of the project area. The length of their stay in the vicinity of a particular village would vary depending on opportunities for temporary farm labor for the adult males, the hospitality of the host village, and availability of pastures for their herds. Gradually, as their industry as workers and their skill and know-how as gardeners and fruit growers came to be valued more by their hosts, their temporary sojourn nearby a particular village turned into permanent association as they began to build their own permanent dwellings on lands offered them by their hosts. Although today the numbers of nomadized Palestinians are rapidly diminishing, their experience

stands as a modern-day example of the fluidity of traditional Arab society and of the nearly completely neglected phenomenon of nomadization.

To provide an idea of the extent to which not only the inhabitants of the project area, but of East Jordan as a whole, expanded the production of fruits and vegetables during the Modern Period, I shall turn to statistics gathered by the Ministry of Agriculture since 1961. According to figures published by the Department of Statistics (Hashemite Kingdom of Jordan 1967), the production of vegetables in East Jordan reached a high of 438,223 tons in 1967, compared with 42,885 tons in 1928 (Konikoff 1943). In 1972, fruit production reached a high of 149,191 tons, compared with 40,000 in 1938. By contrast, the production of wheat increased only modestly from levels reached in 1938, from 168.4 tons to 244.5 tons in 1974, whereas barley production actually declined from 98.0 tons in 1938 to 40.0 tons in 1974. Thus, with the expansion of wheat and barley production which took place mostly in the plateau regions of Jordan during the Early Modern Period, further expansion of vegetable and fruit production also occurred during the Modern Period, particularly in the Jordan Valley and in the well-watered areas along the piedmont and riverine valleys of the eastern highland.

Although production statistics pertaining exclusively to the project area have not been gathered, some insight into how project area lands are currently utilized can be gained from data provided for the Madaba Subdistrict in the Department of Statistics report for 1979 (Hashemite Kingdom of Jordan 1979). In terms of area devoted to producing crops (given in thousands of square meters or dunums, one dunum being equal to about 1/4 acre), the following are listed as *main crops*: wheat (98,051 dunums), barley (29,847), lentils (10,605), chickpeas (2,283), tomato (1,948), okra (1,168), olives (14,966), and grapes (6,167). *Secondary crops* listed are vetch (111), tobacco (258), eggplant (33), summer squash (292), cucumber (78), snake cucumber (33), watermelon (16), onion (16), peas (64), figs (20), pomegranate (17), almonds (117), plums (153), peaches (23), prunes (33), and apples (48).

As the Madaba Subdistrict does not include most of the western descent or the northern hills, it cannot be regarded as perfectly illustrative of landuse within the project area, but rather of

Plate 3.30   Helmi (far left), a Palestinian, by his tent in 1974

Plate 3.31   The author and his son visiting Helmi inside his new cement house in 1980

landuse on the eastern plain. Precise information on how lands were utilized strictly within the project area would reveal a much greater emphasis on vegetables and fruit trees and a lesser emphasis on wheat and barley. This can be demonstrated on the basis of statistics, gathered by Agrar- und Hydrotechnik (1977), regarding the contribution of fruit tree production to total crop area for villages within the project area. For the four respective subregions the percentage of cultivated area devoted by its villages to fruit production is 15% for the western descent, 15% for the plateau ridge, 12% for the northern hills and 4% for the eastern plain. Furthermore, Ministry of Agriculture statistics available for the Naur Subdistrict, to which most of the northern hills belong, and for the Shuna Subdistrict, to which portions of the western descent belong, show a much greater emphasis on vegetable and fruit production in these hilly and well-watered regions than is found in the Madaba Subdistrict.

The fact that the growing of vegetables and fruit trees is a much more labor-intensive undertaking than is cereal production or herding has already been alluded to. In contrast to cereal farming, which today is largely mechanized and involves very little labor input throughout the growing season except for at the beginning and at the end, fruit-tree production is largely manual and involves reliance on animal-draft power, particularly donkeys and mules, where much of the labor expended is in pruning, binding, plowing, and watering the trees. Since most orchards are located on slopes, each plowing involves an initial passage up and down the slopes followed by a passage back and forth against the slope to prevent erosion and conserve water. Such plowing may be repeated up to five times throughout the growing season. Most watering is done manually, donkeys or trucks being used to haul water to tanks situated on the edges of the orchards. Vegetable production can be even more labor intensive, as watering and weeding around the plants must be done by hand throughout the entire growing season.

To the link between increased population growth in project area villages along the plateau ridge and western descent and increased emphasis on labor-intensive cultivation can be added another link, namely increased production of certain types of livestock. Specifically, as cultiva-

tion has increased along the terraced hillsides and slopes of the western descent and plateau ridge the numbers of mules and donkeys have risen as well. This is because these animals are better suited for plowing in such terrain than oxen. Indeed, while the tractor and combine have largely replaced the teams of oxen which used to be seen on the plain, the utilization of mules and donkeys along these terraced hillsides has increased steadily. This local pattern reflects trends in East Jordan as a whole, for since 1938 the cattle population has dropped from 52,700 to 26,309 in 1961, whereas the number of donkeys increased from 24,500 to 36,477 over the same period, as did the quantity of mules, from 1,500 to 8,700. By comparison, over the same period the quantity of sheep and goats increased only slightly, from a combined total in 1938 of 594,000 to 624,718 in 1961 (Konikoff 1943; cf. Hashemite Kingdom of Jordan 1967).

Another trend which appears to be characteristic of the rise of intensive forms of agriculture is the rise in numbers of barnyard animals, especially chickens, but also pigeons, turkeys, ducks, geese and, in certain areas, swine. As was noted earlier, these livestock require little or no pasture, indeed, they thrive on eating the organic refuse which is produced daily in agricultural villages and towns. Statistics indicative of this trend for East Jordan as a whole are suggestive of its magnitude. Thus, between 1938 and 1961 the number of chickens raised in East Jordan increased from a total of 723,000 to 2,370,585 (Konikoff 1943; Hashemite Kingdom of Jordan 1975: 149). This trend is well illustrated in the project area in that a number of chicken farms can be seen on the edges of several villages, particularly those on the eastern plain inhabited by descendants of the Beni Sakhr.

Along with the shift away from village subsistence farming toward market-oriented production of crops and livestock has come a commensurate change in operational conditions such as increases in facilities built and operated by government organizations for producing, processing, storing, and distributing agricultural products. To begin with, to a great degree, the construction of roads and railways, begun during the Early Modern Period played a crucial role in laying the foundation for the take-off of vegetable and fruit production during the Modern Period. As produce of this kind needs to be brought from village to market as quickly as possible or it perishes, this emphasis has obviously continued into the Modern Period as traditional donkey-tracks have been upgraded into a network of paved roads tying villages to local market towns and urban centers. Furthermore, as was discussed earlier, a great deal of emphasis has been given to increasing the water supply through the drilling of deep wells and the installation of water pipes for bringing water to villages and fields. Also characteristic of the Modern Period is the emphasis being given to the construction of public granaries, food processing plants, and market facilities (Pedersen 1968: 25). All of these developments attest to the important role of the state in creating and maintaining the technological, social, and economic infrastructure necessary for local-level food production to intensify to the levels reached during the Modern Period.

The most distinctive feature of the dietary conditions which have emerged during the Modern Period is their variety due to delocalization. As a result of the ease with which foodstuffs can be transported from surrounding localities and even from distant lands, a much greater proportion of the foods consumed are neither locally grown nor seasonally restricted. In other words, the traditional linkage—characteristic of subsistence diets—of foods consumed to foods produced locally has been partially broken, especially in urban areas and among the more market-oriented households in rural areas. Thus, not only is the diet less seasonal, it also is less restricted in terms of variety of food items consumed. This is due to the fact that the Modern Period household can benefit to a much greater extent from regional variability in agricultural production thanks to the interlinkage of widely dispersed regions by means of modern markets and transportation.

It is important to emphasize, however, that the extent to which the traditional village subsistence diet has been abandoned by a particular household today depends to a great degree on the extent to which the economy of the household has been monetarized and modernized. The typical fare in the villages of the project area throughout the '70s, for example, was the traditional village subsistence diet consisting of bread, *leben*, olive oil, eggs, and seasonally available fruits and vegetables. Of meats, chicken was most frequently consumed, sheep or goats' meat being served primarily on special occasions. Such traditional diets prevail in many urban areas as well, especially among the poorer classes, because locally grown produce is generally much more affordable. Such a diet is also often preferred for sentimental reasons by wealthier people, as it provides some continuity with a rapidly disappearing past.

Configurations of Locally Prevailing Food System Conditions

In the foregoing pages, three different configurations of food system conditions have been set forth with reference to our project area. Specifically discussed were some of the ways in which changes in environmental, settlement, landuse, operational, and dietary conditions within a 10-km radius of Hesban have resulted in three successive configurations of prevailing conditions, namely transhumant pastoralism during the Late Ottoman Period, village cereal farming during the Early Modern Period, and urban-oriented intensive agriculture during the Modern Period. In what ways, then, are we now better prepared to begin the task of reconstructing the food system conditions which prevailed during earlier centuries and millennia within the project area?

To begin with, the environmental conditions to which project area populations have had to adapt have come into clearer focus as a result of this undertaking. In many respects these conditions have been found to be reflective of Middle Eastern conditions as a whole, particularly in regards to the inevitability of summer droughts and the consequences of this for human as well as plant and animal survival. Furthermore, a base line understanding of the adaptive strategies which project area populations have pursued throughout the recent past is now in hand, including an appreciation of their uniqueness as well as of their similarity in comparison with other Middle Eastern populations.

Most important for the present study, however, we have become acquainted, in a heuristic sense, with the process of identifying the parts of the local food system, thinking about how these parts are arranged at various points in time, identifying the prevailing features of these arrangements so as to be able to order them into distinctive configurations, and coming up with suitable labels for these configurations. It is this experience in systematic observation and analysis, this opportunity to become intimately acquainted with daily-life conditions throughout the most accessible historical period within the project area, which has best prepared us for the task ahead, namely to make sense of its fragmentary archaeological past.

In anticipation of this task, it is useful at this point to attempt to clarify exactly what is meant when reference is made in the following chapters to *configurations*. In harmony with what has already been attempted with reference to the recent past, it is suggested that the interrelationships which prevail over a given period of time with regards to environment, settlement, landuse, operational, and dietary conditions constitute a distinctive pattern or configuration—a particular arrangement of certain parts of the local food system. Thus, when reference was made above to pastoral transhumance, to village cereal farming, or to urban-oriented intensive agriculture, three analytically distinguishable configurations—three different hypotheses regarding the prevailing arrangements of the parts of the local food system—are what was meant.

Crucial to this analysis as well is the meaning of the word *prevailing*. In order to reckon with the dynamic nature of food systems, their periods of intensification and abatement, which result in constantly changing configurations of daily-life conditions, the term *prevailing* has been employed here to suggest correspondence of the empirical evidence to a particular hypothesized configuration. Thus, the empirical data examined with respect to the Late Ottoman Period seemed to correspond best with the hypothesized transhumant pastoralism configuration, whereas that examined with respect to the Early Modern Period fit best with the hypothesized village cereal farming configuration.

It must be acknowledged, of course, that these hypothesized *prevailing configurations* are, at best, first approximations—useful primarily as heuristic devices in the service of empirical research. It is anticipated, for example, that as a result of further research, discussions, and criticisms dealing with the contents of this chapter, the configurations proposed here might need to be modified somehow or that several additional ones might profitably be added to those already proposed in order to better present the food system conditions which prevailed during times of transition from one to another of these configurations. The same disclaimer obviously applies to configurations proposed in subsequent chapters on the basis of analysis of the archaeological materials from earlier centuries and millennia.

Chapter Four

FROM ARCHAEOLOGICAL INFORMATION
TO FOOD SYSTEM CONFIGURATIONS

Chapter Four

From Archaeological Information to Food System Configurations

Introduction

In the previous chapters, a three-tiered foundation was laid in preparation for the work which begins with the present chapter: piecing together from archaeological information the story of how people at Hesban and vicinity provided for their food needs in the distant past. In Chapter One, the first of these tiers was laid down in the form of a general methodological framework anchored on the concept of the food system. The second tier, laid down in Chapter Two, involved a discussion of how various environmental, cultural, and social factors characteristic of the Middle East as a region cooperate to produce, by means of the processes of sedentarization and nomadization, cyclic patterns of food system intensification and abatement. The third tier, laid down in Chapter Three, involved becoming intimately acquainted with the changes which have taken place within the project area in the recent past so as to obtain a better heuristic understanding of the workings of the local food system. This, as we shall see, has been an essential preparation for the challenging task of piecing together, from the fragmentary archaeological record, the long-term history of food system intensification and abatement within the project area.

In the present chapter my purpose is to make explicit the assumptions, methods, and procedures upon which reconstruction of past food system conditions within the project area is based. As my goal in the succeeding chapters is not merely to offer a descriptive account of raw data, but to interpret it in the light of a particular set of assumptions about what it means, it is important that the reconstruction procedures followed and the extent and limitations of the evidence used for this purpose be made explicit. While this has already been done at a more general level previously, the present chapter deals with specific questions and problems which need to be addressed given the particular nature of the research context and archaeological information that has been dealt with.

Among these questions are, for example, to what extent has previous archaeological research in Jordan prepared the way for the investigation of food system conditions and configurations attempted here? To what extent were the various lines of research carried out in connection with the Heshbon Expedition related to the goals and requirements of the present undertaking? What are the extent and limitations of the findings of the Heshbon Expedition in terms of these goals and requirements? How were data about food system conditions derived from the archaeological information gathered by the Heshbon Expedition? How were food system configurations, in turn, derived from these data in the case of each of the historical periods investigated?

By way of a rationale for the organization of the discussion which follows, something needs to be said about how the empirical evidence generated in connection with the Heshbon Expedition catalyzed and shaped the development of the theoretical framework presented in the previous chapters. To begin with, as was explained briefly in Chapter One, my initial preoccupation with the analysis and interpretation of animal bone information—in searching for some way to connect our findings to what was being discovered in other expedition undertakings such as the regional survey and the stratigraphic excavations on the tell—eventually led to the adoption of the food system concept as a tool in discovering interconnections between these different lines of research (LaBianca 1984).

Additionally, my prioritization, for the purpose of operationalizing the food system concept, of environmental, settlement, landuse, operational, and dietary conditions can be directly attributed to insights gained from previous experience with the empirical materials from Tell Hesban and vicinity. These dimensions, as we shall see further on, could each be linked fairly directly to a number of data points having been generated by the project. For this reason they seemed to furnish a good solution to the problem of how to operationalize the food system concept. Once these tools were put to use in analyzing the data, they led to findings suggestive of the dynamic processes of intensification and abatement and their corollaries in the Middle East, namely sedentarization and nomadization.

In recognition of the priority of the empirical findings, both in terms of their prior availability and their role in stimulating the search for a methodology, I begin the development of this chapter by focusing on the empirical context out of which this research project emerged and end by showing how the food system concept facilitated my analysis of this material. Specifically I shall begin by offering a brief background to the way in which previous archaeological research in Transjordan has prepared the way for the present undertaking. This is followed by a discussion of the procedures used to derive data about food system conditions from the archaeological information on hand from the Heshbon Expedition. Last, I discuss the procedures followed in deriving food system configurations from the data.

Previous Archaeological Research in Transjordan

Before entering upon a discussion of previous and concurrent archaeological research in Transjordan, a question which needs to be addressed is why limit this overview strictly to this region? Certainly, when it comes to the cultural history of Transjordan, the region has been intimately linked to happenings in the Levant as a whole, including modern Israel, Lebanon, and Syria, as well as the larger Middle East. Furthermore, when it comes to the intellectual context in which archaeology in Transjordan has been carried out, an even wider sphere of influences can be pointed to, especially influences emanating from Europe and the United States. While acknowledging this situation, I feel justified in restricting this review to Transjordan for

three reasons: First, such a focus serves to heighten awareness of the extent to which cumulative research dealing specifically with this region has progressed. Second, such a focus is useful as an orientation to what is known about the archaeological history of Transjordan as a cultural area with its own unique physical environment and cultural history. Third, such a focus would logically come first in a hierarchical arrangement of regional foci (next would be Palestine as a whole, the Levant as a whole, the Middle East, and so on). As reviews of these broader regions already exist (*cf.* Albright 1932; Wright 1966; King 1984; Sterud, Strauss, and Abramovitz 1980; Glock 1985) my focus on Transjordan seems appropriate and within the scope of what is practical given the goals of the present study.

An outline of the development of archaeological research in Transjordan has recently been prepared by Geraty and Willis (1986). While acknowledging the historical ties of Transjordan to Cis-Jordan, they argue that the former has its own history of research. This history they divide into seven distinct periods. The first and longest period began during the Byzantine Period and lasted until 1805. This was a period of visits by pilgrims and Arab geographers to Transjordan, many of whom authored accounts of their journeys.

The second period, which Geraty and Willis called "the rediscovery of Transjordan," began in 1805 with the visit to the region of the first of a dozen or more scientifically motivated explorers, namely Ulrich Jasper Seetzen (1813). This period included individuals like Burckhardt (1822, 1831), Irby and Mangles (1823), Buckingham (1825), Tristram (1873), and many others and ended with the visit of Duc de Luynes in 1864. Next came the years between 1868 and 1923 which emphasized mapping and exploration by individuals such as Merrill (1877, 1881), Conder (1889), Schumacher (1886), Brunnow and Domaszewski (1904), and Musil (1907).

The fourth period lasted from 1923-1948 and was a time of pioneer excavations in Transjordan. It was at the beginning of this period that a Department of Antiquities was established in Transjordan by the British Mandate government. Under the initial leadership of John Garstang and subsequent leadership of Lancaster Harding, this department "greatly encouraged and facilitated both further exploration and the first excavation in

Transjordan" (Geraty and Willis 1986: 5). Particularly ambitious and influential was the surface survey of the entire country of Transjordan carried out by Nelson Glueck between 1933 and 1946. Geraty lists 21 excavations as beginning during this period, including undertakings at Qalat al-Rabad, Amman, Jerash (Geresa), Petra, Teleilat el-Ghassul, Wadi Ramm, 'Ader, Baluah, Marwa, Tell el-Kheleifeh, Ma'in, Wadi Dhobai, and el-Husn.

The fifth period of archaeological research in Jordan (1948-1956) concentrated on single-occupation architectural and tomb sites on both sides of the Jordan River and the Dead Sea under the jurisdiction of the Department of Antiquities. Sites mentioned by Geraty and Willis in this connection include Ala Safat, Sahab, Jebel Jofeh (Amman), Madaba, Dhiban, El-Ghrubba, Jerash, Khirbet Iskander, and Petra.

The period beginning in 1956 and ending in 1967 is a time during which stratigraphic excavation methods and *tell archaeology* became perfected in Transjordan as a result of the leadership provided by Dame Kathleen Kenyon at Tell es-Sultan (Kenyon 1952; *cf.* Wright 1966; Petrie 1904). Among the sites which were dug by her students or individuals who had been influenced by her methods were Qweilbeh, Beidha, Umm el-Biyara, Jerash, Wadi Ramm and Risqeh, Tell Deir 'Alla, Teleilat el-Ghassul, 'Araq el-Emir, Tell er-Rumeith, 'Ara'ir, Tell es-Sa'idiyeh, Amman, Bab edh-Dhra, Umm Qeis, Tabaqat Fahil, and Madaba. Also carried out during this period was Mittmann's (1970) survey of northern Transjordan.

The most recent period in the development of archaeological research in Transjordan began in 1967. During this period over 40 different excavation projects have been fielded in Transjordan, a large number of these under the sponsorship of the American Center for Oriental Research (ACOR) which was established in 1967 after the Six-Day War. Characteristic of this period has been the introduction of multidisciplined and regional approaches at several of the major excavation sites, particularly at Tell Hesban (since 1968), Bab edh-Dhra (since 1975), and Pella (since 1976). Another important development, especially in the past decade, has been the escalation of regional surveys (*cf.* Banning 1986; Graf 1980; Henry 1980; Lundquist 1980; MacDonald 1980; McCreery 1980; Miller 1980; Sauer 1980; McGovern 1983, 1985, 1986; Lenzen and McQuitty 1983).

Thanks to all of the above undertakings, Transjordan today is hardly the *terra incognita* it was regarded as three decades ago and earlier from the standpoint of archaeological research. Indeed, in terms of published descriptions of tell-sites, chronologies, stratigraphic horizons, studies of assemblages of artifacts, accounts of architectural remains, epigraphic studies, and histories of isolated periods, especially those relevant to biblical history, a base line of the archaeological history of the country is now in hand. For example, Sauer (1980), who was the director of ACOR between 1971 and 1981, wrote a booklet summarizing what is known of that archaeological history. His booklet presents an overview of representative sites, artifacts, and pottery manufacture traditions in Jordan, from the Palaeolithic through the Late Ottoman Period. His chronological scheme divides Transjordan's history into the following periods: Palaeolithic, Mesolithic, Neolithic, Late Neolithic, Chalcolithic, Early Bronze I-III, Early Bronze IV-Middle Bronze I, Middle Bronze II, Late Bronze I-II, Iron IA-C, Iron II-Persian, Hellenistic, Nabataean (or Roman), Byzantine, Abbasid, Fatimid, Seljuq-Zengid, Crusader, Ayyubid-Mamluk, and Ottoman. The current state of archaeological research in Jordan is well represented in the proceedings of three international symposia dealing with its history and archaeology (Hadidi 1982, 1985, and 1987).

Largely neglected in archaeological research on Transjordan, however, are attempts to understand its cultural history in light of anthropological theory about how and why cultures change. One obvious reason for this state of affairs is that, until recently at least, this problem has largely been outside of the agenda of the scholarly community working in the country, most of whom were not anthropologists, but historians, epigraphers, biblical scholars, and classical archaeologists. As the conventional approach in disciplines such as these entails specialization around problems relating to a specific historical period, a specific assemblage of artifacts or texts, or even a specific personality or historical event, it is understandable that the largely anthropological problem of how cultures change has not surfaced as a primary focus of research. Yet, few places on earth offer a better empirical arena for addressing this question than Transjordan. This is because in addition to a relatively well-preserved archaeological record,

Transjordan is also well represented in the literary records of antiquity. It is therefore among the best suited regions in the world in terms of its potential as an empirical arena for research concerned with longitudinal patterns of culture change.

When it comes to studies specifically concerned with ancient food systems in Transjordan, a paradoxical situation exists. As we have already seen, information relevant to reconstructing ancient food system conditions, such as descriptions of reservoirs, cisterns, wine presses, pottery jars, coins, houses, agricultural implements, economic texts, etc., have been included in nearly every research report dealing with Transjordan since the days of the 19th-century scientific explorers. Yet, most of these reports fail to treat these finds systematically in terms of their function within the local food system. For example, to the extent that descriptions of pottery have been included in excavation reports, they represent a potential source of information about the local food system. Yet, insofar as these same reports fail to deal explicitly with the functional uses of the pottery which they discuss, they fail to contribute to our understanding of the food system in an integrated sense. This is not to minimize the important questions such studies have addressed relative to the dating and spread of a particular type of vessel from one region to another; it is instead to suggest an additional perspective from which to view such materials.

Publications attempting to contribute to our understanding of food systems in a broad sense have, until recently, been few and far between. Notable because of their efforts to change this situation are the recent contributions of individuals such as McCreery (1979, 1980), Franken (1982), Helms (1981, 1982), Henry (1980, 1985), Fuller and Fuller (1983), Piccirillo (1985), Parker (1986, 1987), Rollefson (1985), Rollefson and Simmons (1986), Schaub (1982), McGovern (1986), Banning (1986), Banning and Köhler-Rollefson (1986), Ortner (1978), Prag (1985), and Villeneuve (1985). In the case of each of these scholars is a commitment to understand, in a broader sense, dynamic aspects of the cultural history of ancient Transjordan.

From Archaeological Information
to Food System Conditions

Insofar as the original goals and methods which governed fieldwork at Tell Hesban and vicinity were much the same as those of other leading projects being carried out in Transjordan and Israel at the same time, it cannot be said that, from the start, the goals and fieldwork procedures were designed with a food system perspective in mind. Although, as discussed earlier, this perspective evolved as a result of an ongoing quest to discover how the various findings generated by the project fitted together, the fact remains that what accumulated in the way of archaeological finds on the expedition, for example, resulted more from a firm commitment to *tell archaeology* and a particular method of investigation, namely the Wheeler-Kenyon method of stratigraphic excavation (pl. 4.1) together with careful recording procedures, than from an explicit concern with any particular anthropological problem (*cf.* Wright 1974; Kenyon 1952; *cf.* Barker 1977). Thanks in particular to Roger S. Boraas, the expeditions' Chief Archaeologist (pl. 4.2), who insisted on careful attention to soil layers and their relationship no matter what the historical significance of a particular stratum, a body of stratigraphic findings gradually accumulated from Tell Hesban which covered the entire historical spectrum of Transjordan from the 12th century B.C. to the present (fig. 4.1). A similar situation pertains to the regional survey finds, none of which were collected with an explicit concern, for instance, for matters related to how land was utilized or how food was stored by the ancient inhabitants of the project area.

As a consequence of the manner in which most of the findings from Tell Hesban were generated, I have preferred to refer to the original body of findings with which I have been working as *information*, in the sense of an accumulated corpus of archaeological facts and figures, rather than as *data* or *evidence*, in the sense of empirical findings gathered with reference to an explicitly stated theory of one kind or another. Therefore, because of the fact that the theoretical perspective around which I have organized this analysis emerged largely after these findings had been accumulated, there are many gaps and inadequacies in this body of findings for which the best excuse is simply that such is the cost of attempting to go beyond the empirical materials themselves in order to gain deeper insight into what they mean. An example of this situation would be the fact that few data were gathered dealing directly with the project areas' nonsedentary populations (*cf.* Hole 1978; Orme

Plate 4.1   Wheeler-Kenyon method of excavation as employed at Tell Hesban

Plate 4.2   Chief archaeologist Roger Boraas giving instructions

Stratum		# of Loci	Period	Approximate Dates	Approximate # of years
1	AM01	68	Modern	A.D. 1870-1976	ca. 106 yrs
	gap		Ottoman	A.D. 1456-1870	ca. 414 yrs
2	AM02	379	Late Mamluk	A.D. 1400-1456	ca. 56 yrs
3	AM03	787	Early Mamluk	A.D. 1260-1400	ca. 140 yrs
4	AM04	126	Ayyubid	A.D. 1200-1260	ca. 60 yrs
	gap		Fatimid	A.D. 969-1200	ca. 231 yrs
5	BA01	56	Abbasid	A.D. 750-969	ca. 219 yrs
6	BA02	210	Umayyad	A.D. 661-750	ca. 84 yrs
7	BA03	55	Late Byzantine	A.D. 614-661	ca. 47 yrs
8	BA04	259	Late Byzantine	A.D. 551-614	ca. 63 yrs
9	BA05	340	Early Byzantine	A.D. 408-551	ca. 143 yrs
10	BA06	255	Early Byzantine	A.D. 365-408	ca. 43 yrs
11	HR01	308	Late Roman	A.D. 284-365	ca. 81 yrs
12	HR02	199	Late Roman	A.D. 193-284	ca. 91 yrs
13	HR03	399	Late Roman	A.D. 130-193	ca. 63 yrs
14	HR04	417	Early Roman	63 B.C.-A.D. 130	ca. 193 yrs
15	HR05	290	Late Hellenistic	198-63 B.C.	ca. 135 yrs
	gap		Late Persian	500-198 B.C.	ca. 302 yrs
16	IR01	58	Iron 2	700-500 B.C.	ca. 200 yrs
17	IR02	42	Iron 2	900-700 B.C.	ca. 200 yrs
18	IR03	30	Iron 2	1150-900 B.C.	ca. 250 yrs
19	IR04 & IR05	82	Iron 1	1200-1150 B.C.	ca. 50 yrs

Fig. 4.1 Tell Hesban strata (Mitchel 1980[1]; cf. Boraas and Geraty 1979 [in Appendix A])

1981: 255-272; Robertshaw and Collett 1983; Arnold 1985: 109-126). It simply was not part of either the original excavation goals or the survey goals to do so, as in both cases the ultimate focus of interest was the study of tells. Yet, serendipitously, a limited amount of data was collected which has been utilized as evidence in the present study for this particular problem, especially by the regional survey.

My aim in this section is to describe in further detail the steps which have been taken in order to convert the various lines of information which have resulted from the careful stratigraphic excavations at Tell Hesban and from the regional survey, into a formally organized body of data relevant to the problem being investigated here. Specifically my aim is to describe how, in the case of each of the ten lines of information mentioned in Chapter One, a connection could be made to one or more of the five parameters of the food system. In so doing, the extent and limitations of the available data will become further apparent.

The types of questions which guided the process of converting this information into data about ancient food system conditions were as follows:

To ascertain *environmental conditions*: what do these finds reveal about the types of soils, or about the communities of plants or animals which existed?

To ascertain *settlement conditions*: what do these finds reveal about the mobility status of the population; about its ethnic identity; about its size and composition; about its distribution within the project area?

To ascertain *landuse conditions*: what do these finds reveal about the way in which the land was utilized, whether for collecting or hunting, grazing of livestock, or growing of field crops, gardens, or orchards; about the type of utilization which predominated in the various subregions of the project area at a given point in time?

To ascertain *operational conditions*: what facilities, tools, and equipment were constructed, maintained, and utilized during this particular period judging from the presence of these finds?

To ascertain *dietary conditions*: what do these finds tell us about what people ate and about their nutritional status during this particular period?

An important advantage of the food system perspective came to light as questions such as these were being asked, namely the way in which this perspective made possible a more systematic approach to determining the uses of a number of finds about which several alternative interpretations had been advanced regarding their function. In such cases, this perspective allowed me to follow a process of elimination which always began with the question of how a particular find might be accounted for in the light of its use in the food system. Once the possibility of its having had a function in the food system had been ruled out, other alternative interpretations could be pursued further. Thus where disputes had arisen over alternative interpretations of a particular find, an *a priori principle*—namely that functional uses in terms of the food system must first be ascertained—could be appealed to in weighing the relative merits of competing proposals. The following, then, is an account of how the various lines of archaeological information on hand were converted into data regarding food systems conditions.

Archaeological Stratum Descriptions

Excavations at Tell Hesban were concentrated in sectors of the tell referred to as *areas*, each identified by a capital letter (see fig. 4.2 and pl. 4.3). Four principal excavation areas were begun during the first campaign at Tell Hesban (Boraas and Horn 1969: 102-117). Areas A and D were in the acropolis sector near the summit of the tell in order to ascertain information about the nature of the ruins of public buildings in evidence on the tell.

In order to allow maximum stratigraphic penetration in the first season, a sector on the southern slope of the tell, which was deemed suitable because it was free of any visible surface remains, was opened. This sector was designated Area B. Finally, Area C, which was located on the western slope of the tell, was begun in order to intersect the defense perimeter walls of the site. In subsequent seasons, soundings were carried out in several locations (Areas E and F) on the lower slope of the tell and in the village of Hesban. In addition, as mentioned in Chapter One, over 40 tombs and caves were excavated in Area F. This area was located to the southwest of the tell in what was believed to be the location of the ancient Roman and Byzantine cemetery.

The portions within each area opened for excavation, whatever their geometric shape, were called *squares*. Most of these measured approximately 7 m x 7 m and were excavated to bedrock. Within each square, the fundamental unit of recording was the *locus* which was defined as "any discernible soil layer or any 'thing' (wall, pit, hearth) within or related to a given soil layer" (Boraas and Horn 1969: 112). Locus numbers were assigned in chronological sequence within each square. Thus, any provenience unit or findspot within a square was traceable by means of a standard findspot number including the designation of the campaign season, the area, the square, and the locus (for example, Heshbon '71, Area A, Square 3, Locus 25 or simply H71A.3:25).

It is important to clarify that, as a result of the excavation strategy which was followed, less than one percent of the settlement area considered to belong to Tell Hesban—namely, most of the area today settled by villagers plus the mound where most of the excavations took place (*cf.* Conder 1889)—was actually investigated by means of stratigraphic excavations. Although several small probes (in Area G) were carried out beyond the mound itself in various locations in the village, the conclusions reached with regard to stratigraphy pertain mainly to the mound where Areas A, B, C, and D were excavated. As far as the exposure of architectural remains are concerned, here too, limitations exist as portions of buildings which extended beyond the restricted vertical balks of a certain square or area were normally not uncovered.

It must also be noted that, except in the case of certain occupational surfaces or when the contents of certain cisterns were excavated, sieving was not normally carried out. That a large number of coins, and especially small fish, bird, and mammal bones, were missed because of very restricted use of sieves is certain. This, at least, is the impression gained based on results obtained in a *test square* operated in Area C in 1976 where sieving was done consistently in half of Square C.9 and not at all in the other half of the same square (Boraas and Geraty 1978: 10, 14; LaBianca 1978a: 241).

The findings which resulted from the stratigraphic excavations were recorded on locus sheets. These, in turn, formed the basis for the end-of-the-season preliminary reports authored by the respective area supervisors (Boraas and Horn 1969, 1973, 1975; Boraas and Geraty 1976, 1978). Between 1976 and 1980, the locus information gathered during each of the excavation seasons was comput-

Fig. 4.2 Topographic map of Tell Hesban showing excavation areas

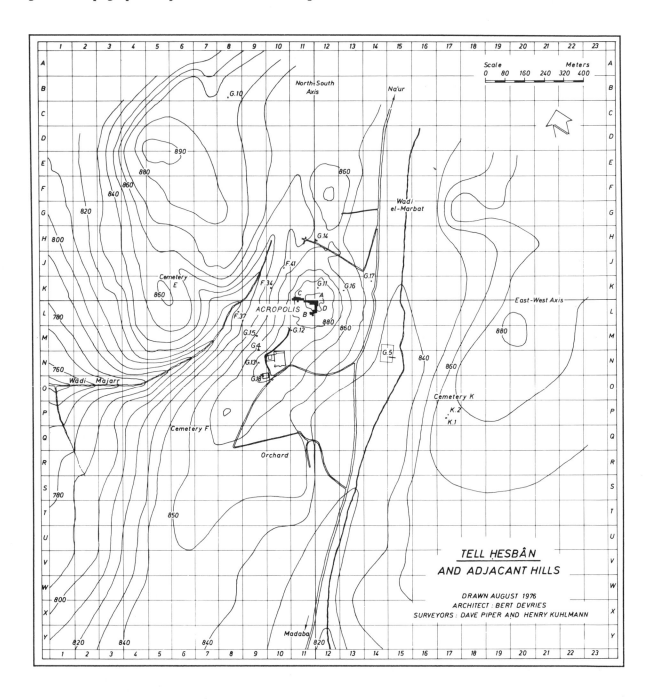

Plate 4.3   Aerial photo of excavation areas (1971); view north

Plate 4.4   Sieving process in A.6

Plate 4.5   Architect Bert de Vries at work in the field

erized as a result of a cooperative endeavor involving James Brower, Bert de Vries, Larry Geraty, Larry Herr, Øystein LaBianca, Larry Mitchel, and Bjørnar Storfjell. Available for use by this investigator were drafts of final reports on the Iron Age (Herr forthcoming), Hellenistic and Roman periods (Mitchel 1980), and the Byzantine and Early Islamic periods (Storfjell 1983) which had been written following completion of the standardized computer-generated listing of all loci resulting from the first five campaigns at Tell Hesban. These loci, in turn, were assigned to one of 19 strata, as mentioned in Chapter One. It is the interpretive results contained in these end-of-the-season preliminary reports and these final report drafts which constitute the first of the ten lines of information examined in this study.

In converting this information into data for use in the present study, the manuscripts which had been prepared on the basis of the computerized locus information were scrutinized for information primarily about operational conditions such as the type and quantity of cisterns, water channels, storage bins, fortification walls, paved streets, baking ovens, kilns, and fire pits. Also noted were proposals regarding the size and nature of settlement conditions during the time of a given stratum.

Pottery Readings

Insofar as field readings of pottery constituted the principal material on the basis of which other finds were dated by association, it played a crucial role in furnishing a temporal framework for chronologically ordering of other types of data relied on in this study. Although ceramic artifacts have great potential also as a source of data about environmental conditions (nature of local clays), settlement conditions (identity of ethnic groups to which potters and users of pottery belonged), operational conditions (arrangements for storage, transportation, and preparations of foods), and dietary conditions (traces of food on insides of sherds), information of this kind was not available for this analysis (*cf.* Crowfoot 1932; Rice 1981; Bishop, Rands, and Holley 1982; Ellison 1984; Arnold 1985).

Registered Small Finds

A computer listing of 2,800 registered small finds ordered according to stratum provided an-

other source of data mainly about operational conditions during successive periods of occupation at Tell Hesban. Such conditions were inferred from analysis of the proportional representation in each stratum of objects such as grinding stones, mullers, spindle whorls, coins, and so on. While much could be learned about local craftsmanship during various historical periods from detailed examination of these objects individually, such analysis has not been attempted in this study (*cf.* Dalman 1964).

Animal Bones

The extensive use made here of animal bone information requires that the many limitations of these data be made as explicit as possible. To begin with, as noted earlier, the quantity of fish, bird, and small mammal remains represented in the animal bone corpus is not what it could have been had sieving been done in all squares (*cf.* Casteel 1972; Payne 1972). Furthermore, during the first four seasons, '68, '71, '73, and '74, a portion of the bone material brought to the *bone tent* by the square supervisors was discarded because it was not judged identifiable at the species level (*cf.* Lawrence 1978). This *scrap* consisted mostly of splinters of long bones, ribs, and vertebrae which were so fragmentary that articulating surfaces were usually altogether absent. Since it was only during the 1976 season that all such scrap could be identified, thanks to the participation of J. Boessneck and A. von den Driesch, quantitative analysis to determine the composition of the domestic animal species during various periods has only been undertaken on the bone corpus from the 1976 season which consisted of about 19,000 fragments. During that same season, however, Professors Boessneck and von den Driesch also analyzed all the boxes of bones saved from previous seasons, measuring all measurable bones and separating out any rare bones which had been missed during the earlier seasons' bone readings (*cf.* Boessneck and von den Driesch 1978a, 1978b).

Another limitation of animal bone data, which also applies to all other small finds, is that a large proportion of it came from *fill* loci. Most productive in terms of bones uncovered were cisterns and the huge Area B reservoir. Because the vast majority of bones were found in such deposits instead of on floor surfaces or on streets or walls, they were preserved better than might have been the case.

Plate 4.6   Jim Sauer (far right) reading pottery (with, from left, Douglas Waterhouse, Larry Geraty, and Robert Ibach)

Plate 4.7   Aina Boraas reconstructing pottery

Plate 4.8   Marion Beegle registering small finds

Plate 4.9   Object conservationist Elizabeth Sanford

Except in the case of the bone finds from the Iron Age reservoir in Area B.1, most of the bone finds came from mixed deposits, *i.e.*, deposits containing pottery from more than one single period, the latest period represented being the one used for assigning a date to the locus or stratum. Because of this situation, the earliest strata, those from the Iron Age, have perhaps the greatest integrity in terms of how representative the bone data are of what was deposited during that period. Unfortunately, however, during the 1976 season Iron Age deposits were not very productive in terms of bone finds when compared to earlier seasons, hence the statistical data from that period are based on a comparatively small sample.

To these limitations must be added those resulting from taphonomic processes, *i.e.*, those physical, chemical and biological agencies whereby skeletal remains are normally disintegrated in nature (Lyman 1982). To begin with, after the butchered parts of food animals were discarded, dogs and other carnivorous wild beasts quickly descended upon them, consuming the vast majority of what was discarded. What was not thus destroyed, such as the hardest parts of the skeleton, was subjected, in the vicinity of people, to further destruction through being shuffled about. To this add the alternating temperatures of night and day and the leaching action of rains, and the fact that less than five percent of what was once discarded actually stood a chance of being preserved for posterity should come as no surprise (LaBianca 1978a: 238).

The fact that such a large quantity of well-preserved fragments was found at Tell Hesban is largely attributable to the protective environments into which most of what had been discarded had been deposited, namely into the deep reservoir in Area B and into numerous cisterns and other subterranean installations inaccessible to scavengers and protective against destruction by the other agencies mentioned above (*cf.* Meadow 1978). The presence of donkeys, horses, and other *unclean* species, including certain wild carnivorous animals in the bone sample is attributable, no doubt, to dogs having hauled the bones into the villages from the surrounding fields, although there is some evidence that equines might have been consumed by the ancient inhabitants of Tell Hesban (Boessneck and von den Driesch 1978a, 1978b).

Two doctoral candidates at the Institut für Palaeoanatomie, Domestikationsforschung und Geschichte der Tiermedizin in Munich, Germany, assisted Drs. Boessneck and von den Driesch with analysis of the bone data in their hands. Thus, as noted, the 18,620 remains of domestic mammals were studied by Detlev Weiler (1981) while the 2,379 chicken bones were examined by Herman Lindner (1979). Also, as noted earlier, the 749 fish bones were identified and analyzed by Johannes Lepiksaar of the Naturhistorksa Museet in Sweden.

In this study, inferences regarding the composition of pasture animals (namely cattle, sheep, goat, pig, camel, horse, and donkey) are based on raw counts of bone fragments of individual species from each stratum. Inferences regarding diet changes, on the other hand, are based on total weight (in grams) of bone fragments of individual species from each stratum. No attempt was made to determine, in the case of principal domestic species, the minimum number of individuals (MNI) present in each stratum (*cf.* Chaplin 1971: 55-71; von den Driesch and Boessneck forthcoming).

In order to obtain an idea of the rate at which animal bone fragments were added to each stratum throughout antiquity, accumulation rates were computed. Such rates were computed by dividing the total weight (weight accumulation rate) and the total number of bones (fragment accumulation rate) of the principal domestic animals (sheep, goat, cattle, horse, donkey, camel, swine) from a given stratum into the total number of years spanned by that stratum.

Carbonized Seeds

In the present study we have relied primarily on Gilliland's (1986) analysis for information about carbonized seeds. After collection by means of judgment sampling procedures from soil and/or ash loci excavated during the 1976 and 1978 field seasons, the carbonized specimens were separated from the soil by means of flotation in water (pls. 4.14, 4.15; see Crawford, LaBianca, and Stewart 1976). A total of 891 carbonized samples were identified (Iron Age = 53; Hellenistic Period = 295; Roman Period = 55; Byzantine Period = 95; Islamic Period = 393). These included three types of cereals (oats, barley, and wheat), four types of legumes (lentils, peas, bitter vetch, and broad beans), olives, and grapes. Given the procedure whereby these palaeobotanical specimens were collected and their limited representation in each

Plate 4.10   Muhammad Tawfik, Asta Sakala LaBianca, and author cleaning animal bones outside the "bone tent" on Tell Hesban

Plate 4.11   Joachim Boessneck and Angela von den Driesch, zooarchaeologists, analyzing animal bones

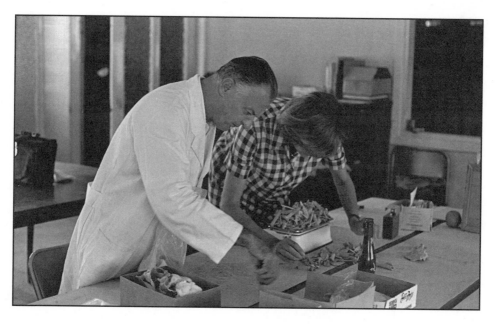

Plate 4.12   Robert Little, physical anthropologist, recording a human bone

Plate 4.13   Mansef remains photographed in the course of taphonomic investigations in 1974

Plate 4.14   Larry Herr (left) and author setting up flotation aparatus; Hal James, geologist, looking on

Plate 4.15   Patricia Crawford, ethnobotanist, examining flotation sample

individual stratum, the most reliable statement that can be made is that a given cultigen either was or was not present during a given period (cf. Renfrew 1973). Although numerical information about the composition of the different species found during various periods is presented, this information must be regarded as suggestive rather than conclusive. Such information has been utilized here as a secondary line of evidence in reconstructing environmental, landuse and dietary conditions.

Archaeological Survey Findings

The archaeological survey which was carried out within a radius of approximately 10 km of Tell Hesban resulted in 155 *sites* being mapped and described (fig. 4.3). The sampling method used was that of judgment sampling (cf. Knudson 1978: 117), whereby sites were found as a result of judgments made by members of the survey team rather than by means of random sampling techniques. Some of the factors which determined the precise limits of the territory surveyed and where the survey team focused their energies were discussed in Chapter One (The Project Area).

Although the definition of *site* offered by Ibach (1976: 119; cf. Redman 1973; Ammerman 1981; Schiffer, Sullivan, and Klinger 1978) is "any significant artifact or group of artifacts in close proximity to one another," the primary emphasis of the survey was oriented toward the discovery and documentation of as many archaeological tells and ruins as could be found within the project area (cf. Schiffer et al. 1978). Thus, observations which were made at each site tended to concentrate on information such as the size of the site (very small, small, medium, large, major tell), observable ruins (vaults and barrel roofs, pillars, building stones, wall, perimeter wall, tomb, cistern, reservoir, rectangular building, cave, tower, circular structure, wine press, foundation, and so on), topographic location (on a natural hill, near wadi, on a steep slope, etc.), and pottery (Iron I, Byzantine, possible Early Roman body sherds, etc.). No attempt was made to specify whether the site could have been an ancient village, farmstead, or campsite.

Extensive study was undertaken of these site descriptions and of the maps which had been prepared of sites from each major historical period in order to convert this information into data about ancient food system conditions. Our study involved examination of changes over time in the distribution of these sites within the project area, of their topographic features and agricultural hinterlands, and of the finds identified at each of them by the survey team. As a result of this undertaking a number of patterns could be identified which contributed significantly to our understanding of changes over time in settlement, landuse, and operational conditions within the project area.

For example, it was possible to determine that a large number of these sites had, during certain periods, served as farmsteads, judging from their location on the edges of fertile agricultural valleys or plains and the presence in the immediate vicinity of each of two or more finds suggestive of an agricultural operation, such as the ruins of at least one watchtower, one or more rectangular buildings, cisterns, terraces, wine presses, caves, family tombs, and a perimeter wall. In other instances sherd scatters were reported in the vicinity of caves or springs. As these showed no signs of buildings or other permanent facilities, and given the fact that most of them were discovered in well-watered locations in the western descent, they were determined to be remains of ancient temporary campsites.

While we recognize that in some instances our identification of a particular site as a farmstead or a campsite may, upon future field inspection, turn out not to be correct, we should point out that where the data seemed too limited to be certain, we applied the *a priori principle* mentioned earlier. In other words, where there was not sufficient data provided to suggest a function for a particular site other than a farmstead or a campsite, we felt justified in treating it, for the purposes of our analysis, as one or the other of these.

Ecological Survey Findings

The various studies mentioned in Chapter One which dealt with the local climate, hydrology, geology, soils, plants, and animals were fundamental to three aspects of this study of the food system. First, they served as a basis for our understanding of the hydrological conditions, the indigenous plant and animal communities, and the successional patterns which prevail within the project area today. Second, this understanding, in turn, served as a basis for our attempts to reconstruct ancient environmental conditions given the information on hand regarding species of plants and animals in existence

Plate 4.16   Robert Ibach and survey team members Douglas Waterhouse and Charlene Hogsten

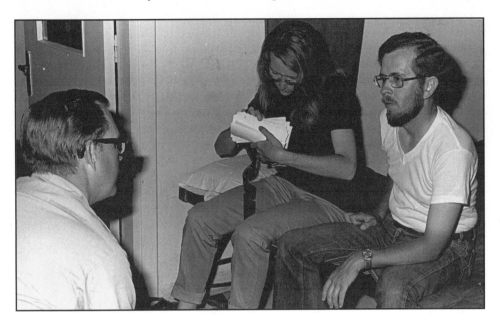

Fig. 4.3   Original Hesban Survey area (after Ibach 1987)

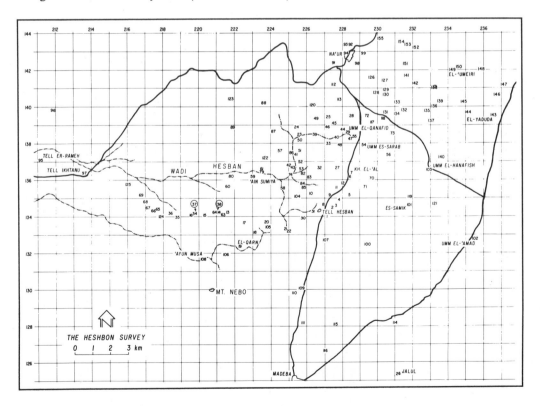

Plate 4.17   Geologist Hal James examining a lithic specimen

Plate 4.18   Robin Brown taking wind speed measurements

at various points in time. Third, they formed a basis for our attempts to understand the project area settlement pattern at various points in time insofar as this pattern, as we have seen already, was greatly influenced by proximity to sources of water and fertile agricultural soils (Evans 1978; Butzer 1982; Vita-Finzi 1978).

Ethnoarchaeological Findings

As was discussed in Chapter Three, the most important way in which our ethnoarchaeological research aided our efforts to reconstruct ancient food system conditions was in enabling us to become more intimately acquainted with its workings at a particularly accessible period in time, namely the recent past (*cf.* Binford 1983). This heightened familiarity, in turn, greatly facilitated our efforts to piece together, from the multiple lines of fragmentary archaeological evidence discussed above, various food system conditions and configurations which prevailed during the successive periods studied. Thus, rather than serving as a basis for direct analogy with the present, this information acquainted us, in a heuristic sense, with certain basic operational principles of the local food system.

Examples of some of these would include our heightened understanding of the fundamental fluidity of social structure in the Middle East, of sedentarization and nomadization as ubiquitous responses to changing social and physical environment, of the relationship between investment in permanent facilities and extent of population mobility, of the connection between species of animals produced and landuse conditions, of the association between types of crops produced and risk of plunderings by others, of the link between intensification of agricultural production and urban interest, and so on. Thus, whereas insights such as these aided in coming up with possible hypotheses to use in making sense out of the archaeological data, exactly what shape transhumance would have taken, for example, during the Byzantine Period, remained a matter to be determined by the available data rather than a supposition based merely on analogy with the present.

Explorers' Accounts

Accounts of ruins and other archaeological findings provided by 19th and early 20th century explorers who visited project area sites were relied upon to flesh out the findings of the Hesban Survey (*cf.* Binford 1983: 19-30). As these accounts were based on surveys carried out before the project area became intensively settled as it is today, they contain descriptions of many sites which today have been obscured by modern building activity and landuse practices. The one major limitation of most of this information, however, is that the temporal framework is very vague because most of these explorers did not have the benefit of knowing about pottery dating techniques. Nevertheless, thanks to the acquaintance of individuals like Tristram and Conder with Greco-Roman and Islamic architecture and alphabets, a large number of ruins dating to these eras were identified as such in their accounts. The information supplied by these sources aided primarily in our reconstruction of past settlement, landuse, and operational conditions.

Secondary Sources

In order to relate developments taking place within the project area to pertinent developments occurring outside this limited region, a number of books and articles were consulted, most of them authored by historians and/or archaeologists. As a general rule, those secondary sources were sought and utilized which offered specific information regarding daily-life conditions in antiquity (as opposed to those primarily concerned with political conditions) and which made specific reference to such conditions in Palestine and especially in Transjordan. It must be acknowledged, however, that it is likely that certain pertinent sources might exist, particularly in non-English languages, which could have been consulted had time and money not been a concern. It is hoped that as this project continues any such gaps will gradually be closed.

Relative Importance of Various Lines of Information

Although the reconstructions of food system conditions and configurations offered in the subsequent chapters rely on all of the above lines of information, certain ones of them can be singled out as having been more extensively exploited than others for this purpose. In terms of extent of time and energy expended in analysis, therefore, the

Plate 4.19   Asta Sakala LaBianca (fourth from left) with Palestinian women

Plate 4.20   Del Downing churning milk

following categorization provides a rough idea of the contribution of each of the ten lines of information to this study: Extensively studied and utilized were the ethnoarchaeological findings, animal bone finds, and archaeological survey finds. Moderately utilized were the ecological survey findings, archaeological stratum findings, explorers' accounts, and secondary sources. Least utilized were the ceramic artifact information (largely because very little except pottery readings was on hand), the registered small finds information (due to time limitations), and the palaeobotanical information (because of the scarcity of available data).

From Food System Conditions
to Food System Configurations

Thus far I have described the procedures employed in converting the various types of information generated by the Heshbon Expedition into data relevant to ascertaining food system conditions. Specifically I've described how environmental conditions were ascertained on the basis of animal bone finds, palaeobotanical finds, and ecological survey finds; how settlement conditions were ascertained from animal bone finds, archaeological stratum descriptions, archaeological survey finds, and explorers' accounts; how landuse conditions were ascertained from animal bone finds, palaeobotanical finds, and archaeological survey finds; how operational conditions were ascertained from archaeological stratum descriptions, registered small finds, and explorers' accounts; and how dietary conditions were ascertained from animal bone finds and the palaeobotanical finds. Throughout the process of identifying these sources of data we were guided by insights derived from our ethnoarchaeological research.

The final step in the process of reconstructing ancient food system configurations was the task of distinguishing between successive ones on the basis of what we had learned about the changing states of the five food system conditions. To begin with, it was necessary to put forth an hypothesis distinguishing between a minimum of three possible configurations of food systems conditions (see fig. 4.4). This hypothesis owes its origin, in part, to Smith and Hill's (1975) proposals regarding energy flow through agroecosystems, which distinguishes between differences in intensity of human management in local ecosystems; and, in part, to insights

gained from the ethnoarchaeological research presented in the previous chapter. Three possible configurations of food system conditions were posited by this hypothesis.

A *low intensity configuration* which is characterized by high diversity of naturally occurring plant and animal species; high seasonal variation in location and intensity of human population due to migration; prevalence of pastoral pursuits and minimal disturbance of soils due to cultivation; prevalence of portable or seasonally abandoned operational facilities; prevalence of a subsistence diet derived from animal by-products, fruits, and grains in season, hunting, and gathering.

A *medium intensity configuration* which is characterized by a moderate diversity of naturally occurring plant and animal species; moderate seasonal variation in location and intensity of human population due to an increased number of permanently settled households; prevalence of field crop pursuits and a moderate disturbance of soils due to cultivation, especially in fertile plains and valleys; prevalence of small-scale water and soil management technologies, fortified farmsteads and villages and extensive utilization of cattle for plowing; prevalence of a subsistence diet derived primarily from field crops, but supplemented by produce resulting from limited gardening, orcharding, and flocks of sheep, goats, and poultry.

A *high intensity configuration* which is characterized by a low diversity of naturally occurring plant and animal species; minimal seasonal variation in location and intensity of human population due to large numbers of permanently settled households; prevalence of field crop pursuits in combination with extensive gardening and orcharding, the latter being especially important in hilly terrain; prevalence of large-scale water and soil management technologies, food processing and storage installations, transportation facilities, markets and urban centers, and extensive utilization of mules and horses for plowing; prevalence, especially in urban areas and to a lesser degree in rural areas, of a diet consisting of greater variety and quantity of exotic items, fruits, and vegetables due to delocalization of food supply by means of long-distance trade.

What this hypothesis provided was a means for arriving at an initial model of the configuration which prevailed during each of the successive periods for which data about food system conditions

Fig. 4.4   Three hypothesized configurations of food system conditions

A low intensity configuration is characterized by:
- high diversity of naturally occurring plant and animal species;
- high seasonal variation in location and intensity of human population due to migration;
- prevalence of pastoral pursuits and minimal disturbance of soils due to cultivation;
- prevalence of portable or seasonally abandoned operational facilities; and
- prevalence of a subsistence diet derived from animal by-products, fruits, and grains in season, hunting, and gathering.

A medium intensity configuration is characterized by:
- moderate diversity of naturally occurring plant and animal species;
- moderate seasonal variation in location and intensity of human population due to an increased number of permanently settled households;
- prevalence of field crop pursuits and a moderate disturbance of soils due to cultivation, especially in fertile plains and valleys;
- prevalence of small-scale water and soil management technologies, fortified farmsteads and villages and extensive utilization of cattle for plowing; and
- prevalence of a subsistence diet derived primarily from field crops, but supplemented by produce resulting from limited gardening, orcharding, and flocks of sheep, goats, and poultry.

A high intensity configuration is characterized by:
- low diversity of naturally occurring plant and animal species;
- minimal seasonal variation in location and intensity of human population due to large numbers of permanently settled households;
- prevalence of field crop pursuits in combination with extensive gardening and orcharding, the latter being especially important in hilly terrain;
- prevalence of large-scale water and soil management technologies, food processing and storage installations, transportation facilities, markets and urban centers, and extensive utilization of mules and horses for plowing; and
- prevalence, especially in urban areas and to a lesser degree in rural areas, of a diet consisting of greater variety and quantity of exotic items, fruits, and vegetables due to delocalization of food supply by means of long-distance trade.

were on hand. In other words, on the basis of comparison of the data for a given period with each of these three models, a first approximation of the prevailing food system configuration could be proposed for each of the successive periods being investigated. Thus, a particular period's configuration would be characterized as being either low, medium, or high in terms of one of these models (*cf.* LaBianca 1984).

Next followed the task of refining the model initially utilized to represent a particular period as extensively as was permitted by the available evidence. In the case of some periods this sometimes led to an intermediate configuration being proposed such as low-to-medium or medium-to-high. In all cases it led to many additional details being introduced into the configuration in order to better characterize the salient features of the period in question. In this manner those aspects of the food system configuration which appeared to be unique to a particular period could be brought into focus while at the same time a sense was preserved of those aspects which recurred during periods initially represented by the same basic model.

After each of the successive historical periods had been examined and, in turn, represented by means of one or the other of these three models, changes became apparent in terms of the food system configurations which prevailed at different points in time. When the change was in the direction of intensification of the food system (increased management of the natural environment), the process of sedentarization was assumed to have occurred at a faster rate than nomadization. When,

on the contrary, change was in the direction of abatement (decreased management of the natural environment), the process of nomadization was assumed to have occurred at a faster rate than sedentarization. That these two processes have historically been simultaneous rather than exclusive of each other in occurrence is a supposition which has its basis both in the ethnoarchaeological materials which preceded this chapter and in the archaeological chapters which follow.

Between *ca.* 1500 B.C. and the present century, the project area food system underwent three major cycles of intensification and abatement involving a *pumping-up* period during which the process of sedentarization gradually gained momentum and prevailed, and a *letting-down* period during which the process of nomadization gradually gained momentum and prevailed. The first of these macrocycles took place between the 15th and the 5th centuries B.C., the second between the 4th century B.C. and the 7th century A.D. and the third between the 8th and 19th centuries A.D. In the following three chapters, each of these cycles is examined respectively.

Endnote

[1]The dates assigned to strata and periods in this volume are those found in Mitchel 1980, except where sociopolitical discussions are based on historical events. These dates should not be regarded as being the final word on dating of strata and periods from this site and survey territory. More authoritative, in this regard, will be the volume dealing specifically with the pottery from Tell Hesban and vicinity (volume 11) which is being prepared by James Sauer.

Chapter Five

CONFIGURATIONS OF THE FOOD SYSTEM DURING THE IRON AGE MILLENNIUM: *CA.* 1200-500 B.C.

Chapter Five

Configurations of the Food System During the Iron Age Millennium: *Ca.* 1200-500 B.C.

Introduction

Over the 1,000 years between 1500 and 500 B.C., the food system of Hesban and vicinity intensified in spurts until a high point of sorts was reached during the 7th and 6th centuries B.C. Side by side throughout this entire millennium transhumant pastoralists and sedentary cultivators pursued their interdependent quests for food, expediently adjusting their variously constituted agropastoral livelihoods in response to an on-again off-again power drive whereby the center of political gravity was gradually shifted in the direction of urban-oriented intensive agriculture, only to revert back from whence it had been moved away, to the ever-present, ever-ready hands of the nomadic pastoralist tribesmen.

In this chapter some of the archaeological residues which were buried in the dust as this power drive ran its course will be set forth. To this end two lines of evidence will be discussed. On the one hand, changes in environmental, settlement, land-use, operational, and dietary conditions will be examined which attest to the occurrence of a cumulative power drive throughout most of the Iron Age millennium. Specifically, evidence will be presented pointing to a transition from a transhumant configuration at the beginning of the millennium, to one involving mixed production of pasture animals and cereals during Iron I (*ca.* 1200-1150 B.C.), to a medium-to-high intensity configuration during Iron II (*ca.* 1150-500 B.C.) based on urban-oriented cultivation of field, garden, and tree crops. On the other hand, the sparse but significant data that bear witness to the activities of the ever-present transhumant population within the project area will also be laid out. But first an introduction is necessary to the sociopolitical context which to a large degree shaped the various patterns of livelihood which manifested themselves during the Iron Age millennium in this region.

The Sociopolitical Context

The Wider Sociopolitical Context

In considering the wider sociopolitical context to which daily life in the vicinity of Hesban was oriented throughout the Iron Age (see fig. 5.1), mention must be made of the impact of iron technology on the whole of the ancient world during this period which owes its name to this metal. While heat-treated metal objects appear to have been manufactured on a limited scale long before the dawn of the Iron Age in Palestine (*cf.* Muhly 1980; Waldbaum 1980; and Heskel 1983), it was not until *ca.* 1200 B.C. that the manufacture of iron tools and weapons began to become an everyday occurrence in the towns and villages of this region. According to Muhly (1982: 43), it was the collapse of international trade during the waning years of the Late Bronze Age which created the conditions for the development of iron metallurgy.

While copper, which constitutes 90% of the alloy known as bronze, was mined in many localities throughout the ancient world, it was the supply of the distantly obtained tin, which makes up the remaining 10% of this metal, that became in jeopardy by the political upheavals at the end of the Late Bronze Age.

As a result of this disruption of international trade, local communities withdrew into themselves and smiths were goaded into experimenting with locally available iron so as to overcome the technological obstacles which had prevented it from gaining popularity over bronze. As Muhly (1982: 45-46)

Fig. 5.1 Palestine in the Iron Age

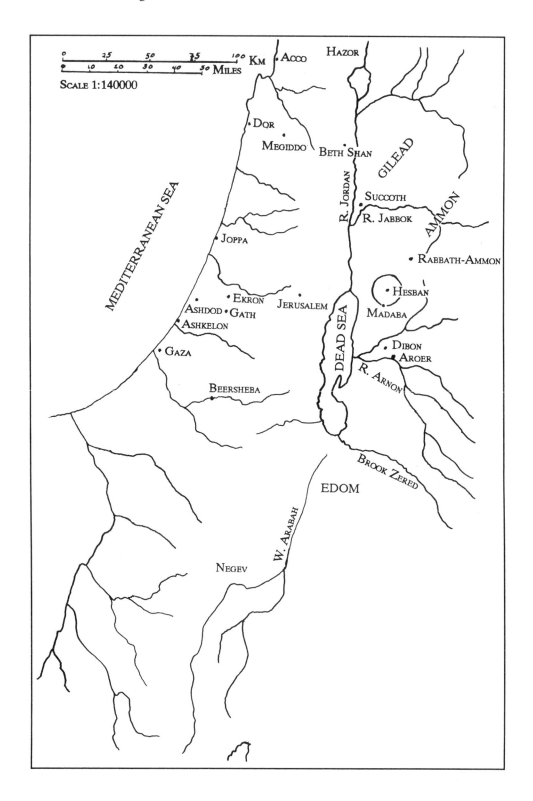

explains, it was when the process of carburization of iron was discovered that iron gained an appreciable edge over bronze:

> The essential factor in the technological development of iron metallurgy was the introduction of up to .8 percent carbon into the red-hot iron, accomplished by a kind of osmosis through prolonged contact with glowing charcoal in the forging furnace. The introduction of this carbon transformed iron from an exotic, semi-precious metal into a metal that would give its name to the age. For carburized iron (iron to which carbon has been added) is, in fact, steel . . . The basic difference between bronze and iron technology determined, to a very great extent, the ways in which the two metals were used. With bronze it was possible to make large, elaborate and intricate castings from the molten metal in shapes impossible to duplicate by forging a bar of iron. A life-size statue was almost commonplace in bronze, but unheard of in iron. Iron came to be used for objects of rather simple shape and design, requiring great hardness and strength. This meant cutting and chopping instruments such as axes, adzes and chisels, digging instruments such as hoes and plowshares, and, above all, weapons. Because of its hardness and its ability to take and hold a sharp cutting edge or point, iron was ideal for swords, spearheads, knives, daggers, and even arrowheads.

Among the many socioeconomic consequences of the development of iron metallurgy was the emergence of a new pattern of economic exchange, necessitated, on the one hand, by the skills required to shape tools out of iron and, on the other hand, by the greater ease with which fields could be cultivated using steel plows. Writes McNeill (1963: 131):

> The fact that metal tools made agricultural work easier and more productive helped to secure a modest surplus to the peasants. Conversely, since the smelting and shaping of metal tools involved special equipment and skills beyond the capacity of any ordinary farmer, the new necessity of buying such tools required the peasants to find such a surplus. . . . [Because of this situation, farmers] were now firmly, if marginally, incorporated within the "great society" which had slowly formed itself around the major urban seats of civilization. Farmers were no longer sufficient unto themselves, as they had been in the fourth millennium B.C.; nor were they simply the victims of their social superiors, supporting the culture of their masters by their own involuntary privation or forced labor, as they had been in the late third and through most of

the second millennium B.C. Instead, the peasants themselves began to enter modestly but significantly into the "'great society," exchanging part of their surpluses for iron implements and other goods that were useful or necessary to their improved methods of farming. The result was to allow the humblest class of society to benefit modestly but really from urban-rural differentiation and specialization. This pattern of local exchange provided the Middle East with a new economic base level. Even when political or military events interrupted long-distance trade and forced local regions back upon their own resources, the social and economic structure allowed for a division of labor between town and country, between artisan and peasant. Under these conditions, urban life could never entirely disappear.

The other development which must be singled out because of its far-reaching consequences was the impetus to invasion and plundering of settled areas resulting from the new metallurgy. In *The Rise of the West* (1963) William McNeill explains how the relative abundance of iron, coupled with the spread of the new iron technology, had the effect of "democratizing warfare" in the ancient Middle East. Indeed, in his view "these technical considerations go far to explain the success of the barbarian invasions that punctuated the political history of the ancient Orient toward the close of the second millennium B.C." (1963: 118).

The Local Sociopolitical Context

The first thing which can safely be said about the local sociopolitical context of Tell Hesban and its environs is that throughout the Iron Age it belonged to a region of Jordan which was much in dispute. To the north and east were the Ammonites, to the west were the Israelites (and later the divided kingdoms of Judah and Israel), and to the south were the Moabites and the Edomites. About the history of these tribes and their disputes between each other and with Israel a considerable amount has been written, particularly by biblical scholars and archaeologists. A partial list of some of the relevant studies include Tristram (1865, 1873), Merrill (1881), Thomson (1880), Conder (1889, 1892), Albright (1924), Glueck (1939, 1946), Baly (1957), Gese (1958), Thompson (1958), Harding (1959), Hentschke (1960), Van Zyl (1960), Fohrer (1961), Reventlow (1963), Oded (1971, 1979), Rosner (1976), (Dever 1977), Boraas and Geraty (1978), Sauer (1978b), Horn (1979), Miller

(1980, 1982), Bennett (1982), Redford (1982), Dornemann (1983), Sawyer and Clines (1983), and Hopkins (1985).

Throughout the Iron Age political domination of the project area was rotated among these four neighboring states. Indeed, the traditional boundary between Ammon and Moab runs right through the northern portion of the project area. Thus, geographically, Tell Hesban was actually much closer to the traditional capital of Ammon, namely Rabbath-Ammon or modern Amman, *ca.* 20 km to the north, than it was to the traditional capital of Moab, namely Qir-hareseth, the present Kerak, *ca.* 80 km to the south of Tell Hesban (*cf.* Glueck 1946: 83-125; Baly 1957: 229-233). According to biblical sources, the strife over control of this territory included not only the Ammonites, the Moabites, and the Israelites, but also the Amorites (Josh 2:10; 9:10; 24:8; Judg 10:8, 11:19-20). According to Num 21:26, for example, "the Amorite King Sihon . . . had fought against the former king of Moab and taken from him all his territory as far as the Arnon." Sihon, whose capital was Heshbon, was subsequently "put to the sword" by the Israelites (Deut 2:33); after which "the Reubenites built Heshbon, Elealeh, Kiriathaim, Nebo, Baal-meon . . . and Sibmah" (Num 32:37, 38). To the southwest of Heshbon, at Dhiban and vicinity, the Gadites, another Israelite tribe, built "walled towns with folds for their sheep" (Num 32:34-36; *cf.* 1 Chr 6:77-81).

It is evident, then, that as seen during the recent past in Chapter Three, the political context during the Iron Age involved complex interactions between several different local sociopolitical entities. Furthermore, during the latter part of the 8th century B.C., the Assyrians and later the Babylonians extended their control into this region as well. Thus, to four centuries of strife between nearby neighbors were added three more centuries of struggle for local autonomy and freedom from the political domination of world powers.

Because of the research cited above, a considerable amount of knowledge has accumulated over the past century about the superficial, rapidly changing history of rulers and nations, of wars and treaties, and of boundaries and fortifications with reference to the Iron Age inhabitants of Hesban and vicinity. Much less is known, however, about the lower undercurrents of activity which represented the daily life of the ordinary people living in this region. One reason for this, of course, is that the structures of everyday life are much less perceptible in the literary sources, although progress has been made in our knowledge of the pertinent languages (Herr 1978; Jackson 1983).

The scholar who perhaps has gone the furthest toward portraying the daily life of the peoples of Ammon, Moab, and Edom is Oded (1971, 1979). Noting that all three of these kingdoms were located along the "King's Highway," an international caravan route connecting Arabia and Egypt with Syria and Mesopotamia, and that to the east of all three nations lay the desert, Oded sums up the sociocultural situation in Moab thus:

> The geographical and economic conditions of Moab made it easy for the Moabites to achieve a suitable blend of their desert heritage with the values of an urban and rural society: this is to be attributed to Moab's position on the border of the desert and to its economy, which was based, on the one hand, upon agriculture, and, on the other, upon cattle raising and trade conducted along the desert routes. Living in a border country, the Moabites, like the Edomites and the Ammonites, were in need of effective defense against sudden attacks by raiders from the desert, as well as against invasion by the regular armies of neighboring countries. For this reason, the Moabites organized themselves into a national kingdom administered from a single center at the beginning of their settlement in Moab; only a permanent and strong leadership was capable of establishing a system of border fortresses, of setting up a permanent force able to match itself against external dangers, and of organizing guards for protection of the section of the "Kings Highway" which passed through Moab (Oded 1971: 191).

As Oded acknowledges, this reconstruction of Moabite culture rests heavily on evidence from "the Middle Iron Age." It is a picture which best fits the culture at the height of its productivity and influence, under its ruler, Mesha, king of Moab, whose achievements he himself summarized on a black basalt stele known as the Moabite Stone (Horn 1979: 751-752). In what follows, an even closer look at the material conditions of the inhabitants of the northern region of Moab is offered, with the dimension of change over time added.

Changes in Environmental Conditions

Given the location of our project area on the western edge of the Arabian Desert, and the varying patterns of human exploitation of this region since prehistoric times, an important question to consider is whether and to what extent the natural resource base, the stage upon which the drama of the food system transformation occurred in antiquity, was the same as today or different from today. Has the climate changed significantly since the Iron Age in this region? Has human activity in this region fundamentally altered the landscape as a natural habitat for plants and animals? Since both of these important questions have been addressed by specialists collaborating with the expedition core staff (*cf.* Geraty and LaBianca 1985; LaBianca and Lacelle 1986), our consideration of them here will be brief and in a summary manner.

The matter of climatic change can be considered at two levels: changes in the local climate (microclimate), and changes in the overall climate of the region (macroclimate). As far as the macroclimate is concerned, conditions which existed during the Iron Age appear to have been basically the same as those existing today. Evidence for this is provided by Gilliland's study of the carbonized seeds from Tell Hesban. He writes (1986: 139-140):

> The paleobotanical evidence presented here gives no compelling reason to conclude that since the initial Iron Age occupation, the Tell Hesban area has ever been either more or less desert-like than at present. For example, *Amaranthus graecizans* is primarily a desert species . . . and either this species or a close relative of it has been present since the Hellenistic period. This situation is also true of *Malva.* . . . *Polygonum*, another wasteland weed, was part of the Iron Age flora, and is still present today. On the other hand, legumes such as *Lens culinaris* would not likely grow in a desert without irrigation . . . and yet this genus has been present since the Iron Age, and even today is cultivated without irrigation.

Others who have addressed this question on behalf of the Hesban project have reached similar conclusions (Boessneck and von den Driesch 1978a; LaBianca and Lacelle 1986).

But while the macroclimate appears not to have changed much since the Iron Age, local changes in climate, plant, and animal life did take place during this millennium. As a result of the deforestation which preceded the spread of plow agriculture onto the fertile plains of the highland plateau, the communities of oak and pine forests which covered much of the land surface in this region during earlier millennia were gradually cut back. This removal of the native forests resulted in less protection of the local soils and soft plants from the ravages of torrential rains and intense sunshine. Consequently, hardier species of plants, such as thorny burnet, common ballota, alkanet, blue eryngo, century, and thistle today live where formerly coniferous and oak forests existed. Thus, while man's activities may not have caused desertification in this region, they have "pushed succession backward to an earlier stage" (Gilliland 1986).

Yet, in contrast to the present landscape, the Iron Age landscape had large quantities of trees, especially on hills and slopes where cultivation was not extensive. Thus, better pasture conditions for cattle and sheep were found than can be found today. This situation is reflected in the relatively large proportion of bones belonging to these animals from Iron Age strata. It is also hinted at in biblical references to the Hesban region which describe it as being "good grazing country" on which "the Reubenites and the Gadites had large and very numerous flocks" (Num 32:1, 3, 4).

Better protection for a variety of wild mammals and birds was another result of the presence of extensive forests. Of the more than 100 species of wild birds and mammals identified in the bone remains from Tell Hesban, only a small proportion of these have survived until today. Gone, for example, is the lion, wild pig, ostrich, and blackbird, to mention only a few of the species which once inhabited this region (*cf.* Boessneck and von den Driesch 1978a).

Changes in Settlement and Landuse Conditions

Intensification of Settlement and Sedentary Life

The first line of evidence suggesting an intensification of the food system of Hesban and vicinity during the Iron Age comes from consideration of the increase in the quantity and location of sites within the project area. As can be seen in figs. 5.2, 5.3, and 5.4, an increase in the quantity of sites occurred from a total of 4 sites during the preceding Late Bronze Age, to a total of 24 sites during Iron I and 51 sites during Iron II. To these can be added an additional 46 sites, most of them very small, which could only be assigned to the Iron-Persian period.

Fig. 5.2 Late Bronze Age sites

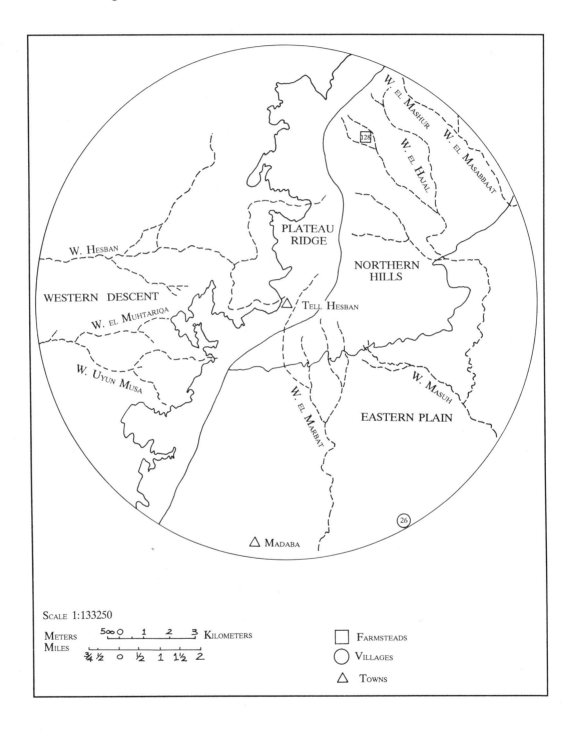

Fig. 5.3 Iron I sites

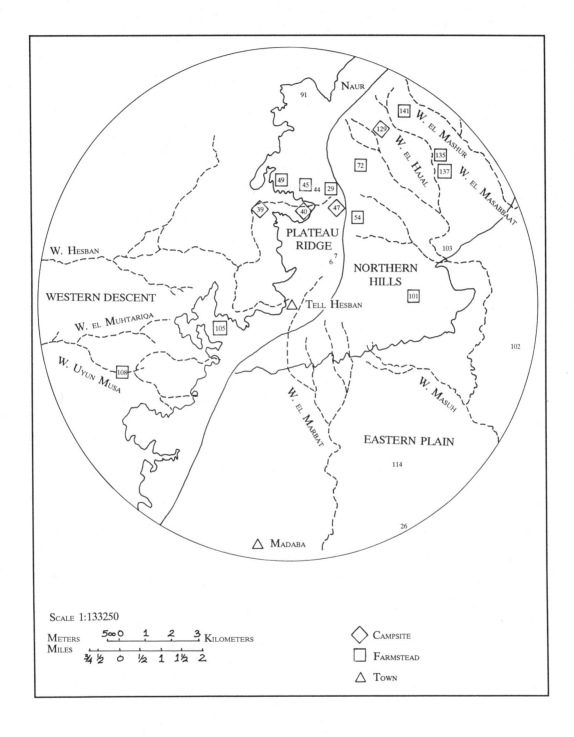

Fig. 5.4 Iron II sites

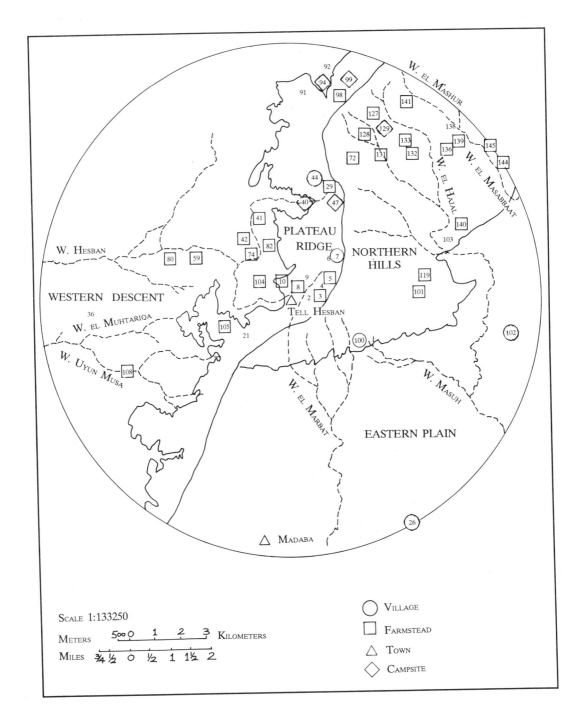

Table 5.1   Number of identified specimens of principal domestic animals from Iron Age strata

Strata	Period	Cattle #	Cattle %	Sheep/Goat #	Sheep/Goat %	Sheep #	Sheep %	Goat #	Goat %	Pig #	Pig %	Camel #	Camel %	Equids #	Equids %	Horse #	Horse %	Donkey #	Donkey %	Total #	Total %	Accumulation Rates
1	Modern	60	5.7	908	86.0	36	3.4	52	4.9	25	2.4	9	0.9	54	5.1	5	0.5	19	1.8	1,056	5.7	9.96
2-3	Mamluk	1,117	13.3	6,901	81.9	353	4.2	402	4.8	139	1.6	215	2.6	57	0.7	6	0.1	14	0.2	8,429	45.3	43.00
4	Ayyubid	9	10.7	71	84.5	4	4.8	6	7.1	--	--	2	2.4	2	2.4	--	--	--	--	84	0.5	1.40
5	Abbasid	8	3.9	188	91.7	14	6.8	11	5.4	2	1.0	5	2.4	2	1.0	--	--	--	--	205	1.1	0.73
6	Umayyad	68	10.4	494	75.3	47	7.2	33	5.0	80	12.2	8	1.2	6	0.9	--	--	3	0.4	656	6.5	7.80
7-10	Byzantine	162	12.5	932	71.6	58	4.5	48	3.7	130	10.0	14	1.1	63	4.8	5	0.4	10	0.8	1,301	7.0	4.39
11-13	Late Roman	286	11.7	1,892	77.6	140	5.7	115	4.7	183	7.5	17	0.7	58	2.4	2	0.1	6	0.2	2,436	13.1	10.36
14	Early Roman	131	15.0	682	78.1	67	7.7	36	4.1	43	4.9	7	0.8	10	1.1	--	--	3	0.3	873	4.7	4.12
15	Late Hellenistic	136	12.0	977	85.9	135	11.9	75	6.6	6	0.5	15	1.3	4	0.4	--	--	1	0.1	1,138	6.1	2.60
16-18	Iron 2	256	14.3	1,406	78.5	137	7.7	83	4.6	94	5.3	5	0.3	29	1.6	--	--	9	0.5	1,790	9.6	3.58
19	Iron 1	145	22.2	460	70.6	38	5.8	29	4.4	31	4.8	3	0.5	13	2.0	--	--	6	0.9	652	3.5	3.26
Sum	All	2,378	12.8	14,911	80.1	1,029	5.5	890	4.8	733	3.9	300	1.6	298	1.6	18	0.1	71	0.4	18,620	100	5.81

Table 5.2   Number of identified specimens of carbonized seeds from Iron Age strata

Strata	Period	Oats #	Oats %	Barley #	Barley %	Wheat #	Wheat %	Lentil #	Lentil %	Pea #	Pea %	Bitter Vetch #	Bitter Vetch %	Broad Bean #	Broad Bean %	Olive #	Olive %	Grape #	Grape %	Garden Heliotrope #	Garden Heliotrope %	Total #	Total %
1-6	Modern-Arabic	--	--	29	15.3	91	48.1	15	7.9	--	--	36	19.0	7	3.7	6	3.2	5	2.6	--	--	189	28.5
7-10	Byzantine	--	--	4	7.5	9	17.0	3	5.7	--	--	8	15.1	--	--	14	26.4	15	28.3	--	--	53	8.0
11-14	Roman	1	0.9	62	58.5	5	4.7	1	0.9	--	--	2	1.9	--	--	--	--	35	33.0	--	--	106	16.0
15	Late Hellenistic	2	1.0	12	5.9	43	21.3	8	4.0	1	0.5	126	62.4	2	1.0	6	3.0	2	1.0	--	--	202	30.4
16-19	Iron	5	4.4	6	5.3	14	12.3	2	1.8	--	--	--	--	--	--	82	72.0	3	2.6	2	1.8	114	17.2
Sum	All	8	1.2	113	17.0	162	24.3	29	4.4	1	0.2	172	25.9	9	1.4	108	16.3	60	9.0	2	0.3	664	100

When the shifts which occurred in the regional distribution of sites between Iron I and Iron II are examined, the same pattern is apparent that was seen during the recent past as discussed in Chapter Three: settlement began along the plateau ridge and in the northern hills and eastern plains, but shifted gradually toward occupation of the western descent region as the food system entered its most intensive phase. Thus, whereas during the Iron I only 8% of the sites from that period are found in the western descent region, during the Iron II settlement in this region had increased to 22% of the sites from that period.

Also reminiscent of the process of settlement accompanying the rise of the modern nation of Jordan is the pattern of reuse of previously settled sites. Thus, the majority of the sites which were settled during the Iron Age had been settled earlier, particularly during the Early Bronze Period. Furthermore, sites were sometimes settled, abandoned, and then resettled again throughout the Iron Age millennium. Thus, the Iron I settlement

at Tell Hesban, which began about 1200 B.C., appears to have been followed by an occupational interruption of ca. 150 years, until the end of the 9th century B.C. when the Iron II settlement appears.

Even within the Iron II Period the site appears to have been totally razed and then rebuilt, as is suggested by the stratigraphic evidence from Stratum 16 (Herr forthcoming). While largely destroying the architectural accomplishments of the previous settlers, this rebuilding activity, which occurred sometime around 700 B.C., was followed by the most intensive build-up of human occupation which took place during the Iron Age.

Changes in Landuse:
From Stock to Crop Production

An important fact to establish at the outset with regard to the bone data from the Iron Age strata (table 5.1) is that, compared to those from the Greco-Roman and Islamic strata, they are the smallest in size, accounting for only approximately

13% of the total assemblage from all periods. This situation is reflected also in the fact that fragment accumulation rates for bones from the Iron Age strata were lower—3.26 for Stratum 19 and 3.58 for Strata 16-18—than the mean accumulation rate for all strata, which was 5.81.

A finding significant to Iron Age bone data is the relative importance of cattle in Iron I (Stratum 19). During this period cattle account for a higher proportion of the finds than at any other time in the tell's history (22.2%), compared with 15%, the highest for the Greco-Roman centuries, and 13.3%, the highest for the Islamic centuries. While it is possible that this finding may be accidental, attributable perhaps to the small size of the bone sample from Iron Age strata, this is unlikely, especially with the fact that this trend was also noted by the author in "bone reading sessions" during earlier seasons at Tell Hesban.

A proposal that might account for this phenomenon is that during the Iron Age centuries, a fundamental shift took place in Transjordan in how cattle were utilized. Thus, whereas in the early Iron Age centuries cattle were raised, along with sheep and goats, as pasture animals, by Iron II times this role was largely superseded by their role as draft animals. This is the principal role which they appear to have played in all subsequent periods. It is significant, in this regard, that as the proportion of cattle in the pasture herds was reduced, the proportion of sheep and goats increased from 70.6% to 78.5% between Iron I and Iron II respectively. The increased role of cattle as draft animals might also account for the slight decline in the proportion of equids between these two periods: from 2.0% in Iron I to 1.6% in Iron II.

Unfortunately very little in the way of ancient plant remains from the Iron Age is available from Tell Hesban. Only six flotation samples were obtained from this period, of which 114 specimens could be identified, as shown in table 5.2. While it is not certain that the garden heliotropes and oats were cultivated locally (Gilliland 1986), the wheat, barley, lentils, and grapes no doubt were grown on the fields of Hesban in the Iron Age as they are today. If the lentils were grown in rotation with wheat or barley, as they are today in Jordan, this would likely have occurred toward the end of Iron I and throughout Iron II as the overall emphasis on crop production intensified at the expense of stock production.

Similarly, grapes and olives were probably produced in much larger quantities during Iron II, as this is the period when settlements increased in number in the western descent region and along the slopes where these crops could be grown on terraces adjacent to nearby villages.

Changes in Operational Conditions

Farmsteads and Farm Towers

At least 10, and possibly as many as 12 of the Hesban Survey sites contain the remains of what appear once to have been isolated farmsteads (see fig. 5.5). All but one of them are located along the plateau ridge and in the northern hills region of the project area. Furthermore, in nearly all instances, they are located either on a natural hill or on a ridge in close proximity to agricultural lands. Judging from the associated pottery, only four of them came from Iron I (49, 105, 108, 137), the remaining ones having come from Iron II (5, 98, 104, 105, 131, 132), except for two which could be dated only to the Iron Age (73, 89).

Associated with many of these isolated Iron Age ruins were other features suggestive of their agricultural function. Site 137 offers a good example. It is located "on a low hill of bedrock surrounded by a cultivated plain." Nearby were "two wine presses cut into bedrock and a small cistern or storage cave" (Ibach 1987: 29). In the case of this site and Sites 98 and 131, the remains of one or more rectangular buildings were also visible. The latter site also included a perimeter wall measuring 192 m along the north and east sides of the site (cf. Johnson 1973; Applebaum, Dar, and Safrai 1977; Edelstein and Gat 1980; Edelstein and Kislev 1981; McGovern 1985).

Sometimes associated with these Iron Age farmstead sites, and other times found in isolation, were the remains of structures which in Ibach's (1987) report were identified as "towers." These towers ranged in size from 8 m to 15 m in diameter (table 5.3), judging from the measurements included in the Hesban Survey account (Ibach 1987). Exactly how these Iron Age towers functioned in the food system of this period is not clear. On the one hand, that they were mere agricultural field towers such as those found in the vicinity of Samaria by Applebaum, Dar, and Safrai (1977) is unlikely, for the sizes of the Samarian field towers range in

Fig. 5.5 Iron Age farmsteads

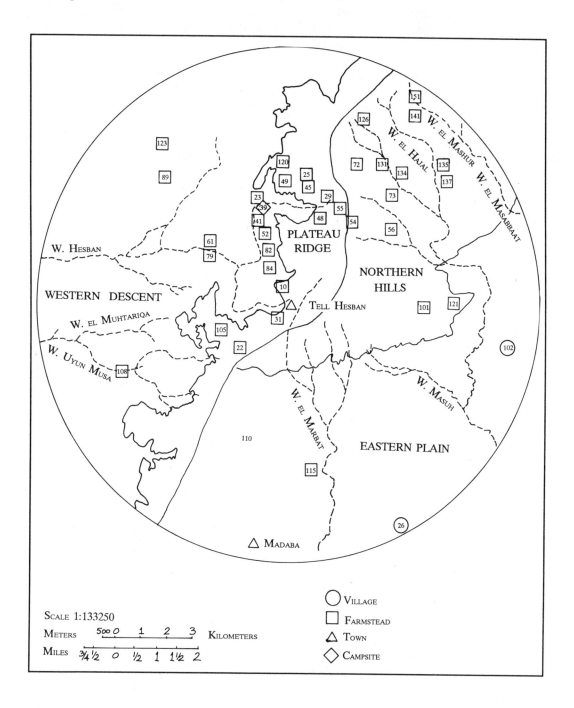

diameter only between 3.7 m and 4.6 m. On the other hand, that these structures represent Ammonite defense towers, as has been suggested by several German scholars (Gese 1958; Hentschke 1960; and Fohrer 1961), is an interpretation which does not seem plausible either, especially given their location adjacent to arable valleys. Furthermore, while the tower structures are too small to house many people (*i.e.* a garrison of troops), their foundation stones are too large for normal houses (Younker personal communication).

Site	Roman Towers	Site	Iron Age Towers
37	7.0 m	5	----
38	6.0 m	49	8.3 m
63	9.8 m	73	12.0 m
64	7.5 m	89	10.9 m
67	7.5 m	98	14.7 m
	9.3 m	104	----
124	5.8 m	105	----
	3.4 m	106	----
125	6.0 m	108	----
	9.0 m	131	----
		132	8.0 m
		137	----
Mean = 7.13 m		Mean = 10.78 m	
Range 3.4-9.8 m		Range 9.3-14.7 m	

Table 5.3 Size of Iron Age and Roman towers

The best explanation for these towers may be that they represent the Iron Age version of the protective dwellings which were in use throughout the Late Ottoman and Early Modern periods in Jordan's history (discussed in Chapter Three). As such they probably served many functions, including service as shelters for cultivators tending nearby orchards and as places for storage of crops and agricultural implements. It is possible, also, that as in the case of the Samarian field towers, their roofs served as places for ripening and drying fruit and as lookout posts for sighting thieves and destructive animals (*cf.* Applebaum, Dar, and Safrai 1977: 97). As in the case of their counterparts in this century, these Iron Age farm towers also very likely provided places of refuge for farm families and protection for flocks of sheep and goats when under the threat of attack by hostile neighbors.

It is important to be able to distinguish these Iron Age farm towers from the watchtowers built by the Romans a thousand years later. Noteworthy,

therefore, are the following differences: first, whereas the Iron Age farm towers were located adjacent to agricultural lands on hills throughout the project area, the Roman watchtowers found by the Hesban Survey were all found adjacent to the remains of ancient Roman roads. Second, the Iron Age farm towers are generally much larger (see table 5.3), having a mean diameter of about 11 m, compared to the Roman towers which averaged *ca.* 7 m in diameter. Third, Iron Age sherds are usually present adjacent to the Iron Age farm towers, and, in some instances, they are the most abundant (Hesban Survey Site 135, compare Fohrer 1961: 60). In most instances, Iron Age sherds are absent, or at least not recognized as such, from the sites containing the Roman watchtowers.

In addition to the towers discovered by Ibach's team, mention must also be made of Saller and Bagatti's (1949) survey of the Nebo region which produced over two dozen "stone circles," many of which very likely were agricultural field towers of the sort found around Samaria. The sizes of two of Nebo region stone circles are 1.24 m (F5) and 3.3 m (B6). While some of them may also have served as burial place markers, as Saller has suggested, the fact that he also noted their function as "camping places for the Arabs" argues for their important function in the local food system as well.

Water Management

It has been stated earlier that a crucial condition for the expansion of settled life in Transjordan is the availability of water. As could be expected, therefore, throughout the Iron Age there is a notable expansion of efforts with regard to this resource. Indeed, of the Iron Age remains from Tell Hesban, none are more impressive in terms of effort expended in construction than are the cisterns, channels, and reservoirs from this period. A closer look at the pertinent findings will illustrate this.

According to Herr (forthcoming), the very first evidence of human occupational activity on Tell Hesban is a "long, straight trench crudely carved out of bedrock in B.2, 3, and D.4. Its depth varied around the 4.00 m. mark . . . and its width was 2.00-2.50 m. at the top and around .75 m. at the bottom." To the extent that it was excavated, it measured 16.85 m long. While the function of this trench is enigmatic, the explanation favored in the end by Herr is that it was a channel whereby water from sources to the east of it could flow into a reservoir believed to have existed to the west of it ("in the general region of B.2").

Given the crucial importance of water for expansion of settled life, this interpretation, insofar as it favors an explanation having to do with water use, is probably as sound as any. It is likely, however, that its function was more than simply that of a channel for transporting water. For this purpose alone it is too big, as it is located near the summit of the tell where its catchment area would have been too small to necessitate the construction of a channel this deep and wide.

More consistent with the concern for water sufficiency would be the suggestion that this trench served both as a channel and as an overflow tank for water overflowing from surrounding cisterns. Cisterns of various sizes and shapes are encountered throughout nearly every stratum at Tell Hesban, beginning with Iron I Stratum 19 (D.1:63). This earliest of the cisterns from Tell Hesban was small, *ca.* 2.25 m wide and 3.50 m long by 1.75 m high, and shaped roughly like an egg. Also, it was coated completely, top to bottom, by a thick (*ca.* .08 m) layer of coarse, but very hard, dark tan plaster. If this suggestion is correct, then already in the Iron I village we encounter a significant water management complex consisting of at least one, and probably many (had our excavations been more extensive) cisterns, and an overflow tank, which possibly also served as a channel for leading water to a yet-to-be-discovered reservoir.

More extensive still were investments in water installations during the Iron II Period. The most striking evidence of this is the large plastered reservoir discovered in Iron II Stratum 17 (B.1 and B.2 [pls. 5.1, 5.2]). Cut *ca.* 7 m deep into bedrock, this roughly square reservoir measured 17 m from its southeastern to its northeastern corner. Also found were various shallow feeder channels carved out of bedrock shelves above it. Herr (forthcoming) estimates that it would have had a capacity of slightly over 2,000,000 liters. Because of the enormity of this reservoir, he has suggested that it might have been built by Mesha, the king of Moab, who claims in the famous Mesha Inscription (Horn 1979) to have built water conservation projects in some of the cities listed in his inscription. The reservoir appears to have been in use throughout most of the Iron II Period.

There can be little doubt that a crucial factor in accounting for the spread of permanent settlements during the Iron Age into regions, such as the eastern plain, where there was no nearby spring or stream to go to for water, was that plastered cisterns came to be relied upon during this period much more than they had been during previous centuries. Thus, cisterns were noted in the Hesban Survey at 7 (or 29%) of the 25 Iron I sites, at 25 (or 49%) of the 51 Iron II sites, and at 8 (or 17%) of the 46 Iron I-II sites. While there is no way of knowing for certain when these cisterns were built and during which periods they were used or not used, short of careful excavation of each, we do know that many of them that are in use today in the villages of Jordan were built in antiquity. We also know that certain of the cisterns excavated at Tell Hesban were in use already in the Iron Age and that they have been used and reused at various points in time since. It may be noted, however, that proportionately more cisterns were found at Iron II than at Iron I sites, a pattern which is consistent with other lines of evidence for the intensification of the food system over these two periods.

Terraces

Nowhere is the blending of the past with the present in Jordan more apparent than when it comes to the maintenance and use of dams and terraces for water and soil erosion control. Indeed, it can safely be said that the majority of terraces currently being utilized by village farmers in Jordan were originally constructed sometime in antiquity. In the case of the majority of these remains, however, it is difficult to be certain about the precise point in time when a given dam or terrace was constructed, used, reused, or neglected.

Examples of terraces can be found in the immediate vicinity of Tell Hesban. In the Wadi el Muhtariqa, a tributary of the Wadi Hesban to the northwest of the tell, a number of retaining walls spaced about 30 m apart can be seen. These form a series of descending platforms, each held in place by these retaining walls. These platforms descend from a large reservoir to the north of the tell which very likely was added sometime during the Roman Period. This whole complex was probably more intact when Musil (1907: 384) visited Hesban, *ca.* 1902, than it is today. By means of these retaining walls, the flow of water resulting from the winter rains would be slowed and diverted onto the banks

Plate 5.1   Wall B.2:84 as part of the eastern face of the Iron Age reservoir in Area B; view east

Plate 5.2   Plaster layers (B.1:145ff) visible in the bottom of the Iron Age reservoir; view west

of the wadi, thereby enlarging the lands available for cultivation. Furthermore, the soils washed off from the higher slopes above the wadi would be captured for agricultural use.

Unfortunately none of these wadi terraces have been investigated to determine their date of origin, but that they were in use in the Iron Age is suggested by the intensity of settlement and agricultural activity at Hesban and vicinity, especially during the Iron II Period. Support for this contention is provided by biblical sources. Thus, Stager (1982: 115) has noted that the word *šadmot* which appears in Isa 16:8 with reference to biblical Heshbon should be translated "terraces." As used in this text, the word *šadmot* is in "a clear agricultural, or more precisely horticultural, context," writes Stager (1982: 114). His translation of the relevant phrases is as follows: "The terraces of Heshbon languish, and the vine of Sibmah." It should also be noted that agricultural terracing is a well-documented Iron Age phenomenon on the other side of the Jordan River (Stager 1976, 1982; Edelstein and Gat 1980; Edelstein and Kislev 1981).

Just as terrace walls crisscross the slopes of the present-day tell, so did they in the Iron Age. Evidence for this is found in Iron II Stratum 16 where the excavators encountered a terrace wall (Wall C.2:49): "Not founded on bedrock, its crude construction precludes the possibility that it was part of a house or other structure." Its use as a terrace wall can be inferred from the pattern of the water-sorted soil layers below it "which hint at slowly flowing water, possibly draining from the terrace" (Herr forthcoming).

Also associated with several of the farm towers and farmsteads are terraces of various sizes and shapes. Some of these farms were also surrounded by extensive perimeter walls such as found at Sites 131 and 148. These perimeter walls no doubt served to enclose the intensively cultivated lands within the wall from grazing animals and would-be thieves.

Food Processing and Storage

Of the 2,800 objects registered during five seasons of excavations at Tell Hesban, only 120 or 4.3% were found in the Iron Age Strata. Included in this tiny proportion were four artifacts associated with the processing of food, specifically with the grinding of grains and other food substances: two mortar fragments (#1594, #1708) and a pestle fragment (#1594) found in Iron I Stratum 19 and a muller fragment (#2596) found in Iron I Stratum 18. These were all made of limestone.

Present in very large quantities, especially in the fill from the Iron II reservoir, were pottery fragments (Sauer 1973), most of which can be assumed to have played a role in the preparation, storage, transportation, and consumption of food. Yet to be completed, however, is a study of the pottery from Hesban from the perspective of its role in the food system. Emphasis thus far has been strictly from the perspective of relative chronology.

Except perhaps for the cave or "storage cellar" encountered in Iron I Stratum 18, no other installations were found in the Iron Age strata which can with confidence be related to food processing activity. Conspicuous because of their absence, in fact, are the remains of mill stones and *tabuns*. This situation is probably the result of the complete razing of the older Iron Age occupational remains which is attested to in Iron II Stratum 16.

Frequently encountered throughout the project area, and often adjacent to present-day olive and/or grape orchards, are the remains of wine/olive presses which have been cut into the bedrock in antiquity. Although it is not possible to say with certainty that any of these were constructed during this period, such presses can be found at the following Iron Age sites: 1, 3, 10, 29, 137. The latter of these, as already mentioned, is located near a farmstead of the sort described above.

Textile and Iron Industries

The discovery of a significant number of textile implements from Tell Hesban suggests that a textile industry may have flourished there, particularly during Iron I when pastoral pursuits were still very significant. Thus of the 120 objects found in the Iron Age strata, 60% were textile implements, mostly loom weight fragments, and all but one of these were found in Iron I Stratum and 19. Also found were 2 spindle rests and 1 spindle whorl (#2310, #1299, #1623).

Knowledge of ferrous metallurgy and the carburization process whereby agricultural and other implements of steel could be manufactured ap-

Strata	Period	Cattle kg	Cattle %	Sheep/Goat kg	Sheep/Goat %	Pig kg	Pig %	Camel kg	Camel %	Total kg	Total %	Accumulation Rates
1	Modern	1.4	27.45	3.0	58.82	0.2	3.92	0.5	9.80	5.1	4.65	0.05
2-3	Mamluk	14.2	30.67	25.2	54.43	0.8	1.73	6.1	13.17	46.3	42.21	0.24
4	Ayyubid	0.1	33.33	0.2	66.67	--	--	--	--	0.3	0.27	0.01
5	Abbasid	0.2	16.67	0.8	66.67	--	--	0.2	16.67	1.2	1.09	0.01
6	Umayyad	1.6	33.33	2.4	50.00	0.6	12.50	0.2	4.17	4.8	4.38	0.06
7-10	Byzantine	2.3	31.51	3.7	50.68	1.1	15.07	0.2	2.74	7.3	6.65	0.02
11-13	Late Roman	4.4	31.43	7.6	54.28	0.9	6.43	1.1	7.86	14.0	12.76	0.06
14	Early Roman	1.9	33.33	3.3	57.89	0.3	5.26	0.2	3.51	5.7	5.20	0.03
15	Late Hellenistic	3.1	46.27	2.8	41.79	--	--	0.8	11.94	6.7	6.11	0.05
16-18	Iron 2	4.6	40.00	6.3	54.78	0.3	2.61	0.3	2.61	11.5	10.48	0.02
19	Iron 1	3.1	45.59	2.9	42.65	0.3	4.41	0.5	7.35	6.8	6.20	0.03

Table 5.4 Weight of principal meat-yielding species from Iron Age strata (in kg)

pears to have arrived at Tell Hesban "at least by the 7th century" B.C. or sometime before then, possibly as early as in the Iron I Period (London forthcoming; *cf.* McGovern 1983, 1985: 147). Because only one iron artifact was found among the Iron Age objects, a blade point (#1329) from Iron II Stratum 16, the question of the extent to which iron metallurgy played a role in the intensification of crop production in this region remains an open one.

Changes in Dietary Conditions

Domesticated Mammals

In considering the food consumption patterns of the Iron Age inhabitants of Tell Hesban, changes in the uses of domesticated mammals are examined first. The reason for beginning with this food group is not because it played the most important role in the Iron Age diet, but because it is the food source for which the evidence is most abundant. This is because of all the different kinds of food groups, including meat, poultry and eggs, cereals, legumes, fruits and vegetables, milk and milk products, etc., none are better and more abundantly preserved by the archaeological record than the discarded bones of domesticated mammals. Yet, even these are far from complete in their representation, as was pointed out in Chapter Four.

The enormous drop in the weight accumulation rates of animal remains between Iron I and II (see table 5.4), suggests an overall decline in the consumption of cattle, sheep, and goats. Proportionately the most important of these in the local diet throughout the entire Iron Age was sheep and goat meat. During the Iron II Period, sheep and goats appear to have been slaughtered and eaten at a younger age.

Beef followed sheep and goats in importance, and may have played a more important role in the Iron I diet than in any subsequent time in this region. Unlike sheep and goats which were sometimes eaten as young animals, cattle were generally not slaughtered until reaching maturity. This conclusion is supported by the absence of remains of young beef in the bone corpus from this era (Boessneck and von den Driesch 1978a; von den Driesch and Boessneck forthcoming).

That horse meat was eaten at various times throughout the history of Tell Hesban is suggested by the fact that butchering marks have been found on many of their bones (Boessneck and von den Driesch 1978a). Whether such marks occur on any of the horse remains from the Iron Age is a question which has yet to be answered. Suffice it to point out here that the remains of horses, along with those of camels and swine, are included in the bone corpus uncovered from this era. That the latter two were eaten, although not in large quantities, is a fact generally not in question (see table 5.1).

Poultry, Fish, and Game

Chickens are the only poultry identified from Iron Age deposits (see table 5.5). These occur in the Iron II strata, as could be expected, but in relatively small quantities when compared to later periods. Of the other forms of poultry encountered in the bone corpus from Tell Hesban, namely the domestic pigeon or house dove and the goose, neither can be said with certainty to come from the Iron Age. Poultry, therefore, apparently really played no significant role in the Iron Age diet.

Strata	Period	# of Bones #	# of Bones %	Min # of Individuals #	Min # of Individuals %	% Young
1	Modern	---	---	---	---	---
2-4	Ayyubid-Mamluk	1566	65.83	128	58.44	22.0
5-6	Umayyad-Abbasid	127	5.34	13	5.94	8.0
7-10	Byzantine	231	9.71	27	12.33	11.5
11-14	Roman	410	17.23	41	18.72	14.2
15	Late Hellenistic	41	1.72	7	3.20	14.6
16-18	Iron 2	3	0.13	2	0.91	---
19	Iron 1	1	0.04	1	0.46	---
Sum	All	2379	100	219	100	

Table 5.5 Number of identified specimens of chicken from Iron Age strata

Type	Iron I	Iron II
Fallow Deer	3	1
Gazelle	11	0
Wild Swine	1	0
Wild Goat	2	0
Wild Sheep or Goat	3	1
Wild Sheep	1	0
Total	21	2
Percentage	95%	5%

Table 5.6 Wild animal bones from Iron Age strata

Three genera of fish were found in Iron Age strata. In Iron I Stratum 19 sea bream (*Sparidæ*) was represented by 5 fragments (out of a total of 11 finds) and in Iron II Stratum 17 parrotfish (*Scaridæ*) and sea perch or bass (*Serrandidæ*) were each represented by one bone fragment (out of a total of 138 and 3 finds respectively, [Lepiksaar forthcoming]). All three of these genera are found in the Red Sea as well as in the Mediterranean Sea. When compared with the total of 872 bones of fish identified from Tell Hesban, the quantity produced by the Iron Age strata is very meager. Again it appears that fish contributed only a small amount to the Iron Age diet.

A wide variety of wildlife is represented in the bone finds from Tell Hesban. While it is not possible at the present time to give the stratum to which every game animal bone belongs, for reasons discussed in the previous chapter, information about the most frequently eaten non-domesticated mammals is presented in table 5.6. Immediately apparent in this table is the paucity of finds from the Iron II strata. While this situation may be simply the result of an overall meagerness of bone finds from Iron II, as was pointed out above, alternatively this fact in itself might reflect an intensifying food system in that formerly unmanaged lands became managed ones with the result that habitats were destroyed for many wild as well as domestic species. The gazelle and the wild sheep could be expected to decline in their numbers just as did domesticated sheep and goats. The same would also hold for wild swine. According to von den Driesch and Boessneck (forthcoming), fallow deer and wild goat were probably not locally hunted animals. They suggest that the presence of these species reflects their importation via the fur trade.

The only wild bird which may have contributed slightly to the Iron Age diet is the partridge (*Alectoris chukar*). This appears to have been the favorite game bird in the Hesban region throughout all periods, judging from the fact that its bones constitute 229 (54%) out of the 420 wild bird bones found on the tell (Boessneck and von den Driesch forthcoming). Other birds which may occasionally have been hunted include the ostrich (*Struthio camelus*), the houbara bustard (*Chlamydotis undulata*), the common quail (*Coturnix couturnix*), and the great bustard (*Otis tarda*). Thirty-seven other species of birds were identified in the Tell Hesban bone corpus (see Boessneck forthcoming), but none of these are likely to have played any significant role in the Iron Age diet.

Cereals, Legumes, Vegetables, and Fruits

Very little can be said with certainty about the relative contribution of various kinds of cereals and produce in the Iron Age diet given the evidence presently on hand. As can be seen in table 5.2, three varieties of grains, namely wheat, barley, and oats were consumed. Of the legumes, only lentils are attested to in the data, while olives and grapes constitute the fruit food group.

In the absence of any other direct lines of evidence regarding the role played by these various food groups, and regarding what other produce might have been consumed, we are left to conjecture on the basis of analogy with the changes in diet which accompanied the intensification of the food system in Jordan over the past 100 years.

Thus it is possible to hypothesize that as the production of pasture animals tapered off, first the field crops, such as wheat, barley, and lentils, and then later the other produce, assumed an increasingly important role in the diet. As the local population became integrated into the wider economy, trade began to account for a relatively greater proportion of the foods consumed as well. Fish, for example, probably was eaten more in Iron II than in Iron I. The Iron II diet generally, in fact, was probably more varied, consisting of a greater variety of locally produced and imported food items. The Iron I diet, on the other hand, was probably less varied, being based primarily on the staple items of wheat, barley, sheep and goat's meat, milk and milk products. Whether eggs were eaten in any appreciable quantity is not known.

Transhumance During the Iron Age

That some type of vertical movement of flocks and households between highland and lowland areas took place during the Iron Age can be inferred from the presence in this region of 17 small sites (numbers 22, 24, 27, 28, 33, 39, 40, 43, 47, 50, 53, 58, 86, 88, 99, 110, 129) which in Ibach's (1987) site list are described as being "very small" or "small" and consist primarily of a concentration of pottery sherds.

As fig. 5.6 shows, these sites are clustered along the edge of the highland plateau north of Tell Hesban and along the upper portions of Wadi Hesban and its tributaries. While all of these sites produced some type of Iron Age sherds, more precise dating was possible in the case of Sites 39, 40, 47, and 129 which were dated to Iron I and Sites 39, 99, 110, and 129 which were dated to Iron II.

Since Ibach's (1987) site list offers no further details about these sites other than their location, relative size, pottery information, and remarks to the effect that no architectural remains were observed, our proposal regarding the users of these sites as having been transhumants must rest on the *a priori principle* (discussed in Chapter Four), on inferences based on historical sources, and on analogy with the situation which existed in this region during the Ottoman Period.

According to the *a priori principle*, the most likely explanation for the presence of these sherd scatters is that they represent activities somehow related to the Iron Age food system. While the possibility that they represent the remains of some component of the sedentary food system must definitely be reckoned with, the likelihood that many of them were camping sites utilized by the transhumant component of the local food system can be hypothesized on both historical and ethnoarchaeological grounds.

On the one hand, the historical basis for this hypothesis has been provided by Israel Eph'al (1982) in his book *The Ancient Arabs: Nomads on the Borders of the Fertile Crescent 9th-5th Centuries B.C.* In this study of contemporary biblical, Assyro-Babylonian, Greek, and ancient Arabic sources, Eph'al presents convincing literary evidence for the presence of nomadic peoples in Transjordan throughout the entire Iron II Period. On the other hand, the ethnoarchaeological basis for this hypothesis was presented in Chapter Three where it was noted that the western part of the project area was used by the Adwan tribesmen throughout the 19th century as spring and summer pasture. During the fall and winter, they would retreat to their more permanent homes in the foothills and plains to the north of the Dead Sea.

That a similar pattern of transhumant migration occurred throughout the Iron Age is suggested by the concentration of these sherd scatters in the western descent where favorable watering and sheltering conditions for people and animals could be found in the Iron Age as they could be in the recent past. It is also very likely that the Iron Age caves which are located along the plateau ridge, in the northern hills and in the eastern plain also were utilized by transhumants as seasonal shelters and campsites, just as they were in the Ottoman Period. While many of these caves were, no doubt, also utilized by the settled population during medium and high intensity periods, they certainly would have been available for use by transhumant herdsmen during the occupational hiatus between Iron I and Iron II as well as during the Hellenistic Period. Caves were noted at the following Iron I sites: 1, 44, 105, 135; and at the following Iron II sites: 10, 29, 44, 72, 105, 127, 131, 132, 139, 145; Iron I and/or II: 113, 115, 121, 123, 134, 137.

Sedentarization and Nomadization

When the various lines of evidence available pertaining to the Iron Age millennium at Hesban and vicinity are brought together, the picture which

Fig. 5.6 Iron Age sherd scatters

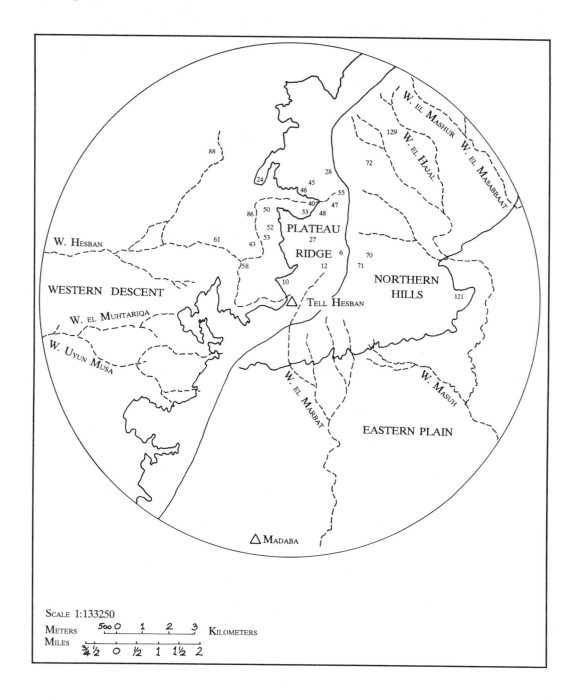

emerges is that of a population responding, by means of movement back and forth along the nomad-sedentary continuum, to shifting political winds. Throughout the entire millennium, transhumant pastoralists were converting to sedentary cultivators and vice versa. Between the 12th and the 6th centuries B.C., the rate at which the population sedentarized exceeded the rate at which it nomadized, resulting in a gradual build-up of sedentary villages and intensification of landuse to where a high-intensity configuration was reached during the 7th and 6th centuries B.C.

Archaeological residues of this high-intensity configuration include widespread occurrences of farmsteads, farm towers, cisterns, and a large reservoir at Tell Hesban. Produced in relatively large amounts during these centuries were fruits and vegetables in combination with cereals, cattle, sheep, and goats. The fact that several cylinder seals (cf. Herr 1978) and other emblems of delegated authority are included in the finds from these two centuries adds further weight to the conclusion that a form of urban-oriented elite-controlled agriculture prevailed during these two centuries.

The return to transhumance, which followed toward the end of the Iron II Period, is evidenced by the abandonment of most of these facilities which began to occur in the 5th century B.C. This process of nomadization continued to occur until a low-intensity configuration was in place by the 4th century B.C. This configuration appears to have prevailed throughout the 3rd and 2nd centuries B.C., judging from the paucity of sites from these centuries.

Chapter Six

CONFIGURATIONS OF THE FOOD SYSTEM DURING THE GRECO-ROMAN MILLENNIUM: *CA.* 333 B.C. TO A.D. 661

Chapter Six

Configurations of the Food System During the Greco-Roman Millennium: *Ca.* 333 B.C. to A.D. 661

Introduction

Over the approximately 1,000 years between the arrival of Alexander the Great in Palestine, *ca.* 333 B.C., and the conquest of the region by the Muslims, *ca.* A.D. 661, several distinct, yet intimately intertwined paths of development took place on the Transjordanian landscape. On the one hand there was the path promoted by the Hellenized and Romanized elite of Palestine which gradually led to the establishment of an urban-oriented production regime in the project area emphasizing, especially during Late Roman and Byzantine times, the cultivation of vine and tree fruits. On the other hand there were the paths chosen by the rural masses, some of which led to close and intimate cooperation within the Greco-Roman production regime, others which led to pastoral-oriented production regimes emphasizing autonomy and self-sufficiency as a means of coping with increasing disinheritance and alienation experienced at the hands of the Hellenized and Romanized majority.

In this chapter some of the evidence leading to this view of the Hesban vicinity food system during Greco-Roman times is presented. As in earlier chapters we shall look at five principal parameters of the food system, namely environmental, settlement, landuse, operational, and dietary conditions. By considering the changes which occurred in each of these five domains of the food system we shall see clearly the development of the Greco-Roman production regime. Much more subtle are the clues indicating the independent paths pursued by certain members of the rural masses.

In the analysis which follows, their paths of resistance will seen by focusing attention on evidence suggestive of the processes of polarization and nomadization within the project area. Not to reckon with several such co-occurring developments is, in our opinion, to fail to properly acknowledge the complexity of the sociocultural situation in Transjordan during this pivotal millennium in the history of the region.

The Sociopolitical Context

The Wider Sociopolitical Context

To interpret the archaeological remains encountered in the vicinity of Hesban from the Greco-Roman centuries, five transforming influences must be reckoned with which catalyzed and shaped the course of the sedentarization and nomadization processes which occurred side by side within the project area during this pivotal era in the history of Palestine and the world. They include first, *Hellenization* of Transjordan; second, *Nabataean sedentarization* in Transjordan; third, the *Romanization* of Transjordan; fourth, the *Christianization* of Transjordan; and fifth, the expansion of *long-distance trade* which resulted from these influences.

While the ways in which each of these influences transformed the lives of individuals and communities throughout this region are extremely wide ranging and certainly too many to enumerate in this brief overview, our aim here is to introduce each of them sufficiently to acknowledge their relevance as factors which must be reckoned with in accounting for alterations in the local food system. We would caution at the outset, however, against the impression that these influences represent sharply segregated and equally pervasive processes. Rather, they were all overlapping and merging developments and not all on parallel footing in terms of their impact on the way of life of the indigenous population.

Fig. 6.1. Palestine in the Greco-Roman period

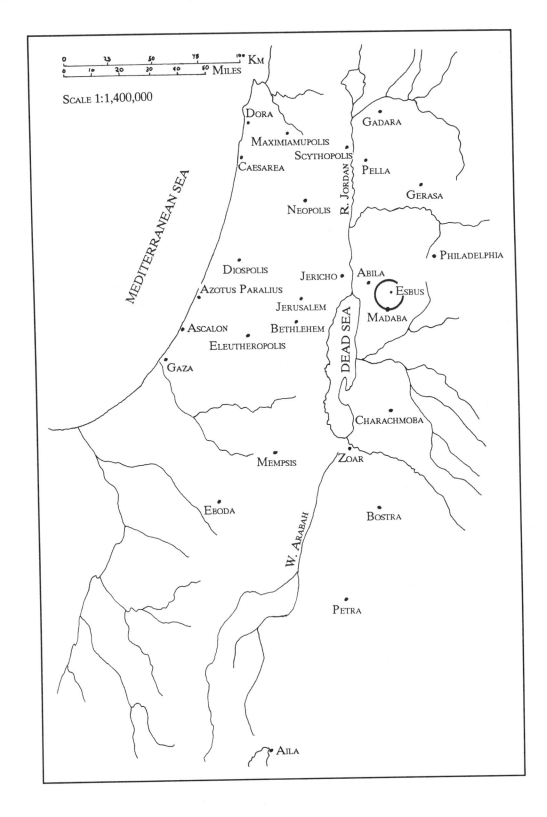

The Hellenization of Transjordan

Hellenization is the process of assimilation of Greek cultural elements by various Oriental populations which followed in the wake of Alexander the Great's campaigns throughout the ancient Near East. The commonly agreed-upon date of Alexander's march through Syria and Palestine is 333 B.C. (Parr 1975: 947). Especially instrumental in carrying out this process in Palestine were two ruling families, the Ptolemies of Egypt and the Seleucids of Syria, who had both emerged as victors in the struggle for power which followed in the wake of Alexander's death. While the Ptolemies managed to maintain the upper hand in Palestine for about a century beginning ca. 301 B.C., in 198 B.C. this disputed region was annexed by the Seleucid Empire. Their control was short-lived, however, for it only lasted a little more than three decades until ca. 164 B.C., when the Seleucid Empire was divided between several rebelling and conquering peoples (Parr 1975: 947; Solomon 1971).

While the Ptolemies' approach to Hellenization emphasized "centralized bureaucratic control of trade, agriculture, industry, and local affairs in Palestine" (Parr 1975: 948), the Seleucids emphasized the development of semiautonomous Greek-style cities (fig. 6.1).

Rostovtzeff (1928b: 192), for example, points out that "in Transjordania side-by-side with the native sheikhs and their tribes, a group of towns with a mainly Greek population" were in existence during the Seleucid reign. Among these were Philadelphia (modern Amman), founded on the site of ancient Rabbath-Ammon (Harding 1960; Avi-Yonah and Stern 1979), located approximately 26 road km northeast of Tell Hesban. Philadelphia was later brought into a league consisting of ten cities which came to be known as the Decapolis (Applebaum 1971: 1449; for an alternative view on the administrative structure of these cities see Parker 1975: 437-441). It remained thus until it was annexed by the Romans during the reign of Domitian (A.D. 51-96; see Bowersock 1983: 91).

The Seleucids were more aggressive in propagating Greek thought and customs than were the earlier Ptolemies, thus creating more ill will. This was especially the case among the Jews, who eventually rebelled and managed to form their own state under the leadership of the priestly Hasmonean family (Tcherikover 1972a, 1972b; Bayer 1971: 1455-1458). This new Jewish state in Palestine prospered under the leadership of a series of Hasmonean rulers and between ca. 164 B.C. and 37 B.C. came to control practically all of Palestine and Transjordan except for certain of the Decapolis cities, one of which was Philadelphia (Parr 1975: 948).

Nabataean Sedentarization in Transjordan

The sedentarization of the Nabataean Arabs in Transjordan appears to have been catalyzed by their initial successes as caravaneers and merchants. Various explanations have been suggested for why these nomadic tribesmen of the North Arabian desert were able to gain such a powerful hold on the overland trade routes of Arabia. On the one hand, the stimulus for trade and industry which resulted when Alexander the Great put into circulation "a vast amount of precious metals, which the Persian kings had hoarded," has been offered as an explanation (Parr 1975: 948). On the other hand, their success has been attributed to the competitive edge which they enjoyed because they had come into possession of the North Arabian saddle. This saddle gave the camel rider, for the first time in history, the ability to fight effectively from camel-back with sword and spear (Bulliet 1975: 92).

Whatever the outcome of the debate over the causes of Nabataean rise to power and influence, the fact remains that the dominance which they were able to exert over the trade routes of Arabia resulted in great profits finding their way back to their capital city, Petra, in southern Jordan (cf. Zayadine 1985; Khairy 1982). To supply food to their growing urban populations, in Petra and in their other major trading centers, increasing numbers of these tribesmen began to settle in the hinterlands behind these centers. There they began to expand and improve upon the agricultural accomplishments of the populations they gradually subjugated, such as the descendants of the Edomites and the Moabites (Glueck 1939: 48). In particular, they introduced deeper into the desert regions of their kingdom enhanced schemes for controlling and taking advantage of floodwaters.

Detailed investigations of the desert farming techniques of the Nabataeans and those who followed them have been carried out by Glueck (1939), Evenari (1956), Mayerson (1962) and by Evenari, Shanan, and Tadmor (1971). In order to take maximum advantage of the 100 mm rainfall which falls between December and March in the dry regions which they cultivated, Nabataean farmers took full advantage of the natural watersheds which made up the catchment areas of the numerous desert wadis.

As was noted in Chapter Two, on the slopes of tributary wadis they constructed terraces consisting of a series of stone shelves. This prevented the floodwater from rushing violently down the slope and instead forced it to flow gently, irrigating each shelf and transporting nutrients to the soil. In the main wadis, into which the tributary wadis eventually emptied out, diversion conduits and dams were constructed of stone which served to divert some of the water to higher plots further down the wadi. In this manner the Nabataean farmer was able to overcome the problem of insufficient rainfall for agriculture in the dry regions in which he lived.

In addition to such floodwater irrigation schemes, the Nabataeans also collected rainwater in strategically located cisterns "fed by conduits which captured and led runoff from the slopes and gullies above them" (Mayerson 1962: 248). While most of these were near or beneath dwellings where they provided drinking water for people, others were adjacent to agricultural fields where they provided supplementary irrigation water after the winter rains had passed (Mayerson 1962: 240).

Where spring water was available, imaginative irrigation schemes were introduced as well. Thus Glueck (1939: 44, 1959: 201-204) has documented the existence of several Nabataean *garden cities* and *garden villages* which arose in the vicinity of springs. In the Wadi Arabah, for example, he discovered a *garden city* (et-Telah) which consisted of "several square miles of carefully walled fields" which were irrigated from spring waters stored in a large *birkeh* or reservoir. These "elaborately walled fields," when later observed from an airplane, "resembled a gigantic checker board" (Glueck 1959: 202). Smaller spring-fed garden villages, which apparently existed on the outskirts of the Nabataean capital, "helped supply the food-requirements of Petra's large population" (Glueck 1939: 44). Furthermore, the inhabitants inside the city watered their gardens by means of elaborate aqueducts and floodwater collection schemes as well (Hammond 1973).

The fact that Nabataean agriculture persisted despite the demise of Nabataean commerce in the 1st century A.D. may partially be attributed to a deliberate policy adopted by several Nabataean kings which had emphasized "urban growth and a peaceful transition from commerce to agriculture" (Bowersock 1983: 69). Seeing evidences of attempts to divert their trade to cities further north such as Gerasa, Bostra, and Palmyra, these Nabataean kings apparently encouraged sedentarization especially along the fertile highland plateau of Transjordan so as to provide for an alternative economic basis for their government. Despite these efforts, however, in A.D. 106 Petra "lost her independence and was absorbed into the Roman Empire by the emperor Trajan" (Bulliet 1975: 101).

Two additional factors come to mind as well in thinking about the persistence of Nabataean agriculture. First, as Evenari *et al.* (1971: 325) have noted, the Nabataean farmers' practices were restorative rather than destructive to the available natural resource. Their maintenance of terraces, for example, helped tame the flood torrents from washing away the soil. Also, because their supply of water was so limited they were prevented from overirrigating. They were thus spared the damaging effects of salinization.

The other factor is that to a large degree, Nabataean agriculture was based on local self-sufficiency (*cf.* Glueck 1959: 253-254; Mayerson 1962). Each village and farmstead developed and maintained its own irrigation system rather than being linked to a region-wide floodwater management system, as was the case in Mesopotamia, for example. Thus, the livelihoods of the farmers were not so intimately tied to the fates of urban elites. Hence the persistence of the Nabataean farmer despite the sudden disappearance of his urban partners at Petra and the other centers of Nabataean commerce in the Negev.

The Romanization of Transjordan

Roman influence in Syria and Palestine began *ca.* 64 B.C. when Pompey and his legions arrived in Syria "to bring an end to the chaos that had followed upon the dissolution of the Seleucid dynasty" (Bowersock 1983: 28). The process of Roman annexation of Transjordan was not completed, however, until Trajan succeeded in annexing the Nabataean Kingdom in A.D. 106. During these intervening years, the Nabataean Arabs retained control of most of southern Transjordan and the desert regions to the east, while the fertile highland of central and northern Transjordan was administered by several competing Roman client states.

Although the Decapolis city of Philadelphia (modern Amman), along with the other cities of the *league*, had been incorporated into the province of Syria, which had been established by Pompey, it was allowed to continue in its autonomous status in the Hellenistic tradition until its annexation into the province of Arabia in A.D. 106 (Applebaum 1971: 1449; Bowersock 1983: 91).

The establishment of the province of Arabia by Trajan marks the completion of Roman annexation of Transjordan. Up to this time, Roman influence in the region had been buffered by the continuance of Arab and Hellenistic traditions kept alive by the Nabataeans and the inhabitants of the Decapolis cities of Gerasa and Philadelphia. Trajan's annexation of the Nabataean Kingdom in A.D. 106

> was followed by the greatest piece of Roman road-building in the Orient, the construction of the *via nova* in the years A.D. 111-114. It was the work of Claudius Severus, the first governor of Provincia Arabia, and ran from Bostra to Aila (Aqaba) on the Red Sea (Avi-Yonah 1950: 56; *cf.* Bowersock 1983: 83).

Other roads were constructed as well, including one built *ca.* A.D. 129-130 by Hadrian connecting Hesban with Jerusalem via Livas and Jericho (Avi-Yonah 1950: 56, 59; see fig. 6.2).

For approximately two centuries, *ca.* A.D. 106 to 315, Transjordan remained unified as a political entity under Rome's *Provincia Arabia*. During this period, the rhythms of daily life in the rural hinterlands and cities had to be adjusted to the concerns and ambitions of the Romanized elite. Besides construction of a network of paved roads throughout the province, these included construction and maintenance of the *limes Arabicus*, the fortified garrisons along the eastern border of the province (Parker 1976; Bowersock 1983: 105). The development of the urban areas was also important. In Transjordan the cities of Petra, Bostra, Philadelphia, and Gerasa, all bear witness to Roman undertakings in the form of temples, theatres, baths, streets with colonnades and monumental gates, mausolea, masonry tombs, and cemeteries (Conder 1889; Brunnow and Domaszewski 1904; Kraeling 1938). Such buildings were also constructed in many of the smaller towns and villages, including, as we shall see, Madaba and Hesban.

The urban dominance of rural hinterlands which had begun to emerge during Hellenistic times throughout the Near East was strengthened during the centuries of Roman control in the re-

gion. Every free and settled person, whether living in the towns or in the country, belonged to a *polis*, a city. Even in Transjordan, where there were relatively few cities, this form of organization appears to have prevailed, except that certain villages also functioned as units of government. Thus, writing with reference to the province of Arabia, Jones (1964: 713) notes that the villages of this "backward area" functioned as

> self-governing communities which managed their own revenues and possessed and erected public buildings: the governing body was a mass meeting . . . which elected annual magistrates and passed decrees. In fact, the villages seem to have differed from small cities only in lacking a council . . . and several were promoted to city ranking in the third and fourth centuries (Jones 1964: 713).

The consequence of this trend toward urban dominance for the rural peasant population was a gradual loss of personal freedom and proprietorship of lands (*cf.* Sperber 1972: 244, 1974). This pattern of social organization continued for the next four centuries until the end of the Byzantine Period.

It is important to note, however, that throughout this entire period, confederations of Arab tribes existed in Transjordan whose way of life did not conform to the lifestyles prescribed by the Romanized majority. The presence, for example, of the Safaitic Arabs in northern Transjordan and the Thamudic Arabs in the south has been noted by Caskel (1959), Beisheh (1973), Bowersock (1983: 97, 131), and Shahid (1984a: 128-141, 1984b). These were literate tribesmen on whom the Roman governors of this province may initially have relied to assist in the administration of inaccessible territories to the east (Bowersock 1983: 97). The role which these played in the local economy, and the polarization which occurred between them and the Roman elite, is a matter which until recently has largely been neglected by scholars concerned with Roman Palestine (*cf.* Banning 1986; Parker 1986, 1987).

The Christianization of Transjordan

The conversion in A.D. 312 of Constantine I to Christianity, along with his founding of Constantinople as the capital of the Eastern Roman Empire, had a profound effect on Syria and Palestine. In Transjordan, many temples were either destroyed or converted into churches, and, especially during the Late Byzantine Period, a number of new churches were built (Sauer 1980: 32). Further-

Fig. 6.2. Road map of Roman Palestine (after Avi-Yonah 1950)

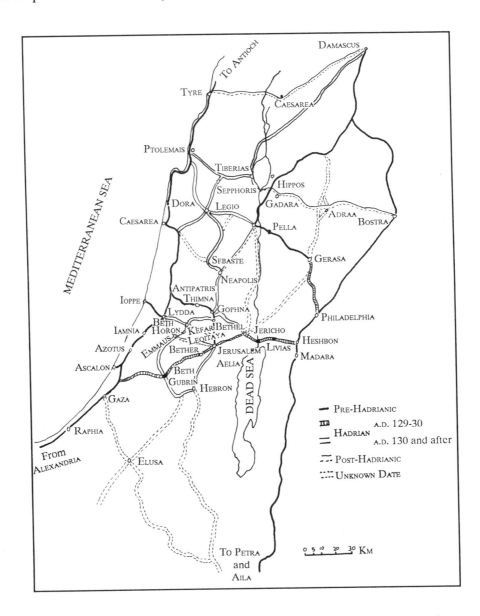

more, "as protectors of the new religion Constantine and his successors evinced a special interest in Palestine, the land of its origins" (Parr 1975: 951). As Avi-Yonah has shown, this resulted in an influx of capital into Palestine which

> revolutionized its position completely; from an obscure province it became the Holy Land, pampered by emperors whatever their treasurers might say. The stream of capital which then began to flow explains better than any other factor the astonishing prosperity of Palestine in the Byzantine Period; its cessation must be accounted among the main causes of its collapse (Avi-Yonah 1958: 41).

By the end of the 3rd century the Arab urban establishment in the Fertile Crescent had been almost completely replaced by a Romanized one; a situation which likely led to a diminished role for transhumants in the control of local affairs. Shahid (1984a: 137) has pointed out that this situation may have caused "a certain degree of nomadization" within the countries of the Fertile Crescent. Furthermore, this alienation of the indigenous population by the Romans no doubt goes a long way toward explaining the explosive conquests of Arabs under the banner of Islam three centuries later. Indeed, by their determination to rely on major sheikhs in the region for assistance in pacifying their fellow tribesmen, the Byzantine government may well have encouraged what had been disparate groups of tribes to join together into the larger social and administrative units which had come into existence by the time of the Arab conquest (Bowersock personal communication).

A new element in the social fabric of Palestine during the Byzantine Period was the monastic movement which no doubt played an important role in the Christianization of the Transjordan. Monasteries not only provided a refuge for persons seeking spiritual nourishment for their souls, they also provided places to stay for pilgrims. The agricultural sector of the economy was enlarged as well as a consequence of monks extending the cultivated areas into inaccessible regions (Avi-Yonah 1958: 48). Of the many monasteries in Jordan, the one at Mt. Nebo is perhaps the best known (Saller and Bagatti 1949). Its famous mosaics with depictions of orchards, game animals, and daily life support the impression that the Byzantine centuries in Palestine were indeed prosperous ones (Parr 1975: 951).

Increased Long-Distance Trade

Over the centuries between the conquests of Alexander and the conversion of Constantine I, long-distance trade in the ancient world was extended to where all four of Eurasia's major civilizations—China, India, the Near East, and Greece-Rome—were tied together by a network of interconnected sea and overland trade routes. During this period the famous caravan route known as the *Silk Road* came into existence and, as a result, greatly increased the movement of goods between China and the Middle East. Furthermore, sea routes were discovered which made mercantile shipping between the Mediterranean ports, Arabia, India, Malaysia, and China a matter of routine (McNeill 1963: 295-298).

As already noted, Transjordan and the Nabataeans played an important role in the development of long-distance trade during this period. To begin with they were among the chief suppliers of Arabian products such as incense, which was transported via the Arabian *incense route* through Petra, to Rome (Thorley 1969: 211). They also held a tight grip on the trade between the Mediterranean lands and the Far East. For example, they maintained a monopoly on the *timber route* whereby ebony and other woods, such as teak, blackwood, and sandalwood, were transported from India and other distant lands to the furniture manufacturers of the Eastern Mediterranean (Thorley 1969: 218). Petra was also one of principal distribution centers for silk imported overland from China (Thorley 1969: 217). Other products from India and the Far East which very likely passed through Nabataean hands included cinnamon, cassia, spikenard, costus, cardamum, betel, pepper, pearls, ivory, precious stones, parrots, animal skins, rice, cotton, and even tigers and snakes (Thorley 1969: 219-223; see also Raschke 1976).

In addition to such long-distance trade there was also extensive trade between the countries of the Mediterranean. For example, Sperber (1976) has shown that between the 1st and 5th centuries A.D. there was extensive commercial contact between Palestine and Egypt. While imports from Egypt consisted of beer, wheat, fish, linen, wine, natron, materia medica, baskets, and rope, exports from Palestine to Egypt included linen, tar, bitumen, hides, gum, wine, oil, and balsam (Sperber 1976: 147). The most active century in terms of this commercial contact was the third. This century was for Palestine a time of rapid expansion in the wine industry (Sperber 1976: 113, 141).

Varied Impact of Influences

In concluding this overview of the wider socio-political context it is necessary to again reiterate what was briefly cautioned against at the outset, that the five transforming forces discussed above were not sharply segregated and equal in their influence. Not only did they represent merging and overlapping developments, the extent of their impact varied considerably. For example, as Bowersock (personal communication) has pointed out, the Roman presence in the East generally took a Hellenized form. Thus Romanization was effected in the Greek language and through the use of Hellenic institutions (*polis* organization, *agora*, etc.). Latin was scarcely used in the administration of the region. As for Christianization, while it represented a confrontation with Hellenized institutions insofar as it promoted a diversion of capital into ecclesiastical coffers for the construction of churches and monasteries, it cannot be regarded as being on parallel footing with either Romanization or Hellenization in terms of its overall impact on the way of life of the indigenous population.

The Local Sociopolitical Context

Throughout the first half of the Greco-Roman millennium, the Hesban region was as unstable politically as it had been during the previous Iron Age millennium. To fully appreciate how unstable and fragmented the situation in this region really was, it is instructive to scrutinize its changing boundaries as shown on political maps such as those prepared by Abel (1933), Amiran (1970), and Parr (1975). Summarized below (cf. fig. 6.1), is the changing political landscape within the 10-km radius Hesban project area as represented in the historical atlas prepared by Amiran 1970.

500-333 B.C. (Persian Period)

Except for the area to the north and west along the perimeter of the project area, which apparently was in the hands of the Tobiads during the Persian Period, the political situation which prevailed in the rest of the project area is uncertain (cf. Mazar 1957; Tcherikover 1972a, 1972b; Elazary and Porten 1971). Only the town of Madaba is shown on the map from this period.

333-198 B.C. (Early Hellenistic Period)

Throughout the Early Hellenistic Period the project area remained divided between four different political entities. The northern hills region belonged to the hinterlands of the autonomous Decapolis city of Philadelphia. The eastern perimeter bordered on the lands of the Nabataean Arabs. The central and southern portions belonged to the Ptolemian eparchy of Idumea and the western perimeter bordered on the hyparchy of the Tobiads, a predominantly Jewish settlement within the eparchy of Samaria. The map shows Madaba as a town and Esbus (Hesban) as a village during this period. However, no archaeological evidence exists for a village at Tell Hesban until the end of the 2nd century B.C.

198-63 B.C. (Late Hellenistic Period)

After the breakup of the Seleucid Empire which followed in the wake of the Hasmonean revolt, most of the project area was annexed by the Nabataean Kingdom. It remained thus until the conquests of John I Hyrcanus (Feliks 1971), leader of the new and rapidly expanding Hasmonean Kingdom of Judea between 135 and 104 B.C., brought most of the project area under Jewish rule. The northeastern portion, which belonged to the independent city of Philadelphia, was not conquered, however. During this period both Hesban and Madaba are represented as towns on the map, and Samage is shown as a village.

63-40 B.C. (Early Roman Period)

The breakout of civil war within the Hasmonean Kingdom and the simultaneous arrival of the Roman legions in Palestine resulted in the Hasmonean Kingdom being greatly reduced. Thus the towns of Esbus and Madaba along with most of the rest of the project area was handed over to the Nabataeans. Only the northeastern portion continued to be ruled as before, namely as part of the territory of the independent city of Philadelphia.

40-4 B.C. (Early Roman Period Continued)

In 40 B.C. the Hasmonean Kingdom became a client state under Rome when Herod, son of Antipater the Idumaean, was proclaimed king of Judea. Under Herod's rule the boundaries of Judea again expanded. To protect the eastern frontier of Herod's kingdom, Esbus and vicinity were turned into a military colony. Parker (personal communication) has suggested that the population which occupied Esbus during this period very likely were Hellenistic mercenaries of mixed origin. Madaba, however, remained in Nabataean hands and the northeastern portion continued as before under the rule of the independent city of Philadelphia.

4 B.C.-A.D. 106 (Early Roman Period Continued)

After Herod's death in 4 B.C. Esbus and vicinity were again incorporated under Nabataean rule. The status of Madaba remained unchanged, continuing under Nabataean rule. The northeastern portion of the project area remained unchanged as well, continuing under the control of the independent city of Philadelphia. During this period of relative tranquility in Transjordan, however, Judea and Samaria underwent severe political upheavals, including the first of two Jewish revolts against Roman rule. That the peace may also have been disturbed at Hesban in A.D. 66 is suggested by the fact that the Jews apparently sacked Hesban and its region in that year (Josephus BJ 2.18.1, 458).

A.D. 106-365 (Late Roman Period)

In A.D. 106 Trajan annexed the Nabataean Kingdom and installed the Roman Province of Arabia in its place. Along with the cities of Philadelphia, Gerasa, and Bostra, the towns of Esbus and Madaba and their hinterlands were organized under one provincial government. Thus began the period of the Pax Romana in Transjordan.

A.D. 365-661 (Byzantine Period)

Throughout the three centuries of the Byzantine Period Palestine was divided among four provinces. One of these was again called Province of Arabia and to it belonged the towns of Madaba and Esbus (Hesban) along with the cities of Philadelphia and Gerasa. Each of these settlements represented a polis with its own local government and dependent agricultural population, as explained earlier.

Changes in Environmental Conditions

No major changes in the macroclimate appear to have taken place during the Greco-Roman millennium which would have significantly altered the natural environment, making it, for example, more or less desert-like. This is evidenced, for instance, by the fact that species of wildlife such as the dorcas gazelle, fallow deer, wild boar, chukar partridge, houbara bustard, and other forms of indigenous wildlife continue to exist in the finds from this millennium (Boessneck and von den Driesch 1978a; von den Driesch and Boessneck forthcoming). This is not to say, however, that no changes occurred at all in the natural resource during this period. In fact, a number of cataclysmic events as well as long-term destructive processes did indeed occur which had great consequences for the human population in this region.

Mention must be made, for example, of a series of earthquakes which rocked the lands along the earthquake-prone Jordan rift valley during this period. Based on his examination of references to earthquakes and their consequences in various ancient sources, Amiran has put together an Earthquake Catalogue of Palestine (1950; Amiran et al. 1952; cf. Russell 1985) which gives the year and location of 27 earthquakes occurring at various locations throughout Palestine between 64 B.C. and A.D. 632. Earthquakes which apparently affected Palestine as a whole include those which occurred in A.D. 48, 130, 344, 362, 365, 394, 396, 419, 447, 551, 554, 580, 583, 631, and 632. Of these, the one in A.D. 130 is believed to have been responsible for the destruction of Early Roman Stratum 14 at Tell Hesban (Mitchel 1980: 96; cf. Sauer 1978a, 1978b); the one in 365 is blamed for the massive damages observed in Late Roman Stratum 11 (Mitchel 1980: 193); and one occurring "around the end of the first quarter of the 6th century" A.D. is mentioned by Storfjell (1983: 113; cf. Russell 1985: 37; Parker 1986) as a possible cause of the destruction evidenced in Byzantine Stratum 9.

Even though no major alterations in the macroclimate of Palestine appear to have taken place during the Greco-Roman centuries, as mentioned above, climatic ups and downs appear nevertheless to have been sufficient to cause a growing concern among the Jews of Palestine beginning in the 2nd century A.D. and especially during the 3rd. This is the impression which Sperber (1974) has communicated following his examination of references in the rabbinic literature from these centuries to communal concern about insufficient rainfall and drought. Apparently irregularities "of seasons and successive droughts, followed by famine and pestilence, took their toll of both population and the land" (Sperber 1974). The partial retreat from the land by cultivators which occurred in the vicinity of Hesban during the Late Roman Period may be partially attributable to conditions such as these, as will be discussed below.

To these evidences of cataclysmic and extreme events must be added the cumulative damage to natural resources which resulted from the gradual, but constant destruction of trees and forests which took place also during the Greco-Roman millennium. This deforestation was attributable to a number of factors: First, to the plains and valleys already opened for cultivation during previous millennia, uplands and slopes were added as well, judging from the intensification of settlements in these subregions during the Roman Period. As will be discussed in greater detail below, in the vicinity of Hesban, formerly uncultivated uplands, slopes and ridges, especially in the western descent, were cleared and terraced for cultivation of tree and vegetable crops. Second, this expansion of cultivation reduced further the available pasturage, increasing the problem of overgrazing in the pastures still remaining. Third, as if the damage thus sustained were not enough, trees were also cut in great quantities for military purposes (Sperber 1972: 239).

The cumulative effect of this denudation, especially of the forests in hilly regions, was that more and more soil was washed away by the heavy seasonal rains. As a result, what had been perennial streams watering the lower areas became occasional torrents washing stones and boulders down into the plains and valleys below and generally worsening the situation for the farmer. This situation very likely contributed as much as did irregularities in rainfall to the drought, famine, and pestilence with which the local farmers had to contend during the latter half of the Greco-Roman millennium in Palestine.

Changes in Settlement and Landuse Conditions

Hellenistic Period (*ca.* 333-63 B.C.)

Pottery dating to the Hellenistic Period was found at 17 of the 148 sites visited by the Hesban Survey (fig. 6.3). In contrast to the quantities of pottery representing other periods, the number of Hellenistic sherds found at these sites was few. At

Umm es Sarab (Site 54), for example, Hellenistic pottery turned up in only one of the six pails of pottery from that site (Ibach 1987: 148). At other sites only two or three sherds were attested from this period.

Of the 17 Hellenistic sites, 15 were located on sites which had been settled during earlier periods. Possibly settled for the first time during Hellenistic times were Sites 130 and 142, both located in the northern hills region of the project area. Altogether 7 Hellenistic sites were located in this region, compared with 4 along the plateau ridge, 4 in the western descent, and 2 in the eastern plain. As would be expected, the majority of these sites are located in close proximity to either springs or cisterns. Caves and tombs are other features common to many of them. The modest level of settlement in the region surrounding Tell Hesban is reflected in the occupation of the site itself (Stratum 15). Judging from the pottery found, resettlement of the site began in the Late Hellenistic Period or between *ca.* 198-63 B.C.

Perhaps the most impressive evidence from this period, unearthed in Areas A and D, is "a massive 1.80-meter-thick stone wall that apparently completely surrounded the summit of the tell" (Mitchel 1980: 29). The discovery of this massive perimeter wall, along with the high proportion of artifacts from this period of a military nature, such as armor scales, slingstones, maceheads and arrowheads, has led the excavators to the conclusion that Hellenistic Hesban (Esbus) "began its life as a type of border fort" (Mitchel 1980: 67).

Inferences about landuse during the Hellenistic Period can be made on the basis of our knowledge of the local sociopolitical context, the location and density of settlements, and the plant and animal remains from the period. These lines of evidence point to a low-to-medium intensity configuration involving the production of field crops on the eastern plain and in the fertile valleys in the northern hills and western descent regions and the raising of sheep, goats, cattle, and camels on pastures and stubble fields throughout the entire project area.

To begin with, this inference makes sense in light of the local sociopolitical context which, as noted earlier, was very unstable during the Hellenistic Period. Esbus itself changed hands four times between 300 and 63 B.C. (Mitchel 1980: 21), and the project area as a whole was divided and redivided several times between the armies of the

Fig. 6.3. Hellenistic Period sites

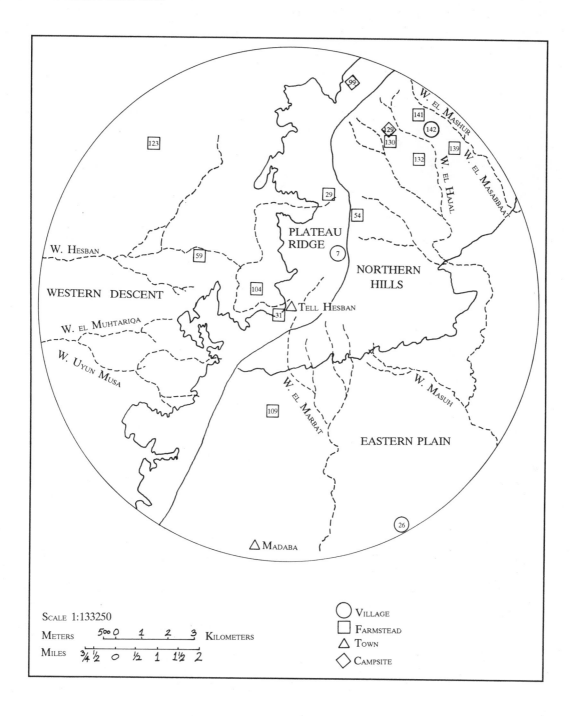

Table 6.1 Number of identified specimens of principal domestic animals from Greco-Roman strata

Strata	Period	Cattle #	%	Sheep/Goat #	%	Sheep #	%	Goat #	%	Pig #	%	Camel #	%	Equids #	%	Horse #	%	Donkey #	%	Total #	%	Accumulation Rates
1	Modern	60	5.7	908	86.0	36	3.4	52	4.9	25	2.4	9	0.9	54	5.1	5	0.5	19	1.8	1,056	5.7	9.96
2-3	Mamluk	1,117	13.3	6,901	81.9	353	4.2	402	4.8	139	1.6	215	2.6	57	0.7	6	0.1	14	0.2	8,429	45.3	43.00
4	Ayyubid	9	10.7	71	84.5	4	4.8	6	7.1	--	--	2	2.4	2	2.4	--	--	--	--	84	0.5	1.40
5	Abbasid	8	3.9	188	91.7	14	6.8	11	5.4	2	1.0	5	2.4	2	1.0	--	--	--	--	205	1.1	0.73
6	Umayyad	68	10.4	494	75.3	47	7.2	33	5.0	80	12.2	8	1.2	6	0.9	--	--	3	0.4	656	6.5	7.80
7-10	Byzantine	162	12.5	932	71.6	58	4.5	48	3.7	130	10.0	14	1.1	63	4.8	5	0.4	10	0.8	1,301	7.0	4.39
11-13	Late Roman	286	11.7	1,892	77.6	140	5.7	115	4.7	183	7.5	17	0.7	58	2.4	2	0.1	6	0.2	2,436	13.1	10.36
14	Early Roman	131	15.0	682	78.1	67	7.7	36	4.1	43	4.9	7	0.8	10	1.1	--	--	3	0.3	873	4.7	4.12
15	Late Hellenistic	136	12.0	977	85.9	135	11.9	75	6.6	6	0.5	15	1.3	4	0.4	--	--	1	0.1	1,138	6.1	2.60
16-18	Iron 2	256	14.3	1,406	78.5	137	7.7	83	4.6	94	5.3	5	0.3	29	1.6	--	--	9	0.5	1,790	9.6	3.58
19	Iron 1	145	22.2	460	70.6	38	5.8	29	4.4	31	4.8	3	0.5	13	2.0	--	--	6	0.9	652	3.5	3.26
Sum	All	2,378	12.8	14,911	80.1	1,029	5.5	890	4.8	733	3.9	300	1.6	298	1.6	18	0.1	71	0.4	18,620	100	5.81

Table 6.2 Number of identified specimens of carbonized seeds from Greco-Roman strata

Strata	Period	Oats #	%	Barley #	%	Wheat #	%	Lentil #	%	Pea #	%	Bitter Vetch #	%	Broad Bean #	%	Olive #	%	Grape #	%	Garden Heliotrope #	%	Total #	%
1-6	Modern-Arabic	--	--	29	15.3	91	48.1	15	7.9	--	--	36	19.0	7	3.7	6	3.2	5	2.6	--	--	189	28.5
7-10	Byzantine	--	--	4	7.5	9	17.0	3	5.7	--	--	8	15.1	--	--	14	26.4	15	28.3	--	--	53	8.0
11-14	Roman	1	0.9	62	58.5	5	4.7	1	0.9	--	--	2	1.9	--	--	--	--	35	33.0	--	--	106	16.0
15	Late Hellenistic	2	1.0	12	5.9	43	21.3	8	4.0	1	0.5	126	62.4	2	1.0	6	3.0	2	1.0	--	--	202	30.4
16-19	Iron	5	4.4	6	5.3	14	12.3	2	1.8	--	--	--	--	--	--	82	72.0	3	2.6	2	1.8	114	17.2
Sum	All	8	1.2	113	17.0	162	24.3	29	4.4	1	0.2	172	25.9	9	1.4	108	16.3	60	9.0	2	0.3	664	100

Ptolemies, Seleucids, Nabataeans, Hasmoneans, Romans, and the independent city of Philadelphia. Under such unstable conditions landuse strategies permitting quick return on investments, as do field crops and pasture animals, would have represented the least risk to the producers.

Second, the low density of population, judging from the small quantity of settled sites, and the fact that most sites were located in the northern hilly region adds further weight to this impression. The location of the majority of the sites on natural hills and ridges enhanced possibilities for self-defense and permitted, at the same time, easy access to the fertile wadi bottoms for purposes of cultivation. Furthermore, most of the sites thus occupied already had cisterns to collect water in place, caves for use as temporary shelters for people and animals, and building stones for the construction of more permanent homes and facilities.

Third, both the substantial quantity of cattle (table 6.1) from this period and the range of plants (table 6.2) utilized by the inhabitants of Late Hellenistic Tell Hesban (Esbus) are indicative of a people well acquainted with sedentary life. Indeed, the inhabitants of this site may well have been local leaders, along with the populations of Philadelphia and Madaba, in the drive to sedentarize and Hellenize the transhumant pastoralists and semisedentary mixed-farmers who no doubt made up the majority of the population in this region during these turbulent centuries.

Early Roman Period (ca. 63 B.C.-A.D. 130)

Pottery dating to the Roman Period was found at 118 of the 148 sites surveyed by the Hesban Survey (fig. 6.4). Of these 44 contained sherds datable to the Early Roman Period and 36 contained sherds from the Late Roman Period.

A total of 38 sites either could not be subperiodized into early or late or belonged to the Roman road which was dated to both periods. That an increase in sedentary activity took place during the Early Roman Period is evident from the significant

Fig. 6.4 Early Roman Period sites

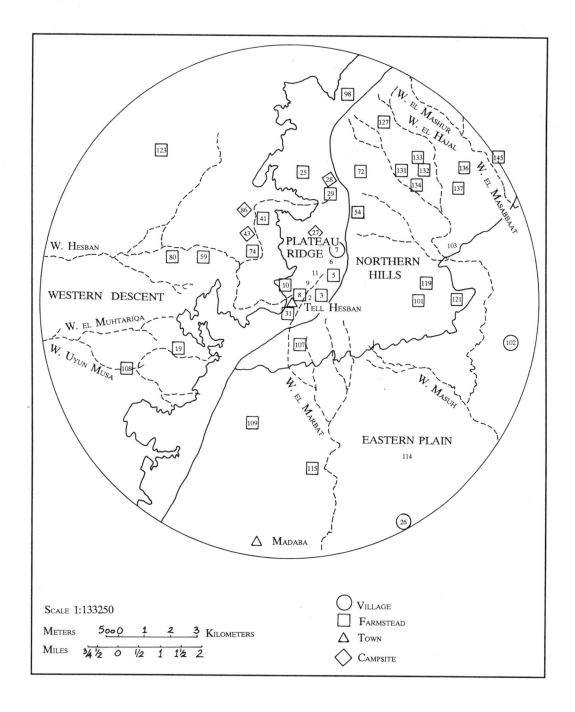

rise in the number of sites with Late Roman Period sherds (44 sites) over sites with Hellenistic Period sherds (17 sites). While this intensification of settlement occurred throughout the whole project area, it is most marked along the plateau ridge, where there was an increase from 4 to 16 sites during this period. Increases in the number of sites in the other subregions went from 2 to 5 sites in the eastern plain, from 7 to 15 sites in the northern hills, and from 4 to 10 sites in the western descent. It is significant to note that all sites yielding Early Roman pottery also evidenced pottery from earlier periods. Thus, as was the case during previous centuries, reuse of old sites was the rule rather than the exception during this period as well. As during the earlier Hellenistic Period, a large proportion of the sites tended to be located on natural hills (22 sites) or plateau ridges (5 sites).

Also frequently encountered at these sites are cisterns (20 sites), tombs (17 sites), and caves (14 sites). The discovery of 10 sites containing remains of agricultural towers, especially along the plateau ridge and in the northern hills subregions, no doubt indicates the growing importance of permanent farmstead operations during the Early Roman Period. Farmstead sites are discussed below.

When attention is turned to the pattern of occupation at Tell Hesban itself during the Early Roman Period (Stratum 14), a situation reflecting that of the wider region and reminiscent of the earlier Hellenistic Period is clearly in evidence. On the one hand, the massive perimeter wall continues in use, suggesting the presence of a fort of some kind at the site also during the Early Roman Period (Mitchel 1980: 76). On the other hand, a prominent feature of the occupation pattern on the tell is that caves were extensively used as dwellings (Mitchel 1980: 71). One of these caves, as will be discussed further below, was entered via rock-cut steps (Mitchel 1980: 86). Other remains of sedentary life on the tell during this period included several cobblestone and soil surfaces, a few unconnected wall fragments, storage silos, a *tabun*, and a fire pit (Mitchel 1980).

The landuse pattern which characterized the Early Roman Period was much like that of the earlier Hellenistic Period, except that greater strides were made in the direction of increased production of field crops and, to a limited degree, tree crops. On the one hand, that landuse intensified somewhat is suggested, for example, by the discovery of

17 farmsteads from this period, compared with only 4 from Hellenistic times. Furthermore, the significantly higher number of settlements along the plateau ridge and in the western descent—in areas ideal for tree fruit production, but not for field crops—lends further support to this inference.

On the other hand, there is also evidence that transhumant pastoralists continued to live side by side with the more permanently settled population. This is suggested by the continued popularity of caves—relied upon for shelter in the winter months by transhumants—throughout the region. The presence of several possibly transhumant campsites containing only sherd scatters, two in the western descent region (Sites 43 and 86) and three along the plateau ridge (Sites 6, 27, and 28), adds further to this impression.

This side-by-side existence of transhumant pastoralists and settled farmers appears to have been the case at Esbus as well. On the one hand there were the occupants of the fort who, according to Josephus (cited in Mitchel 1980: 106), during Herod's reign may have been military veterans eager to take possession of their own plots of land. On the other hand, there were the inhabitants of the caves surrounding the fortress, and apparently also within it (whether contemporaneously with the veteran colony or before and after is not possible to say) whose livelihoods were less influenced by the ruling elite, dependent no doubt on more traditional enterprises for their survival.

Compared with the earlier Late Hellenistic Period, there is a drop-off of about 8% in the relative abundance rates for sheep and goats and slight increases in these rates for cattle and donkeys. This is suggestive of a general trend toward sedentarization in that reliance on flocks of sheep and goats now began to give way to greater reliance on oxen for plowing and donkeys for local travel. Furthermore, raising pigs became increasingly important because they would survive on the wastes and offal which are left over after the harvest of plants and animals and the preparation and eating of meals.

The pattern of side-by-side transhumance and village farming which appears to have persisted throughout the Early Roman Period, despite the steady advance of sedentarizing forces, is understandable in light of the continuing unrest which prevailed until the region was annexed by Rome. Not only did the fort at Esbus change hands several times again during this period; much of the project area was alternately controlled by the Nabataeans and Herodian Judea.

Furthermore, the late-1st-century A.D. Jewish revolt against Rome very likely had repercussions which contributed to the uncertain political climate of the Hesban region as well. Under such unstable conditions, extensive investments in vineyards and orchards would simply not be worth the risk. Thus, there was a predominance of a medium-intensity food system based on field crops and pasture animals with at best limited orchard production during this period.

Late Roman Period (*ca.* A.D. 130-365)

Pottery dating to the Late Roman Period was encountered at 36 of the 148 sites surveyed by the Hesban Survey, not counting Roman road sites (fig. 6.5). This represents a reduction in settlements from the Early Roman Period in the eastern plain (from 5 to 3 sites), western descent (from 10 to 7 sites), and northern hills (from 15 to 8 sites), but an increase along the plateau ridge from 16 to 18 sites. As was the case in the previous period as well, every one of the Late Roman sites had been occupied in former times.

The most commonly encountered ruins at Late Roman sites were tombs and cemeteries found at 14 of the 36 sites (pls. 6.1, 6.2). Caves were relatively less common, for they were noted at only 7 sites. Farmstead sites appear also to have been reduced somewhat in number, from 10 to 8. But the most striking feature of the Late Roman settlement pattern is the intensification of sites along the plateau ridge. If we assume that the 21 sites which could not be distinguished as early or late all were occupied during Late Roman times, this pattern is even more apparent.

One factor which very likely contributed to the concentration of sites along the plateau ridge was the new Roman road which appears to have been built at the beginning of the 2nd century A.D. This road, which may have been a segment of the famous *via nova Traiana*, ran from Philadelphia (modern Amman) via El 'Al to Esbus and on to Madaba (Thomsen 1917: 34-57; Avi-Yonah 1977; Ibach 1987). Its passage along the plateau ridge of the project area no doubt accounts for the concentration of tomb and cemetery sites in this region, for it was a common Roman practice to locate such sites "alongside of, or at least in association

with, the roads that led from the gates into the open country" (Toynbee 1971: 73). Not surprisingly, therefore, 10 of the 14 tomb and cemetery sites were found along the route of this road between Esbus and present-day Naur.

In addition to cemeteries and tombs, this new road also appears to have accelerated urbanization in the project area. This is evident at Esbus itself, as has been shown by Mitchel (1980). For example, Late Roman Stratum 13 (*ca.* A.D. 130-193) reflects a "complete change in living patterns" (Mitchel 1980: 121). Filled in and/or sealed over were the caves which had been so prominent during Early Roman times. Nor did the fort continue to be used. Instead, walls outlining rooms are seen all over, and in Areas B and D were found a series of rooms surrounding a central plaza. After ruling out a number of possible alternative interpretations of these remains, Mitchel comes down in favor of viewing them as being the remains of an inn. As such it "would have provided housing and food— perhaps even some entertainment—for travelers and caravaneers" (Mitchel 1980: 142) using the Philadelphia-Madaba road and the Esbus-Jericho road which branched off from it at Esbus.

Late Roman Stratum 12 (*ca.* A.D. 193-284) provides evidence of continuing build-up of the town of Esbus. The remains from this stratum attest "without much doubt the most extensive settlement of the site up to this time" (Mitchel 1980: 155). Indeed, according to Tristram (1865: 540) who visited the site before it was settled, "the whole city must have had the circuit of about a mile." Not only did the inn continue in use, a Roman temple (pl. 6.3) and very likely other public buildings as well were added in the acropolis area of the tell during this period. Furthermore, Esbus was granted the right to mint its own coins, several of which were found at the site (pl. 6.4). Thus it became a poor cousin, at least, of such famous Roman cities as Philadelphia and Gerasa.

The momentum which was built up during these earlier two Late Roman strata maintained itself to the end of the period, judging from the remains of Stratum 11 (*ca.* A.D. 284-365). For example, additions were made to the Roman temple and a monumental stairway was constructed leading up to the top of the acropolis area (see pl. 6.5), at the foot of which was laid down an "extensive plaza." Thus, in addition to the fact that earlier buildings and walls continued to be used, there are signs all over

Fig. 6.5   Late Roman Period sites

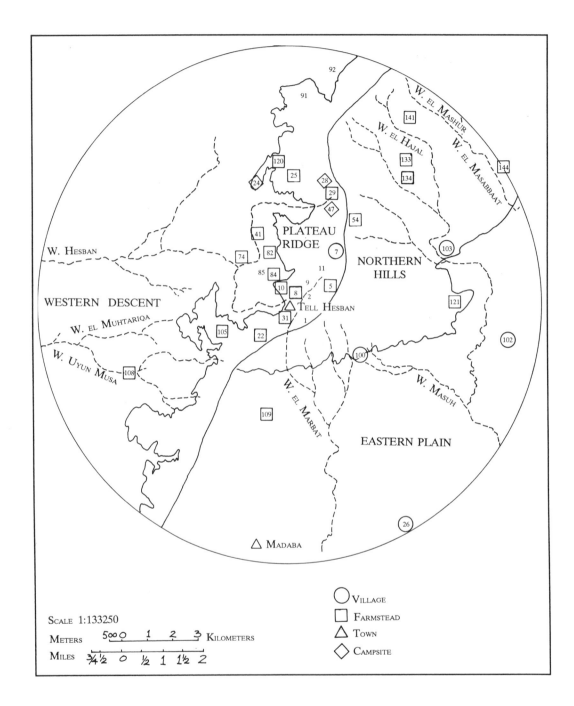

Plate 6.1   Entrance and forecourt of Early Roman chamber tomb with radiating loculi (Tomb F.1)

Plate 6.2   Interior doorway of Late Roman-Early Byzantine arcosolium Tomb F.5

Plate 6.3   Front foundation wall (A.6:65) of Roman temple portico; view south

Plate 6.4   Reverse of Esbus coin (Object #1522) minted during the reign of Elagabalus (A.D. 218-222)

Plate 6.5   Part of Late Roman stairway (B.7:20) which led to temple precinct on the acropolis; view north

Plate 6.6   Interior doorway of Late Roman Cave A.1:44, part of a two-cave complex; view west

the tell that Stratum 11 was as active as any of the earlier ones in terms of construction and rebuilding (Mitchel 1980: 180-196).

Inferences about landuse throughout the Late Roman Period must be made with much caution. On the one hand, increase in settlements along the plateau ridge very likely reflects expansion in the orcharding sector of the local economy. On the other hand, reduction of settlements in the other subregions of the project area suggests that a certain amount of desertion might have occurred among the peasant cultivators in the more distant hinterlands of Esbus. Such desertions were indeed common in Palestine and Syria at the end of the Late Roman Period (Jones 1970; Sperber 1972; Mitchel 1980).

The most striking evidence for intensification of landuse in the direction of orcharding is the increased abundance of horses, mules, and donkeys for plowing on slopes and terraces: from 1.1% in the Early Roman Period to 2.4% in the Late Roman Period (table 6.1). These animals appear to have increased in abundance at the expense of the cattle, which declined in importance from 15% to 11.7% over the same period. Along with this increase in tree-crop production came increased reliance on pigs: from 4.9% during the Early Roman Period to 7.5% during the Late Roman Period.

Byzantine Period (*ca.* A.D. 365-661)

Pottery dating to the Byzantine Period was found at 107 of the 148 sites visited by the Hesban Survey (fig. 6.6). Minimally, this represents an increase of 50 sites over a maximum total of 57 Late Roman sites, assuming that the 21 Roman sites which could not be distinguished as to early or late were all Late Roman. This means that Byzantine pottery was present at 83% of all surveyed sites, not counting road sites. As in previous periods, the large majority of these sites had been settled in earlier times.

The most drastic changes occurred in the western descent region where the number of sites with Byzantine pottery increased fivefold: from 7 in Late Roman times to 35. A fourfold increase took place in the northern hills: from 8 to 31. Along the plateau ridge and in the eastern plain the increases were twofold: from 18 to 34 sites in the former case and from 3 to 7 sites in the latter case.

Since differentiation of the Byzantine sites into subperiods was not feasible, given the pottery readings on hand, not much can be said about how the regional settlement pattern of the Early Byzantine Period differed from that of the late on the basis of the survey data alone. Something about the temporal dimension can be learned, however, from the Byzantine strata at Tell Hesban. In this regard it will be recalled that the changes observed in the site survey data between the Early Roman and the Late Roman periods were generally reflected in stratigraphic evidence from the tell.

According to Storfjell (1983), whose dissertation covered the Byzantine strata at Tell Hesban, "there was no evidence of any clearly defined break between the Late Roman and the Early Byzantine periods." Stratum 10 (A.D. 365-408) represents, therefore, a continuation of the Late Roman culture encountered in the earlier Stratum 11.

Thus, the monumental stairway, the plaza below, and the Roman temple and colonnade all appear to have been in use during this stratum. Unlike the earlier stratum, however, there was no evidence of any new building activity at Esbus in Stratum 10, a situation which very likely reflects the hard times which seem to have come to Transjordan in the latter days of the Roman regime.

It was not until the 5th century A.D. that the effects of Constantine I's conversion became evident at Esbus. This is clearly seen in Stratum 9 (A.D 408-551), which not only gives evidence of a build-up on the tell itself, as well as in its outerlying areas, but also offers proof of the arrival of Christianity at Esbus. Erected on the acropolis, right on top of the Roman colonnade area and re-using much of the Roman masonry, was a Christian basilica with an inscribed apse and a mosaic floor (*cf.* pls. 6.7, 6.8). Although the precise date of its construction could not be ascertained, it is clear that it was built sometime during the period covered by Stratum 9.

Stratum 8 (A.D. 551-614) gives evidence of further expansion of Esbus onto surrounding slopes and hills. This growth in population was probably the reason for the construction of two additional Christian churches at Esbus during this period. Furthermore, the original basilica on top of the acropolis appears to have been rebuilt and possibly also enlarged. A peak of some sort appears to have been reached during the time of this stratum, however, for signs of neglect and retrenchment be-

Fig. 6.6 Byzantine Period sites

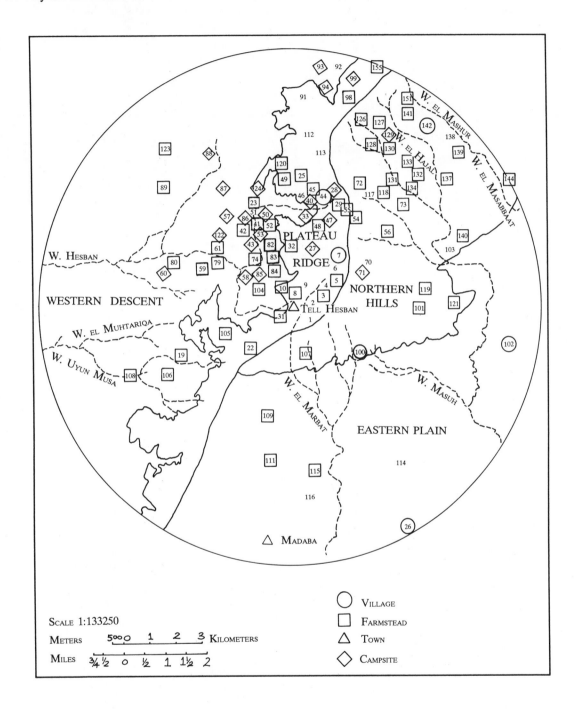

Plate 6.7   Architect's sketches of tentative reconstruction of Early Christian church at Heshbon (after Boraas and Horn 1969). Top: view southwest—entrance. Bottom: view northeast—apsidal end

Plate 6.8   Byzantine mosaic Floor A.4:8 from Hesban

come noticeable in the upkeep of the church building itself and in the tapering off of activity in certain of the residential areas on and beyond the tell. Stratum 7 (A.D. 614-661) reinforces this impression. It covers three decades during which no new buildings were begun. People were living, it appears, in buildings constructed during earlier times, for only occupational debris was found.

At no other time in the history of the project area did landuse intensify to the level it did during the Byzantine Period. To begin with, this is clearly evidenced in the quantity of farmsteads and villages which were occupied during this period. As already noted, there was a fivefold increase in the number of sites in the western descent region, the majority of which were farmsteads and villages, and a fourfold one along the plateau ridge. On the terraces and slopes above the springs and streams tree fruits were grown in larger quantities than ever before. Suggestive of the importance of tree fruits during this period are representations of scenes depicting orchards and harvesting of tree fruits which can be found in several mosaics discovered within the project area (cf. Saller and Bagatti 1949; van Elderen 1986; see also Piccirillo 1985). While grapes and olives were probably the most common, others, such as pomegranate, apricots, pears, and apples were also likely produced. Fruit tree production was also very likely important in the northern hills region, but there and in the eastern plain, staple crops like wheat and lentils probably continued to use up most of the land.

It is by no means a coincidence, then, that the quantity of donkeys, mules and horses reaches its highest peak (4.8%) during the Byzantine Period (table 6.1). These animals, as noted in earlier chapters, are much better suited than teams of oxen to plowing on steep and winding slopes. The continued high demand for pigs (10%) is also consistent with what we would expect, given the reduced availability of pastures.

Changes in Operational Conditions

Caravan Routes and Roads

Caravan Routes

That a caravan route existed which ran along the path of the ancient King's Highway through the Wadi el Arabah, via Kerak, Dhiban, Madaba, and Umm el Amad to Amman, has been shown by Glueck (1939: 113). While Nabataean sherds have been found at Madaba (Glueck 1939: 139), the Hesban Survey did not find any Nabataean sherds at Umm el Amad (Ibach 1987), a likely way-station along this route.

Another camel track running from Amman via El 'Al, Hesban, Mushaqqar, Khirbet el Mehatta, to Livias and across the Jordan to Jericho and Jerusalem no doubt also existed in Hellenistic-Early Roman times. It very likely followed the path of the Roman road which was subsequently built along this passageway. That Hellenistic and Early Roman pottery was attested to at most of these sites, including the fort at Khirbet el Mehatta, adds weight to this inference.

Roads

The road which connected Esbus to the West Bank via Livias and Jericho is well attested to in the survey results (cf. 6.7). This road is represented by curbstones, watchtowers, and ruins of buildings which probably belonged to way-stations (see pls. 6.9, 6.10). To the southeast of Tell Hesban is found a reservoir which probably served as a watering place for animals employed by travelers along this road. The approximate time when this road was constructed is believed to be about A.D. 130 (Avi-Yonah 1950: 59; Ibach 1987: 160), or during the first three decades after the establishment of the Roman Province of Arabia in A.D. 106. This road appears to have remained in use at least until the end of the Byzantine Period (cf. Ibach 1987).

The relationship of Esbus (Tell Hesban) to the via nova Traiana constructed by Emperor Trajan in the beginning of the 2nd century A.D. is a matter of some dispute (Mitchel 1980: 111). While Avi-Yonah (1977: 187) places Esbus on the route, as does Sauer (1973: 54), others have expressed doubts because of the complete absence of any milestones or other road remains in the vicinity of the site (Germer-Durand 1904: 4; Ibach 1987). The absence of remains, however, is not conclusive proof that this road did not pass by Esbus. Indeed, as Parker has noted (personal communication) the road was called the via nova Traiana, i.e., Trajan's new road, implying that it replaced an old road that existed before the early 2nd century A.D. This old road is almost certainly the King's Highway of the Old Testament and that later used by the Nabataeans through Edom and Moab northward.

Fig. 6.7 Esbus-Livias road sites

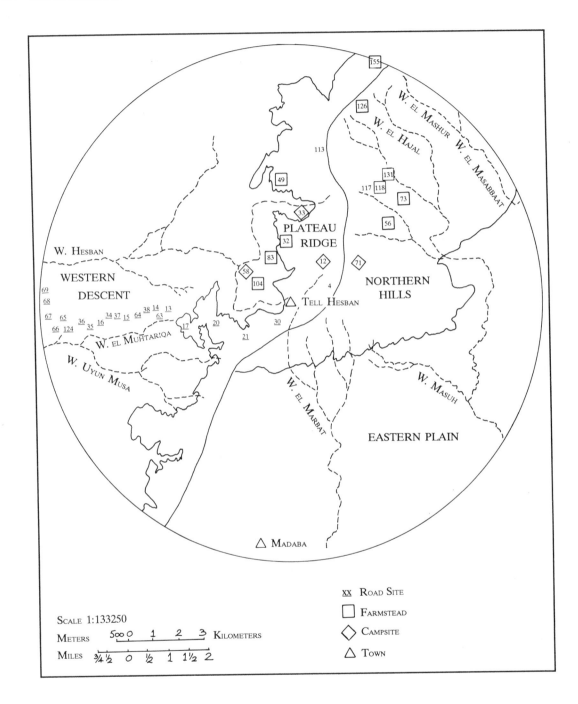

Plate 6.9   Roman cobblestone road east of Hesban Survey Site 35; view southeast

Plate 6.10   Roman curbstones between Hesban Survey Sites 13 and 17; view west

Farmsteads, Farming Villages, and Monastic Settlements

Farmsteads

The location of farm sites and farmsteads throughout Greco-Roman times corresponds pretty much to the pattern noted with regards to all sites from each of the different periods discussed above. During the Hellenistic centuries, 11 sites were occupied, more than half of which were located in the northern hills region. During the Early Roman centuries, 31 sites were occupied, the majority along the plateau ridge and in the northern hills regions. During Late Roman times 21 sites were occupied, this time primarily along the plateau ridge; and during Byzantine times, 61 sites were occupied, including 18 in the western descent region. Throughout the Greco-Roman centuries, therefore, there appears to have been a fairly steady intensification in sedentary farming activity along the plateau ridge, whereas in the other sub-regions such intensification was interrupted at least once by a century or two of abatement.

In terms of buildings and facilities, much of what had been utilized in the earlier Iron Age Period continued to be used during the Greco-Roman Period. For example, a typical, well-established farmstead would be located on a natural hill or on the slopes of a wadi above a fertile field of land. It would be surrounded by a perimeter wall with an opening leading onto a private access road, which, in the case of some larger estates, was paved (Geraty et al. 1986). Within the walls could be found one or more rectangular buildings of varying sizes (10 m x 20 m, 13 m x 20 m, 19 m x 21 m), a round or square agricultural tower ranging about an average of 11 m in diameter, one or more cisterns, and in some instances, a wine press, and a cave or two. In the case of some estates, even a family tomb was located nearby. Where the hillsides inside the perimeter walls were steep, some terrace walls would also be found. Sites fitting this pattern existed in varying quantities, as we have seen, throughout all of the centuries of the Greco-Roman Period within the project area.

In the absence of any detailed excavation data pertaining to either Iron Age or Roman farms in the project area, we can only speak in general terms about some of the ways in which the latter differed from the former. It is safe to assume, however, that the Roman and Byzantine farmsteads were more advanced in terms of how they collected and stored water, in their methods of storing, processing, and transporting foodstuffs, and also with regard to methods of cultivation and animal husbandry. Not only did the farmers of this period have the experience of the Nabataean farmers to draw upon right in their own backyard—including the opportunity in some instances to benefit directly where Nabataean terraces and farmsteads were reuseable—they also benefited from the farming know-how, new seeds, and new species of domestic animals introduced into the region by Nabataean merchants and Greek and Roman administrators and settlers in the region (cf. White 1970).

Farming Villages and Towns

In addition to the isolated farmsteads, farming villages and towns played an important role in the local economy. During the Hellenistic and Early Roman periods, Tell Hesban was the site of one such village, and Madaba was perhaps a slightly larger version of the same. Not only did these villages provide shelter for people and animals, they also served an important role as local centers of trade and manufacture of farm implements and ceramic storage vessels. While these two villages grew to become municipalities in their own right during the later Roman and Byzantine periods, other villages sprang up which took their place, as seen on the map from each of the periods.

The role of villages and towns as places of refuge for the farmstead population during times of uncertainty and trouble explains, perhaps, the persistence of such settlements during Late Roman times. As has already been noted, during this period there appears to have been a retreat of farming families from the farmsteads to the larger towns and villages. By contrast, the town of Hesban actually expanded during Late Roman times and all of the other major tell settlements within the project area (Sites 7, 26, 100, 102, 103)—sites where smaller villages and towns very likely existed—continued to survive as well. Indeed, there may actually have been an increase in the number of such village settlements between the Early and Late Roman periods.

An idea of the extent to which people were settled in villages and towns during the Late Roman and Byzantine periods can be gained from analysis of the detailed descriptions of settlements

Fig. 6.8 Byzantine Period sites (after Conder 1889 and Ibach 1987)

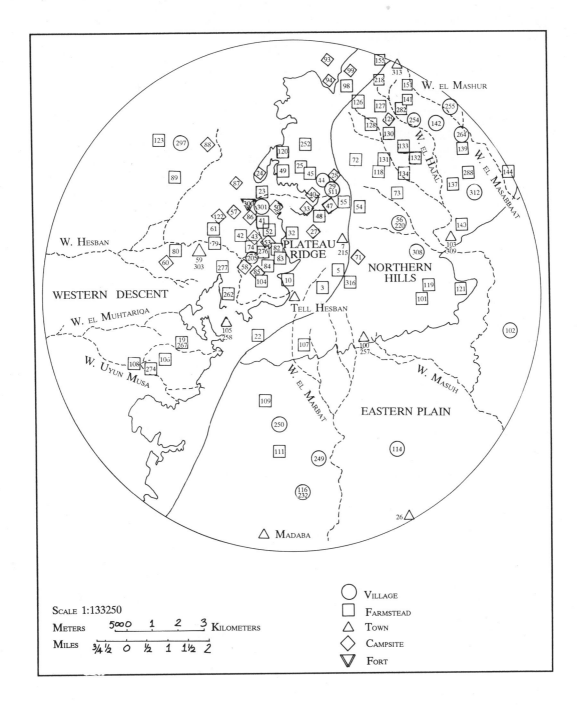

from this period recorded by Conder (1889). At the time of his visit to the Hesban region, the ruins from these periods (and also from the more recent Ayyubid-Mamluk period) were apparently much better preserved than they are today. One reason for this state of affairs, was, of course, that where he witnessed the ruins of houses with "vaults and barrel roofs"—the tell-tale mark of Roman and Byzantine construction—we today encounter villages and towns. Indeed, these were the vaults reused by the late 19th-century settlers in this region—at Madaba, Hesban, Umm el Hanafish, and so many of the other recently settled villages and towns—as framing for their first houses, as discussed in this chapter. Based on the information provided by both Conder (1889) and Ibach (1987), therefore, a much more complete picture can be gained of the Late Roman and Byzantine settlement pattern within the project area (fig. 6.8).

That Esbus and Madaba were sizable settlements during the Late Roman and Byzantine periods can be seen from the town plans prepared by Musil (1907) on his visit to both in 1902 (figs. 6.9 and 6.10). The fact that their ruins were much

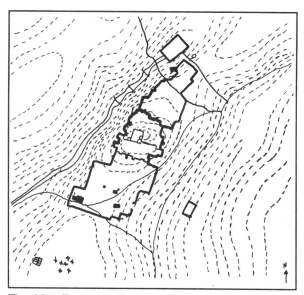

Fig. 6.9 Byzantine Esbus as sketched by Musil in 1902 (1907)

more extensive at the time of his visit is evident not only from the details he is able to include in his sketch, but also from his discussion in the text and that of others who spent some time inspecting the ruins, such as Conder (1889) and Brunnow and Domaszewski (1904).

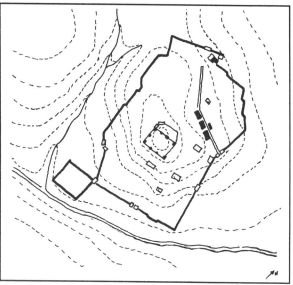

Fig. 6.10 Byzantine Madaba as sketched by Musil in 1902 (1907)

Hermitages and Monasteries

During Byzantine times, Christian hermitages and monasteries were established in several locations within the project area, including Mount Nebo, Uyun Musa, Umm el Qanafid, and Ain Sumia. Regarding the hermitages at Uyun Musa and the monastery at Mount Nebo, Saller and Bagatti (1949) have written in considerable detail. According to a 4th-century pilgrim account, monks had originally taken up residence in the caves surrounding Uyun Musa, but had by the 5th century "established themselves near the memorial of Moses on the top of Mount Nebo" (Saller and Bagatti 1949: 109). There they constructed a basilica with several chapels and a monastery complex consisting of a series of courtyards with buildings grouped around them. Both at Uyun Musa and on Mount Nebo, monks survived in monasteries and hermit caves from the 4th through the 7th centuries. In these places they cultivated gardens and "grew fruit and vegetables for the benefit of pilgrims" (Avi-Yonah 1958: 48). Perhaps some of them also engaged in pig breeding, especially in the vicinity of the springs at Uyun Musa (Avi-Yonah 1958: 48).

At Ain Sumia, Conder (1889: 221) encountered a building measuring

> 120 feet along its east wall, and 80 feet along the south wall. . . . There was a courtyard, with a vault or cistern beneath, and with chambers to

the north and south. On the east was an entrance-gate, approached by a narrow path on the face of a very steep slope.

These, according to Conder, may be the remains of either a fort or a monastery dating to Byzantine times. At Umm el Qanafid (Umm el Kenafid), Conder (1889: 249) encountered another monastic site, namely the remains of a hermit's cave. He offers no further details, however.

Marketplaces

Throughout the entire Greco-Roman millennium the settlements at Madaba and Hesban appear to have played an important role as local marketplaces. Their role as centers of trade is evidenced both by their comparatively large size and by the presence of public buildings of various kinds among their ruins. At Hesban, the remains of a "public plaza" are found in the Late Roman Period (Mitchel 1980: 150), and in subsequent periods, as has already been pointed out, the summit of the tell was turned into an acropolis with a paved colonnade, streets, and stairs. The same kind of facilities were located at Madaba as well during the Late Roman and Byzantine periods. Their strategic location on important highway crossings in Transjordan no doubt also contributed to their role as market towns. Furthermore, both towns also minted their own coins during Late Roman times, another sign of their status as centers of commerce.

Other locations within the project area which very likely served as local marketplaces during the Late Roman and Byzantine periods are those sites which have been designated as towns on fig. 6.8. These include the ruins located at Umm es Summaq (313), Umm el Hanafish (309), Jalul (26), Masuh (100, 257), El 'Al (7, 215), Ain Sumia (59, 303), Mushaqqar (105, 258), and Qaryat el Mukheiyat (172). At all of these locations, the remains of numerous buildings and monumental architecture are suggestive of their role as gathering places for the surrounding population.

Fortifications

The most famous fortification located within the project area is the one at Khirbet el Mehatta (36). Located on a high ridge overlooking the Jordan Valley, it has the shape of a triangular structure which was traced by Ibach (1987) for over 600 m. A popular site with visitors to this region, it has been commented upon frequently in reports by Tristram (1865), Thomson (1880), Conder (1889), and Henke (1959). As already noted, this site was settled already in Hellenistic times and continued in use right through to the end of the Byzantine Period.

Other than this major military installation which, as was noted earlier, may also have been converted into a monastery in Byzantine times, only one other site is described as being a "fort" in Conder's (1889) account, namely the one at Shunet edh Dhiabeh (300). It is "a small fort built on the hillside west of the stream of Wadi Hesban" which "measures 35 paces square outside, with a courtyard on the south, measuring 150 feet by 100 feet" (Conder 1889: 27). Mention has already been made of the fort which apparently existed at Tell Hesban during the Hellenistic Period.

The Water Supply System

Crucial to the sedentarization which occurred in the project area during the Greco-Roman millennium was the construction of facilities for collecting and storing water (fig. 6.11). This was particularly the case at places like Hesban and Madaba where large concentrations of people had to survive the dry season without having easy access to a spring or stream. To begin to meet this challenge, the Romans undertook the construction of several large reservoirs in the major towns, and cisterns were added in great profusion.

Reservoirs

The largest reservoir discovered in the project area is the one at Madaba which is commented upon by almost every one of the explorers who visited the place (Tristram 1880: 252; Thomson 1880: 637; Conder 1889: 182; Brunnow and Domaszewski 1904: 19; Musil 1907: 113). Thomson's description of it highlights both the massiveness of the undertaking it represents and its likely uses in antiquity:

> Between the hill on which the church stood and the city in the shallow vale is a large reservoir or tank. It is about three hundred and thirty feet long from east to west, and three hundred and twelve feet broad from north to south, measuring from the inside. It is over fifteen feet deep from the top of the wall to the soil which now covers

Fig. 6.11 Project area water supply

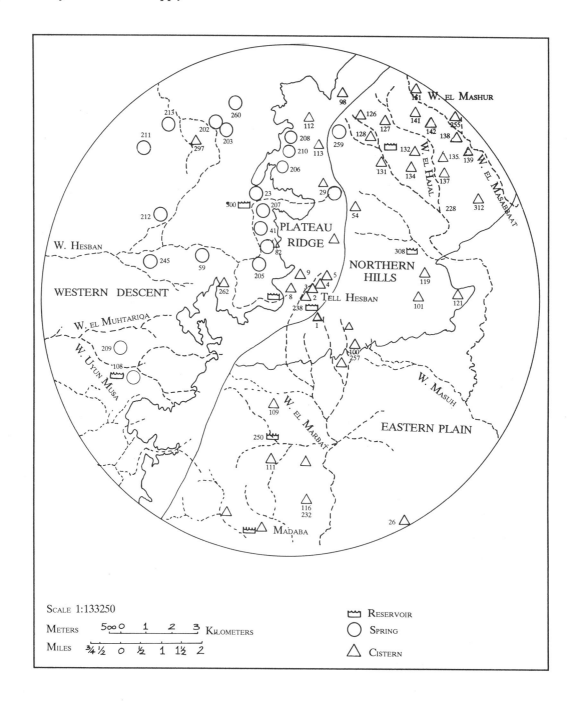

the bottom, and which is often planted with tobacco.

At the south-east and north-east corners stone steps led down to the water, and on the latter corner was a strongly built tower, probably for the defence of the reservoir. The wall is in excellent preservation, and is about twenty feet high and twelve feet thick; but on the east side at the base it is over eighteen feet wide, diminishing to twelve feet at the top, and further strengthened by a massive embankment, as it was exposed on that side to the heaviest pressure from the great body of water within the reservoir.

A strong dam was carried across the shallow valley southward to lead the water into the tank during the rainy season. It has long since been washed away, and the reservoir is now always empty. It would require but little expense to put that large reservoir into complete repair, and thus secure an abundant supply of water, not only for all necessary domestic purposes but also to irrigate the fertile fields below it to the south-east (Thomson 1880: 637).

Other dams as well were found at Madaba. Tristram (1880: 252) reports seeing a reservoir in the town itself "that had been roofed over, which was thirty feet deep, and still another which was one hundred feet in one direction; but in the other direction it could not be measured, as it had been covered by fallen ruin." In the vicinity of Tell Hesban the remains of at least two reservoirs were noted by explorers at the turn of the century (Warren 1869: 289; Fish 1876: 320; Conder 1889: 104; Musil 1907: 384). For example, Musil's account includes the measurements of two reservoirs, one to the north of the tell in the Wadi Majarr and another in the Wadi el Marbat to the south. The one to the north of Tell Hesban measured 14 m or 46 ft² (cf. Conder 1889: 104) and it had four wide stairs leading down into it (Musil 1907: 386). The one to the south of the tell was 67 m (219 ft) long and 46 m (150 ft) wide. Additional details about it were recorded by Conder (1889: 105):

On the south of the Tell is the flat open valley which leads to the southern plateau, the city being mainly on a saddle dividing this valley head from the true watershed. In the open valley is the great tank to which the name "Alwan" appears to apply. It measures 191 ft. north and south by 139 ft. east and west, and is about 10 ft. deep. The masonry is well dressed, but the stones are not drafted; the walls have been apparently shaken by earthquake; stones were measured 15 in. long by 11 in. high, and 10 in. by 15 in., representing

the average dimensions of the ashlar. In the south-east corner of this tank lies a trough measuring 6 ft. 2 in. by 3 ft. outside, and 5 ft. by 20 in. inside; the height 18 in. outside and 12 in. inside. It has probably fallen from above, and was no doubt used for watering animals when the tank was full of water.

In 1974 a probe was carried out in this reservoir by the Hesban excavation staff (Herr 1976: 107-108; Storfjell 1983: 107, 171). Measurements taken at that time correspond roughly to those taken by Conder and Musil. Excavations revealed that this reservoir had been constructed in Early Byzantine times (Stratum 9) and that it had a plastered bottom. Because of damages sustained as a result of an earthquake, its walls were repaired again in Late Byzantine times (Stratum 8).

Elsewhere in the project area reservoirs of varying sizes can be found as well, especially in the vicinity of ruins of larger settlements. Between Conder's (1889) and Ibach's (1987) surveys, a total of 19 sites containing reservoirs have been found within the project area, including those at Hesban and Madaba. Of these 5 sites were located in the western descent region, 2 along the plateau ridge, 6 in the northern hills, and 6 in the eastern plain.

Not only were these reservoirs used to collect drinking water for animals, they were also frequently used as tanks for holding irrigation water. This type of use was clearly the case with the reservoirs at Hesban. The one in the Wadi Majarr, for example, had a step-wise series of cultivable shelves below it, each shelf being held in place by a retaining wall of stones. A similar use was no doubt also made of the tank to the south of the tell, although traces of retaining walls have still to be searched for.

Cisterns and Water Channels

Throughout the project area are cisterns of varying shapes and sizes, the majority of which were no doubt in use during Late Roman and Byzantine times. The combined sightings of Conder (1889) and Ibach (1987) yielded a total of 49 sites containing cisterns within the project area. Of these, 3 are located in the western descent, 14 along the plateau ridge, 22 in the northern hills and 10 in the eastern plain. More often than not several cisterns existed at each of these sites.

The manner in which concern with water collection intensified over the Greco-Roman millennium is exemplified in the stratigraphic evidence from

Plate 6.11   Byzantine plastered floor (Locus 26) of Reservoir G.5A; view west

Plate 6.12   Late Hellenistic underground plastered circular Pool B.4:265 cut in bedrock Cave B.4:247; view southeast

Plate 6.13   Water system in C.4. In right foreground are Water Channels C.4:68; mouth of Cistern C.4.7 on left; opening to Basin C.4:71 visible in center of picture in south balk; view south

Plate 6.14   Mouth of Cistern C.5:228; view east down

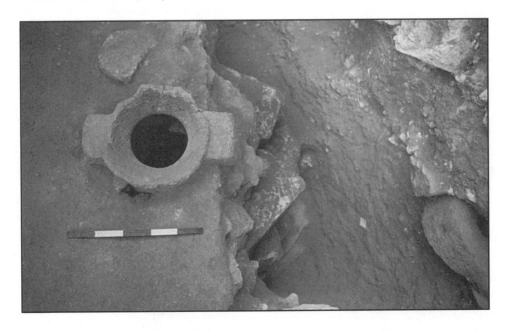

Tell Hesban, despite the limited horizontal exposure of the excavations. Thus, neither during the Late Hellenistic (Stratum 15), nor during the Early Roman times (Stratum 14) was any evidence of construction activity having to do with water collection encountered. Very likely, the population was taking advantage of cisterns already constructed in Iron Age times to meet their water supply needs.

As could be expected, perhaps, it was during Late Roman times (Strata 13-11) that construction activity aimed at improving the water supply appears. This concern is evidenced by the discovery of two drainage channels which "were installed in the uppermost Stratum 13 layers or surfaces." One of these "was built of side stones and capstones" (Mitchel 1980: 136). Another such channel was found in Stratum 12, while in Stratum 11 a large cistern (C.5:228) was discovered (Mitchel 1980: 159, 191, 194).

This concern with water supply clearly escalated during Byzantine times. In the four strata dating to this period (Strata 10-7) at least nine separate water channels were found to be in use (C.4:68; A.7:65; D.6:63; D.5:20; D.1:89; D.2:30; D.6:53; D.5:16; and C.1:15). One of these was actually a catch basin for rain water (D.6:63), others were simply channels draining water into cisterns, and in one case (C.4:68—see pl. 6.13), the channel actually served as an overflow drain directing the water to cisterns below (Storfjell 1983: 31, 39). Several cisterns were also uncovered which were in use during this period.

The fact that many cisterns are located in places where there are no other ruins except, perhaps, a wine press, suggests that in addition to serving as storage places for drinking water, many of these cisterns were also used to hold water for irrigation of crops and watering of animals. By this means, fruit trees and vegetables could be produced in the absence of any other perennial sources of water. This was very likely the case in the northern hills region during Late Roman and Byzantine times. In this region several of the farmsteads very likely irrigated fruit and vegetable crops by means of cistern water.

Springs and Streams

There can be no doubt that the springs and streams which are abundant in the western descent region remained a constant resource for the trans-humant population of the project area throughout the entire Greco-Roman millennium. During the Roman, and especially the Byzantine Period, however, many springs such as those at Uyun Musa, Ain Sumia, Ain Hesban, Ain el Fudeli, Ain Jamus, and El Rawda became sources of irrigation water for cultivators growing fruits and vegetables on terraced slopes below them. Even some of the nearby slopes above these springs were often terraced and watered by means of animals hauling water in skins to the cultivated areas. The best example in the project area of this type of use of spring waters is found at Uyun Musa.

Aqueducts

Evidence of aqueducts is sparse in the project area. That they were used in a limited way to transport water from certain of the springs in the western descent region is possible, however. Conder (1889: 4-5) discovered near the spring at Ain el Fudeli, for example, that "numerous dams and lades lead from the spring towards the remains of former irrigated places. Traces of one little aqueduct lead to the Jineinet Belkis, or 'Zenobia's garden,' which is a mere barren plot."

Wine Presses

In the vicinity of ancient farmsteads, villages and vineyard sites throughout the project area can be found the remains of numerous rock-cut wine presses (fig. 6.12). As could be expected, such presses are most abundant along the plateau ridge and in the western descent subregions, although they occur also on certain of the slopes in the northern hills subregion.

Such presses are particularly abundant in the vicinity of the town of Nebo and at Siyagha where the Byzantine monastery is located. Here dozens of presses of varying shapes and dimensions have been found, including ones with fan-shaped basins, rectangular basins, and "irregular" basins (Saller and Bagatti 1949: 13). A similar variety was noted by Conder at other sites throughout the western descent and plateau ridge subregions (cf. Conder 1889: 146, 151, 157, 171).

As with so many other agricultural installations in this region, it is not possible to say exactly when these wine presses were built and when they were used. Certainly, some of them predate the Greco-Roman millennium, having been built sometime during the Iron Age or possibly even earlier. There

Fig. 6.12 Project area wine presses and water-driven mills

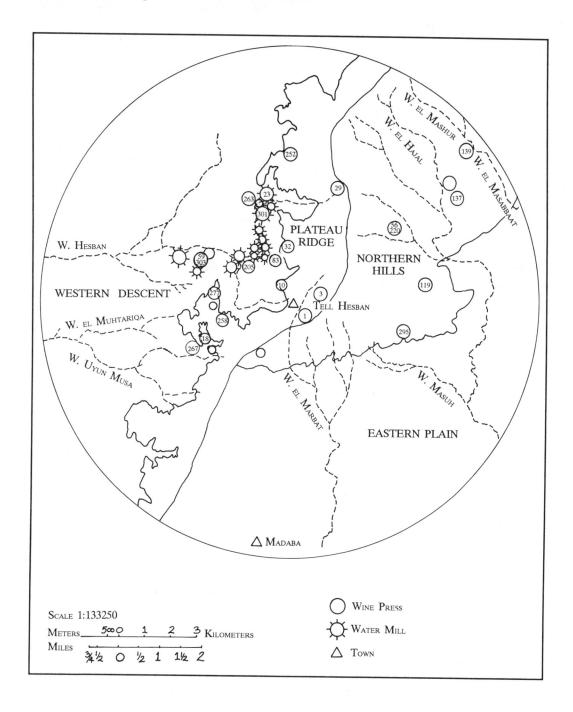

can be little doubt, however, that the vast majority of them were in use during the Byzantine Period. Thus, of the 10 presses sherded by Ibach's team (Ibach 1987), Byzantine pottery was found at 9 of them. This was evidently also a period during which some of the finest presses were built. In the monastery at Mount Nebo, for example, a press was uncovered which had a mosaic floor and masonry lining (Saller and Bagatti 1949: 13).

Water-driven Mills

While nearly a dozen water-driven flour mills were noted by the Hesban Survey (Ibach 1987) in the Wadi Hesban, most were not sherded or catalogued as sites except for one, namely the one at Ain Hesban (Site 23); and it turned up Roman and Byzantine pottery. The possibility that most of these mills might originally have been constructed during the 4th or 5th century A.D. should be seriously considered, however, despite the limited pottery evidence on hand. This is because water-driven flour mills of various kinds became a widespread phenomenon throughout the Roman Empire during these times (Dalman 1964: 243-249; Forbes 1955 vol. 2: 88-111; Landels 1981: 16-26; Parker 1982: 18, 1985: 19).

Of all the wadis in the project area, the Wadi Hesban was certainly the most natural place to install these mills, given its perennial flow. Furthermore, given the intensity of human settlement in the vicinity of this wadi during the 4th and 5th centuries, the conditions were unquestionably right for the adoption of a device which would harness the springs and streams of this wadi to the benefit of people. Finally, it might also be pointed out that the Wadi Hesban was not the only stream in Jordan thus exploited. At least a dozen such mills are located in the Wadi Ajlun further north in Jordan as well (Merrill 1881: 374).

Storage Facilities

Of all the various operational facilities encountered on the tell and in the survey territory, none are more varied than are the arrangements for storing food supplies. On the one hand are the installations which apparently were specifically constructed for the purpose of food storage, such as the storage silos discovered at Late Hellenistic Hesban (Stratum 15). These silos, which the excavator believes were used for grain storage, can with confidence be distinguished from cisterns because

they were connected by a network of tunnels and showed no signs of plastering (Mitchel 1980: 35).

On the other hand are the great range of makeshift storage facilities such as caves, tombs, rooms restored from ruined buildings, and so forth. Of these, caves were the most frequently encountered both on the tell and in the survey territory. Such caves were represented at Tell Hesban in strata from both Roman and Byzantine times as well as at dozens of the sites with pottery from these periods. Inside these storage installations and makeshift facilities, flour and other dry goods, along with supplies of drinking water and wine, were preserved in pottery storage jars, a great variety of which have been uncovered in the finds from Tell Hesban (Lugenbeal and Sauer 1972).

The near absence of storage silos in the Late Roman and Byzantine strata at Tell Hesban does not necessarily mean that they did not exist elsewhere on the tell during these periods. Indeed, they very likely did. What accounts for this is very likely the fact that much of what was excavated from these periods came from the acropolis area of the town. Domestic storage installations of this type, therefore, were not likely to be encountered. Public and commercial buildings specifically constructed for the purpose of food storage would be more likely occurrences in this location during these periods. Such may well have been the case in Early Byzantine Stratum 9 where a storage facility of a "commercial nature" may have existed, judging from the remains in Square B.4 (Storfjell 1983: 106). Other types of buildings devoted primarily to food storage which could be expected during the Late Roman and Byzantine periods would be public granaries, although no such facilities have been discovered either on the tell or in the project area to date.

Fire Pits and Tabuns

Several fire pits were encountered at Tell Hesban, one in Late Hellenistic Stratum 15 (C.2:46), one in Early Roman Stratum 14 (D.3:54), one each in Late Roman Strata 12 (A.7:77) and 11 (A.1:62), and one in Early Byzantine Stratum 10 (A.5:23). Typically these fire pits consisted of deposits of ash or burnt materials indicating that fires had once been burned in this spot. The fact that only one fire pit was found in strata from the Byzantine Period is another sign of the gradual evolution of occupational activity on the summit of the tell away

Plate 6.15   Wine press at Hesban Survey Site 36 (Ateyig); view west

Plate 6.16   Early Roman *Tabun* B.4:84 with air intake hole at bottom; view north

from domestic toward public and commercial affairs.

Baking ovens or *tabuns* were encountered only in Early Roman Stratum 14 (B.4:66, 84, 261, 262). Whereas *Tabun* B.4:261 measured *ca.* 0.50 m in diameter, the one in B.4:262 had a diameter of *ca.* 0.35 m (Sauer 1976: 51). The presence of four *tabuns* in this Early Roman stratum suggests that a sizable population had come to rely on the oven-baked bread of villagers rather than the pan-baked bread of transhumants. The process of sedentarization was clearly well on its way by the Early Roman Period.

Enclosure Walls

During Greco-Roman times, as in other times, enclosure walls played an important role in keeping animals and people from entering orchards, gardens, and private courtyards. As already noted, such walls surrounded the farmsteads and orchards in the survey territory. They also make up a significant proportion of the structures encountered in the various strata on the tell. Although the evidence on hand does not permit any quantitative statement about the increase in the density of walls per unit of land, that such an increase occurred over the Greco-Roman millennium is very likely. As the food system intensified, more land was set aside for intensive orcharding and vegetable production. Such uses of the land necessitated greater concern with protection of the crops, something which, in part at least, could be achieved by the raising of increasing numbers of walls and fences.

Animal Folds and Shelters

The most common form of shelters for animals since prehistoric times in the survey territory has no doubt been caves. Indeed, most caves found in this region have surfaces which consist of layers of dung, mostly sheep and goat dung. In addition to these, make-shift shelters are sometimes constructed in partially standing ruins. That animals and people shared the same shelters is very likely. One of the tombs in Cemetery F, for example, appears to have served as a shelter for both people and animals during the Early Roman Period.

That numerous animal folds existed throughout the project area during the Greco-Roman millennium can safely be assumed. Conder (1889: 208), for example, makes brief mention of the existence of a "Byzantine cattle enclosure" at Rujm Serarah.

On his map he also pinpoints several "goat folds." Typically, folds consist of enclosures made of un-hewn stones. In many cases these enclosures are divided into several distinct partitions for separating herds into smaller groups (*cf.* Murray and Chang 1980).

Draft Power

Besides people themselves, the most important source of draft power during all periods in the project area was cattle. As already noted, oxen were harnessed to the plow primarily on the eastern plain and on the gentle slopes, whereas horses, asses, and especially mules were preferred on the steep slopes. The increase in use of horses, mules, and donkeys which is evident in the Late Roman and Byzantine periods is, as has already been suggested, a sign of the more intensive exploitation of steep slopes for vineyards during these periods. As can still be seen today, mounted transport was provided by camels, horses, mules, and donkeys in the Greco-Roman millennium as well.

Sanitation

Of the structures uncovered in the Greco-Roman strata from Tell Hesban none appear to have been built specifically for the purpose of sewage drainage, as can be found at Gerasa, for example (Kraeling 1938). That sanitary measures were taken by the people of this site can be inferred, however, from the fact that the bones of traditionally unclean animals such as horses, mules, and donkeys were deposited away from the settled areas. The remains of these animals, therefore, are less plentiful in the bone finds than are the remains of cattle, sheep, and goats. What was found of equine bones in deposits on the tell owes its location there to dogs and other scavenging animals that took the bones back into the settled area.

Indeed, the most important agency in getting rid of scraps of food and other organic garbage were, no doubt, the domestic cat, dog, pig, and chicken. Between these and other wild scavengers, such as jackals and hyenas, anything edible would be disposed of which was within their reach. As has been noted elsewhere (LaBianca 1978a), it is thanks to the cisterns and other subterranean installations on the tell into which literally hundreds of bones were washed during the rainy season in this region that bones of any kind survived to be included in this study.

Table 6.3 Weight of principal meat-yielding species from Greco-Roman strata (in kg)

Strata	Period	Cattle kg	Cattle %	Sheep/Goat kg	Sheep/Goat %	Pig kg	Pig %	Camel kg	Camel %	Total kg	Total %	Accumulation Rates
1	Modern	1.4	27.45	3.0	58.82	0.2	3.92	0.5	9.80	5.1	4.65	0.05
2-3	Mamluk	14.2	30.67	25.2	54.43	0.8	1.73	6.1	13.17	46.3	42.21	0.24
4	Ayyubid	0.1	33.33	0.2	66.67	--	--	--	--	0.3	0.27	0.01
5	Abbasid	0.2	16.67	0.8	66.67	--	--	0.2	16.67	1.2	1.09	0.01
6	Umayyad	1.6	33.33	2.4	50.00	0.6	12.50	0.2	4.17	4.8	4.38	0.06
7-10	Byzantine	2.3	31.51	3.7	50.68	1.1	15.07	0.2	2.74	7.3	6.65	0.02
11-13	Late Roman	4.4	31.43	7.6	54.28	0.9	6.43	1.1	7.86	14.0	12.76	0.06
14	Early Roman	1.9	33.33	3.3	57.89	0.3	5.26	0.2	3.51	5.7	5.20	0.03
15	Late Hellenistic	3.1	46.27	2.8	41.79	--	--	0.8	11.94	6.7	6.11	0.05
16-18	Iron 2	4.6	40.00	6.3	54.78	0.3	2.61	0.3	2.61	11.5	10.48	0.02
19	Iron 1	3.1	45.59	2.9	42.65	0.3	4.41	0.5	7.35	6.8	6.20	0.03

Table 6.4 Number of identified specimens of fish from Greco-Roman strata

Strata	Period	Family Cichildæ Combs #	%	Family Claridæ Catfish #	%	Family Cyprinidæ Minnows #	%	Family Mugilidæ Grey Mullets #	%	Family Scaridæ Parrot Fish #	%	Family Sciænidæ Drums & Croakers #	%	Family Scombridæ Mackerel-like Fish #	%	Family Serranidæ Bass #	%	Family Sparidæ Sea Breams #	%	Total #	%
1	Modern	1	50.0	1	50.0	--	--	--	--	--	--	--	--	--	--	--	--	--	--	2	0.3
2-3	Mamluk	18	12.3	33	22.6	5	3.4	4	2.7	84	57.5	1	0.7	--	--	--	--	1	0.7	146	19.5
4	Ayyubid	--	--	--	--	--	--	--	--	--	--	--	--	--	--	--	--	--	--		
5	Abbasid	--	--	3	75.0	--	--	--	--	1	25.0	--	--	--	--	--	--	--	--	4	5.6
6	Umayyad	25	59.5	8	19.0	--	--	1	2.4	7	16.7	--	--	--	--	1	2.4	--	--	4	0.5
7-10	Byzantine	8	33.3	8	33.3	--	--	--	--	5	20.8	1	4.2	1	4.2	--	--	1	4.2	24	3.2
11-13	Late Roman	1	1.2	1	1.2	--	--	--	--	1	1.2	--	--	79	96.3	--	--	--	--	82	10.9
14	Early Roman	1	1.4	1	1.4	--	--	--	--	1	1.4	62	89.9	4	5.8	--	--	--	--	69	9.2
15	Late Hellenistic	--	--	1	0.3	--	--	--	--	--	--	--	--	372	99.7	--	--	--	--	373	49.8
16-18	Iron 2	--	--	--	--	--	--	--	--	1	14.3	--	--	--	--	1	14.3	5	71.4	7	0.9
19	Iron 1	--	--	--	--	--	--	--	--	--	--	--	--	--	--	--	--	--	--	--	--
Sum	All	54	7.2	56	7.5	5	0.7	5	0.7	100	13.3	64	8.5	456	60.9	2	0.3	7	0.9	749	100

Changes in Dietary Conditions

Introduction

The first point to keep in mind as the evidence for dietary changes during the Greco-Roman millennium is evaluated, is that direct evidence in the form of plant and animal remains is available only from the excavations at Tell Hesban and not from any other sites in the surrounding project area. Given, as we have seen, the existence of a heterogenous population in this region throughout the Greco-Roman millennium, it is obvious that the practices attested to in the remains from Tell Hesban cannot be attributed to the population of the project area as a whole. Indeed, as we shall see, Tell Hesban offers information primarily regarding the dietary preference of a Hellenized, Romanized and Christianized population respectively. The site has little to offer in understanding dietary changes which occurred among other, more traditional members inhabiting the hinterlands of the site.

A second point to keep in mind is the changing occupational context from which the data on hand were recovered. As we noted earlier, the activity pattern on the tell's summit where most of the excavation areas were located underwent a gradual transformation away from domestic use toward public use during this millennium. This transformation, as we have seen, gained considerable momentum in Late Roman times and continued until the latter part of the Byzantine Period. This situation is partially to blame for the diminishing rate at which both plant and animal remains accumulated in tell deposits during the latter part of this millennium.

A third point to keep in mind is that the best represented food remains are the bones of domestic ungulates, especially sheep, goats, and cattle. This is due, of course, to the fact that their remains are more resistant than plant remains to destruction. Thus, the fact that animal remains generally receive more attention in this discussion than do plant remains should not be taken as a sign that they were more important in meeting the nutritional needs of the population. Indeed, to a large degree, the diets in antiquity consisted for the most part of plant foods, as do those of most people in the nonindustrialized world today. In the discussion which follows, reference will be made to the data presented in tables 6.1-6.5.

The Late Hellenistic Diet at Esbus (Tell Hesban)

The diet of the Late Hellenistic inhabitants at Tell Hesban is clearly reflective of the Greek palate and, therefore, as discussed earlier, of the role of these inhabitants as agents of Hellenization in this corner of Palestine. In support of this impression is the discovery in Late Hellenistic Stratum 15 of 372 bone fragments belonging to the *Scombridæ* family of fish (mackerels and tunnies). As has been noted by von den Driesch and Boessneck (forthcoming), and also by Tannahill (1973: 96-100), mackerels and tunnies were used in the production of *liquamen* (or *garum*), a type of Greek, and later Roman, fish sauce used to season foods. This sauce was possibly transported to the site in Rhodian amphora jars, several of which were found in Late Hellenistic deposits at Tell Hesban (Cox 1976: 149-155).

Another possible evidence of the Greek palate at Tell Hesban in the Hellenistic Period is the high proportion of pulses, especially peas and vetches. As the Brothwells (1969: 106) have noted, "the Greeks made great use of the pulses in their diet, indeed they even had a god of Beans, and held a 'bean feast' in honour of Apollo. Pea soup was made and could be bought hot in the streets."

Another important feature about the Late Hellenistic diet at Esbus was the relative importance of camel meat in it. As noted earlier, transhumant camel nomads existed side by side with settled cultivators in this region during Hellenistic times. These nomads were very likely the producers of much of the camel meat consumed by the Greek settlers at Esbus.

The fact that cattle are represented so prominently in the Late Hellenistic stratum is suggestive not only of their importance as draft animals, but also of their importance in the diet. Beef appears, in fact, to have been consumed in greater propor-

tions during the Hellenistic Period than during any subsequent period in this millennium. Mutton and goats' meat were also consumed, but in proportionately smaller quantities than during later centuries.

Other items in the Late Hellenistic diet at Esbus included, of course, wheat, barley, and oats. These were used by the Greeks to make various kinds of breads, pastes, and porridges (Tannahill 1973: 80). Chicken and swine were eaten as well, but not in the quantities they were consumed in the subsequent Roman and Byzantine centuries (cf. Boessneck and von den Driesch forthcoming). Olives and grapes were also eaten, but again, not in the amounts they were consumed in these later centuries.

Strata	Period	# of Bones #	# of Bones %	Min # of Individuals #	Min # of Individuals %	% Young
1	Modern	---	---	---	---	---
2-4	Ayyubid-Mamluk	1566	65.83	128	58.44	22.0
5-6	Umayyad-Abbasid	127	5.34	13	5.94	8.0
7-10	Byzantine	231	9.71	27	12.33	11.5
11-14	Roman	410	17.23	41	18.72	14.2
15	Late Hellenistic	41	1.72	7	3.20	14.6
16-18	Iron 2	3	0.13	2	0.91	---
19	Iron 1	1	0.04	1	0.46	---
Sum	All	2379	100	219	100	

Table 6.5 Number of identified specimens of chicken from Greco-Roman strata

The Roman Diet at Esbus

The most distinctive feature of the changes in dietary preferences which occurred during the Roman centuries, judging from the data on hand, was increased eating of swine. Between the Late Hellenistic and Late Roman periods the rate of swine consumption jumped from 0.3% to 14%.

Along with this came an increase in the eating of poultry, especially chicken, but also geese and pigeons (Boessneck and von den Driesch 1978a: 266-267). The use of *garum* appears to have continued as well. In addition, a wider variety of both fresh-water and salt-water fish was being imported, including combs (family *Chiclidæ*), parrotfishes (family *Scaridæ*), catfishes (order *Cypriniformes*), drums and croakers (family *Sciænidæ*), sea breams (family *Sparidæ*), mackerels and tunnies (family *Scombridæ*). The fact that Mediterranean species, especially drums, croakers, and mackerels, are the most abundantly represented is an indication of the active trade which went on between Transjordan and coastal cities in Palestine during the Roman Period. More will be said about the implications of the fish finds for our understanding of ancient trade routes in Chapter Eight.

This increased reliance on swine, poultry, and exotic items like the various types of fish, is to be expected, especially during Late Roman times, when Esbus was transformed from a small village into a moderate-sized town located at the crossing of several major highways. The Esbus-Livias-Jerusalem road would have been especially important in facilitating the transportation of fish from the Mediterranean and the Jordan River to Esbus.

Increases in the eating of swine and poultry appears to have gradually diminished the use of beef in the diet, especially during Late Roman times. The shifts in the pattern of consumption of camels' meat are, as we have suggested earlier, understandable in light of the side-by-side existence of transhumant camel nomads and settled cultivators in this region during Roman times as well. Thus, the increased percentage of camels' meat in the diet during the latest Roman stratum can be viewed as being a reflection of a return to camel nomadism by disinherited tribes in the hinterlands. This process would have led to an increase in the supply of camels' meat.

The diminishing importance of sheep and goats between the Early Roman strata and the later ones is probably reflective of a combination of factors, including the increasing role of swine and poultry raising in the towns and villages, and the aforementioned return to camel nomadism among hinterland tribes. Regarding grains, pulses, vegetables, and fruits, not much can be said given the meagerness of the plant remains on hand. It can safely be inferred, however, from the other lines of evidence discussed above, that the principal field crops of antiquity were used in the diet, including wheat, barley, oats, lentils, peas, and beans.

Besides grapes and olives, other fruits, including figs, dates, apples, apricots, and pears, were also very likely consumed (Forbes 1955 vol. 3: 54). The variety of such grains, pulses, fruits, and vegetables in the Roman diet very likely increased, just as was the case with the fish, poultry, and meat supply, after the Roman road network made interregional exchange of produce more feasible and profitable.

The Byzantine Diet at Esbus

The Byzantine diet was, to a large degree, much like that of the earlier Roman Period. Thus swine, poultry, and fish remained popular substitutes for beef, mutton, and goats' meat, the latter being in relatively short supply in this era of orchards, gardens, and field crops. The drastic increase, however, in equine remains during this period, and the fact that butchering marks were encountered on the pelvis bones of at least one equine find, may be indicative of the consumption of horse meat by certain classes at Esbus during Byzantine times (Boessneck and von den Driesch 1978a: 265).

The sharp drop-off in the percentages of camel remains from the Byzantine strata may be a measure of the extent to which camel pastoralists were excluded from their traditional pastures in the hinterlands of Esbus. Given the density of human settlement during this period, and the wide extent to which cultivation was pushed, there simply were not sufficient grazing areas left in the plains and valleys to permit large herds of camels to graze. Instead, herds of sheep and, especially goats were kept which could better exploit the less accessible grazing lands along the steep slopes and ridges of the western descent region. A slight rise in the quantity of sheep and, especially goats gives added support to this explanation.

The diversity which characterized the Late Roman diet, and the reliance on imported items such as fish, may have been even more apparent during Byzantine times. This is the impression gained, at least, from the fish finds which show comparatively higher quantities across the various species represented than during previous periods.

While field crops like wheat, barley, oats, lentils, peas, beans, and vetch no doubt continued to play a role as staple items in the diet, it is very likely that fruits and vegetables were eaten in greater quantities as well, given the widespread presence of gardens and orchards throughout the project area during Byzantine times. Exotic foods and spices were also very likely more common than ever before, given the trade network to which the people at Esbus had access.

Sedentarization and Nomadization

The foregoing analysis of the changes which took place in the food system of Esbus (Tell Hesban) and vicinity between *ca.* 333 B.C. and A.D. 661 has focused attention on the changes which were introduced as a result of the Greco-Roman power drive in this region as well as on the response to this situation by the rural population. Specifically, data gathered by means of surface surveys and stratigraphic excavations were examined to ascertain what changes were observable with reference to five interrelated aspects of the food system, namely environment, settlement, landuse, operational facilities, and diet. On the one hand, the evidence available reveals a gradual process of intensification of the food system. This was brought about as the result of several powerful forces set in motion by the Greeks and the Romans. To begin with, the process of Hellenization which followed Alexander the Great's conquest of the Orient in 333 B.C. led to new markets and long-distance trade opening up from India and China to Egypt and Greece. In Transjordan, this catalyzed the rise to power of the Nabataean Arabs who with their camels and knowledge of the desert caravan routes were able to capitalize on the new opportunities for caravaneering and commercial exchange.

With the arrival of the Romans in Palestine *ca.* 63 B.C., the Nabataeans were slowly forced to relinquish their control of the trade routes. Gradually they turned their skills to the improvement of the desert agricultural techniques for which they have also become famous. Their accomplishments in agriculture laid the foundation for the subsequent development and expansion of floodwater cultivation techniques in Transjordan in the Greco-Roman millennium, especially during the Late Roman and Byzantine centuries.

During the Hellenistic centuries, the Hesban region was the home of both settled villagers and transhumant camel nomads. Tell Hesban or Esbus itself was not settled until Late Hellenistic times. Its rebuilders were persons with Greek tastes and concerns, for the site functioned primarily as a fort and appears to have been occupied by soldiers who also were farmers. Extensively cultivated were field crops including wheat, barley, oats, peas, lentils, beans, and vetch. The inhabitants of Esbus may very well have played an important role not only as agents of Hellenization, but also as local leaders in reintroducing sedentary agriculture in this region.

During the Early Roman Period, Esbus continued to be used as a fort and as a temporary place of shelter and work for semisedentary cul-

tivators and transhumant pastoralists. The Late Roman Period, however, was a time of rapid urbanization at Esbus and intensification of landuse in its hinterlands. An important catalyst in this transformation was that during this period Esbus became a way-station on the Esbus-Livias road. The town was also connected to the *via nova Traiana*, the main highway running north-south in Transjordan.

The process of urbanization which took hold during the Late Roman Period was accompanied by expansion of the tree-fruit production sector of the local economy, especially in the vicinity of Esbus and along the road between it and Amman. At the same time, however, there are signs of cultivators actually abandoning their farms in the northern hills and on the plains to the east of Esbus. Thus a process of polarization appears to have gained momentum in the region during Late Roman times as well. While certain of the rural population migrated to the larger towns and villages, others returned to pastoral pursuits.

The Hesban region reached the height of its maximization drive during the Early Byzantine Period. Not only is there evidence of extensive use of Nabataean-style floodwater irrigation technology during this period, Roman-style reservoirs and water mills were added on a scale never before seen in the region as well. This is also the period during which more villages and towns were settled than in any previous age. What catalyzed this intensification was, among other factors, the influx of capital to the region in the wake of Constantine I's conversion to Christianity. As Avi-Yonah (1958) has pointed out, this event led to a new influx of capital to Palestine, as pilgrims and pious men and women in other lands bestowed their wealth on the region.

One apparent consequence of this intensification was that there was little room left for the traditional camel nomads in Transjordan. Their way of life could no longer be accommodated because of the intensity with which every potential plot of pasture was exploited for cultivation or herding of swine, goats, and sheep. This alienation of the camel-pastoralists in Transjordan and elsewhere in the Byzantine world led, as is well known, to the build-up of a reservoir of Arab tribesmen in the desert, which, in time, became the rallying point for the Muslim takeover of the ancient Greco-Roman world under the banner of Islam.

Chapter Seven

CONFIGURATIONS OF THE FOOD SYSTEM DURING THE ISLAMIC CENTURIES: *CA.* A.D. 661 to 1870

Chapter Seven

Configurations of the Food System During the Islamic Centuries: *Ca.* A.D. 661 to 1870

Introduction

During the centuries between the end of the Greco-Roman millennium and today, a cultural synthesis prevailed throughout the Middle East which blended the interests of rural tribesmen, the ambitions of literate townsmen, and the exhortations of a spiritual messenger, namely the prophet Muhammad. This new blend of institutions and peoples resulted in the emergence of dynasties in Arabia, Syria, North Africa, Mesopotamia, Persia, and Asia Minor which advanced significantly upon the accomplishments of the Greco-Roman millennium while, at the same time, it strengthened "a spirit of independence which conflicted with the forms of servitude demanded by the bureaucratic states of antiquity" (Hess 1985: 33).

In Transjordan the Islamic cultural synthesis was experienced at its creative, turbulent center in the sense that its inhabitants had to cope with competing factions of Islam, conflicting dynastic ambitions, and shifting flows of communication and commerce. The history of Transjordan during the Islamic centuries, therefore, is a history of human resilience in the face of constantly changing winds of political dominance and economic opportunity. This situation is reflected at the level of material existence in widely fluctuating conditions of settlement and landuse. What predominates in Islamic Transjordan are those modes of livelihood found toward the middle and low points of the food system intensity continuum (see Chapter Four), for these are the modes which have resonated the best with the survival instincts of the inhabitants in this turbulent corner of the Islamic world.

Tell Hesban and vicinity offer proof of this, for although there is evidence of a wide range of configurations of livelihoods during the Islamic cen-

turies, the predominant ones are those between the medium and low intensity points of the food system continuum. Thus, on the local level, the political center of gravity appears to have been in the domain of independent tribal cultivators and pastoralists for many more centuries than it was in the domain of literate townsmen under the protection of rulers in Egypt, Mesopotamia, or Syria.

The Sociopolitical Context

The Wider Sociopolitical Context

A New Cultural Synthesis

The emergence, on the Arabian peninsula, of a spiritual message with the power to blend the aspirations of independent tribesmen of the desert with the ambitions of cosmopolitan townsmen in their towns and cities along the trade routes of the ancient world was by no means an accidental development. To begin with, the pre-Islamic inhabitants of the Arabian peninsula consisted of both groups. Whereas those who inhabited the south "had a highly developed urban civilization, with great temples and palaces, a highly organized and stable social system, and an advanced economy based partly on agriculture and partly on sea trade from the Orient," those who inhabited the north were, for the most part, nomadic pastoralists of various types (Jeffery 1952: 90). Furthermore, to the extent that the interests of these two groups converged and conflicted, the search for solutions and new opportunities was particularly intense among the sedentarized Quraysh clans of Mecca, the leading tribesmen of that oasis-town and the group of kindred in whose midst Muhammad was born and raised. This was because, to a greater degree than was the case among the people living in the southern coastal settlements of the Arabian peninsula, the way of life of these Meccan clans depended upon their ability to maintain a balance between these two groups.

A son of the Hashemite family of the tribe of the Quraysh, Muhammad proclaimed a message which sought to (Polk 1980: 19)

> transcend the limits of kinship and neighborhood of the tribe and village by creating a sense of community which would embrace rival groups of kindred, men of different hamlets, and even men separated by the frontiers of religion.

As his message was initially rejected by the establishment of Mecca, Muhammad was forced to retreat to the oasis-town of Medina. From there he summoned those who would listen to abandon their pagan ways and to join his new political community (*umma*).

The emergence of the Islamic state was an "organizational breakthrough of proportions unparalleled in the history of Arabian society until modern times" (Donner 1981: 269). Among the elements which, according to Donner, account for the integrative power and durability of this new state were

> the prevalence of an overriding concept of law, the focusing of political authority in God, the *umma*, and Muhammad, the systematization of taxation and justice, the establishment of a network of administrative agents to supervise member groups (1981: 75).

Given, on the one hand, the integrative power of the early Islamic state, and given, on the other hand, the exhaustion of both the Sassanian and the Byzantine civilizations due to prolonged war, and the rising tide of feeling against Hellenism and the Byzantine Greeks among the peoples of Syria, Egypt, and other provinces, the reasons for the rapid expansion of Muhammad's community become evident (*cf.* Donner 1981: 269). Thus, by means of a series of holy wars and astute political maneuvers, Muhammad and his followers eventually succeeded not only in subduing Mecca, but also in bringing into the new political community the vast majority of the population of western Arabia and the Fertile Crescent (*cf.* Spuler 1960; Polk 1980; Donner 1981). The specific events which led to Transjordan's subjugation by the Muslim army (*ca.* A.D. 636) have been recounted by Salibi (1977: 18) and Donner (1981: 91-155).

To a degree far greater than any previous system of beliefs to emerge out of the ancient Near East, the religion of Islam succeeded in blending the aspirations of desert tribesmen with those of the agricultural communities and cosmopolitan trading centers of the Near East. In the long run, however, the consequence of this assimilation of the desert tribesmen was that "the weight of the pastoralist weakened the ability of central government to conduct its affairs in the manner of previous regimes" (Hess 1985: 33). Thus, even though the ruling elite that emerged in the wake of the conquests were to survive for many centuries, the Arabian-Islamic state soon began to disintegrate (Donner 1981: 273; *cf.* Crone 1980).

It is in light of this insight that the political story of Islamic civilization must be understood. This story is a tale of shifting political centers of gravity between the north and the south, between the town and the steppe, and between proponents of competing definitions of Islam. For our purposes here, it is convenient to divide this history into four periods: 1) Caliphate Period (*ca.* A.D. 661-1055); 2) Seljuq Period (*ca.* A.D. 1055-1200); 3) Ayyubid-Mamluk Period (*ca.* A.D. 1200-1456); and 4) Ottoman Period (*ca.* A.D. 1456-1870). A brief overview of each of these periods, with particular reference to the Levant, follows.

The Caliphate Period (ca. A.D. 661-1055)

The first Muslim empire to emerge in the wake of the Prophet's death (in A.D. 632) was that of the Umayyads in A.D. 661. From their capital in Damascus, Syria, the Umayyad caliphs expanded the domain of the Muslim empire to Spain in the west and to the Indus Valley in the East. Although politically they were organized along Arab tribal lines, they retained, for the most part, the administrative bureaucracies they inherited from the Byzantines and Persians in their respective provinces. This did not prevent them, however, from embarking on an aggressive program of Arabization. Thus Arabic was adopted as the official state language throughout the empire and a new Arabic coinage was introduced. Where Greek and Persian personnel had served in previous administrations, they were replaced by Arabs.

An important consequence of the Islamic conquests and the ensuing program of Arabization was that it facilitated the movement of goods, people, and technology which made possible what has been called the "Arab agricultural revolution" (Watson 1974; *cf.* 1981; Ashtor 1981). This revolution, which took place over the first four centuries of Islam, involved the introduction into the lands of the Arabs of a number of new crops and farming practices originating mainly in India. Among the crops involved in this diffusion were "sixteen food crops and one fiber crop," including the following: "rice, sorghum, hard wheat, sugar cane, cotton, watermelons, eggplants, spinach, artichokes, colocasia, sour oranges, lemons, limes, bananas, plantains, mangos and coconut palms" (Watson 1974: 9). Also involved in this revolution was the introduction of a new agricultural season. Writes Watson (1974: 10):

> Hand in hand with the new crops came changes in farming practices. For one thing, a number of the new crops led to the opening of a virtually new agricultural season. In the lands of the Middle East and Mediterranean the traditional growing season had always been winter, the crops being sown around the time of the autumn rains and harvested in the spring; in the summer the land almost always lay fallow, usually even in irrigated regions where at least some of the crops available to the ancients could, with special care, have given satisfactory yields. Those crops mentioned as summer crops in the classical Roman manuals—barley, *trimestre* wheat, sesame and various legumes—played a minor role in some parts of the northern Mediterranean, where the summer was relatively cool, though even there they seem to have been little used and were not integrated into any systematic rotation. But in the southern and eastern parts of the Mediterranean they were practically never grown, at least not as summer crops. There the summer season was to all intents and purposes dead. Since, however, many of the new crops originated in tropical regions of India, Southeast Asia, and Central Africa, they could be grown only in conditions of great heat. In particular, rice, cotton, sugar cane, eggplants, watermelons, hard wheat and sorghum were all summer crops in the Islamic world, though rice and hard wheat could also be winter crops in certain very warm areas. Several other important new crops which we have not been able to study in detail, such as indigo and henna, were also grown in summer. Through the introduction of summer crops on a wide scale, therefore, the rhythm of the agricultural year was radically altered as land and labor which had previously lain idle were made productive.

Along with this opening of a summer season of sowing and harvesting came other practices which were needed in order to "combat exhaustion and even improve the soils," such as "extensive use of all kinds of animal and green manures, each with its special qualities and uses, as well as ashes, rags,

marl, chalk and crushed bricks or tiles" (Watson 1974: 11). Also intensified was the extent to which artificial irrigation was practiced. In addition to embarking upon extensive programs of repairing ancient irrigation works to which they fell heir, the Muslim conquerors introduced "a profusion of devices, borrowed rather than invented by the Arabs, for catching, storing, channeling and lifting water" (Watson 1974: 13). Among the more important of these borrowed devices were the underground canals or *qanats* and "a variety of wheels turned by animal or water power and used for lifting water—sometimes to great heights—out of rivers, canals, wells and storage basins" (Watson 1974: 13). The cumulative outcome of this diffusion of irrigation technology has been summarized by Watson (1974: 13-14) as follows:

> The result was to bring much more water to much more land; to irrigate lands which in earlier systems were not, and often could not have been reached, and to improve the quality of irrigation, that is to increase the flow of water on many lands watered by more primitive techniques in earlier times. So great indeed was the progress made that it would be only a slight exaggeration to claim that by the eleventh century there was hardly a river, stream, oasis, spring, known aquifer or predictable flood that went unused. Many were fully or almost fully exploited, though not always by irrigators, who had to compete with other users. The combined effect of all these advances was to create across the Islamic world a patchwork of heavily irrigated areas, great and small, into which the new agriculture could move, to transform an environment fundamentally hostile to many of the new crops into one in which, for a time at least, they were grown with astonishing success.

But the agricultural revolution was by no means confined to heavily irrigated and fertile areas where multiple cropping on the Indian model could be introduced. On the contrary, though the impact of the revolution was greatest in such areas and though they may perhaps be regarded as the spearheads of agricultural advance, the new agriculture overflowed their bounds to affect the whole spectrum of land types—from best to worst—that the early-Islamic peasant tilled. Virtually all categories of land came to be farmed more intensively. In part, this spillover was made possible by the fact that there was no sharp break between irrigated and unirrigated lands. Rather the various advances in irrigation had endowed the early Islamic world with a gradation of artificially watered lands: at one end of it were those which were under heavy, perennial irrigation and could support the Indian system of cropping; in the middle was a wide range of lands watered less heavily through the year or only parts of the year; and at the opposite end were lands watered only once or twice in a season through the capture, for instance, of a flash flood or through sparing use of small amounts of water stored in a cistern. The possibilities which partial irrigation opened up for intensifying land use were compounded by the fact that the authors of the Arab farming manuals identified far more types of soils than are mentioned by the ancients. By taking into account structure, temperature and moisture of the soil, they were able to see much more clearly than their predecessors the potential of each soil type. They assumed that all soils would be used to their full capacity—even inferior and downright bad lands, which the ancient writers did not deign to consider.

As a consequence of this agricultural revolution, urban growth—particularly involving inland cities and towns—ensued throughout much of the Islamic world. Some well-known examples include Cordoba, Seville, Damascus, Aleppo, Baghdad, and Cairo. Significantly, however, neither the Arab agricultural revolution, nor the urbanization which it facilitated, appears to have noticeably impacted central Transjordan, at least not during the first four centuries of Islam. Several explanations can be advanced to account for why this was the case.

To begin with, when the Umayyad caliphate, with its seat at Damascus, came to an end in A.D. 750, Transjordan, along with the rest of Palestine, was caught in the middle of a long-lasting strife between rival powers—one centered in the Tigris-Euphrates valley and the other in the valley of the Nile. On the one hand, there were the Abbasids (A.D. 750-1258) who, with their seat of power at Baghdad and with their generally eastward orientation, had a difficult time holding on to and administrating their western provinces in Syria, Palestine, and North Africa. Indeed, they may even have subjected Syria and Palestine to intentional neglect, as it had been the Umayyad's base of power (Donner personal communication). On the other hand, there were the Tulunids (A.D. 868-905), Ikhshidids (A.D. 935-969), and Fatimids (A.D. 969-1200) with their power base in Egypt, whose expansionist policies and, in the case of the Fatimids, whose competing definition of Islam, led to repeated confrontations, many of them on Transjordanian soil, with the rulers of the Abbasid dynasty

in Baghdad. Thus, while the fruits of the Arab agricultural revolution were enabling urban growth and the development of highly sophisticated urban cultures in valleys of Egypt and Mesopotamia, the Levant was undergoing an extended period of unstable governance due to the inability of these rival powers to sustain their hold upon the region for more than a few decades at a time (Salibi 1977).

Contributing to this process of political fragmentation and general decline in Levantine provinces during the first four centuries of Islam were a number of factors of which two will be briefly mentioned. The first was the decline of commercial traffic along the trade routes of Transjordan and Syria because trade between central Asia and eastern Europe passed into the hands of merchants in Iraq and Persia, while "the Red Sea which carried the eastern trade directly to Egypt and Syria was to a great extent replaced as a maritime highway by the Persian Gulf" (Salibi 1977: 35).

The second was the ascent of rival tribal confederacies within the Levantine provinces in the wake of the impoverishment which followed from the loss of commerce and the failure of both the Egyptian-based and Mesopotamian-based dynasties to develop effective administrative structures for governing them (cf. Crone 1980). Thus, throughout most of the period of caliphate reign in Transjordan and Syria, feuding persisted between tribesmen belonging to the Kalb (also known as Yaman) Confederacy and those belonging to the Qays (also known as Mudar) Confederacy (Salibi 1977: 25). Of these two groups, the Kalb were the more settled, having existed in Transjordan and Syria as tribal peasants (ashair) since before the conquest. Among their numbers could be found those who were primarily agricultural in their way of making a living and those who practiced some form of transhumance (Salibi 1977: 10-11).

The Qays, on the other hand, appear to have arrived in Transjordan and Syria with the conquest. Although fewer in number than the Kalb, they were an aggressive tribe of Bedouins (qabail) whose demands had to be taken seriously (Salibi 1977: 11, 25). Indeed, so widespread and persistent was the feud between these two groups that it appears to have been a major factor in the collapse of the Umayyad caliphate and in accounting for the failure of subsequent caliphs to establish effective administration in Transjordan and Syria (cf. Salibi 1977).

Toward the end of Abbasid rule in Transjordan, in the year A.D. 968, another tribal confederacy, that of the Tayy Arabs, rose to political prominence in Palestine and Transjordan. Being closely allied with the Fatimids of Egypt, their chiefs actually became, for a time, the representatives of Fatimid authority in this region (Salibi 1977: 91).

Seljuq Period (ca. A.D. 1055-1200)

Beginning in the 11th century, the Islamic world and what remained of the Byzantine Christian empire in Asia Minor and Europe were confronted by invasions of Turks, many of them led by the Seljuq family. Having begun their conquests in the east, in Iran and Iraq, the Seljuqs, who had recently converted to Islam, began their domination of the Muslim world by establishing, in A.D. 1055, a protectorate over the Abbasid caliphate in Baghdad. A similar arrangement was soon to follow in Fatimid Egypt where, in A.D. 1073, the caliph yielded his power to Badr al-Jamali, an army commander.

In due course, the Seljuqs moved westward into Syria and Palestine, where they occupied Damascus and Jerusalem, meeting little unified resistance due to the fragmented and largely autonomous state of the Fatimid provinces in central and southern Syria. In northern Syria and Asia Minor they also encountered the Byzantines, who were forced to turn to the pope in Rome for assistance in resisting them. This appeal triggered the organization of the First Crusade to reconquer the Holy Land by European Christians (cf. Spuler 1960: 89).

Seljuq occupation of the Levantine region turned out to be brief, lasting only from A.D. 1071-1097 (Salibi 1977: 122-160). Because of their staunchly Sunnite convictions, their track record as capable administrators, and their zeal in reviving commerce in their provinces, the Seljuqs were generally well received by the urban population of Syria. They failed, however, to capture the loyalties of the heterodox inland tribal peasants, many of whom were Ismailis, and therefore sympathetic with the Fatimid regime in Egypt. Consequently, except for in such urban centers as Damascus and Aleppo, the Seljuqs failed to bring an end to the anarchy which had persisted in the rural hinterlands of Syria and Transjordan since the fall of the Umayyad caliphate in A.D. 750.

The capture of Jerusalem and Antioch by the Seljuqs was the event which ultimately catalyzed the first march of crusaders, whom the Muslims referred to as the "Franks," to Palestine (Perowne and Prawer 1987: 359B). With this first crusade, the period of Seljuq domination in Syria and Palestine came to an end and the Kingdom of Jerusalem, which lasted from A.D. 1099 until 1187, came into existence (cf. fig. 7.1). Attached to this kingdom were several Christian feudal principalities located northward along the coast—Antioch, Edessa, Tripoli, and others (Spuler 1960: 90). With the exception of Transjordan, the Franks rarely penetrated far into the interior and could maintain their territorial domain only as long as the surrounding Muslim community remained divided.

Ayyubid-Mamluk Period (A.D. 1200-1456)

The emergence of the Ayyubids in the late 12th century as a major unifying force in the Levant was a direct result of the invasions of the Franks. First under the leadership of Nur al-Din of Damascus, then later, in Egypt, under Salah al-Din, or as the Franks called him, Saladin, a unified Muslim front against the Franks was created (cf. Ziadeh 1953: 3; Spuler 1960: 92). After encircling the Kingdom of Jerusalem, Saladin led a holy war against the Franks which culminated in the capture of Jerusalem in A.D. 1187. The decisive confrontation was the Battle of Hattin, near the Sea of Galilee, where the Franks lost most of their army. Also recovered by the Muslims in the wake of this battle were most of the other crusader strongholds along the coast and in Transjordan. This victory was short-lived, however, for in their Third Crusade, the Franks were able to recover many of these strongholds and hold on to them for nearly a century. This crusade did not succeed in recovering the city of Jerusalem itself, however, although its gates were again opened to Christian pilgrims after a treaty negotiated between Saladin and Richard I the Lion-Hearted in 1192 (Baldwin 1987: 887).

After Saladin's death in A.D. 1193, the Ayyubid dynasty (which was named after his father, Ayyub) was divided between members of his family. Thus principalities were established in Aleppo, Hamah, Homs, Damascus, Baalbek, and Transjordan. Disputes between the rulers of these principalities weakened Ayyubid solidarity, however, resulting in restoration of Jerusalem to the Christians and renewed unrest among the Arab tribal peasants.

Fig. 7.1   Kingdom of Jerusalem (after *Encyclopædia Britannica* 1987, vol. 16)

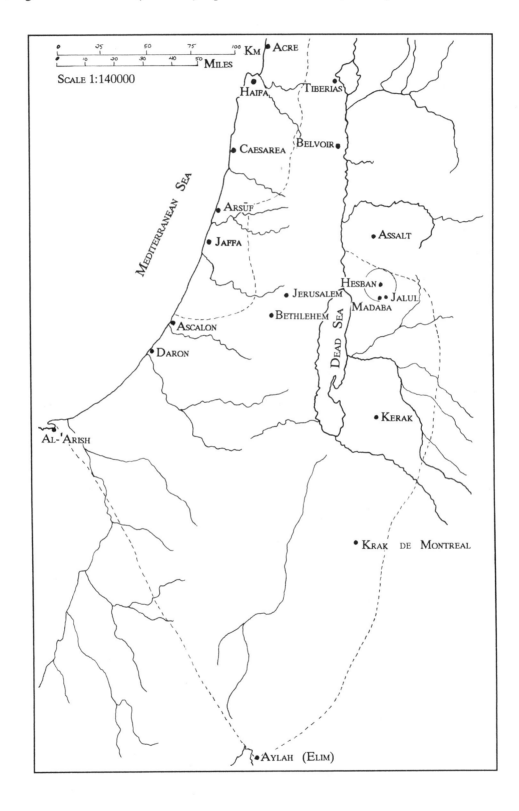

Their decline was ended by Mamluk accession to power in A.D. 1250.

Although the practice of using slave soldiers in the service of the state was not a new phenomenon among the Muslims, having come into existence already in the 9th century under the Abbasid caliphs in Baghdad, it had evolved by the 13th century to where a dynasty ruled by Mamluks, which means "slave soldiers," could rise to power in Egypt (cf. Crone 1980). After annexing the Ayyubid principalities of the Levant to Egypt, the Mamluk sultans proceeded to strengthen their position in the eyes of their Muslim subjects by undertaking a series of raids against the Franks between A.D. 1261 and 1291 which culminated in the complete expulsion of the crusaders from Palestine (cf. Ziadeh 1953: 5-7). Their success at thwarting the Mongol threat to the security of Egypt and Syria was also a significant achievement.

The revival of commercial activity in Palestine and Syria which began in the 10th and 11th centuries under the Fatimids and Seljuqs continued under the Franks and under the Ayyubid-Mamluk sultans. While along the coast maritime trade had been encouraged by Italian and other European entrepreneurs, including the Franks themselves, inland, along the fringes of the desert in Transjordan, the trade route between the Red Sea and Damascus was being revived, partially as a consequence of the Franks occupying the coastal routes (cf. Ziadeh 1953: 58; Salibi 1977: 87; Russell 1989). Along with this increase in trade and communication came advances in agriculture and manufacturing industries. Among the ones which apparently thrived were those which had sprung up around the production of sugar, textiles, glassware, and paper (Ziadeh 1953: 132-133).

The decline of the Mamluk Sultanate was caused by a number of different factors. To begin with, toward the end of the 14th century, a policy emphasizing ethnic affiliation rather than proven skill in the art of war was instituted as a criterion for advancement within the Mamluk administration. The result of this was a general weakening of the central administration. This, in turn, led to loss of solidarity in the task of protecting agriculture and trade from the predation of Bedouins and from ambitious Mongol warlords. When finally Damascus and other Syrian towns were devastated by the Mongol invader, Timur (Tamerlane) in A.D. 1401, the damage was too severe for the weak

Mamluk administration to repair. Thus famine and pestilence followed, and in their wake came the plague, which in the 14th century decimated a large percentage of the population (Dols 1977). To these already severe blows must be added yet another, namely the assault on the Red Sea trade which followed the discovery, by the Portuguese, of a direct sea route linking India and Europe. The end of the Mamluk Sultanate came in A.D. 1517 when they were defeated in battle by the Ottomans in both Syria and Egypt.

The Ottoman Period (ca. 1456-1870)

At the time of its conquest of Syria and Egypt, the Ottoman empire was already in its heyday, having undergone a period of almost continuous expansion since the beginning of the 14th century. In Syria, as elsewhere in their empire, the Ottoman sultans established provinces, each under a governor. The system of taxation which they instituted "continued in principle to be that of Muslim law—land tax, poll tax on Christians and Jews, and customs duties" (Hourani and Irvine 1975: 955).

Throughout most of their rule, the Ottomans left the governance of their provinces to their governors. In parts of Syria, where the governors paid attention to agriculture, it flourished and was particularly the case in parts of central and northern Syria during the 16th and 17th centuries. Consequently commerce and trade revived some in this region during these centuries. During the 18th and 19th centuries, however, things did not fare as well. Because of a weakened central administration in Istanbul, the Ottoman standard of administration declined. Thus rather than protecting the farmers from Bedouin predation, the Janissaries, the elite army of soldiers of the sultan, began themselves to exploit the farmers. This led to rapid decrease of sedentary agriculture and to a new ascendancy of tribalism. It also opened the door wide for sedentarization in Transjordan and Syria of northward-pushing tribesmen from the Hejaz.

The Local Sociopolitical Context

Since an in-depth history of central Transjordan during the Islamic centuries has yet to be written, the following attempt to sketch the local sociopolitical situation which prevailed in the immediate vicinity of the project area since the Islamic conquest can at best be regarded as a first approximation. What follows is a mere outline, a synthesis based entirely on secondary sources such as those cited already in the previous section. It is intended more as a vehicle for launching discussion and further research on this important subject, than as a completed piece of in-depth research.

As was noted in our discussion earlier, following the collapse of the Umayyad dynasty, Transjordan (along with the rest of Syria) was caught in the midst of the rivalry between the Abbasids in Mesopotamia and the Fatimids and their successors in Egypt. Rather than benefiting from the economic and cultural gains which were made in the vicinity of each of these centers of early Islamic civilization, the region entered a period of shifting and elusive dynastic domination. One consequence of this was that neither caliphate managed to establish viable administrative bureaucracies within the region. Its inhabitants, therefore, were forced to turn back upon their own resources, which meant a return to less capital-intensive, more self-reliant forms of food production. These strategies, in turn, were facilitated by increased emphasis on migration and tribal forms of social organization.

Throughout the Caliphate Period, the population of Transjordan was made up of peoples whose modes of livelihood represented varying degrees of sedentarism/nomadization. The predominant group, according to Salibi (1977: 10-11), were the *ashair* or tribal peasants, some of whom were primarily village-based cereal farmers and some of whom were transhumants. Also occupying the country on a seasonal basis were various Bedouin tribesmen whose original homeland was the Hejaz. As in former and subsequent times, these Bedouin tribesmen presented a constant threat to the older, more established population of tribal peasants. Over time, however, they too tended to settle, only to experience themselves the oncoming of new tribes of Bedouin.

About the fact that tribal peasants and Bedouin representing varying degrees of sedentarization/ nomadization continued to occupy Transjordan throughout the Seljuq, Ayyubid-Mamluk, and Ottoman periods there can be little doubt. The extent to which they dominated the sociopolitical scene appears to have abated considerably during Ayyubid and Early Mamluk times, however. As has already been noted, during these periods, Transjordan (along with the rest of Syria) experienced a temporary return to widespread sedentarization, to more intensive and market-oriented forms of agriculture, and to a modest degree of cosmopolitanism. In Late Mamluk times, however, this trend appears to be reversing itself. Thus, in the ensuing Ottoman Period, the population of Transjordan is again gradually turned back upon its own resources, to the hands of its most resilient residents—its independent tribal peasants and Bedouin.

In the following paragraphs a brief overview is offered of some of the political and ethnic entities which have been identified as having existed in central Transjordan throughout each of the major Islamic periods. Mention will also be made of the extent to which the archaeological record from each period attests sedentary occupation. The dates to which each period is assigned below are those which are commonly used with reference to central Transjordan (*cf.* Sauer 1982). They are therefore not always the same as those which apply for a particular dynasty from its original rise to power to its collapse.

A.D. 661-750 (The Umayyad Period)

For about a century and a half after the Islamic conquest, Transjordan continued to prosper because of its proximity to Damascus, the seat of Umayyad power and the center of political and commercial activity in the emerging Muslim world. Under the Umayyads, Syria and Transjordan were divided into four (and eventually five) military provinces (*jund*). These included the jund of Hims to the north of Damascus, the jund of Damascus which included most of central Syria, the jund of Jordan which included the territory to the west and east of the Sea of Galilee, the jund of Palestine which included the territory to the west and east of the lower half of the Jordan River and the Dead Sea (*cf.* Salibi 1977: 23). It was to the jund of Palestine that the project area belonged during the Umayyad Period.

Judging from the archaeological evidence, sedentary occupation in Transjordan during the Umayyad Period appears to have abated somewhat when compared with the preceding Late Byzantine Period (Sauer 1982). That the region continued to prosper, however, is clear from the size and quantity of settlements and from the impressive architectural accomplishments of the period (*cf.* Almagro and Olavarri 1982; McNicoll and Walmsley 1982; Sauer 1982; Tell 1982; Russell

1989). Particularly well known are the so-called Umayyad "palaces," many of which were converted from old Roman buildings and forts by elites emulating their caliphs. That these were not merely, in the words of Grabar (1955: 7) "places for high princely living and entertainment, but also centers for agricultural exploitation" is a point to which we shall return later.

Prominent among the Arab tribes which occupied Transjordan during the Umayyad Period were the Ghassanids, who in the 6th century had existed as a vassal kingdom of the Byzantine empire, helping to protect the spice trade and serving as a buffer against the desert Bedouin. While their kingdom had been weakened by the Muslim conquerors, some of its tribal constituents apparently continued to play a part in Transjordan's affairs during the Umayyad Period (Salibi 1977: 14-15; cf. Crone 1980: 34-36). According to Donner (1981: 103-105), the Belqa region was occupied by the Beni Irasha, a section of the Bali. Also living in this region were tribesmen belonging to the Judham and Lakhm (cf. Rotter 1982: 126-133). Both of these tribes were apparently allies of the Byzantines at the time of the Islamic conquest.

A.D. 750-969 (Abbasid Period)

In contrast to the relatively orderly and prosperous Umayyad Period, the Abbasid Period in Transjordan was a time of elusive dominion by the caliphs of Baghdad and Egypt. Consequently many of the major cities and towns of Transjordan appear to have suffered setbacks, and a number appear to have been abandoned (cf. Sauer 1982). Among the tribes which rose to prominence during this period were several groups of tribal peasants (ashair), among whom were the Lakhm and the Judham tribes. These were apparently among the more sedentarized of the tribes which inhabited Transjordan (Salibi 1977: 43-47, 74). Less sedentarized, and considered as being newcomers to the region during the 9th century, were the Tayy Arabs. In A.D. 883, a revolt by this tribe against representatives of the Tulunid Dynasty in Transjordan led to the cancellation of the annual pilgrimage from Damascus to Mecca for three years in a row (Salibi 1977: 47).

A.D. 969-1071 (The Early Fatimid Period)

The domination of central Transjordan by tribal peasants and Bedouins which had taken hold during the Abbasid Period continued unabated throughout Early Fatimid times. Just as in the preceding Abbasid centuries, the cities and towns of the earlier Byzantines and Umayyads continued to lie in ruins. Where archaeological signs of sedentary occupation occur, they suggest a "rural character, with smaller villages rather than major cities" (Sauer 1982: 333).

During the Early Fatimid Period, the power of the Tayy chiefs in southern Syria and Palestine appears to have reached new heights. Indeed, for a time, they came to represent Fatimid authority in Palestine and Transjordan (Salibi 1977: 85, 91). Also apparently still in the vicinity were the tribal peasants of the Yaman Confederacy, many of them probably settled, to varying degrees, in small cereal villages and hamlets in the highlands of Transjordan (Salibi 1977: 85-86). Numerous lesser clans were also in existence, but not much is known about them.

A.D. 1071-1200 (The Late Fatimid Period)

About the Late Fatimid Period in central Transjordan, which overlaps both with the Seljuq conquest of Syria (A.D. 1071) and the Franks' (Crusaders) arrival in Palestine (A.D. 1099), very little is known either archaeologically or historically. Two events, both of which were mentioned earlier, bear repetition in this context, however. One was the establishment of a principality of the Latin Kingdom of Jerusalem in Transjordan known as Oultre Jourdain. At Kerak and at esh-Shoubak two fortresses were built (Musil 1907: 45-64, 324-327; Brunnow and Domaszewski 1904: 113-119). The former was built on the site of an ancient Moabite fortress. It fell into Muslim hands in A.D. 1188, the year after the Battle of Hattin. These strongholds served to protect the crusader states in vulnerable positions in southern Transjordan.

Also noted earlier was the revival of the eastern caravan route which was stimulated, in part, by the expansion of trade between the Fatimids and the Europeans; in part, by the Seljuqs' restoration of law and order in Damascus and other cities in Syria and Palestine; and most important perhaps, by the Franks' occupation of the regions of western Palestine and Syria through which the western routes passed. These events created new opportunities to prosper for the Tayy, Yaman, and other tribal peasants and Bedouin occupying the highlands and deserts of Fatimid Transjordan.

A.D. 1200-1456 (Ayyubid-Mamluk Period)

With the establishment of an Ayyubid principality in Transjordan following the Battle of Hattin in A.D. 1187, the gains made during the Late Fatimid Period were consolidated. Thanks, in part, to a new system of land tenure whereby grants of rights over land could be obtained in return for military service, security improved along the trade routes and in the rural countryside (Hourani and Irvine 1975). This, in turn, stimulated further development of commerce and the revival of more intensive forms of agriculture. In due course these improvements led to increases in the growth and prosperity of villages and towns, a fact which is well attested by the archaeological remains from the period (Sauer 1982). The lingering presence of the Franks throughout this period is particularly evident, however, in the amount of energy which was devoted to the construction of fortresses. A good example is the Qalat er-Rabad, an Ayyubid castle near Ajlun "which was constructed during the time of Saladin to counter the Crusaders" (Sauer 1982: 334).

With the arrival of the Mamluks, the Levant was reorganized into *mamlakas* or "kingdoms" (*cf.* fig. 7.2). According to information provided by Ziadeh (1953: 13), the project area belonged to the *Mamlaka of Dimashq* (Damascus) which "extended from the north of Hims to the north of al-Karak." Each mamlaka, in turn, was divided into several sections and subsections called *wilayas*. According to the same author (1953: 13) Hesban and vicinity belonged to what is known as "the southern section." Its "administrative center" was Busra with "smaller centers" at the wilayas of "Sarkhad and Ajlun (Niyabas) and Baysan, Banyas and Subayba, Shaara, Idhraat, Husban and Salt."

Under the Early Mamluks, central Transjordan reached another peak in its multimillennial history. Among the factors which no doubt played a role in stimulating the attainment of this peak were one, Transjordan's role as a communication and transportation corridor linking Egypt and Syria; two, the gains of the Arab agricultural revolution which now could be capitalized upon; and three, the demand for agricultural products stimulated by the rapidly growing urban centers of the empire and beyond.

That conditions may have been particularly prosperous during this period at Hesban has been suggested by Russell (1989). Not only was it the capital of Belqa during Mamluk times, it also "served as a rest stop on the postal route from Damascus to al-Kerak" (Russell 1989: 29). Furthermore, the status of the Karak district as a more or less independent kingdom may also have contributed somewhat to Hesban's prosperity during Mamluk times (Russell 1989).

An idea of the extent of sedentary occupation which existed during Early Mamluk times is provided by contemporary Arab geographers. According to Ziadeh (1953: 71), who has studied some of the pertinent accounts, the town of Hesban, which functioned as a "smaller center," had a total of 300 villages attached to it. When regional survey results from Transjordan in general are taken into account, they, too, give support to the conclusion that sedentary activity was intense during this period (Sauer 1982).

An example of how the gains of the Arab agricultural revolution could be capitalized upon during this period is the sugar production industry. Being one of the crops introduced into Western Asia by the Arabs, sugar cane was apparently being produced in the Jordan Valley even before the arrival of the Franks (Ziadeh 1953: 132). Seeing that its production was profitable, they continued it, as did the Ayyubids and the Mamluks after them. In order to obtain sugar from the sugar cane, the Mamluks operated numerous water-driven sugar mills in the Jordan Valley, many of which have been found by archaeologists (Sauer 1982: 334; *cf.* Ashtor 1981). That some of these mills had been constructed even as early as Late Fatimid times is possible.

That tribal peoples continued to make up a significant portion of central Transjordan's population throughout Ayyubid and Mamluk times is not to be doubted. Ziadeh (1953: 45), for example, has examined the pertinent contemporary accounts which, he claims, mention the Batn Mahdi tribe as "the masters of al-Balqa" and the Batn Zubayd as another important Bedouin tribe of the period. It is also very likely that many of the older, more established tribes of central Transjordan in the 19th and 20th centuries also were known during Mamluk times (*cf.* Al-Bakhit 1982).

A.D. 1456-1870 (The Ottoman Period)

Throughout most of the Ottoman Period, central Transjordan belonged to the province of Damascus. This province, in turn, was divided into

Fig. 7.2 Syria under the Mamluks (after Ziadah 1953)

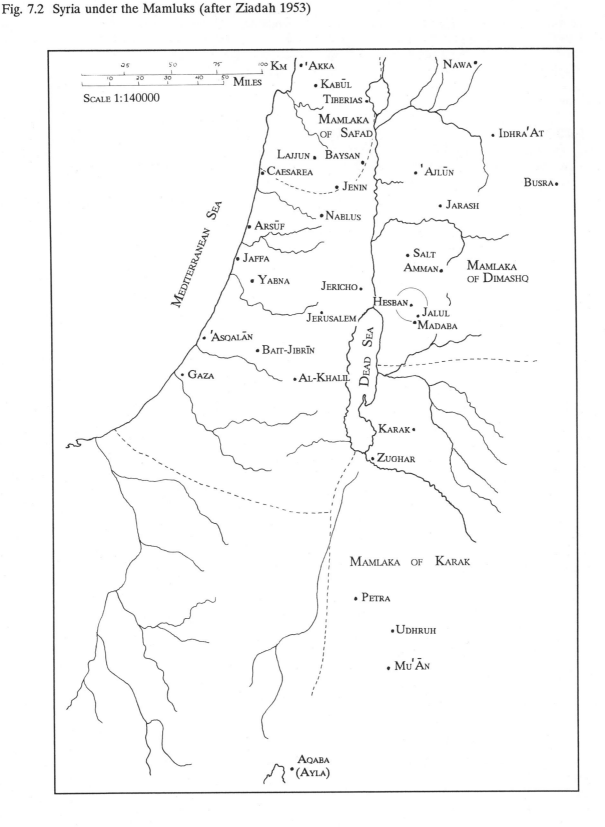

several "sanjaks." In Transjordan there were three such sanjaks, one headquartered at Kerak, another at Salt, and a third at Ajlun. The project area belonged to the region which was administered from Salt (*cf.* Hutteroth 1975).

Recently attempts have been made to reconstruct, on the basis of census and tax information recorded by Turkish government officials, the cultural landscape of Palestine and Transjordan during the Ottoman Period. An example is Hutteroth's (1975) research which focused on conditions prevailing during the last quarter of the 16th century. The settlement map he prepared shows that, in Transjordan, villages clustered around the administrative headquarters of Kerak, Salt, and Ajlun. Of the three regions (sanjaks), Ajlun appears to have been the most densely settled. The Salt region was settled mostly by nomadic tribes, while the Kerak region was inhabited by an even mixture of villagers and nomads.

That a gradual process of nomadization was under way in central Transjordan already in the 16th century is evident from the data in Hutteroth's study. He notes, for example, that "progressive decay" was especially evident in the case of the ten villages attached to Salt, for in the tax record were "entered the remark that either no taxes could be collected from them or that their peasants had run away" (Hutteroth 1975: 8).

By the 17th century, this process of abatement in sedentary occupation had further reduced the number of villages and towns. By this time central and southern Transjordan, with the exception of Kerak and its nearby villages, had largely reverted to the control of transhumants. Indeed, most of the project area tribal entities included in Peake's *A History of Jordan and Its Tribes* (1958) appear to have had a presence in central Transjordan by this time, including—in the case of Hesban and vicinity—the Adwan, the Beni Sakhr, the Ajarmeh, and the other tribes discussed in Chapter Three.

Changes in Environmental Conditions

Some years ago, Reifenberg (1955) expressed the view that since the demise of the Byzantine civilization, an unabated process of environmental degradation has occurred in Palestine. More recently, the same view has been repeated by Naveh and Dan (1973: 375). According to these authors, starting after the Muslim conquest a period of "increasing agricultural decline and landscape desiccation" occurred in Palestine which lasted for more than 1,300 years. To what extent do our findings from Tell Hesban and vicinity support this view?

To answer this question, notice will be taken of two pertinent lines of evidence. On the one hand, as was discussed in the previous chapter, there is what is known from literary sources about environmental conditions in the Hesban region during the last three centuries of the Greco-Roman millennium. On the other hand, there are the zooarchaeological and other environmental data generated by the Heshbon Expedition. When these two lines of evidence are examined, the suspicion that the above appraisal is altogether too sweeping, and even misleading, is strengthened.

To begin with, as was noted in Chapter Six, the process of environmental degradation in Palestine was well on its way already in the 3rd and 4th centuries A.D., judging from the literary information available from these periods. Furthermore, that this process continued unabated, as is implied in the above paragraph, is very unlikely. Thus, as will be seen later on in this chapter, in Ayyubid-Mamluk times there appears to have been great effort made to restore the terraces, embankments, and diversion dams built by earlier inhabitants of the project area.

The presence in the bone finds from this same period of an impressive array of wild birds, most of which are either extinct or rarely seen today in the project area, is another indication of the state of the environmental conditions which prevailed throughout the Islamic centuries. Among the species of wild birds identified in the bone corpus from the Islamic strata by Boessneck and von den Driesch (1978a) are the little owl (*Athene noctua*), stone curlew (*Burhinus oedicnemus*), chukar partridge (*Alectoris chukar*), corn-crake (*Crex crex*), houbara bustard (*Chlamydotis undulata*), palm dove (*Streptopelia sp.*), white stork (*Ciconia ciconia*), flamingo (*Phoenicopterus ruber*), dotterel (*Eudromias morinellus*), kestrel (*Falco tinnuculus*), and lesser kestrel (*Falco naumanni*).

When the zooarchaeological evidence from the Islamic strata at Tell Hesban is reflected upon, along with the accounts of environmental conditions in Moab provided by travelers such as Tristram (1873, 1880; see Chapter Three), alternatives to the "unabated degradation hypothesis" come to mind. For example, the possibility must be considered that in Jordan, as in other developed and developing countries, the degraded state of the natural environment today may be due, to a larger degree than generally acknowledged, to more recent events and causes. In other words, rather than attributing these conditions primarily to "centuries of neglect" by ignorant pastoralists and tribal cultivators, the devastating impact of un-bridled development, accompanied by unprecedented rates of sedentarization and intensification of agriculture, must also be reckoned with in assigning blame. There exists, in any case, very little to support the unabated degradation hypothesis in the data from Tell Hesban and vicinity. As in pre-Islamic and modern times, there have been periods of intensive management of the natural environment, and periods of little such management during the Islamic centuries as well. Whether the Islamic centuries witnessed a greater degree of neglect and mismanagement than previous centuries is still an open question. The answer to this question depends in part, of course, on the extent to which low intensity use of the land by Bedouin and tribal cultivators is to be equated with neglect and mismanagement.

Changes in Settlement and Landuse Conditions

Caliphate and Seljuq Periods

Having offered an overview of the sociopolitical and environmental conditions which prevailed throughout the Islamic centuries in Transjordan as a whole, we return again to consideration of the food system conditions attested by the archaeological remains from these centuries at Tell Hesban and vicinity. To begin with, when attention is focused on changes in settlement and landuse conditions during the Caliphate and Seljuq periods, it is apparent that what is known of conditions in central Transjordan as a whole is generally affirmed by the empirical evidence from the project area. Thus, as happened elsewhere in central Transjordan, while life in villages and towns within the Hesban project area persisted into the Umayyad period, it ebbs considerably with the coming of Abbasid rule and remains at a low intensity level for over four hundred years until it again flows throughout Ayyubid-Mamluk times.

This pattern is evident, first, in the results of the Hesban Survey. Significant with respect to the Umayyad Period sites (cf. fig. 7.3) is their location and quantity when compared with the preceding Byzantine Period (fig. 6.6) and the succeeding Abbasid Period (fig. 7.4). In quantity, the number of sites where pottery from these three successive periods was found decreases from 107 (Byzantine), out of a total of 148 sites surveyed, to 23 (Umayyad), to 5 (Abbasid). Along with this abatement in intensity of settlement was a retreat of sedentary occupation away from the eastern plain and western descent regions into the north-ern hills and plateau ridge. During the Umayyad Period, the quantity of sites in each of these four subregions numbered 2, 4, 10, and 7 respectively. In the ensuing Abbasid Period sedentary occupa-tion was further reduced to five sites, three in the northern hills (Sites 132, 144, 145), one on the plateau ridge (Tell Hesban), and one in the eastern plain (Tell Jalul).

An even closer view of the transition from Byz-antine to Early Islamic times is provided by the results of excavations at Tell Hesban. To begin with, there is a noticeable reduction in the quantity of archaeological loci assigned to the Early Islamic strata–210 assigned to Stratum 6 (Umayyad Period) and 56 assigned to Stratum 5 (Abbasid Period), compared with 909 from the earlier Byz-antine strata (i.e. Strata 10-7). This decline in occu-pational activity is also evidenced by the fact that one excavation area, namely Area B, was devoid of Umayyad remains altogether throughout the five seasons of excavations.

During the 1968 campaign, Phyllis Bird (1969), who served as the field supervisor for Area D, attempted to ascertain whether the transition from the Byzantine to the Arab Period was one of basic continuity or radical change. On the basis of care-ful consideration of the accumulated evidence from her field, she reached the conclusion that it "was one of basic continuity, involving the reuse of ear-lier structures, rebuilding and adaptation of others and some new building within the older structural framework" (Bird 1969: 193). This "continuity of construction" thesis remained unchallenged by the field supervisors who continued the work in Area D during the subsequent four campaigns.

As has already been indicated, very little was unearthed at Tell Hesban from the Abbasid Period (Stratum 5). Apart from a fire pit in Area A

Fig. 7.3 Umayyad Period sites

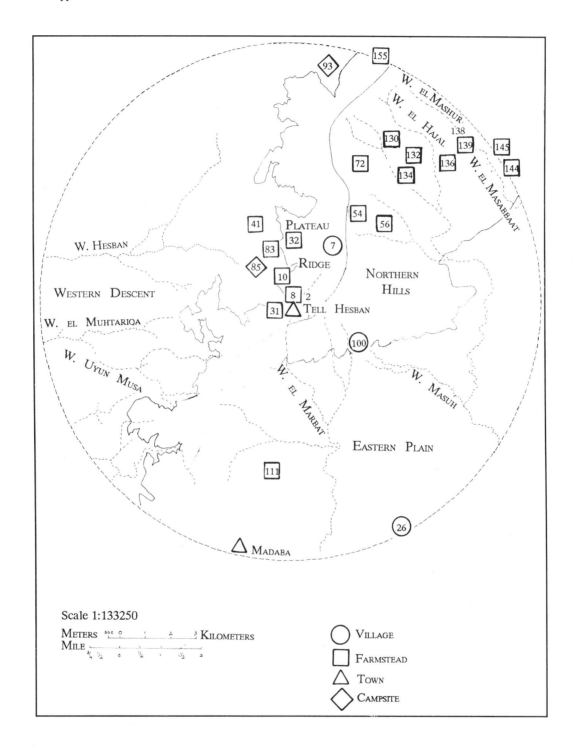

Fig. 7.4 Abbasid Period sites

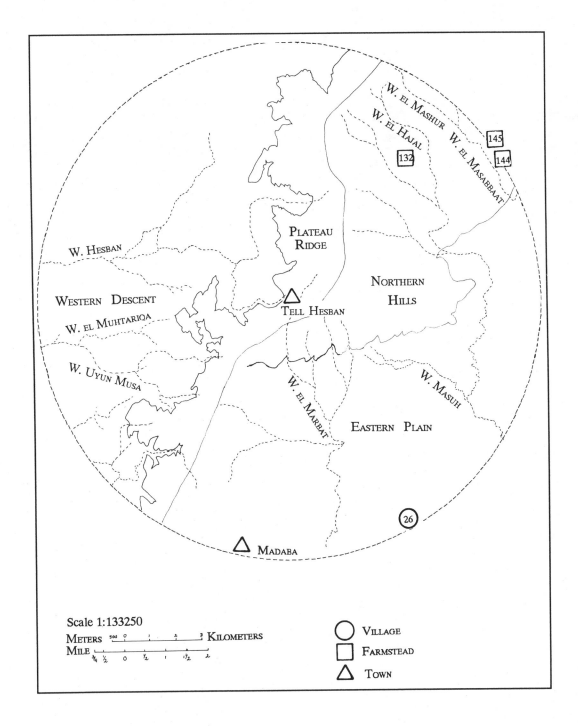

(A.9:80), a pit in Area B (B.6:2), and an enclosure wall in Area D (D.1:4c), the remains from this period consisted mostly of layers of soil, fill, tumble and *huwwar* containing Abbasid pottery mixed in with sherds from earlier periods. No evidence was found on the tell itself of buildings or other installations associated with permanent settlement. That seasonal use was made of the tell and its environs during the Abbasid period is a good possibility, however (see discussion under Changes in Operational Conditions below).

No signs were reported indicating permanent occupation of the tell and its environs during the Fatimid and Seljuq periods. As in the case of the Abbasid Period, however, some sort of seasonal settlement may have existed at Tell Hesban also during these centuries. Until the problems of distinguishing pottery from these periods are overcome, however, this suggestion must obviously be taken not as fact, but as a reasonable conjecture based on ethnohistorical analogy.

Turning next to consideration of landuse changes during the Early Islamic centuries, the story which is suggested by the available evidence is about a gradual change away from the high intensity configuration of the Byzantine centuries toward a medium intensity one during the Umayyad Period followed by a low intensity one during the Abbasid, Fatimid, and Seljuq centuries. The principal basis for this story is the changing pattern of settlement discussed above. Thus, the retreat of the sedentary population, during the Umayyad Period, away from the western descent and the eastern plain into the northern hills and plateau ridge is indicative, for reasons discussed in chapters Three and Four, of a return to mixed farming involving cereals and pasture animals. The further retreat, in turn, of towns and permanent villages during the Abbasid Period, and their continued sparsity during the Fatimid and Seljuq periods, would suggest further abatement during these periods in the intensity of the local food system in the direction of pastoral nomadization. This interpretation of the evidence is, of course, consistent with the literary evidence discussed above which indicates that the project area was under the control of tribal villagers, such as the Kalb Arabs, and Bedouins, such as the Tayy, during this part of the Caliphate Period.

Closer examination of the number of specimens of animal bones from the Umayyad and Abbasid strata provide further clues to the changes in patterns of landuse during these periods (table 7.1). To begin with, the relative importance of cattle appears to drop from 12.5% in the Byzantine strata to 3.9% in the Abbasid stratum. At the same time the importance of the camel seems to increase slightly over the same time span, from 1.1% to 2.4%. Concurrent with these changes is an increased interest in sheep and goat production, from 71.6% in the Byzantine Period to 91.7% in the Abbasid Period. Taken together, these changes suggest a gradual shift away from the intensive plow agriculture, involving teams of oxen, which prevailed during Byzantine and early Umayyad times toward greater emphasis on herding of sheep, goats, and camels during Abbasid times.

Ayyubid-Mamluk Period

The increased prosperity of life in villages and towns, documented with regard to the Ayyubid-Mamluk periods elsewhere in central Transjordan, is an undisputable occurrence also within the Hesban project area. This is attested, first, by the results of the Hesban Survey (fig. 7.5). Pottery from these periods was found at 47 sites, of which 18 were located along the plateau ridge, 13 in the northern hills, 9 in the western descent, and 7 on the eastern plain. Significantly, every one of these sites had been settled before, *i.e.* none were settled for the first time during Ayyubid-Mamluk times.

To gain further understanding of how sedentarization intensified, then abated during these periods, it is necessary to turn to the results of the excavations at Tell Hesban. To begin with, there is the measure provided by the quantity of archaeological loci assigned to each of the three Ayyubid-Mamluk strata: specifically 126 to Stratum 4 (Ayyubid, *ca.* A.D. 1200-1260), 787 to Stratum 3 (Early Mamluk, *ca.* A.D. 1260-1400), and 379 to Stratum 2 (Late Mamluk, *ca.* A.D. 1400-1456). The most intensively built-up and sedentarized of these three periods, then, was the Early Mamluk Period.

Closer examination of the architectural remains from these three strata yields additional evidence suggestive of this process of intensification and abatement. Thus, whereas the purely Ayyubid stratum consisted primarily of soil layers, a number of pits, a few floor surfaces, and one significant installation, namely a *tabun* (Area A), the subsequent Ayyubid-Mamluk strata were made up of a

Fig. 7.5 Ayyubid-Mamluk period sites

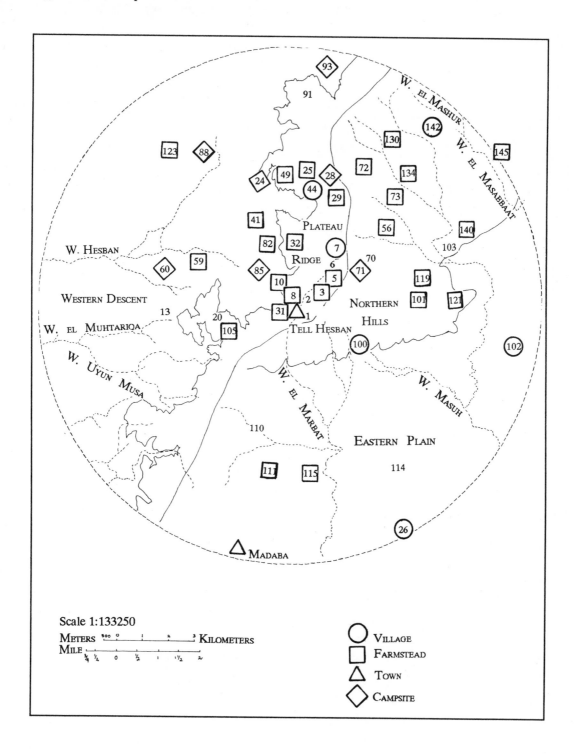

Table 7.1   Number of identified specimens of principal domestic animals from Islamic strata

Strata	Period	Cattle #	%	Sheep/Goat #	%	Sheep #	%	Goat #	%	Pig #	%	Camel #	%	Equids #	%	Horse #	%	Donkey #	%	Total #	%	Accumulation Rates
1	Modern	60	5.7	908	86.0	36	3.4	52	4.9	25	2.4	9	0.9	54	5.1	5	0.5	19	1.8	1,056	5.7	9.96
2-3	Mamluk	1,117	13.3	6,901	81.9	353	4.2	402	4.8	139	1.6	215	2.6	57	0.7	6	0.1	14	0.2	8,429	45.3	43.00
4	Ayyubid	9	10.7	71	84.5	4	4.8	6	7.1	--	--	2	2.4	2	2.4	--	--	--	--	84	0.5	1.40
5	Abbasid	8	3.9	188	91.7	14	6.8	11	5.4	2	1.0	5	2.4	2	1.0	--	--	--	--	205	1.1	0.73
6	Umayyad	68	10.4	494	75.3	47	7.2	33	5.0	80	12.2	8	1.2	6	0.9	--	--	3	0.4	656	6.5	7.80
7-10	Byzantine	162	12.5	932	71.6	58	4.5	48	3.7	130	10.0	14	1.1	63	4.8	5	0.4	10	0.8	1,301	7.0	4.39
11-13	Late Roman	286	11.7	1,892	77.6	140	5.7	115	4.7	183	7.5	17	0.7	58	2.4	2	0.1	6	0.2	2,436	13.1	10.36
14	Early Roman	131	15.0	682	78.1	67	7.7	36	4.1	43	4.9	7	0.8	10	1.1	--	--	3	0.3	873	4.7	4.12
15	Late Hellenistic	136	12.0	977	85.9	135	11.9	75	6.6	6	0.5	15	1.3	4	0.4	--	--	1	0.1	1,138	6.1	2.60
16-18	Iron 2	256	14.3	1,406	78.5	137	7.7	83	4.6	94	5.3	5	0.3	29	1.6	--	--	9	0.5	1,790	9.6	3.58
19	Iron 1	145	22.2	460	70.6	38	5.8	29	4.4	31	4.8	3	0.5	13	2.0	--	--	6	0.9	652	3.5	3.26
Sum	All	2,378	12.8	14,911	80.1	1,029	5.5	890	4.8	733	3.9	300	1.6	298	1.6	18	0.1	71	0.4	18,620	100	5.81

Table 7.2   Number of identified specimens of carbonized seeds from Islamic strata

Strata	Period	Oats #	%	Barley #	%	Wheat #	%	Lentil #	%	Pea #	%	Bitter Vetch #	%	Broad Bean #	%	Olive #	%	Grape #	%	Garden Heliotrope #	%	Total #	%
1-6	Modern-Arabic	--	--	29	15.3	91	48.1	15	7.9	--	--	36	19.0	7	3.7	6	3.2	5	2.6	--	--	189	28.5
7-10	Byzantine	--	--	4	7.5	9	17.0	3	5.7	--	--	8	15.1	--	--	14	26.4	15	28.3	--	--	53	8.0
11-14	Roman	1	0.9	62	58.5	5	4.7	1	0.9	--	--	2	1.9	--	--	--	--	35	33.0	--	--	106	16.0
15	Late Hellenistic	2	1.0	12	5.9	43	21.3	8	4.0	1	0.5	126	62.4	2	1.0	6	3.0	2	1.0	--	--	202	30.4
16-19	Iron	5	4.4	6	5.3	14	12.3	2	1.8	--	--	--	--	--	--	82	72.0	3	2.6	2	1.8	114	17.2
Sum	All	8	1.2	113	17.0	162	24.3	29	4.4	1	0.2	172	25.9	9	1.4	108	16.3	60	9.0	2	0.3	664	100

complex, site-wide assemblage of foundation trenches, walls, floors, pits, *tabuns*, caves, channels, and cisterns, along with massive quantities of tumble and fill. Among the remains of buildings recognizable in this assemblage of ruins was an elaborate bath complex (in Area A; see pl. 7.1) which included both hot and cold water tanks (de Vries 1986); several instances of buildings with vaulted rooms surrounding a courtyard (pl. 7.2)—the one in Area D large enough to qualify as having once been a caravansary; several large cave-complexes (Area B, G.4) that appear to have served as permanent residences; and in Area A, a large baking facility. In Area B, a large kiln was dated to the Ayyubid-Mamluk period as well. When, precisely, most of these buildings and installations were constructed—whether in Ayyubid or Early Mamluk times is not certain, because of difficulties in distinguishing the pottery and the mixed contents of most of the loci from these periods. The excavators, however, believe that the most active period of construction and habitation

at Tell Hesban during these centuries was the Early Mamluk Period (Geraty 1976: 47).

Along with the build-up of sedentary occupation during the Ayyubid-Mamluk centuries came significant intensification of landuse. To begin with, this intensification is reflected in the expansion of villages and farmsteads along the plateau ridge and into the northern hills. There is also limited expansion into the western descent and the eastern plain. Judging from the modest increase in the total number of settlements during these periods, and from the location of most of the sites along the plateau ridge and northern hills, a medium-intensity food system appears to have been achieved during these periods.

Consonant with this interpretation are the animal bone finds from Tell Hesban. As can be seen in table 7.1, which presents number of bone specimens of the principal domestic animals, there is an increase again in the relative importance of cattle, from 3.9% during Abbasid times to 13.3% in the Mamluk Period. A corresponding decrease

Plate 7.1   Southern half of Islamic bath complex (Squares A.7, A.8). From right: entrance hall, lounge, access hallway, bath room; view east

Plate 7.2   Mamluk courtyard (Squares A.7-10) surrounded by rooms with arched entrances to left and bath complex to right; view north

in the relative importance in sheep and goats is also noticeable over the same time span, from 91.7% to 81.9%. These changes are what one could expect, given the above-mentioned changes in settlement patterns; namely an increase in the proportion of cattle for use in plowing the fields and a corresponding decrease in the proportion of pasture animals as grazing lands are again returned to cereal cultivation. While vegetables and tree crops no doubt also were raised in significant quantities, they probably did not contribute as much to the local economy during the Ayyubid-Mamluk period as they had during the previous Roman and Byzantine periods.

The presence in the bone finds from Ayyubid-Mamluk times of zebu or humped-back cattle is noteworthy (Boessneck and von den Driesch 1978a: 264). Although these drought-resistant draft animals had been introduced to Palestine several centuries earlier, perhaps during Roman or Byzantine times, their numbers very likely increased in the rural regions in wake of the Arab agricultural revolution discussed earlier. This, at least, is a possibility suggested by their presence at Hesban during these centuries.

Ottoman Period

The decline in the number of permanent villages and towns which had begun during the Late Mamluk Period continued unabated into the Ottoman Period. This decline is attested by the drop in the number of survey sites (fig. 7.6) attesting Ottoman pottery and by the sparsity of occupational debris from this period. On the tell, for example, all that was unearthed from this period was a cave/cistern complex found in Area G.4. containing "probable" Ottoman pottery (Wimmer 1978: 150). Had more caves been investigated, it is likely that a better picture would have been obtained of the village, which according to Ottoman tax records (Hutteroth and Abdulfattah 1977) existed at Hesban in A.D. 1596. The fact that this settlement was one of only two villages located in the Transjordanian highland between Salt in the north and the Wadi Mujib in the south is noteworthy. Being entirely surrounded by nomadic tribes, it is not surprising that, although mentioned in the records as a village, it yielded no taxes on the basis of which agricultural production statistics could be obtained.

During the Ottoman centuries, therefore, the center of gravity, in terms of landuse, tended to remain on the side of pastoral pursuits by seminomadic tribesmen (see Chapter Three for a more detailed discussion of landuse during the Late Ottoman Period). While wheat, barley, and other field crops were no doubt planted to varying degrees by most of these tribesmen on the fertile slopes and wadi bottoms surrounding Hesban (cf. Hutteroth and Abdulfattah 1977, Agricultural Production Map), the extent to which this was done from one year to the next no doubt waxed and waned as local political and economic winds encouraged or discouraged it.

As was discussed in Chapter Three, the most pastoral of the tribesmen who inhabited the project area during the Ottoman Period were the camel-breeding Beni Sakhr. By contrast, the sheep-and-goat-breeding Ajarmeh tribesmen were widely known for their wheat which they cultivated in the slopes and valleys surrounding seasonally-inhabited villages (see below). These villages could be found along the northern highland, along the plateau ridge and in the valleys of the western descent. As was discussed in Chapter Three, both the Beni Sakhr and the Ajarmeh, whose ancestors have utilized the project area since the earliest decades of the Ottoman Period, have over the past two centuries gradually abandoned their nomadic ways in favor of a more sedentary existence. The same also is true with regard to other Ottoman Period residents of the project, such as the Adwan, the Belqawiya, and the Beni Hamida (Glubb 1938; Peake 1958).

Changes in Operational Conditions

The Qasr or Fortified Farm Compound

One of the most distinctive architectural features of the rural landscape of the Islamic centuries was the so-called qasr (plural qusur). As a background to the following discussion of qusur at Tell Hesban and vicinity, note will be taken of Conrad's article on the subject of "The Qusur of Medieval Islam" (Conrad 1981). Conrad begins his article by dispelling the idea that the Arabic term qasr always is used with reference to luxurious or fortified places, such as castles, palaces, or fortified mansions of various kinds (cf. Grabar 1955). This, he argues, is a meaning that has been "imposed on

Fig. 7.6 Ottoman Period sites

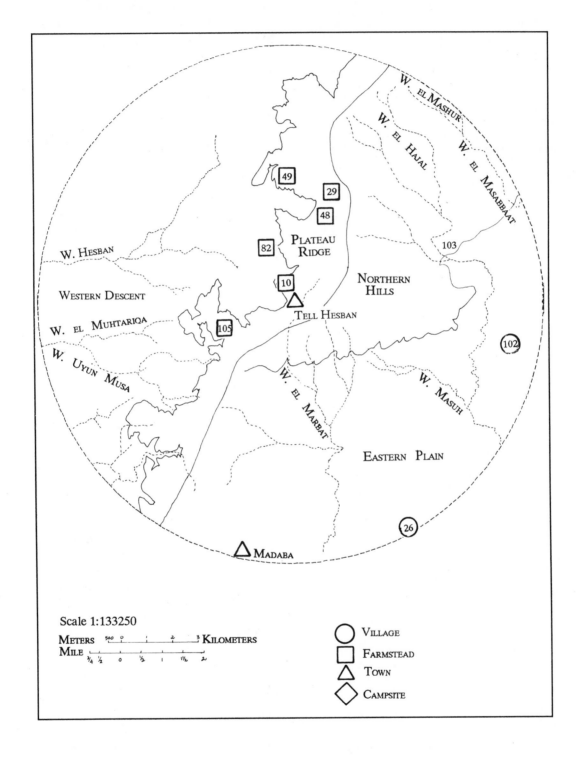

the term" and which has led to "substantial misunderstanding" in our interpretation of it.

Contrary to views advanced by several medieval Arabic lexicographers, Conrad sees "no justification" for viewing the term *qasr* as an instance of Arabization of some Latin or Greek word. Instead, he prefers to view the word as "a perfectly regular Arabic" term meaning "enclosure, confinement, or restriction" (Conrad 1981: 7-9).

Indeed, when careful attention is paid to the actual usage of the term *qasr* by the Arabs themselves, a wide range of meanings and connotations is found to exist. For example, among the Rwala Bedouins, "*qasr* is the name of any house built of stone or mud brick" (Musil 1928: 160 as quoted in Conrad 1981: 11). A similar usage for the term was noted by Canaan (1933), whose lifework was focused on documenting the construction techniques of the fellahin of Palestine (Conrad 1981: 13). In other instances, the term is used with reference to agrarian installations, such as permanent structures for storing or guarding garden crops. In still other cases, the term is used with reference to "substantial agricultural compounds" or "fortified farms" (Conrad 1981: 14-15; *cf.* Musil 1927: 370).

The term *qasr*, then, connotes the opposite of "ephemeral structures" such as tents and reed houses. In terms of its social context, it reflects "a direct response" to the problem of "endemic insecurity" faced by permanently settled members of the Islamic rural landscape. As Conrad (1981: 18-19) explains:

> Our Near Eastern *qusur* were not outposts garrisoned by imperial troops or allies acting on their behalf. They were the preserves of powerful local clans or tribal leaders, and in many towns and villages there were multiple *qusur* controlled by separate and sometimes rival groups. We would not expect to find such a phenomenon in a society organized as a single harmonious entity, and the fact that we do find it so prominently at so early a date indicates, again, how profoundly urban and village life in many parts of the Near East was affected by the realities of tribalism.

It is important to note that these fortified residential compounds or *qusur* did not always exist as isolated entities. As was pointed out in the previous paragraph, clusters of *qusur* could be found which together made up a village or a town. Individually, most of these compounds were usually "much less than a fortress or a palace," yet they

represented "a vital social institution," given the constant exposure of the sedentary population to attacks by marauding tribesmen. For warding off such threats the *qusur* were well suited. Writes Conrad (1981: 10):

> The compound was generally small and simple, and in its construction groups of families or related clansmen would have encountered no difficulty in the way of expense or technological requirements. The enclosure wall was but a slight obstacle to an organized attack by trained troops, but was sufficient to deter marauders who had neither the time nor the patience for a siege. In time of danger, the villagers withdrew to the *qusur*, drove their livestock into the courtyard, and barred the gate against the raiders. The latter, though unable to penetrate the *qasr*, could still force the settlement to come to terms by threatening to burn or trample crops, cut down trees, fill wells, and smash irrigation works. Usually an arrangement was reached whereby the intruders agreed to spare the exposed fields and facilities of the settlement, and to leave peacefully in exchange for money or goods.

Perhaps the most distinctive architectural feature of the *qusur* of Transjordan is the "vaults and barrel roofs" construction. While this construction technique predates the Islamic era, it appears to have been used widely throughout the villages and towns of the Ayyubid-Mamluk period, judging from the frequent association of this type of architecture with pottery from this period throughout the project area. Among the project area sites which contained ruins of this type are: Jalul (Site 26; pls. 7.5 and 7.6), Beit Zira (Site 56), Masuh (Site 100), Kefeir Abu Khinan-west (Site 111), and east (Site 115), Dubaiyan (Site 134), Umm es Summaq (Site 154), and Sites 130 and 145 (Ibach 1987: 192-193). To varying degrees, all of these villages and towns were made up of clusters of fortified residential compounds, or groups of *qusur*.

Whether one or more *qusur* existed at Tell Hesban throughout the early Islamic centuries is not certain. Excavation results from the Early Mamluk Period at this site, however, suggest the presence of several. The most impressive of these, "the acropolis building complex," was a structure, built upon the ruins of the Byzantine church, containing a courtyard surrounded by interconnected rooms (*cf.* pl. 7.2). These rooms were constructed using the vault and barrel roof method noted earlier. Arranged in a U-shape, they "formed a large open courtyard in the middle, which

Plate 7.3   Ayyubid-Mamluk Vault G.6:9 made of rough hewn blocks of *nari* and biomicrite; view east

Plate 7.4   Ayyubid-Mamluk vaulted Room D.4:24 with Bedrock D.4:25 in left foreground; view southeast

Plate 7.5   Islamic architecture at Tell Jalul (Hesban Survey Site 26); view southwest

Plate 7.6   Close up of Islamic architecture at Tell Jalul (Hesban Survey Site 26); view south-southeast

appeared to have been open on the east side" (van Elderen 1978: 20). A perimeter wall sealed off the top of the U. Also included within this compound was an exceptionally well-preserved bath complex (de Vries 1986; cf. Grabar 1955: 13; pl. 7.1).

To the west of this acropolis qasr several smaller "domestic houses" were uncovered, all of which conform to the basic pattern of the qasr noted above. These "houses" had been constructed using the same vaulting method as was used in the acropolis qasr and each consisted of a cluster of rooms around a central open court. Unlike the town which had existed during the Roman-Byzantine period, the "houses were placed haphazardly in the available space without any street apparent."

These finds suggest the presence during Early Mamluk times at Tell Hesban of a classic medieval qusur town, complete with a qasr of mansion proportions on the acropolis summit itself, and a cluster of less imposing residential qusur surrounding it in a more or less haphazard fashion. Associated with all of these compounds were numerous reused cisterns, water channels, baking ovens, and storage and habitation caves. The large reservoir east of the tell along the Wadi el Marbat was also in use.

The existance in the midst of the present-day village of Hesban of a building which the villagers call the qasr should also be noted. While the building is today used only as a store house for agricultural products, villagers say that it used to be the residence of the landowner who "owned" the village and the fields cultivated by its inhabitants. Unfortunately, no attempt was made to ascertain the building's construction date, nor was its use-history investigated. What was determined, however, was that it had been constructed on top of walls dating back at least to the Ayyubid-Mamluk period (Brown 1978: 181-183; cf. Conder 1889: 210).

Habitation Caves

Another noteworthy feature of the Ayyubid-Mamluk settlement at Tell Hesban is the presence on and surrounding the tell of numerous habitation caves (Geraty 1976: 47; Ibach 1987: 192). The largest of these was discovered at the end of the 1976 season. It measured 100 m in length and was,

in some places two stories high. Too large to excavate in the final season, it was only explored;

from off the surface came two large, beautifully glazed Mamluk bowls—one patterned in brown and yellow, the other in black and green (Geraty 1976: 47).

That such habitation caves were widely in use throughout project area villages in Ayyubid-Mamluk times is quite certain. Indeed, as Ibach (1987: 191-192) has noted, Ayyubid-Mamluk sites may be recognized by their "sharply undulating surface" and by the presence of "small mounds" "interspersed with depressions and cave entrances." These features "are caused by several architectural features of the period, namely, arches, vaulted buildings, semisubterranean rooms and caves. In some cases these have collapsed, forming depressions." Nearly all of the Ayyubid-Mamluk period sites mentioned above exhibit these features.

Seasonal Villages

Another type of rural settlement which existed in the project area throughout the Islamic centuries was the seasonal "village." These were villages in which people lived for part of the year in caves and for part of the year in tents. What made them seasonal was the fact that their populations fluctuated significantly on a seasonal basis.

An example of this is provided by the Ajarmeh. During the winter months, they would move out of their tents in the vicinity of fields and pastures and into caves nestled in depressions and slopes of ancient tells. From here they would come forth daily to concentrate their efforts on plowing and planting wheat in the fertile valleys surrounding their "village."

But not everyone would move into caves in the winter. Others would migrate to the Ghor or into the eastern desert in order to spare their flocks of cattle, sheep, and goats from the worst of the winter weather. These members of the tribe would return in time to assist with the wheat harvest and to graze their flocks on the stubble. Later in the summer, the flocks would again need to be taken to distant pastures, which resulted in another fluctuation of the village population.

Typically seasonal villages flourished during periods when villages, in the traditional sense of clusters of permanently occupied stone buildings, were abandoned. That the populations of these villages were capable of completely abandoning them, if need be, was a source of considerable frustration to Ottoman tax collectors. Thus, efforts at collection were frequently blunted by villagers moving out on hearing of the arrival of tax authorities (*cf.* Hutteroth 1975).

While the most important feature of these villages was their habitation caves, each of which typically had a masonry entrance, other distinguishing features can be pointed to as well. For example, all of them had a threshing ground, a primary water source such as a well or one or more cisterns, several animal corrals, and a burial ground. Significantly, they also had names, as in the case of the Ottoman seasonal villages of Hesban and Masuh, both of which were known by those names before they were rebuilt at the end of the 19th century.

That Hesban itself was used as a seasonal village site by members of the Ajarmeh tribe during the Ottoman Period has already been suggested. Evidence for this is the existence of numerous caves throughout the village. Most of these have black ceilings and contain the remains of some sort of fire pit. At least one of them was still in use as residential quarters for humans in 1976, although such use of caves was by then the exception. Much more common today are instances where these caves are used as storage places and animal shelters.

Only one of these Ottoman habitation caves, G.4, was explored by the archaeological team. It turned up "probable" Ottoman pottery along with an interesting array of objects, including a large key, a stirrup, a small iron horseshoe, a Turkish clay pipe, a bronze bracelet, an iron hook, a machine part, a plastic comb, a loom weight, and a piece of worked flint (Wimmer 1978: 150-151).

In Chapter Three it was suggested that transhumant pastoralism was the prevailing form of landuse within the project area throughout the Ottoman Period. The extent, however, to which this subsistence pattern involved a commitment to cultivation of field crops is reflected in what has already been stated previously about the nature of the seasonal village. Indeed the raison d'être of the seasonal village was to allow people to concentrate their energies on cultivation during the wheat growing season. The maintenance of such villages by the Ajarmeh, therefore, is consonant with their reputation as being skillful agriculturalists known for outstanding wheat harvests (see Chapter Three).

Sacred Stone Circles

Another important feature of the rural landscape of the project area during Islamic times is, as was noted briefly in Chapter Three, the sacred stone circle. In essence, these were burial sites which also served as tool and equipment depots for storing plows and other articles used by tribesmen in this area. Such places were noted by Conder (1889) at Ain Hesban (1889: 6-7), El 'Al (1889: 16-19), Butmet et Terki (1889: 93-94), Hesban (1889: 104), El Jereineh (El Jureina) (1889: 110), Kabr 'Abdullah (1889: 113), Khurbet el 'Amriyeh (1889: 146), Khurbet Umm el 'Akak (1889: 156-157), Rujm Saaur (1889: 207-208), and Umm el Hanafish (1889: 246-248). All of these sites are located within 10-km radius of Hesban (see Ibach 1987: 201-232).

The iconography associated with these sacred circles provides some insight into what the tribesmen considered to be valued attributes of individual members. Carved in relief on one of the stones at Ain Hesban, for example, were the tribal marks of the Ajarmeh, along with "rude designs representing a bow, a coffee-mortar and pestle, and finally a man on a horse with a sword and a bow above him." On another stone at this site were carved "representations of a coffee-mortar and pestle, four coffee-cups, or finajin, and a spoon (Mihmasah) for roasting, and a little jug or pot for boiling the coffee." Similar representations were noted on stones at Kabr Abdallah (Conder 1889: 6-7; 113). Concludes Conder (1889: 7): "These designs are modern Arab work, and are interesting . . . because they are intended by an illiterate people to be symbols of the warlike valor and of the hospitable character of the chief here buried."

Changes in Dietary Conditions

The information available regarding the dietary practices which prevailed during the Islamic centuries comes primarily from the animal bone finds and carbonized seeds excavated at Tell Hesban. These finds, it will be recalled, stem primarily from the Umayyad and Ayyubid-Mamluk periods, as these were the times during which the tell was extensively settled on a year-round basis.

In comparison to other periods, none is better represented in the faunal assemblage from Tell Hesban than the Mamluk Period. For example,

Table 7.3 Weight of principal meat-yielding species from Islamic strata (in kg)

Strata	Period	Cattle kg	Cattle %	Sheep/Goat kg	Sheep/Goat %	Pig kg	Pig %	Camel kg	Camel %	Total kg	Total %	Accumulation Rates
1	Modern	1.4	27.45	3.0	58.82	0.2	3.92	0.5	9.80	5.1	4.65	0.05
2-3	Mamluk	14.2	30.67	25.2	54.43	0.8	1.73	6.1	13.17	46.3	42.21	0.24
4	Ayyubid	0.1	33.33	0.2	66.67	--	--	--	--	0.3	0.27	0.01
5	Abbasid	0.2	16.67	0.8	66.67	--	--	0.2	16.67	1.2	1.09	0.01
6	Umayyad	1.6	33.33	2.4	50.00	0.6	12.50	0.2	4.17	4.8	4.38	0.06
7-10	Byzantine	2.3	31.51	3.7	50.68	1.1	15.07	0.2	2.74	7.3	6.65	0.02
11-13	Late Roman	4.4	31.43	7.6	54.28	0.9	6.43	1.1	7.86	14.0	12.76	0.06
14	Early Roman	1.9	33.33	3.3	57.89	0.3	5.26	0.2	3.51	5.7	5.20	0.03
15	Late Hellenistic	3.1	46.27	2.8	41.79	--	--	0.8	11.94	6.7	6.11	0.05
16-18	Iron 2	4.6	40.00	6.3	54.78	0.3	2.61	0.3	2.61	11.5	10.48	0.02
19	Iron 1	3.1	45.59	2.9	42.65	0.3	4.41	0.5	7.35	6.8	6.20	0.03

Table 7.4 Number of identified specimens of fish from Islamic strata

Strata	Period	Family Cichlidæ Combs #	%	Family Clariidæ Catfish #	%	Family Cyprinidæ Minnows #	%	Family Mugilidæ Grey Mullets #	%	Family Scaridæ Parrot Fish #	%	Family Sciænidæ Drums & Croakers #	%	Family Scombridæ Mackerel-like Fish #	%	Family Serranidæ Bass #	%	Family Sparidæ Sea Breams #	%	Total #	%
1	Modern	1	50.0	1	50.0	--	--	--	--	--	--	--	--	--	--	--	--	--	--	2	0.3
2-3	Mamluk	18	12.3	33	22.6	5	3.4	4	2.7	84	57.5	1	0.7	--	--	--	--	1	0.7	146	19.5
4	Ayyubid	--	--	--	--	--	--	--	--	--	--	--	--	--	--	--	--	--	--	--	--
5	Abbasid	--	--	3	75.0	--	--	--	--	1	25.0	--	--	--	--	--	--	--	--	4	0.5
6	Umayyad	25	59.5	8	19.0	--	--	1	2.4	7	16.7	--	--	--	--	1	2.4	--	--	42	5.6
7-10	Byzantine	8	33.3	8	33.3	--	--	--	--	5	20.8	1	4.2	1	4.2	--	--	1	4.2	24	3.2
11-13	Late Roman	1	1.2	1	1.2	--	--	--	--	1	1.2	--	--	79	96.3	--	--	--	--	82	10.9
14	Early Roman	1	1.4	1	1.4	--	--	--	--	1	1.4	62	89.9	4	5.8	--	--	--	--	69	9.2
15	Late Hellenistic	--	--	1	0.3	--	--	--	--	--	--	--	--	372	99.7	--	--	--	--	373	49.8
16-18	Iron 2	--	--	--	--	--	--	--	--	1	14.3	--	--	--	--	1	14.3	5	71.4	7	0.9
19	Iron 1	--	--	--	--	--	--	--	--	--	--	--	--	--	--	--	--	--	--	--	--
Sum	All	54	7.2	56	7.5	5	0.7	5	0.7	100	13.3	64	8.5	456	60.9	2	0.3	7	0.9	749	100

the combined weight of bones of cattle, sheep-goat, pig, and camel from the Mamluk period accounts for fully 42% of the bones of these species from all periods. This large assemblage of domestic species is also accompanied by a large quantity of fish, poultry, and game.

What the diet might have consisted of during the low intensity times which prevailed throughout the Abbasid, and later on throughout the Ottoman Period, is a question about which little can be said on the basis of the faunal remains on hand. An idea of what it might have been like, however, is suggested by the discussion of diets during the transhumance phase in Chapter Three.

Domesticated Mammals

As in all previous periods, the principal source of meat for the inhabitants of Hesban was sheep and goats. However (see table 7.3), there appears to have been considerable variation in the extent to which these animals were eaten from one period to the next. They played, for example, a more important role in the diet during the Abbasid and Ayyubid periods than they did in the Umayyad and Mamluk periods. Of the two species, goats may have played a proportionately larger role in the Mamluk diet than in previous times (von den Driesch and Boessneck forthcoming).

Another significant source of meat was cattle and camel, especially during Mamluk times. Together, these two species contributed over 44% of the red meat, compared with 54% for sheep-goat. In no other period, except for the Abbasid, does camel play as large a role in the diet as here. During Abbasid times camel account for almost 17% of the red meat consumed.

As could be expected with the coming of Islam, there is a marked drop in the consumption of pigs, especially in Mamluk times. Compared to Byzantine times, when pigs accounted for over 15% of the red meat, they accounted for 12.5% during

Umayyad times and for less than 2% during Mamluk times. Evidence for the consumption of horse or donkey meat is also very sparse from the Islamic periods.

Fish

According to Johannes Lepiksaar (forth-coming), who analyzed the fish bones from Tell Hesban, species of fish attested during the Islamic millennium at Hesban came primarily from the Jordan River and the Red Sea. Fish (table 7.4) from the Jordan River or its tributaries include one species (45 out of 56 specimens) belonging to the order *Cypriniformes* or catfish (*Clarias lazera*), two species (44 out of 54 specimens) belonging to the family *Cichlidæ* or combs (*Tilapia galilæa* or *Tilapia nilotica*, *Tristramella sacra* or *Tristramella simonis*) and two or possibly three species (5 out of 5 specimens) belonging to the family *Cyprinidæ* or minnows (*Barbus longiceps*, *Barbus canis* and *Varicorhinus damascinus*).

Fish from the Red Sea include two species (92 out of 100 specimens) from the family *Scaridæ* or parrotfishes (*Sparisoma sp.* and *Pseudoscarus sp.*) Fish which may have come from either the Red Sea or the Mediterranean Sea include two species (5 out of 5 specimens) belonging to the family *Mugilidæ* or grey mullets (probably *Mugil labrosus* and *Mugil ramada*).

Striking because of its poor representation in the Islamic corpus are fish from the Mediterranean Sea. For example, only one out of 64 specimens from the family *Sciænidæ* or drums and croakers is represented (found in the Mamluk strata); only one specimen out of seven from the family *Sparidæ* or sea breams is represented (also found in the Mamluk strata). Completely absent from the Islamic strata is the family *Scombridæ* or mackerels and tunnies. As noted above, fish belonging to the family *Mugilidæ* or grey mullets is found only in the Islamic strata, as is the family *Cyprinidæ* or minnows.

The fact that such a large proportion of the remains of the order *Cypriniformes* (catfish) and of the families *Chiclidæ* (combs) and *Scaridæ* (par-rotfish) come from the Islamic strata, and the fact that the families *Sciænidæ* (drums and croakers), *Sparidæ* (sea breams) and *Scombridæ* (mackerels and tunnies) are so poorly represented in these strata, very likely is indicative of changes in trade

routes which resulted from the Islamic conquest. Whereas in the Roman and Byzantine periods contact with Mediterranean ports was very likely more frequent, such contacts appear to have decreased during the Islamic centuries, and instead, contact with ports on the Red Sea increased. One reason for this shift may be the fact that the Mamluks systematically destroyed coastal forts on the Mediterranean coast to prevent the return of the Franks. This would also have dislocated the local fishing industry centered in these towns (Donner personal communication). Also, especially during the Mamluk Period, fish from the Jordan River and its tributaries became more important in the diet.

Poultry

Poultry, especially chicken, played a greater role in the diet of the Ayyubid-Mamluk inhabitants of the tell than it had in any previous period (table 7.5). Thus, the number of bones of chicken from the three Ayyubid-Mamluk strata was 1566, com-pared with 231 from the four Byzantine strata and 410 from the four Roman strata. Compared with these earlier periods, significantly more young chickens were eaten during Ayyubid-Mamluk times. Other poultry included the domestic goose and domestic pigeons, although the remains of these species are too few to allow any general statement of their relative importance during the various Islamic periods.

Strata	Period	# of Bones #	%	Min # of Individuals #	%	% Young
1	Modern	---	---	---	---	---
2-4	Ayyubid-Mamluk	1566	65.83	128	58.44	22.0
5-6	Umayyad-Abbasid	127	5.34	13	5.94	8.0
7-10	Byzantine	231	9.71	27	12.33	11.5
11-14	Roman	410	17.23	41	18.72	14.2
15	Late Hellenistic	41	1.72	7	3.20	14.6
16-18	Iron 2	3	0.13	2	0.91	---
19	Iron 1	1	0.04	1	0.46	---
Sum	All	2379	100	219	100	

Table 7.5 Number of identified specimens of chicken from Islamic strata

Game

As in previous periods at Tell Hesban, the most commonly hunted species of game during the

Islamic centuries were gazelles. Other species which appear to have been hunted for the table include red deer and wild boar. The most commonly hunted game bird appears to have been the chukar. Other birds which very likely were hunted and eaten during the Islamic centuries include sand partridges, ostriches, and bustards. A much more detailed discussion of the wild animals and birds which may have contributed to the diet during the Islamic centuries will be included in a separate volume in this series (see Appendix B).

Cereals, Legumes, Vegetables, and Fruits

Collected from the Umayyad and Ayyubid-Mamluk strata at Tell Hesban were a total of 189 carbonized seeds (see table 7.2). Cereals identified include wheat and barley. Legumes identified include lentil, bitter vetch, and broad beans. Fruits identified include olive and grape.

Sedentarization and Nomadization

One of the challenges of attempting to reconstruct long-term changes in Hesban's food system during the Islamic centuries is the large "gaps" in the archaeological data from the tell and surrounding region. These gaps, which were noted in Chapter Four, both preceded and followed the prosperous Ayyubid-Mamluk period. The factors to which these gaps are attributable are at least three, two of which have been noted earlier. They include, first, the expedition's research strategy which was primarily tell-oriented and hence not sensitive to lighter forms of permanent and semipermanent occupation as exemplified by seasonal cave villages; second, the limited extent of knowledge of how to date pottery from the Islamic centuries in the late '60s and early '70s when this project was in the field; and third, the fact that settlement and landuse during these "gap" periods actually, and in reality, *were* comparatively lighter than during the heavily occupied Roman-Byzantine and Ayyubid-Mamluk periods.

In this chapter, an attempt has been made to create a picture of how people lived at Hesban and vicinity during these "gap" periods. To this end, the role of the fortified residential compound, or *qasr*, and of the seasonal cave village was discussed. While both of these forms of settlements very likely were in use throughout the entire Islamic

Period, they represent a lighter form of occupation and landuse than do villages and towns of the kind that prospered and exploited the hinterlands during the Ayyubid-Mamluk period. Furthermore, the existence of this form of settlement in central Transjordan should serve to caution against the impression that there were *no* permanently settled people in this part of Jordan during, for example, the Abbasid or Ottoman periods. Indeed, Hesban itself very likely was occupied more or less permanently in this way throughout these "gap" periods. This statement, however, is made with the benefit of the hindsight which comes from a food-system oriented, rather than a tell-oriented examination of the finds from Tell Hesban and vicinity.

Another important by-product of this attempt to understand how people lived during the "gap" periods at Hesban is the insight it provides into the settlement pattern and social structure of periods when villages and towns prospered. For example, during the Ayyubid-Mamluk period, residents of Hesban not only lived in clusters of enclosed residential compounds or *qusur*, there is evidence that many also lived in caves. As was the case at Hesban in the early part of this century, very likely those who could afford to build and move into the *qusur* compounds were relatively wealthier than those who remained in caves. Further examination of this proposal would be desirable and would involve comparisons of pottery, objects, and bones from the caves with those of the residential compounds to ascertain the extent to which differentiation into rich and poor is noticeable.

This research on the Islamic centuries at Hesban also raises interesting questions about what happens to the rich and the poor when a town ceases to prosper and begins to be abandoned. Presumably, the greater adjustment must be made by the rich, many of whom would have had to abandon their comfortable residential compounds and either move away, or adopt a simpler form of life involving a return to living in caves and tents. To the extent that the poor were already living this way, they could go on with their lives, although very likely, their lives too would be disrupted to some degree. Furthermore, it is significant to note, in this context, that it is those people who have persisted in living in caves and tents, even during times of prosperity, that have preserved, by their total way of life, the know-how by means of which survival is possible during periods of abatement.

The examples of long-term residents of the project area, such as the Ajarmeh, provide some insight into structural arrangements which traditionally have enabled people in central Transjordan to cope during times of political and economic uncertainty. In their case five strategies can be pointed to. These include one, maintaining the ability to be mobile when necessary; two, maintaining—by means of tribal organization—access to a variety of natural resources; three, combining livestock production with limited cereal cultivation; four, knowing how to hunt and gather wild roots and plants; and five, being satisfied, and knowing how, to make their homes in tents and caves. By these means, the Ajarmeh minimized their exposure to exploitation by tax authorities, capricious townsmen, and hostile tribesmen throughout the Ottoman centuries.

Finally, this analysis of the Islamic centuries adds further to our general understanding of the processes of sedentarization and nomadization in the vicinity of Hesban. Since prehistoric times, these processes have involved gradual changes at the level of the individual household which, in turn, resulted in a spectrum of slightly different food procurement and residential arrangements within a given tribe or village at any given point in time. It is as the center of gravity of this spectrum has shifted, either in the direction of nomadization or sedentarization, that changes in the intensity of the local food system have oscillated over the centuries between the low and high ends of the continuum.

Chapter Eight

INTENSIFICATION AND ABATEMENT:
SUMMARY AND REFLECTIONS

Chapter Eight

Intensification and Abatement: Summary and Reflections

Introduction

In concluding this study the following questions will be considered: What were the transitions, in terms of changing configurations of food system conditions, which occurred over the past three and half millennia at Hesban and vicinity? What were the mechanisms of intensification and abatement accounting for these transitions? In what ways did food system configurations differ in each millennium and how were they the same? What are the strengths and limitations of food system analysis? What are some implications of this undertaking for research and planning concerned with the future of Jordan and its people?

Over the past three and a half millennia, the project area food system reached variously constituted high-intensity food system configurations at least four times (see fig. 8.1): during the 7th and 6th centuries B.C. (Iron II Period), during the 3rd through 6th centuries A.D. (Late Roman and Byzantine periods), during the 12th and 13th centuries A.D. (Ayyubid-Mamluk periods), and since *ca.* A.D. 1950 (Modern Period). A closer look at the processes of intensification and abatement which led up to and followed each of these peaks will serve to illustrate how sedentarization and nomadization occurred from one millennium to the next within the project area.

Overview of Food System Transitions

Iron Age Millennium

At the beginning of the Iron Age millennium (*ca.* 1200 B.C.), a low-to-medium intensity food system configuration prevailed. Apart from a few permanent cereal-farming settlements such as those which existed at Jalul, El 'Umeiri, and Iktanu, the prevailing form of landuse consisted of pastoralism involving transhumants who specialized in raising large flocks of cattle and sheep on the fertile pastures of Hesban and vicinity. Gradually over the ensuing centuries, farmsteads were established in the vicinity of certain of the larger permanent settlements, first in the northern hills and along the plateau ridge, then later on also in the western descent. With these farmsteads came increased production of grapes and olives and other tree fruits. This process of sedentarization and population growth reached its high point during the 7th and 6th centuries B.C. This is evidenced by the large number of farmsteads dated to these centuries throughout the project area, by the impressive undertakings related to water collection and storage at places like Hesban, and by the evidence of bureaucratization (in the form of Iron II cylinder seals and scarabs from Tell Hesban) of certain activities related to the maintenance of the sociopolitical infrastructure during this period.

Among the large number of cooperating factors which played a role in fueling the power drive during the Iron Age millennium, four have been identified archaeologically that deserve further research. First was the emergence within the project area of a new pattern of rural-based craft specialization and economic exchange similar to that which was emerging elsewhere throughout the ancient Near East during this millennium. At Tell Hesban, for example, a flourishing textile industry thrived throughout this millennium. This pattern contrasts with the situation which existed throughout the ancient Near East during the previous millennium, when craft specialization was primarily an urban as opposed to a rural-based phenomenon.

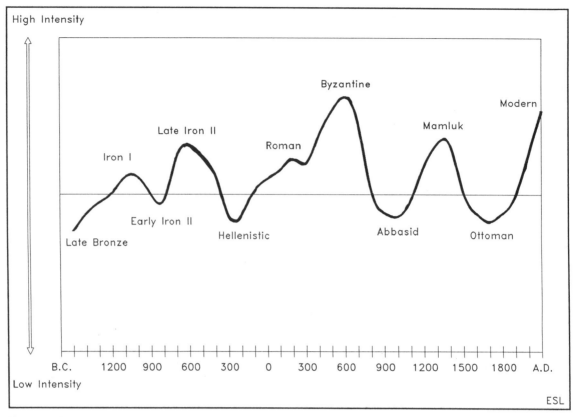

Fig. 8.1 Temporal variability in intensity of project area food system: a first approximation

A second factor that played a crucial role in harnessing the rural population to producing food surpluses was the formation of local state governments (in Israel, Ammon, Moab, and Edom) with kings and armies on both sides of the Jordan during this millennium. While throughout most of the Iron Age millennium, the project area remained politically unstable as a result of successive wars between these various local kings or between them and warlords from Egypt or Mesopotamia, Transjordan appears to have enjoyed its longest and most peaceful period politically following the rise of King Mesha to the throne of the Moabite Kingdom. Over the next two centuries, the bureaucracy and socioeconomic infrastructure needed to further intensify the rural economy was improved to the point where a high-intensity food system configuration could be maintained. The modest delocalization of the diet at Tell Hesban during the Iron II Period no doubt reflects the region-wide trade in foodstuffs which occurred during these latter centuries of the Iron Age millennium.

A third factor was the increase in long-distance trade along the King's Highway and other international trade routes in use in Transjordan during the Iron Age millennium. Not only was such trade promoted by local kings, such as King Solomon of the Israelite Kingdom, as in earlier centuries, the Transjordan trade corridor continued to be useful to merchants from both Egypt and Mesopotamia as well. That traffic along the King's Highway reached a high point of some kind during the Iron II Period is likely, given the relatively secure conditions which prevailed during those centuries (cf. Eph'al 1982).

A fourth factor which played a role in facilitating the establishment of farmsteads and villages on natural hills and slopes away from readily available sources of water, such as springs and streams, was the spread within the project area sometime early on in the Iron Age millennium of plastering techniques whereby cisterns could be effectively sealed for use in year-round water storage. Not only did such techniques facilitate the establishment of permanent settlement at Hesban, but numerous other sites which were similarly distant from springs or streams were also settled for the first time during the Iron Age, particularly in the eastern plain, northern hills and along the plateau ridge in places where readily available sources of spring or stream water did not exist. That similarly effective plastering techniques were not widely used during the Early Bronze Period, when the project area was undergoing an earlier power drive, is evident from the survey finds which locate most of the sites from this period near readily available sources of water, especially in the slopes along the western descent.

The high-intensity peak which was reached during the 7th and 6th centuries B.C. was followed by a period of abatement during most of the Hellenistic Period, involving a return to a low-to-medium-intensity configuration which lasted until the 1st century B.C. While a few cereal villages may have remained in existence throughout most of this period, especially in the northern hills region in the hinterland of the city of Philadelphia (Amman), transhumant pastoralism appears to have prevailed throughout most of the rest of the project area. Among the factors which very likely contributed to this abatement was the collapse of the state apparatus which had promoted and nourished the power drive during the immediately preceding centuries. Along with this collapse came decreased security for people and their belongings, leading to less regular traffic along the international trade routes which ran through or adjacent to the project area. Under diminished public security and lost opportunities for trade and exchange, the local population which remained was forced to turn back upon their own resources. This included a return to subsistence-oriented production of cereals and small flocks of sheep and goats in such readily defendable locations as those which exist in the northern hills and along the plateau ridge.

Greco-Roman Millennium

Between the 5th and the 2nd centuries B.C. such low-to-medium intensity configurations remained the status quo throughout the project area. During these centuries, Tell Hesban, for example, is described by its excavators as undergoing an "occupational hiatus," although its caves, ruins, and cisterns were no doubt being used seasonally for sheltering and watering by certain of the shepherd households still making a living within the project area. By the end of the 2nd century B.C., a foothold was established by the Greeks within the project area. Not only can these Hellenized soldier-farmers be recognized by the discovery of Greek pottery in the fortified settlement they established at Hesban, their eating habits give them away as well. This resettlement signals the beginning of another power drive—a drive which has not been equaled in its peak intensity by any before it or after it, including the most recent one.

Over the centuries which followed the initial establishment of Hellenized cereal farmers at Hesban, several intertwined paths of development took place within the project area. On the one hand, there was the path pursued by Hellenized and Romanized elite which gradually led to the establishment of urban-oriented, moisture-maximizing agriculture on a grand scale. On the other hand there were the paths chosen by the rural masses, some of which led to close and intimate cooperation within the Greco-Roman production regime, others which led to pastoral-oriented production regimes emphasizing autonomy and self-sufficiency as a counter measure to increasing disinheritance and alienation experienced at the hands of the urban elite.

As in the earlier Iron Age, the process of sedentarization began with cereal farming centered in fortified villages and farmsteads on the plateau. Resettled were most of the farmsteads and villages which had originally been settled in the previous millennium, plus several new ones. As subsistence farming of cereals gave way to increasingly urban-oriented fruit, vine, and vegetable production, settlements increased in size and number along the plateau ridge and especially along the well-watered slopes and valleys of the western descent. In these areas aqueducts and terraces were constructed on a scale never before seen in this region, especially during Byzantine times. Not only were mules and donkeys raised in large numbers in order to supply draft power along these terraced slopes and hillsides, swine and poultry were also produced on a large scale, especially during this same period, to compensate for the diminished availability of meats from pasture animals. In order also to increase the water supply on the plateau, massive reservoirs were built on a grand scale in wadis running nearby or at the foot of densely settled hilltop

Plate 8.1 Cycles of intensification and abatement at Hesban. Portrayed in this painting are changes over time in types of settlements over which existed at Tell Hesban. The 13 ascending circles represent successive historical periods over the past 3,500 years. The agricultural scenes represent predominant methods of food production on the fields surrounding this tell and include producing cereals in the plains and wadi bottoms, growing vine and tree crops on terraces and slopes, raising flocks of sheep and goats, and being camel pastoralists.

Three major cycles of settlement and landuse have occurred at Tell Hesban and vicinity. At the beginning of each cycle, predominant methods of landuse were cultivation of cereals and raising of sheep and goats. At the peak of each cycle, when settlement was most intense, vine and tree crops played an important role as well. In the periods between each cycle, when settlement was least intense, pastoralists utilized Tell Hesban and vicinity on a seasonal basis.

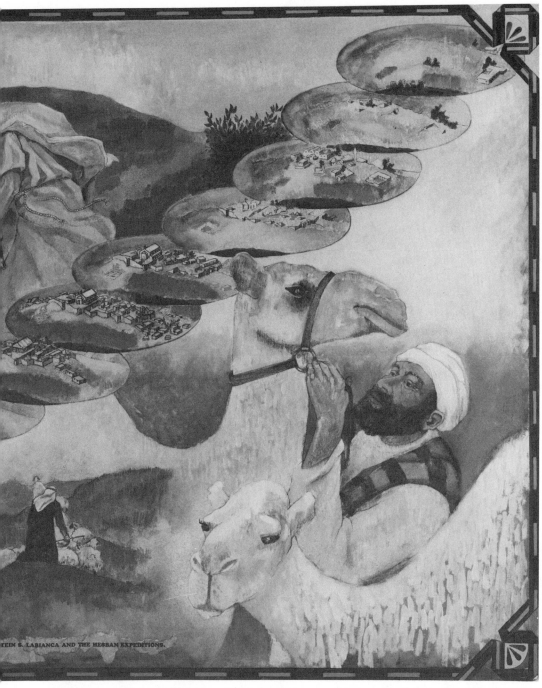

Plate 8.1 Cycles of intensification and abatement at Hesban (*continued*). The first cycle began about 1200 B.C. and ended about 500 B.C. This cycle corresponds to the Iron Age and is represented by the 2nd (Iron I) and 3rd circles (Iron II) on this painting, starting from the bottom left corner. The second cycle began about 200 B.C. and ended about A.D. 750. It corresponds to Roman-Byzantine-Umayyad times and is represented by the 5th through 9th circles (Late Hellenistic, Early Roman, Late Roman, Byzantine, Umayyad). The third cycle began about A.D. 1200 and ended about A.D. 1450. This corresponds to Ayyubid-Mamluk times and is represented by the 10th circle.

The 1st (Late Bronze), 4th (Late Persian-Early Hellenistic), 10th (Abbasid and Fatimid) and 12th (Ottoman) circles represent times when there was little or no permanent occupation of Tell Hesban. The 13th circle represents the present-day resettlement of the tell by members of the Ajarmeh tribe.

villages and towns, as in the case of Madaba and Hesban. Along with major highways, such as the *via nova Traiana*, subsidiary roads were also built, some of these serving individual estates and farmsteads as well as local villages and towns.

As these changes were taking place certain members of the rural population appear to have followed a different course involving a quest for self-sufficiency and independence from the Greco-Roman power drive. Thus, while Hesban (now called Esbus) and certain of the other villages along the plateau ridge entered upon a phase of growing urbanization and delocalization of the food supply during Late Roman times, certain of the farmers in the hinterlands to the east appear to have gradually abandoned their lands either to settle in the towns or to return to transhumance. By Byzantine times, therefore, as a consequence of the ubiquitous spread of permanent settlement and moisture-maximizing agriculture, those segments of the population having returned to pastoral pursuits as their primary occupation were pushed further into the desert, judging from the fact that their contribution to the local economy gradually fades during the period.

Five transforming influences must be reckoned with in accounting for the power drive which occurred during the Greco-Roman millennium. Each of these represent, in various ways, a steady advance of new opportunities for the people of Transjordan in general and of the project area in particular. To begin with, the Hellenization of Palestine revitalized international trade routes and certain strategically located caravan cities along the Transjordanian highland, including Philadelphia (Amman). Second, the sedentarization of the Nabataean Arabs to the south resulted in remarkable advances in moisture-maximizing agricultural techniques, which laid the technological foundation for the advance of such agriculture also within the project area. Third, the Romanization of Palestine resulted not only in improved public security in rural areas through the establishment of Roman military forts along the eastern frontier of the country, but also in heightened bureaucratization and delocalization of the food system, increased craft specialization, urbanization and trade. Fourth, the Christianization of Palestine during Byzantine times further strengthened the infrastructure put in place by the Romans. Additionally, European wealth began to be pumped into the local economy

by pious believers and pilgrims in the form of donations toward the construction of churches, monasteries, and memorials in places like Nebo, Madaba, and Hesban. Fifth, all of the above led to continual population growth which, in turn, steadily heightened the pressure on local farmers for intensified food production.

Among the many cooperating factors which eventually led to the collapse of the Greco-Roman power drive, at least two may be attributed to the shortsighted policies of the Hellenized and Romanized elite. First is the gradual disinheritance and alienation of certain members of the rural population, which began during the Early Roman Period and continued until the end of the Byzantine Period. This situation would account for the continuous process of nomadization which occurred side-by-side with the sedentarization promoted by the Greco-Roman elite in the region. As a consequence of this, a large reservoir of nomadized peoples was built up in the Arabian desert. It was the energies and disaffections of these peoples which Muhammad, under the banner of Islam, was able to harness in mobilizing the Arab conquest of Palestine and the rest of the Middle East during the 6th and 7th centuries A.D.

Second is the gradual worsening of the lot of the rural farming population of Palestine during the 2nd and 3rd centuries A.D. (*cf.* Sperber 1974). As a result of increasing taxation and bureaucratization of production, formerly free peasant proprietors were forced to become servile tenant farmers. As the demand for food surpluses by the increasingly urbanized populace escalated, shortages became more frequent both in the countryside and among the subservient classes in the towns. This, we may conjecture, led to increasing prevalence of malnutrition and weakened resistance to disease among a large segment of the populace. At the same time, the spread of infectious disease agents was facilitated by the delocalized food supply which heightened the chances of disease agents from distant places reaching the population in places like Hesban. It was, very likely, this synergism of social and biological factors that set the stage for the sudden demographic collapse which appears to have occurred during the 6th and 7th centuries in Transjordan.

A third factor which deserves to be mentioned is the impact of repeated earthquakes and droughts on the stability of the Greco-Roman production regime. While such natural hazards had existed in Transjordan during previous millennia, the extent to which the Greco-Roman regime depended upon large reservoirs and aqueducts for its water supply would have made it more vulnerable to temporary setbacks resulting from earthquakes or successive years of drought. While such setbacks could be overcome as long as a sufficient supply of laborers was on hand to make repairs or haul water, when this supply was diminished due to weakening of the state's coercive powers and other causes, the work of repairing these massive structures would have fallen short of what was needed. This, in turn, heightened the problem of providing sufficient water for future generations, thus further intensifying the accumulation of hazards with which the populace had to cope.

Finally, the gradual loss of income from pilgrims and believers in other parts of the world, which took place following the Islamic conquest of the Holy Land, along with the shift from Damascus to Baghdad of the political center of Islam under the Abbasids in A.D. 750, added further to the problems of the sedentary population of Transjordan. These circumstances, with those mentioned above, worked together to bring back a low-intensity food system configuration within the project area by the end of the 7th century A.D. Basic to this configuration was, no doubt, the camel which by this time had become a favored animal by the nomadized Arabs of the Arabian desert. As in Late Ottoman times, however, configurations involving various combinations of sheep, goats, camels, and limited cereal cultivation by tribal peasants and transhumants was very likely the prevailing pattern. Very little in the way of direct evidence of what the food system was like between the 7th and the 11th centuries A.D. is on hand from the project area, however. What is known is that neither at Tell Hesban nor in the surrounding project area is there any architectural evidence that has been firmly dated to these centuries, either in the form of ruins of settled towns, villages, or farmsteads. This situation reflects that of central Transjordan as a whole during the Abbasid, Fatimid, and Seljuq-Zengid centuries (Sauer 1980).

Islamic Centuries

Between the beginning of the 12th and the end of the 14th centuries A.D. another power drive completed its cycle within the project area. While in intensity the Ayyubid-Mamluk power drive was much less powerful than the previous Greco-Roman one, it reached a medium-to-high configuration in terms of food system conditions. Hesban itself appears to have been a regional market center of some importance, judging from the intensity of rebuilding and the extent to which the tell as a whole was settled. At its high point the town consisted of a cluster of qusur, each with its own courtyard. One of these buildings included a bath complex requiring about six attendants for its operation (de Vries 1986). While these qusur were probably the residences of the elite, the majority of the town's inhabitants very likely lived in less expensive buildings and caves.

As most of the settlements during the Ayyubid-Mamluk period were along the plateau ridge and in the northern hills, it seems that a mixed agro-pastoral production regime emphasizing sheep, goat, and cereals prevailed during this period. Particularly abundant in our finds, in fact, are sheep and goats, although poultry appears also to have been raised in large numbers. The degree to which the diet was delocalized (fish from the Gulf of Aqaba are abundant in the finds from this period) and the presence of a rich variety of coins and other market-related items from the tell give further evidence of its regional importance.

Three factors must be considered to account for the intensification peak which was reached during the Ayyubid-Mamluk period. The first of these was the new opportunity for trade and commerce which followed in the wake of the revival of the eastern caravan route during the preceding Late Fatimid Period. A second factor was the occupation of portions of Syria, Palestine, and Transjordan by the Franks, which provided a common threat against which the indigenous tribesmen had to unify. Thus the stage was set for the emergence of a great hero, namely Saladin, under whose leadership greater Syria was liberated from occupation by the Franks. A third factor was the earlier gains of the Arab agricultural revolution which could be capitalized upon by the population in this area now that markets were again expanding.

To account for the abatement which followed this peak, three factors are of particular importance. The first was the weakening of the Mamluk Sultanate's central administration, which led to loss of resolve in the task of protecting trade and the agricultural hinterlands of the Eastern Mediterranean. The second was the invasion of Palestine by the Mongols, which resulted in devastation of Damascus and other important administrative and commercial centers throughout Syria. The third was the plague, which in the 14th century decimated a large percentage of the population of Palestine and Syria.

As a consequence of these events, a low-intensity food system configuration gradually established itself again within the project area. This system was presided over by the Ottoman Turks, who occupied Palestine from the beginning of the 16th to the beginning of the 20th century A.D. It involved movement of people and animals between pastures in lowland areas such as the Ghor and the eastern desert and various campsites and cave villages located in the highlands surrounding Tell Hesban. To the various transhumant tribesmen who vied for control of the project area, the reservoirs, cisterns, caves, and ruined buildings left by the Greco-Roman and Ayyubid-Mamluk cultures represented resources which had their own meaning and use within their economies and lifestyles. Such installations provided temporary places for sheltering their families and watering their herds, and in many instances ruins on top of mounds and hills were utilized to construct rude burial grounds and storage depots.

Modern Period

The most rapidly advancing power drive to take place within the project area is the present one which began about 150 years ago. Although in terms of density of villages and farmsteads and in terms of the spread of moisture-maximizing agriculture the Modern Period has not yet surpassed what existed during Byzantine times, it is only a matter of a few decades before it will, assuming that population growth and agricultural development continues at its present pace. Already a high-intensity configuration has been reached in terms of food system conditions, including the sedentarization of most of the local inhabitants and extensive undertakings in such areas as water management, road construction, market-oriented production of crop and animal products, and delocalization of the diet, especially in the larger villages and towns. Outstanding among the factors which account for this intensification are the role

of the state in introducing the infrastructure necessary in order to support a high-intensity configuration, the new opportunities for trade and exchange which have come with the rise of world capitalism, and the massive influx to Transjordan of skilled agricultural labor which resulted from the wars with Israel.

Configuration Differences and Similarities

Having presented an overview of the food system transitions which occurred over the past three and a half millennia within the project area, and some of the factors contributing to the completion of the Iron Age and the Greco-Roman cycles, we shall next briefly consider some ways in which the food system configurations prevailing during these different millennia were alike and differed from each other in how they were constituted. Rather than attempting to state all of the various ways in which differences and similarities occur, the aim here is to highlight certain outstanding examples in order to orient to the type of insights which may come from such an undertaking.

One dimension along which temporal differences may be noted is that of water provisioning. Here is seen an instance of a cumulative development of sorts in terms of increasing capacities for supplying water. Thus, during the Iron Age a major improvement over the preceding millennia was the spread of plastering techniques which enabled people to settle year-round in locations which had no nearby source of running water. While cisterns continued to be built and used by the Romans, their power drive required even larger capacities for water provisioning which led to the widespread construction of reservoirs on the plateau and aqueducts in the western descent area. During the Modern Period, cisterns continue to be used in rural areas, but not reservoirs. What has been improved in the present era is people's capacity to exploit sources of water lying deep below the surface. Thus, by means of mechanical pumps, water is today being transported from underground aquifers or from springs to villages and fields on the plateau.

Another dimension along which temporal differences may be noted is that of the habitation of the farming population during high-intensity configurations. During the Iron Age, for example, fortified farmsteads inhabited by only one or a few households appear to have been the prevailing pattern whereas, during the Late Roman and Byzantine periods, the farming population appears to have been concentrated in large estates, villages, and towns. Today villages serve as the principal place of residence for the farming population.

That temporal differences existed along a number of other dimensions between same-intensity configurations can safely be assumed. As research progresses it will no doubt be possible, for instance, to identify a number of ways in which transhumance differed during each of these millennia. For example, that the camel played a more important role among pastoralists during the Islamic centuries than it did for pastoralists during the preceding ones (during which the donkey and mule very likely were relied on more for hauling purposes) has already been suggested.

Whereas temporal differences such as these will come more clearly into view as the particulars of each millennium and of each different configuration occurring within them are brought to light, continuity from one millennium to the next exists primarily at the general level of the three models presented in Chapter Four, namely between the conditions which characterize low-, medium-, and high-intensity configurations, respectively. Thus, high seasonal variation in location and intensity of the human population is a situation which recurs in various ways within the low-intensity configurations of all three millennia. In the case of medium-intensity configurations, an emphasis on field crops of different kinds and settlement in variously fortified residences appears to have recurred as well from one millennium to the next. At the level of high-intensity configurations, delocalization of the diet in various ways can also be counted on across the successive millennia. To these many others could be added. An example would be the link between tribalism and low-intensity configurations and that between centralized governments and high-intensity ones, and so on.

When an attempt is made to compare the rate at which the processes of sedentarization and nomadization occurred across these successive millennia, the impression is gained that the former process tended to occur at a slower rate than the latter. Thus, on the one hand, for the Iron Age power drive to reach its peak it took at least four centuries, and for the Greco-Roman one at least three centuries were needed. The abatement process, on the other hand, took less than two centuries in both instances. An exception to this pattern is the modern power drive which has occurred at the unprecedented speed of less than a century.

The reason why this difference should exist in the case of the preindustrial rates is actually quite simple. It has to do with the fact that to build the infrastructure needed to support high-intensity configurations required both planning, material resources of various kinds, and large amounts of labor, whereas to reverse such a power drive all that in theory would be required would be a severe natural event such as a prolonged drought, an earthquake, or a plague. A massive military assault aimed directly at disabling the infrastructure upon which a particular high-intensity configuration rested would have a similar effect.

This point leads back to a proposal stated in Chapter Two regarding the difference between the processes of sedentarization and nomadization as general sociocultural phenomena in the Middle East. It was suggested there that whereas the process of sedentarization tends to be directly promoted by the policies and actions of a state apparatus of some sort, the process of nomadization is best understood as a form of resistance, a sort of natural response by the rural population to the shortsighted and often exploitative undertakings of those at the center of sedentary power. Rather than being a process that is deliberately instituted by pastoralists, it represents instead a form of escape, a return to greater independence, and a distancing on the part of some members of the rural population from the cultural and economic domination of sedentary elites.

This ability to choose alternative actions, to remain resilient in the face of hazards and changing social conditions, has traditionally been valued by the rural populace of the Middle East. It is precisely because of such orientations that metaphors based on the unilineal principle of kinship have tended to play an important role in structuring social relations among cultivators and shepherds alike. Not only have such metaphors facilitated the process of organizing people at various levels, whether it be the household, the village, the camping unit, or the tribe, they have also served to enable the changing organizational needs which tended to arise as individual households moved back and forth along the mobility continuum between nomadic and sedentary. It is not surprising at all, therefore, that whereas various forms of state organization have come and gone throughout different times and regions of the Middle East, tribal organization in various forms has remained a constant since recorded history, even to the present day.

A matter requiring further study is the extent to which the repeated oscillations between low- and high-intensity configurations in Transjordan might be attributed to the cooperative effect of the persistence of tribalism as an indigenous risk-management institution and the relatively greater degree to which this region is prone to droughts than is nearby Cis-Jordan. In other words, given that droughts are likely to occur more frequently and for longer periods along the Transjordanian highland than along the highlands and plains to the west of the Jordan River, to what extent has this situation heightened the persistence of tribalism in Transjordan and, as a consequence of this, resistance to power drives promoted by would-be builders of nation states? Could it be that the transience of high-intensity configurations in Transjordan is a consequence of stronger pull toward low-intensity food system configurations exerted by the collective will of the indigenous population of this region, given the greater challenges to survival presented by Transjordan as a natural habitat?

Of relevance in regards to these questions is the fact that in every historical instance involving a high-intensity food system configuration in Transjordan, including the present, the region has been integrated economically and politically with other, less vulnerable regions as a buffer against the inevitability of drought and the threat of famine. In other words, in order to overcome traditional resistance to power drives, Transjordan's rulers have historically needed to rely on bonds of friendship and economic cooperation with other states as a fundamental prerequisite of sustained development and stability. To the extent, therefore, that such relationships were able to ward off the effects of locally recurring droughts and other natural hazards, high-intensity food system configurations have survived.

Conclusions

Finally, a few remarks are in order regarding the limitations and strengths of the concept and method of food system analysis by means of which the present investigation of sedentarization and nomadization in Transjordan has been carried out. Following are some ways in which this perspective has facilitated the present undertaking.

First, the delineation of five archaeologically traceable parameters of the food system organized our analysis and discussion throughout this study. Second, the perspective served to focus attention on the recent past within the project area as a means to become acquainted, in a heuristic sense, with the workings of the local food system. Third, our acquaintance with the recent past enabled the formulation of procedures for converting archaeological information from Tell Hesban and vicinity into data about food system conditions throughout the past. Fourth, this acquaintance with the recent past also facilitated the formulation of a hypothesis setting forth three models or configurations regarding how the archaeological data about food system conditions in the past could be expected to be correlated under different states of intensity of the food system. Fifth, this perspective offered a unified framework for examining change over time in the intensity states of food system configurations from one period to the next. Sixth, it provided an orientation to a number of mechanisms whereby temporal changes from one food system intensity state to another could be accounted for. Seventh, insofar as this perspective focused attention on the interaction of environmental and social conditions in people's quest for food, it served to bring to light some possible explanations for the transience of high-intensity food system configurations in Transjordan. And eighth, as a result of all of the above, integration was possible of a wide range of lines of research and information which in the past have tended to progress in isolation one from another.

Several important limitations of the food system approach need also to be stated. To begin with, there is no necessary connection between adherence to a food system framework and some form of uniformitarianism or some species of environmental or historical determinism. As has been emphasized many times throughout the foregoing pages, the use of this perspective has been as an aid to integration and interpretation, in a heuristic sense, of the diverse lines of research generated by multidisciplinary archaeological undertakings such as the Heshbon Expedition.

Another limitation of the food system approach is that it is not equally applicable everywhere. It has worked well in this particular case because the empirical context has been primarily a rural one where the quest for food has been a fundamental and pervasive activity structuring the lives of the local population throughout most periods. Where, for instance, the empirical context involves an industrial setting of some kind, or a place of ritual or worship of one sort or another, other frameworks are likely to be needed, although to the extent that the quest for food, or symbolic behaviors related to this quest accounts for at least a portion of the daily activities of populations in such places, the present perspective may be useful.

A third potential drawback with this approach is that, even where the quest for food constitutes a fundamental and pervasive activity, other activities not directly related to this quest may be overlooked as a result of this focus. While this need not become a problem, it is one that deserves a note of caution.

In addition to these limitations of the food system perspective, shortcomings having to do with the nature of the empirical materials available must again be noted. For example, neither the excavation results nor the survey results were such that reliable estimates of project area population sizes and characteristics could be ascertained for the various historical periods. Such estimates would obviously have been useful in helping to answer questions regarding the causes of food system intensification and abatement. Not even the extant analysis of the human skeletal remains from Hesban and nearby cemeteries was of much help in this regard.

In planning for the future well-being of the people of Transjordan, much can be learned from continued research concerned with the country's food system. We have noted already some of the potential dangers inherent in power drives leading to high-intensity configurations, including the tendency toward environmental degradation and nomadization as a traditional response to policies perceived to be stifling to the traditional emphasis on resilience through diversified household economies. We have also noted the connection between the survival of high-intensity food system configurations and leadership capable of building and maintaining broadly based ties of friendships and economic cooperation.

To what extent these lessons from the past are applicable to planning for the future is an important question. Certainly there are some lessons to be learned from the Nabataean ancestors of the present population whose moisture-maximizing agriculture survived for centuries after their eclipse as monopolizers of the Arabian caravan trade. The widespread use of large reservoirs by Transjordanian peoples during Roman times is another practice worthy of consideration in planning for the water needs of Jordan's population in the future. Much can also still be learned from closer examination of the traditional risk-management strategies of Jordan's rural families whose traditions have enabled them to survive despite wide fluctuations in the region's political and economic integration over the past centuries. In deepening our understanding of concerns such as these there is much room for cooperation between scholars and scientists knowledgeable about Jordan's past and national leaders concerned with the country's present and future.

Appendix A

BIBLIOGRAPHY OF HESBAN-RELATED
SCHOLARLY PUBLICATIONS

Appendix A

Bibliography of Hesban-Related Scholarly Publications[1]

Editor's note: the following abbreviations have been used in this appendix. *ADAJ* (*Annual of the Department of Antiquities of Jordan*), *AUSS* (*Andrews University Seminary Studies*, and ASOR (American Schools for Oriental Research).

Alomia, M. K.
1978   Tell Hesban 1976: Notes on the Present Avifauna of Tell Hesban. *AUSS* 16: 289-303.

Ayalon, M.
1973   Tell Hesban 1971: Heshbon Ostracon III. *AUSS* 11: 132.

Battenfield, J. R.
1974   Tell Hesban 1974. *Newsletter of the Near East Archaeological Society* No. 2: 3.

Beegle, D. M.
1969   Tell Hesban 1968: Area B. *AUSS* 7: 118-126.

1975a   Tell Hesban 1973: Necropolis Area F. *AUSS* 13: 203-211.

1975b   Tell Hesban 1973: Soundings—Area G. *AUSS* 13: 213-215.

Bird, P. A.
1969   Tell Hesban 1968: Area D. *AUSS* 7: 165-216.

Blaine, M.
1978   Tell Hesban 1976: Area G.12. *AUSS* 16: 183-188.

Boessneck, J., and von den Driesch, A.
1978   Tell Hesban 1976: Preliminary Analysis of the Animal Bones from Tell Hesban. *AUSS* 16: 259-288.

1981   Erste Ergebnisse unserer Bestimmung-sarbeit am dem Tierknochenfunden vom Tell Hesban/Jordanien. *Archaeologie und Naturwissenschaften* 2: 55-71.

Boraas, R. S.
1974   Notes and Reviews. *Palestine Exploration Quarterly* CVI,1: 5, 6.

1977   The Annual Heshbon Preliminary Reports. Paper presented at the Annual Meeting of ASOR. December 28, San Francisco.

Boraas, R. S., and Geraty, L. T.
1976   The Fourth Campaign at Tell Hesban (1974). *AUSS* 14: 1-16.

1978   The Fifth Campaign at Tell Hesban (1976). *AUSS* 16: 1-18.

1979   The Long Life of Tell Hesban, Jordan. *Archaeology* 32: 10-20.

Boraas, R. S., Geraty, L. T., *et al.*
1976   *Heshbon 1974: The Fourth Campaign at Tell Hesban. A Preliminary Report.* Andrews University Monographs. Vol. 9. Berrien Springs, MI: Andrews University.

1978   *Heshbon 1976: The Fifth Campaign at Tell Hesban. A Preliminary Report.*

Andrews University Monographs. Vol. 10. Berrien Springs, MI: Andrews University.

Boraas, R. S., and Horn, S. H.
1969a   The First Campaign at Tell Hesban (1968). *AUSS* 7: 97-117.

1969b   Heshbon. *Revue Biblique* 76: 395-398.

1969c   Tell Hesban 1968: The Results of the First Season's Work. *AUSS* 7: 217-222.

1973   The Second Campaign at Tell Hesban (1971). *AUSS* 11: 1-16.

1975   The Third Campaign at Tell Hesban (1973). *AUSS* 13: 101-116.

Boraas, R. S.; Horn, S. H.; *et al.*
1969   *Heshbon 1968: The First Campaign at Tell Hesban. A Preliminary Report.* Andrews University Monographs. Vol. 2. Berrien Springs, MI: Andrews University.

1973   *Heshbon 1971: The Second Campaign at Tell Hesban. A Preliminary Report.* Andrews University Monographs. Vol. 6. Berrien Springs, MI: Andrews University.

1975   *Heshbon 1973: The Third Campaign at Tell Hesban. A Preliminary Report.* Andrews University Monographs. Vol. 8. Berrien Springs, MI: Andrews University.

Brower, J. K.; LaBianca, Ø. S.; and Mitchel, L. A.
1982   Stages in the Development of an Archaeological Data Base: Goals Envisioned, Work Done, and Lessons Learned in an Effort to Computerize Stratigraphic and Typological Data from the Excavations at Tell Hesban, Jordan. Unpublished manuscript.

Brower, J. K., and Storfjell, J. B.
1982   The Use of Coins for Findspot Dating. Paper Presented at the Annual Meeting of ASOR. December 20, New York.

Brown, R. M.
1978   Tell Hesban 1976: Area G.11, 16, 17, 18. *AUSS* 16: 167-182.

Bullard, R. G.
1972   Geological Study of the Heshbon Area. *AUSS* 10: 129-141.

Campbell, E. F.
1977   Conclusion to Symposium: An Evaluation of the Heshbon Project. Paper Presented at the Annual Meeting of ASOR. December 29, San Francisco.

Chapman, B. C.
1983   Heshbon. Pp. 236-237 in *The New Dictionary of Biblical Archaeology*, eds. E. M. Blaiklock and R. K. Harrison. Grand Rapids: Zondervan.

Coleman, R. O.
1981   Heshbon. *Biblical Illustrator* 7, 4: 56-61.

Cox, J. J. C.
1976   Tell Hesban 1974: A Rhodian Potter's Date-Stamp. *AUSS* 14: 149-156.

Crawford, P.
1976   Tell Hesban 1974: The Mollusca of Tell Hesban. *AUSS* 14: 171-176.

Crawford, P., and Gilliland, D. R.
1978   Botanical Studies at Tell Hesban. Paper Presented at the Annual Meeting of ASOR. November 21, New Orleans.

Crawford, P., and LaBianca, Ø. S.
1976   Tell Hesban 1974: The Flora of Hesban, a Preliminary Report. *AUSS* 14: 177-184.

Crawford, P.; LaBianca, Ø. S.; and Stewart, R. B.
1976   Tell Hesban 1974: The Flotation Remains, a Preliminary Report. *AUSS* 14: 185-188.

Cross, F. M.
1969   Tell Hesban 1968: An Ostracon from Heshbon. *AUSS* 7: 223-229.

1973   Tell Hesban 1971: Heshbon Ostracon II. *AUSS* 11: 126-131.

1975   Tell Hesban 1973: Ammonite Ostraca from Heshbon: Heshbon Ostraca IV-VIII. *AUSS* 13: appendix I-20.

1976   Tell Hesban 1974: Heshbon Ostracon XI. *AUSS* 14: 145-148.

1979   Heshbon in the Iron Age: An Epigraphic Perspective. Paper Presented at the Annual Meeting of ASOR. November 15, New York.

1986   An Unpublished Ammorite Ostracon from Hesban. Pp. 475-489 *The Archaeology of Jordan and Other Studies*, eds. L. T. Geraty and L. G. Herr. Berrien Springs, MI: Andrews University Press.

Davis, J. J.
1977   The Roman/Byzantine Cemeteries at Heshbon. Paper Presented at the Annual Meeting of ASOR. December 28, San Francisco.

1978   Tell Hesban 1976: Areas F and K. *AUSS* 16: 129-148.

De Vries, B.
1977   The Ayyubid/Mamluk Periods at Heshbon. Paper Presented at the Annual Meeting of ASOR. December 28, San Francisco.

1979   Archaeological Remains in the Ayyubid-Mamluk Period. Paper Presented at Annual Meeting of the Middle East Studies Association of North America. November 7, Salt Lake City.

1986   The Islamic Bath at Tell Hesban. Pp. 223-235 in *The Archaeology of Jordan and Other Studies*, eds. L. T. Geraty and L. G. Herr. Berrien Springs, MI: Andrews University Press.

Geraty, L. T.
1973   Tell Hesban 1971: Area D. *AUSS* 11: 89-112.

1974a   Hesban 1974: The Roman/Byzantine Results. *Newsletter for Roman/Byzantine Archaeologists in the Middle East* 1,3: 3-4.

1974b   Tell Hesban—A Roman/Byzantine Excavation in Jordan. *Newsletter for Roman/Byzantine Archaeologists in the Middle East* 1,1: 2-4.

1974c   The Excavations of Tell Hesban, 1974. *ASOR Newsletter* No. 5: 1-8.

1975a   Hesban (Heshbon). *Revue Biblique* 82: 576-586.

1975b   Tell Hesban 1973: Area D. *AUSS* 13: 183-202.

1975c   The 1974 Season of Excavations at Tell Hesban. *ADAJ* 20: 47-56.

1976a   Tell Hesban 1974: Heshbon Ostracon X. *AUSS* 14: 143-144.

1976b   The 1976 Season of Excavations at Tell Hesban. *ADAJ* 21: 41-53.

1977a   Excavations at Tell Hesban, 1976. *ASOR Newsletter* No. 8: 1-15.

1977b   Hesban (Heshbon). *Revue Biblique* 84: 404-408.

1977c   Heshbon in the Bible, Literary Sources, and Archaeology. Paper Presented at the Annual Meeting of ASOR. December 29, San Francisco.

1977d   Introduction to Symposium: Heshbon 1968-1976: History, Significance, Plan of Publication. Paper Presented at the Annual Meeting of ASOR. December 28, San Francisco.

1978   Heshbon Final Publication Project: A Progress Report. Paper Presented at the Annual Meeting of ASOR. November 21, New Orleans.

1980   Tell Hesban (1976). *Archiv für Orientforschung* 27,1: 251-255.

1981   Heshbon Exhibit and Lectures. *Biblical Archaeologist* 44: 247.

1982   Heshbon. Pp. 699-702 in Vol. 2 of *The International Standard Bible Encyclopedia*, ed. G. W. Bromiley. Grand Rapids, MI: Eerdmans.

1983   Heshbon: The First Casualty in the Israelite Quest for the Kingdom of God. Pp. 239-248 in *The Quest for the Kingdom of God: Essays in Honor of George E. Mendenhall*, eds. A. Green, H. B. Huffmon, and F. A. Spina. Winona Lake, IN: Eisenbrauns.

Geraty, L. T., and Boraas, R. S.
[*See* Boraas, R. S., and Geraty, L. T.]

Geraty, L. T., and LaBianca, Ø. S.
1986   The Local Environment and Human Food Procuring Strategies in Jordan: The Case of Tell Hesban and its Surrounding Region. *Proceedings of the Second International Conference on the History and Archaeology of Jordan.*

Geraty, L. T., *et al.*
1977   Outline of Final Publication Procedures for the Tell Hesban Excavations: The Period Reports. Unpublished paper.

Gilliland, D. R.
1979   Introduction to the Paleoethnobotany and Paleoenvironment of Tell Hesban, Jordan. M. A. Thesis, Walla Walla College.

Gilliland, D. R., and Crawford, P.
[*See* Crawford, P., and Gilliland, D. R.]

Goldstein, S. M.
1976   Tell Hesban 1974: Glass Fragments from Tell Hesban, a Preliminary Report. *AUSS* 14: 127-131.

Groot, J. C.
1978   Tell Hesban 1976: The Prometheus Bone Carving from Area B. *AUSS* 16: 225-228.

Hare, P. E., and LaBianca, Ø. S.
1978   Depositional and Post Depositional Processes Affecting Animal Remains (Taphonomy). Paper Presented at the Annual Meeting of ASOR. November 21, New Orleans.

Harvey, D.
1973   Tell Hesban 1971: Area A. *AUSS* 11: 17-34.

Herr, L.
1976a   Tell Hesban 1974: Area D. *AUSS* 14: 79-100.

1976b   Tell Hesban 1974: Area G.5. *AUSS* 14: 107-108.

1977   The Iron Age at Heshbon. Paper Presented at the Annual Meeting of ASOR. December 28, San Francisco.

1978   Tell Hesban 1976: Area D. *AUSS* 16: 109-128.

Horn, S. H.
1968a   The First Season of Excavations at Heshbon, Jordan. *ASOR Newsletter* No. 3: 1-5.

1968b   Discoveries at Ancient Heshbon. *ADAJ* 12-13: 51-52.

1969a   The 1968 Heshbon Expedition. *Biblical Archaeologist* 32: 26-41.

1969b   Heshbon (Jordanie). *Revue Biblique* 76: 395-398, Plates 10-11a.

1971   The Second Season of Excavation at Heshbon. *ASOR Newsletter* No. 4: 1-4.

1972a   Hesban (Heshbon). *Revue Biblique* 79: 422-426, Plates 41-42a.

1972b   The 1971 Season of Excavation at Tell Hesban. *ADAJ* 17: 15-22, 111-115.

1973   The Excavations at Tell Hesban, 1973, *ASOR Newsletter* No. 2: 1-4.

1974   The 1973 Season of Excavation at Tell Hesban. *ADAJ* 19: 151-156.

1975   Tell Hesban. *Revue Biblique* 82: 100-105.

1976a   Heshbon. Pp. 510-514 in Vol. 2 of *Encyclopedia of Archaeological Excavations in the Holy Land*, ed. M. Avi-Yonah. Englewood Cliffs, NJ: Prentice-Hall.

1976b   Heshbon. Pp. 410-411 in Supplementary Volume of *The Interpreter's Dictionary of the Bible*, ed. K. Crim. Nashville: Abingdon.

1977   The Heshbon Objects. Paper Presented at the Annual Meeting of ASOR. December 29, San Francisco.

1978   Tell Hesban 1976: An Egyptian Scarab in Early Roman Tomb F.31. *AUSS* 16: 223-224.

1982   *Heshbon in the Bible and Archaeology.* Occasional Papers of the Horn Archaeological Museum, Andrews University 2. Berrien Springs, MI: Horn Archaeological Museum.

Horn, S. H., and Boraas, R. S.
[*See* Boraas, R. S., and Horn, S. H.]

Horn, S. H.; Maxwell, C. M.; and Waterhouse, S. D.
   1968   The Heshbon Expedition. *Andrews University Focus* 4,6: 2-8.

Ibach, R.
   1973   1973 Expedition at Tell Hisban. *Newsletter of the Near East Archaeological Society* No. 2: 2-5.

   1974   Heshbon Regional Survey. *Newsletter of the Near East Archaeological Society* No. 2: 4-5.

1976a   Tell Hesban 1974: Archaeological Survey of the Tell Hesban Region. *AUSS* 14: 119-126.

1976b   Tell Hesban 1974: Area G.8 (Umm es-Sarab). *AUSS* 14: 113-118.

1977   The Heshbon Regional Survey and Roman Road System. Paper Presented at the Annual Meeting of ASOR. December 28, San Francisco.

1978a   Tell Hesban 1976: An Intensive Surface Survey at Jalul. *AUSS* 16: 215-222.

1978b   Tell Hesban 1976: Expanded Archaeological Survey of the Hesban Region. *AUSS* 16: 201-214.

1980   Hesban Region. Paper Presented at the Annual Meeting of ASOR. November 8, Dallas.

Ibach, R., and Waterhouse, S. D.
[*See* Waterhouse, S. D., and Ibach, R.]

James, H. E.
   1976   Geological Study at Tell Hesban, 1974, a Preliminary Report. *AUSS* 14: 165-170.

Kotter, W. R.
   1979   Objects of Stone, Clay, Bone and Ivory from the Heshbon Excavations. MA project report, Andrews University.

Kritzeck, J.
   1976   Tell Hesban 1974: Two Early Arabic Glass Weights. *AUSS* 14: 157-162.

Kritzeck, J. A., and Nitowski, E. L.
   1980   The Rolling-Stone Tomb F.1 at Tell Hesban. *AUSS* 18: 77-100.

LaBianca, Ø. S.
   1973   Tell Hesban 1971: The Zooarchaeological Remains. *AUSS* 11: 133-144.

   1974   A Preliminary Research Design for Ethnographic Studies at Heshbon in Jordan. Unpublished Manuscript.

Andrews University Institute of Archaeology.

1975a Pertinence and Procedures for Knowing Bones. *ASOR Newsletter* No. 1: 1-4.

1975b A System for Analyzing, Recording and Computer Processing Faunal Remains. Unpublished Manuscript. Andrews University Institute of Archaeology.

1975c Tell Hesban: Some Environmental and Zooarchaeological Inquiries. Master's thesis, Loma Linda University.

1976 Tell Hesban 1974: The Village of Hesban, an Ethnographic Preliminary Report. *AUSS* 14: 189-200.

1977 Local Habitat and Modes of Livelihood at Heshbon through Time: A Summary of Methods and Emerging Conclusions. Paper Presented at the Annual Meeting of ASOR. December 29, San Francisco.

1978a Computer-Assisted Management of Archaeological Information as a Vehicle for Multiple-Disciplinary Teamwork. Paper Presented at the ASOR Workshop on Heshbon. November 21, New Orleans.

1978b Ethnoarchaeological and Taphonomical Investigations in the Vicinity of Tell Hesban in Jordan. Paper Presented at Annual Meeting of the ASOR. November 21, New Orleans.

1978c The Logistic and Strategic Aspects of Faunal Analysis in Palestine. *Approaches to Faunal Analysis in the Middle East.* Edited by R. H. Meadow and M. A. Zeder. Peabody Museum Bulletin 2: 3-9.

1978d Tell Hesban 1976: Man, Animals, and Habitat at Hesban—An Integrated Overview. *AUSS* 16: 229-252.

1979a Agricultural Production on Hesban's Hinterland in the Iron Age. Paper Pre-

sented at the Annual Meeting of ASOR. November 15, New York.

1979b Agricultural Production on Hesban's Hinterland, 198BC-AD969. Paper Presented at 81st General Meeting of Archaeological Institute of America. December 30, Boston.

1979c Reconstructing Cultural Processes from Livestock Remains. Unpublished Manuscript. Andrews University Institute of Archaeology.

1979d Temporal Variability in Nomad-Sedentary Relations in Central Transjordan during the Islamic Era. Paper Presented at Annual Meeting of Middle East Studies Association of North America. November 7, Salt Lake City.

1979e Temporal Variability in Nomad-Sedentary Relations in Central Transjordan: The Zooarchaeological Evidence. Paper Presented at Annual Meeting of the American Anthropological Association. November 30, Cincinnati.

1981a Food Production on the Fields of Hesban: A General Model. Paper Presented at Heshbon Authors' Conference. March, Andrews University.

1981b The Diachronic Study of Food Production Systems. Unpublished Manuscript. Andrews University Institute of Archaeology.

1982a Toward a Dynamic Perspective on Transjordanian Food Systems. Paper Presented at the Annual Meeting of ASOR. December 22, New York.

1982b Transience and Resilience in Transjordanian Food Systems. Paper Presented at the Annual Meeting of the Society for American Archaeology. April, Minneapolis.

1983 The Little Man of Hesban: A Micro-historical Analysis of a Jordanian Food

System. Paper Presented at the Symposium on Ancient Mediterranean Food Systems during the Annual Meeting of ASOR. December 21, Dallas.

1984   Objectives, Procedures, and Findings of Ethnoarchaeological Research in the Vicinity of Hesban in Jordan. *ADAJ* 28: 269-287.

1985   The Return of the Nomad. *ADAJ* 29: 251-254.

1986a   The Diachronic Study of Animal Exploitation at Hesban. Pp. 167-181 in *The Archaeology of Jordan and Other Studies*, eds. L. T. Geraty and L. G. Herr. Berrien Springs, MI: Andrews University Press.

1986b   An Anthropological Perspective on Sociocultural Change in Central Transjordan. Paper presented at the Annual Meeting of ASOR, November 24, Atlanta.

1987   Sedentarization and Nomadization: Food System Cycles in Hesban and Vicinity in Transjordan. Doctoral dissertation, Brandeis University.

LaBianca, Ø. S., Brower, J. K., and Mitchel, L. A.
[*See* Brower, J. K.; LaBianca, Ø. S.; and Mitchel, L. A.]

LaBianca, Ø. S. and Crawford, P.
[*See* Crawford, P., and LaBianca, Ø. S.]

LaBianca, Ø. S.; Crawford, P.; and Stewart, R. B.
[*See* Crawford, P.; LaBianca, Ø. S.; and Stewart, R. B.]

LaBianca, Ø. S., and Geraty, L. T.
1984   Sedentarization and Nomadization: Toward an Agenda for Future Research in Central Jordan. Paper presented at the Annual Meeting of ASOR, December 10, Chicago.

LaBianca, Ø. S., and Hare, P. E.
[*See* Hare, P. E., and LaBianca, Ø. S.]

LaBianca, Ø. S., and LaBianca, A. S.
1976a   Tell Hesban 1973: The Anthropological Work. *AUSS* 13: 235-247.

1976b   Tell Hesban 1974: Domestic Animals of the Early Roman Period at Tell Hesban. *AUSS* 14: 205-216.

LaBianca, Ø. S.; Mitchel, L. A.; and Perkins, P. W.
1977   Computer-Assisted Management of Heshbon Data. Paper Presented at the Annual Meeting of ASOR. November 21, New Orleans.

Langholf, V.
1969   A Latin Potter's Seal Impression. *AUSS* 7: 230-231.

Lawlor, J. I.
1978   Tell Hesban 1976: Area G.14. *AUSS* 16: 189-200.

1979a   Hesban (Heshbon) 1978. *Revue Biblique* 86: 115-117.

1979b   The 1978 Hesban North Church Project. *ASOR Newsletter* No. 4: 1-8.

1980a   The Excavation of the North Church at Hesban, Jordan: A Preliminary Report. *AUSS* 18: 65-76.

1980b   The 1978 Excavation of the Hesban North Church. *ADAJ* 24: 95-105, 275-280.

Lindner, H.
1979   Zur Fruehgeschichte des Haushuhns im Vorderen Orient. Doctor of Veterinary Medicine Dissertation, Ludwig-Maximilian University, Munich.

Little, R. M.
1969   An Anthropological Preliminary Note on the First Season at Tell Hesban. *AUSS* 7: 232-239.

London, B. D.
1981   The Metallurgy of Archaeological Samples from Tell Hesban. Under-

graduate Thesis Report, Drexel University.

Lugenbeal, E. N., and Sauer, J. A.
1972 Seventh-Sixth Century B.C. Pottery from Area B at Heshbon. *AUSS* 10: 21-69.

Mare, W. H.
1975 The 1974 Excavation at Tell Heshbon and its Bearing on the date of the Exodus. *Near East Archaeological Society Bulletin* No. 5: 21-46.

1976a Tell Hesban 1974: Area C. *AUSS* 14: 63-78.

1976b Tell Hesban 1974: Area G.6, 7, 9. *AUSS* 14: 109-112.

1978 Tell Hesban 1976: Area C.1, 2, 3, 5, 7. *AUSS* 16: 51-70.

Maxwell, C. M.; Horn, S. H.; and Waterhouse, S. D.
[*See* Horn, S. H.; Maxwell, C. M.; and Waterhouse, S. D.]

Mitchel, L. A.
1977 The Hellenistic/Roman Periods at Heshbon. Paper Presented at the Annual Meeting of ASOR. December 28, San Francisco.

1979 Tell Hesban, Jordan: The Hellenistic and Roman Remains. Paper Presented at Annual Meeting of Archaeological Institute of America. December 30, Boston.

1980 The Hellenistic and Roman Periods at Tell Hesban, Jordan. Th.D. dissertation, Andrews University.

1982 The Hellenistic and Roman Periods at Tell Hesban, Jordan. *AUSS* 20: 67-68.

Mitchel, L. A.; Brower, J. K.; and LaBianca, Ø. S.
[*See* Brower, J. K.; Mitchel, L. A.; and LaBianca, Ø. S.]

Mitchel, L. A.; LaBianca, Ø. S.; and Perkins, P. W.
[*See* LaBianca, Ø. S.; Mitchel, L. A.; and Perkins, P. W.]

Nitowski, E. L.
1976 Tell Hesban 1974: An Inscribed Mamluk Sherd. *AUSS* 14: 163-164.

Nitowski, E. L., and Kritzeck, J. A.
[*See* Kritzeck, J. A., and Nitowski, E. L.]

Parker, S. T.
1978 Tell Hesban 1976: Area C.4, 6, 8, 9, 10. *AUSS* 16: 71-108.

Perkins, P. W.; LaBianca, Ø. S.; and Mitchel, L. A.
[*See* LaBianca, Ø. S.; Mitchel, L. A.; and Perkins, P. W.]

Platt, E. E.
1977 The Heshbon Jewelry. Paper Presented at the Annual Meeting of ASOR. December 29, San Francisco.

Russell, M. B.
1979 Hesban in Mamluk Times: Prosperity in the Midst of Decay? Paper Presented at Annual Meeting of the Middle East Studies Association of North America. November 7, Salt Lake City.

Sauer, J. A.
1973a Tell Hesban 1971: Area B. *AUSS* 11: 35-71.

1973b *Heshbon Pottery 1971: A Preliminary Report on the Pottery from the 1971 Excavations at Tell Hesban.* Berrien Springs, MI: Andrews University.

1975a Tell Hesban 1973: Area B and Square D.4. *AUSS* 13: 133-168.

1975b Heshbon Pottery 1973. Unpublished manuscript.

1976 Tell Hesban 1974: Area B and Square D.4. *AUSS* 14: 29-62.

1978a   Tell Hesban 1976: Area B and Square D.4. *AUSS* 16: 31-50.

1978b   Tell Hesban's Pottery Corpus. Paper Presented at the Annual Meeting of ASOR. November 21, New Orleans.

Sauer, J. A., and Lugenbeal, E. N.
[*See* Lugenbeal, E. N., and Sauer, J. A.]

Shea, W. H.
1977   Ostracon II from Heshbon. *AUSS* 15: 217-222.

1979   Heshbon in the Iron Age: An Historical Perspective. Paper Presented at the Annual Meeting of ASOR. November 15, New York.

Stewart, R. B.; Crawford, P.; and LaBianca, Ø. S.
[*See* Crawford, P.; Stewart, R. B.; and LaBianca, Ø. S.]

Stirling, J. H.
1976a   Tell Hesban 1974: Areas E, F, and G.10. *AUSS* 14: 101-106.

1976b   Skeletal Remains from Tell Hesban, 1974. *AUSS* 14: 201-204.

1978   Tell Hesban 1976: The Human Skeletal Remains from Hesban's Cemeteries. *AUSS* 16: 253-258.

Storfjell, J. B.
1977   The Byzantine/Early Arabic Periods at Heshbon. Paper Presented at the Annual Meeting of ASOR. December 28, San Francisco.

1979   Tell Hesban, Jordan: The Byzantine and Early Arab Remains. Paper Presented at Annual Meeting of the Archaeological Institute of America. December 30, Boston.

1980   Tell Hesban, Jordan: The Byzantine and Early Arab Remains. *American Journal of Archaeology* 84: 234-235.

1981a   The Byzantine and Early Arab Periods at Tell Hesban. Paper Presented at

Heshbon Authors' Conference. March, Andrews University.

1981b   The Use of Coins for Stratigraphic Dating. Paper Presented at Heshbon Authors' Conference. March, Andrews University.

1983   The Stratigraphy of Tell Hesban, Jordan in the Byzantine Period. Ph.D. dissertation, Andrews University.

Storfjell, J. B., and Brower, J. K.
[*See* Brower, J. K., and Storfjell, J. B.]

Terian, A.
1971   Coins from the 1968 Excavations at Heshbon. *AUSS* 9: 147-160.

1974   Coins from the 1971 Excavations at Heshbon. *AUSS* 12: 35-46.

1976   Coins from the 1973 and 1974 Excavations at Heshbon. *AUSS* 14: 133-141.

1977   The Heshbon Coins. Paper Presented at the Annual Meeting of ASOR. December 29, San Francisco.

1980   Coins from the 1976 Excavation at Heshbon. *AUSS* 18: 173-180.

Thompson, H. O.
1969   Tell Hesban 1968: Area C. *AUSS* 7: 127-141.

1973   Tell Hesban 1971: Area C. *AUSS* 11: 72-88.

1975   Tell Hesban 1973: Area C. *AUSS* 13: 169-182.

Van Elderen, B.
1969   Tell Hesban 1968: Area A. *AUSS* 7: 142-164.

1975a   Tell Hesban 1973: A Greek Ostracon from Heshbon. *AUSS* 13: 21-22.

1975b   Tell Hesban 1973: Area A. *AUSS* 13: 117-132.

1976   Tell Hesban 1974: Area A. *AUSS* 14: 17-28.

1978   Tell Hesban 1976: Area A. *AUSS* 16: 19-30.

Von den Driesch, A., and Boessneck, J.
[*See* Boessneck, J., and von den Driesch, A.]

Vyhmeister, W. K.
1967   The History of Heshbon from the Literary Sources. B.D. thesis, Andrews University.

1968   The History of Heshbon from Literary Sources. *AUSS* 6: 158-177.

Waterhouse, S. D.
1973   Tell Hesban 1971: Areas E and F. *AUSS* 11: 113-125.

Waterhouse, S. D.; Horn, S. H.; and Ibach, R.

[*See* Horn, S. H.; Waterhouse, S. D.; and Ibach, R.]

Waterhouse, S. D., and Ibach, R.
1975   Tell Hesban 1973: The Topographical Survey. *AUSS* 13: 217-234.

Weiler, D.
1981   Saeugetierknochenfunde vom Tell Hesban in Jordanien. Doctor of Veterinary Medicine Dissertation, Ludwig-Maximilian University, Munich.

Wimmer, D. H.
1978   Tell Hesban 1976: Area G.4, 13, 15. *AUSS* 16: 149-166.

Endnote

[1]This list does not include manuscripts for the Hesban Final Publication Series. See Appendix B for the list of volumes in this series.

Appendix B

OVERVIEW OF
THE HESBAN FINAL PUBLICATION SERIES

Appendix B

Overview of the Hesban Final Publication Series

Editor's Note: When completed, the Hesban Final Publication Series will consist of 14 volumes in five parts.

The first part (Hesban 1) offers an integrative account of cultural changes at Hesban and vicinity from a food systems perspective.

The second part (Hesban 2-4) contains background studies of Hesban's local environment, history from literary sources, and present-day inhabitants.

The third part (Hesban 5-9) discusses the archaeological survey of the Hesban region with stratigraphy interpretation from the Iron Age, Hellenistic-Roman, Byzantine-Early Islamic, and Ayyubid-Mamluk periods.

The fourth part (Hesban 10-13) presents the results of specialists' studies of the Roman-Byzantine cemetery, the pottery, the objects, and the animal remains.

The fifth part (Hesban 14) evaluates the implications of all of the above studies for our understanding of biblical and ancient Near Eastern history. The volumes are being made available as work on the various manuscripts is completed and not necessarily in numerical order.

Hesban 1: Sedentarization and Nomadization
Øystein Sakala LaBianca (Andrews University)

This volume pulls together the various lines of evidence presented in the other 13 volumes to reconstruct and explain the cultural changes which have taken place over the past 3,500 years at Hesban and vicinity. To this end, the volume employs the food system concept and related theoretical constructs, such as sedentarization and nomadization, upon which our understanding of cultural change at Hesban pivots.

Contents: Introduction to the Food System Concept and the Heshbon Expedition; Sedentarization and Nomadization; The Hesban Area Food System during the Recent Past; From Archaeological Information to Food System Configurations; Configurations of the Food System during the Iron Age Millennium: *Ca.* 1200-500 B.C.; Configurations of the Food System during the Greco-Roman Millennium: *Ca.* 333 B.C. to A.D. 630; Configurations of the Food System during the Islamic Centuries: *Ca.* A. D.630 to 1900; Intensification and Abatement: Summary and Reflections; Appendex A: Bibliography of Hesban-Related Scholarly Publicatiaons; Appendix B: Overview of the Hesban Final Pubiblication Series; Appendix C: Sponsors and Participants of the Heshbon Expedition; Arabic Summary; Author Index; General Index. Includes 47 figures, 83 plates, and 16 tables. 350 pages.

Hesban 2: Environmental Foundations
Edited by Øystein Sakala LaBianca (Andrews University) and Larry Lacelle (British Columbia Ministry of Environment)

An introduction to the climate and landscape to which successive generations of Hesbanites have had to adapt.

Contents: Introduction; Climate of Tell Hesban and Area; Bedrock, Surficial Geology, and Soils; Surface and Groundwater Resources of Tell Hesban and Area, Jordan; Flora of Tell Hesban and Area, Jordan; Ecology of the Flora of Tell Hesban and Area, Jordan; Paleoethnobotany and Paleoenvironment; Conclusion; Index. Includes 26 figures, 42 plates, and 9 tables; 174 pages.

Contributors: Patricia Crawford (Boston University), Kevin Ferguson (Clark University),

Dennis R. Gilliland (Walla Walla College), Tim Hudson (University of Southern Mississippi), Øystein S. LaBianca (Andrews University), and Larry Lacelle (British Columbia Ministry of Environment).

Hesban 3: Historical Foundations

Edited by Lawrence T. Geraty (Atlantic Union College) and Leona G. Running (Andrews University)

Volume 3 presents an analysis of Old Testament, Egyptian, Greek, Arab, and European literary references to Tell Hesban and its surrounding region.

Contents: The History of Heshbon from the Literary Sources; Hesban During the Arab Period: A.D. 635 to the Present; A Review of Critical Studies of Old Testament References to Heshbon; Appendix A: Heshbon Through the Centuries; Appendix B: Hesban in the Literary Sources Since 1806; Author Index; Biblical Reference Index; General Index. Includes 4 figures and 1 plate; 97 pages.

Contributors: Arthur J. Ferch (Andrews University), Malcolm B. Russell (Andrews University), Werner K. Vyhmeister (SDA Theological Seminary Far East)

Hesban 4: Ethnoarchaeological Foundations

Øystein Sakala LaBianca (Andrews University)

Volume 4 tells, from the perspective of an archaeologist-turned-ethnographer, how the people of Hesban and vicinity gradually converted from wandering pastoralists to villagers and townsmen over the past 150 years.

Hesban 5: Archaeological Survey of the Hesban Region

Robert D. Ibach, Jr. (Dallas Theological Seminary)

This volume offers systematic descriptions, including numerous maps and photographs, of the 148 archaeological sites visited by the expedition's regional survey team within a 10-km radius of Tell Hesban.

Contents: Introduction; Catalogue of Sites; Characterization of Periods; Summary and Conclusions; Appendix A: Project Area Sites visited by C. R. Conder in 1881-1882; Appendix B: Sample Site Report Form; Index. Includes 18 figures, 198 plates, 34 tables; 299 pages.

Hesban 6: Iron Age Strata

Edited by Lawrence T. Geraty (Atlantic Union College

This volume presents a layer-by-layer account, including numerous plans and photographs, of the discoveries made in Tell Hesban's four Iron Age strata (12th to 5th centuries B.C.). These discoveries are interpreted in the light of contemporary natural, cultural, and historical events.

Contributors: Roger S. Boraas (Upsala College), James Brower (Andrews University), Gary Christopherson (University of Arizona), and Larry G. Herr (Canadian Union College).

Hesban 7: Hellenistic and Roman Strata

Larry A. Mitchel (Andrews University)

A layer-by-layer account of Tell Hesban's five Hellenistic and Roman strata (2nd century B.C. to the 4th century A.D.) is presented, including numerous plans and photographs of discoveries made. These discoveries are interpreted in the light of contemporary natural, cultural, and historical events.

Hesban 8: Byzantine and Early Islamic Strata

J. Bjørnar Storfjell (Andrews University)

Volume 8 presents a layer-by-layer account, with numerous plans and photographs, of the discoveries made in Tell Hesban's six Byzantine and Early Islamic strata (4th to the 10th centuries A.D.). These discoveries are interpreted in the light of contemporary natural, cultural, and historical events.

Hesban 9: Ayyubid-Mamluk Strata

Bert de Vries (Calvin College)

The discoveries of Tell Hesban's four Ayyubid-Mamluk strata (12th to the 15th centuries A.D.) are presented in a layer-by-layer account, including numerous plans and photographs. These discoveries are interpreted in the light of contemporary natural, cultural, and historical events.

Hesban 10: The Necropolis of Heshbon

Edited by Øystein Sakala LaBianca (Andrews University) and Lawrence T. Geraty (Atlantic Union College)

Volume 10 offers a tomb-by-tomb account, with plans and photographs, of the 41 Roman and Byzantine tombs excavated in the vicinity of Hesban's cemetery.

Contributors: George Armelagos (University of Massachusetts), John Davis (Grace Theological Seminary), Ann Grauer (University of Massachusetts), and Douglas Waterhouse (Andrews University).

Hesban 11: Ceramic Finds
James A. Sauer (American Schools of Oriental Research)

A definitive work by Jordan's ceramic expert, this volume is devoted to typological analysis and descriptions, including numerous drawings, of the large corpus of pottery from Tell Hesban and vicinity.

Hesban 12: Small Finds
Edited by Lawrence T. Geraty (Atlantic Union College)

Volume 12 presents in text and numerous drawings and photographs studies of the large quantity of ivory, stone, iron, glass, and jewelry objects uncovered at Tell Hesban and the nearby cemetery.

Contributors: Abdel-Jalil 'Amr (University of Jordan), Ghazi Bisheh (Department of Antiquities, Jordan), James Cox (Columbia Union College), Frank M. Cross, Jr. (Harvard University), Lawrence T. Geraty (Atlantic Union College), Siegfried H. Horn (Andrews University), Wade Kotter (University of Arizona), Heather Lechtman (Massachusetts Institute of Technology), Elizabeth E. Platt (Dubuque Theological

Seminary), Mort Sajadian (University of Missouri, Columbia), Ervin Taylor (University of California, Riverside), Abraham Terian (Andrews University), and Bastian van Elderen (Free University of Amsterdam).

Hesban 13: Faunal Remains
Edited by Øystein S. LaBianca (Andrews University)

This volume is devoted to the presentation of the zooarchaeological analysis of the nearly 100,000 animal bones uncovered in the excavations at Tell Hesban.

Contributors: Joachim Boessneck (University of Munich), Angela von den Driesch (University of Munich), Lori A. Haynes (Andrews University), Øystein Sakala LaBianca (Andrews University), Johannes Lepiksaar (Museum of Natural History, Sweden), and Herman Lindner (University of Munich).

Hesban 14: Hesban and Biblical History
Lawrence T. Geraty (Atlantic Union College and Øystein S. LaBianca (Andrews University

Volume 14 offers conclusions regarding the significance of the Hesban project for our understanding of biblical and ancient Near Eastern history. In particular, the volume will re-examine the numerous references to Hesban and vicinity throughout the Old Testament in light of the findings reported in the previous volumes.

Appendix C

SPONSORS AND PARTICIPANTS OF THE HESHBON EXPEDITION

Appendix C

Sponsors and Participants
of the Heshbon Expedition

Editor's note: Listed here are participants and sponsors from the five seasons at Heshbon as found in the preliminary reports. Also listed are the participants' main responsibilities. Institutional affiliation is listed for core staff only, including field supervisors. To save space, the following abbreviations have been used: Arch Sur (Archaeological Survey), Architec (Architectural), Assist (Assistant), Assoc (Associate), AU (Andrews University), BU (Brandeis University), CalTS (Calvin Theological Seminary), CC (Calvin College), CovTS (Covenant Theological Seminary), Eco Lab (Ecology Lab), EW (Earthwatch), F Sup (Field Supervisor), GNYA (Greater New York Academy), GTS (Grace Theological Seminary), HU (Harvard University), IU (Indiana University), LLU (Loma Linda University), NYTS (New York Theological Seminary), Photo (Photography), Pt (Part-Time), Rep–Dept of Ant (representative, Jordan Department of Antiquities), Sq Sup (Square Supervisor), UC (Upsala College), UMun (University of Munich), vol (volunteer), Western TS (Western Theological Seminary), WTS (Wesley Theological Seminary).

1968 Campaign

Major Institutional Sponsors
Andrews University, Berrien Springs, MI, *Principal Sponsor*
Department of Antiquities, Amman, Jordan
American Center for Oriental Research, Amman
Archaeological Research Foundation of New York
Calvin Theological Seminary, Grand Rapids, MI
Middle East Division of Seventh-day Adventists

Participants
Siegfried H. Horn (AU)	*Director*
Roger S. Boraas (UC)	*Chief Archaeologist*
Mohammed Adawi (ACOR)	*Cook*
Aina E. Boraas	*Pottery Restoration*

Dewey Beegle (WTS)	*F Sup–Area B*
Marion Beegle	*Object Registrar*
Geoffrey Belton	*Architec Draft Staff*
Paul Belton	*Architec Draft Staff*
Barbara Bergsma	*Sq Sup–Area A*
Paul Bergsma	*Sq Sup–Area C & Photo Staff*
Phyllis Bird (HU)	*F Sup–Area D*
Ghazi Bisheh	*Rep–Dep of Ant*
Andrew Bowling	*Sq Sup–Area B*
James Brashler	*Sq Sup–Area A*
Lenore Brashler	*Sq Sup–Area C*
Keith Bulthuis	*Sq Sup–Area D*
Bert de Vries (CC)	*Head–Architec Draft Staff*
Avery Dick	*Chief–Photo Staff*
Paul Evans	*Architec Draft Staff*
Lawrence T. Geraty	*Assoc F Sup–Area D*
Ed Grohman	*Assoc F Sup–Area B*
Sarah Grohman	*Assist to Pottery Registrar*
Marvin Hoekstra	*Sq Sup–Area A*
Kathy Hoekstra	*Sq Sup–Area C*
Elaine Hutt	*Sq Sup–Area B*
Norman Johnson	*Sq Sup–Area D*
Chris Leys	*Sq Sup–Area D*
Wayne Leys	*Sq Sup–Area C*
Robert Little (IU)	*Physical Anthropologist*
Mervyn Maxwell	*Assoc F Sup–Area A*
Paul Meier	*Sq Sup–Area C*
Mohammed Odeh	*Rep–Dept of Ant*
Siegfried Schwantes	*Sq Sup–Area C*
Arthur Spenst	*Sq Sup–Area D*
Lois Stetler	*Sq Sup–Area A*
Richard Stetler	*Sq Sup–Area B*
Mustafa Tawfiq	*Foreman*
Henry Thompson (NYTS)	*F Sup–Area C*
Hester Thomsen (GNYA)	*Pottery Registrar*
Peter Thorne	*Sq Sup–Area A*
George Unger	*Photo Staff*
Anita Van Elderen	*Messenger Girl*
Bastiaan Van Elderen (CalTS)	*F Sup–Area A*
Vivolyn Van Elderen	*Camp Director*
Douglas Waterhouse	*Assoc F Sup–Area C*
Fawzi Zayadin	*Rep–Dept of Ant*

Plate C.1   1968 Heshbon Expedition staff

Plate C.2   1971 Heshbon Expedition staff

1971 Campaign

Major Institutional Sponsors
Andrews University, Berrien Springs, MI, *Principal Sponsor*
Department of Antiquities, Amman, Jordan
American Center for Oriental Research, Amman, Jordan
American Community School, Amman, Jordan
Archaeological Research Foundation of New York
Calvin Theological Seminary, Grand Rapids, MI
University of Jordan, Amman, Jordan

Participants

Siegfried H. Horn (AU)	*Director*
Roger S. Boraas (UC)	*Chief Archaeologist*
Adeb Abu Schmais	*Sq Sup—Area B*
Mohammad Adawi (ACOR)	*Cook*
Charles Armistead	*Sq Sup—Area C*
George van Arragon	*Sq Sup—Area D*
Mary Bachmann	*Photo Staff*
Miriam Boraas	*Sq Sup—Area D*
Reuben G. Bullard (U of Cincinnati)	*Geologist*
Benjamin C. Chapman	*Assoc F Sup—Area A*
Judy Chapman	*Messenger Girl*
Marlyn Chapman	*Camp Director*
Bert de Vries (CC)	*Head—Architec Draft Staff*
Carl H. Dropper	*Architec Draft Staff*
Carney E. S. Gavin	*Assoc F Sup—Area B*
Lawrence T. Geraty (HU)	*F Sup—Area D*
Samir Ghishan	*Sq Sup—Area C*
Andy Glasbergen	*Sq Sup—Area B*
Rahab Hadid	*Sq Sup—Area A*
Dorothea Harvey (Urbana College)	*F Sup—Area A*
Gerhard F. Hasel	*Assoc F Sup—Area D*
Larry Herr	*Sq Sup—Area B*
Ralph O. Hjelm	*Assoc F Sup—Area C*
Robert Ibach	*Sq Sup—Area C*
Taysir Islim	*Sq Sup—Area B*
G. Arthur Keough	*Sq Sup—Area B*
Mohammad Murshed Khadija	*Foreman*
Øystein LaBianca (LLU)	*Zooarchaeologist*
Robert M. Little (IU)	*Physical Anthropologist*
Nabil Khairy	*Sq Sup—Area B*
John Lorntz	*Sq Sup—Area D*
Bonita Meyer	*Sq Sup—Area C*
Marvin Meyer	*Sq Sup—Area A*
Joyce Miller	*Sq Sup—Area A*
Kathleen Mitchell (AU)	*Object Registrar*
Julia Neuffer	*Assist—Various Areas*
Eugenia Nitowski	*Assist—Areas E & F*
Lutfi Ostah	*Sq Supr—Area D*
Philip Post	*Sq Sup—Area B*
Nabil Salim Qadi	*Sq Sup—Area C*

Hussein Qandil	*Rep—Dept of Ant*
Ghassan Ahmad el-Ramahi	*Sq Sup—Area A*
Lina Sa'adi	*Sq Sup—Area D*
James A. Sauer (HU)	*F Sup—Area B*
William H. Shea	*Sq Sup—Area C*
Wayne Stiles	*Sq Sup—Areas E & F*
Abraham Terian (AU)	*Coins*
Henry O. Thompson (ACOR)	*F Sup—Area C*
Hester Thomsen (GNYA)	*Pottery Registrar*
Tim Smith	*Assist—Various Areas*
Alvin Trace	*Head—Photo Staff*
David Undeland	*Assist—Various Areas*
Douglas Waterhouse (AU)	*F Sup—Areas E & F*
Udo Worschech	*Sq Sup—Area A*

1973 Campaign

Major Institutional Sponsors
Andrews University, Berrien Springs, MI, *Principal Sponsor*
Department of Antiquities, Amman, Jordan
American Center for Oriental Research, Amman, Jordan
American Community School, Amman, Jordan
Archaeological Research Foundation of New York
Calvin Theological Seminary, Grand Rapids, MI
University of Jordan, Amman, Jordan

Participants

Siegfried H. Horn (AU)	*Director*
Roger S. Boraas (UC)	*Chief Archaeologist*
Sami Abadi	*Arch Sur Staff*
Adib Abu Shmais	*Sq Sup—Area B*
Mohamad Adawi (ACOR)	*Cook*
Emmet A. Barnes	*Sq Sup—Area A*
James R. Battenfield	*Sq Sup—Area B*
Dewey M. Beegle (WTS)	*F Sup—Areas F & G*
Marion E. Beegle	*Object Registrar*
Paul J. Bergsma	*Photo Staff*
Michael Blaine	*Sq Sup—Area C*
Jack B. Bohannon	*Sq Sup—Area D*
Elisabeth G. Burr	*Sq Sup—Area D*
Douglas R. Clark	*Sq Sup—Area A*
Omar Daoud	*Sq Sup—Area C*
Avery V. Dick	*Head—Photo Staff*
Bert de Vries (CC)	*Head—Architec Draft Staff*
Lillian A. Foster	*Sq Sup—Area D*
Lawrence T. Geraty (AU)	*F Sup—Area D*
Samir Ghishan	*Sq Sup—Area D*
Susan A. Hamilton	*Sq Sup—Area C*
Ibrahim Hajj Hasan	*Rep—Dept of Ant*
B. Charlene Hogsten	*Arch Sur Staff*
Robert D. Ibach	*Arch Sur Staff*
Norman Johnson	*Sq Sup—Area B*

Plate C.3   1973 Heshbon Expedition staff

Plate C.4   1974 Heshbon Expedition staff

Mohammad Murshed Khadija	*Foreman*
Ann O. Koloski	*Sq Sup—Area A*
Asta Sakala LaBianca	*Assist—Eco Lab*
Øystein Sakala LaBianca (BU)	*Head—Eco Lab*
Richard C. Mannell	*Sq Sup—Area D*
Ali Musa	*Sq Sup—Area D*
Thomas J. Meyer	*Sq Sup—Area C*
Paul E. Moore	*Sq Sup—Area A*
Ali Musa	*Rep—Dep of Ant*
Julia Neuffer	*Sq Sup—Area D*
Eugenia L. Nitowski	*Arch Sur & Darkroom*
Lutfi Ostah	*Sq Sup—Area D*
Philip J. Post	*Sq Sup—Area B*
Nabil Salim Qadi	*Sq Sup—Area C*
Ghassan Ahmad el-Ramahi	*Assist—Area G*
Gary Roozeboom	*Architect Draft Staff*
Elizabeth C. Sanford	*Conservator*
James A. Sauer (ACOR)	*Ceramicist &*
	F Sup—Area B
Catherine Schilperoort	*Sq Sup—Area D*
Eric C. Schilperoort	*Sq Sup—Area A*
Timothy Smith	*Assist—Area F*
Douglas J. Stek	*Sq Sup—Area C*
Mary Stek	*Architec Draft Staff*
Abraham Terian (AU)	*Coins*
Henry O. Thompson (ACOR)	*F Sup—Area C*
Hester Thomsen (GNYA)	*Pottery Registrar*
Leonard P. Tolhurst	*Assist—Area G*
David Undeland	*Sq Sup—Area B*
Anita Van Elderen	*Assist—Area F*
Bastiaan Van Elderen (CalTS)	*F Sup—Area A*
Vivolyn Van Elderen	*Camp Director*
Douglas Waterhouse (AU)	*Head—Arch Sur*
Donald H. Wimmer	*Sq Sup—Area F*
John W. Wood	*Sq Sup—Area D*
Udo Worschech	*Sq Sup—Area B*
James H. Zachary	*Photo Staff*

1974 Campaign

Major Institutional Sponsors

Andrews University, Berrien Springs, MI, *Principal Sponsor*

Department of Antiquities, Amman, Jordan

American Center for Oriental Research, Amman, Jordan

Calvin Theological Seminary, Grand Rapids, MI

Covenant Theological Seminary, St. Louis, MO

Grace Theological Seminary, Winona Lake, IN

Kyle-Kelso Archaeological Fund, Holland, MI

Loma Linda University School of Graduate Studies, Loma Linda, CA

United Nations Relief and Works Agency, Amman, Jordan

Worthington Foods, Worthington, OH

Major Individual Sponsors

Mrs. Ruth Kaune Baucom

Eleanor and William Berecz, Jr.

Wilber A. Bishop, Sr.

Dr. and Mrs. Bernard Brandstater

Dr. and Mrs. Bruce Branson

Dr. Harvey A. Elder

Dr. and Mrs. W. H. Lesovsky

Dr. and Mrs. John Wm. Schnepper

Walter E. Sooy

Dr. Lester G. Storz

Participants

Lawrence T. Geraty (AU)	*Director*
Roger S. Boraas (UC)	*Chief Archaeologist*
Sabri Abbadi	*Rep—Dept of Ant*
Abdel Samia Abu Dayya	*Arch Sur Staff*
Adib Abu Shmais	*Sq Sup—Area B*
Muhammad Adawi (ACOR)	*Cook*
Kim Baker	*Sq Sup—Area A*
James Battenfield	*Sq Sup—Area B*
Michael Blaine	*Sq Sup—Area C*
Paul Bonney	*Photo Staff*
Glenn Bowen	*Sq Sup—Area D*
Kerry Brandstater	*Sq Sup—Area D*
Suzanne Brandstater	*Assist—Areas E & F*
Paul Brohl	*Architec Draft Staff*
Theodore Chamberlain	*Arch Sur Staff*
James Cox	*Sq Sup—Area B*
Mika Damanik	*Sq Sup—Area C*
Omar Daud	*Sq Sup—Area C*
Trevor Delafield	*Sq Sup—Area B*
Paul H. Denton (AU)	*Head—Photo Staff*
Patricia Derbeck	*Arch Sur Staff*
Bert de Vries (CC)	*Head—Architec Draft*
Margaret Dittemore	*Sq Sup—Area C*
Richard Dorsett	*Assist—Areas E & F*
Stephen Emmel	*Sq Sup—Area A*
Gerald Finneman	*Sq Sup—Area C*
Shirley Finneman	*Assist—Eco Lab*
Douglas Fuller	*Assist—Eco Lab*
Samir Ghishan	*Sq Sup—Area B*
Jennifer Groot	*Sq Sup—Area A*
Rose Habaybeh	*Sq Sup—Area A*
Larry G. Herr (HU)	*F Sup—Areas D & G*
Siegfried H. Horn (AU)	*Object Registrar*
Inge—Lise Howse	*Assist to Camp Director*
Kevin Howse	*Sq Sup—Area B*
Robert D. Ibach (GTS)	*Head—Arch Sur*
Harold James (AU)	*Geologist*
Zeidan Kafafi	*Sq Sup—Area D*
Muhammad Murshed Khadija	*Foreman*
Øystein Sakala LaBianca (BU)	*Head—Eco Lab*
Henry Lamberton	*Photo Staff*
John Lawlor	*Sq Sup—Area D*
Melissa Lloyd	*Assist to Pottery Registrar*

Robert Lloyd	*Photo Staff*
Lynn Malvitz	*Sq Sup—Area D*
Richard Mannell	*Arch Sur Staff*
Myra Mare	*Sq Sup—Areas C & G*
W. Harold Mare (CovTS)	*F Sup—Area C*
David Merling	*Sq Sup—Area D*
Kathleen Mitchell	*Sq Sup—Area B*
Mogahed Mohaisin	*Sq Sup—Area D*
Orlyn Nelson	*Sq Sup—Area D*
Nola Opperwaal	*Sq Sup—Area A*
Eunice Post	*Sq Sup—Area C*
Nabil Qadi	*Sq Sup—Area C*
John Reeves	*Assist—Areas E & F*
Mahmoud Rusan	*Rep—Dept of Ant*
James A. Sauer (ACOR)	*Ceramicist &*
	F Sup—Area B
Susan Sauer	*Sq Sup—Area B*
Oscar Schultz	*Sq Sup—Area A*
James H. Stirling (LLU)	*F Sup—Areas E & F*
Ralph Stirling	*Assist—Eco Lab*
George Terzibashian	*Sq Sup—Area A*
Hester Thomsen	*Pottery Registrar*
Michael Toplyn	*Assist—Eco Lab*
Anita Van Elderen	*Architect Draft Staff*
Bastiaan Van Elderen (CalTS)	*F Sup—Area A*
Vivolyn Van Elderen	*Camp Director*
Thomas Walters	*Architect Draft Staff*
Wesley Walters	*Sq Sup—Area C*
Kerry Wiessmann	*Assist—Areas E & F*

1976 Campaign

Major Institutional Sponsors
Andrews University, Berrien Springs, MI, *Principal Sponsor*
Department of Antiquities, Amman, Jordan
American Center for Oriental Research, Amman, Jordan
Calvin Theological Seminary, Grand Rapids, MI
Covenant Theological Seminary, St. Louis, MO
Earthwatch Center for Field Research, Belmont, MA
Friends of Archaeology, Riverside, CA
Grace Theological Seminary, Winona Lake, IN
Kyle-Kelso Archaeological Fund, Holland, MI
United Nations Relief and Works Agency, Amman, Jordan
Winebrenner Theological Seminary, Findlay, OH
Worthington Foods, Worthington, OH

Major Individual Sponsors
Dr. and Mrs. Charles L. Anderson
Mrs. Ruth Kaune Baucom
Eleanor and William Berecz, Jr.
Wilber A. Bishop, Sr.

Dr. and Mrs. Bernard Brandstater
Dr. and Mrs. Bruce Branson
Dr. Irvin N. Kuhn
Dr. and Mrs. John Wm. Schnepper
Walter E. Sooy
John H. Weidner

Participants

Lawrence T. Geraty (AU)	*Director*
Roger S. Boraas (UC)	*Chief Archaeologist*
Arif Abul-Ghannim	*Rep—Dept of Ant &*
	Arch Sur Staff
Mohammad Adawi (ACOR)	*Cook*
Merling Alomia	*Architect Draft Staff &*
	Ornithology
Kim Baker	*Sq Sup—Area A*
Raymond Bankes	*Sq Sup—Areas F & G*
Kaye Barton	*Photo Staff*
Esther Benton	*Assist—Eco Lab*
B. Michael Blaine	*Sq Sup—Area G*
Joachim Boessneck (UMun)	
	Zooarcheologist—Eco Lab
Miriam Boraas	*Sq Sup—Area C East*
Kerry Brandstater	*Sq Sup—Area D & G*
Robin M. Brown	*Sq Sup—Area G*
Pamela Butterworth	*Artist—Eco Lab*
Loren Calvert	*Photo Staff*
Donald Casebolt	*Sq Sup—Area B*
Mary Ann Casebolt	*Assist—Eco Lab*
Douglas Clark	*Sq Sup—Area A*
Vincent Clark	*Sq Sup—Area D & C East*
John Coughenour	*Sq Sup—Area C East*
Robert Coughenour (Western TS)	
	Director of Education & Area A
Robin Cox	*Assist—Eco Lab*
Patricia Crawford (BU)	*Ethnobotanist—Eco Lab*
John J. Davis (GTS)	*F Sup—Area F*
Paul H. Denton	*Head—Photo Staff*
Bert de Vries (CC)	*Head—Architec Draft*
Adelma Downing	*Assist—Eco Lab*
Anna Eaton	*Photo Staff*
Mary Fenske	*Pt vol—Various Areas*
Remie Fenske	*Pt vol—Various Areas*
Theresa Fuentes	*Assist—Eco Lab*
Ronald Geraty	*Sq Sup—Area B & Physician*
Sheila Geraty	*Assist—Areas F & G*
Samir Ghishan	*Assist—Eco Lab*
Jelmer Groenewold	*Sq Sup—Area C West*
Jennifer Groot	*Sq Sup—Area C West*
P. Edgar Hare (Carnegie Geophysical Inst)	
	Geologist—Eco Lab
Larry G. Herr (HU)	*F Sup—Areas B & D*
Siegried H. Horn (AU)	*Object Registrar*
Elisabeth Horner	*EW vol—Eco Lab*
Robert D. Ibach (GTS)	*Head—Arch Sur*
Kenneth Knutsen	*Sq Sup—Areas B & G*

Lorrie Knutsen	*Receptionist–Secretary*	James A. Sauer (ACOR)	*Ceramicist &*
Andrew Kramer	*Photo Staff*		*F Sup–Area B*
Henry Kuhlman	*Architect Draft Staff*	Patricia Schmidt	*Assist–Area F*
Asta Sakala LaBianca	*Assist–Eco Lab*	Helen Shafer	*EW vol–Eco Lab*
Øystein Sakala LaBianca (BU)	*Head–Eco Lab*	Oscar Shultz	*Sq Sup–Area A*
Lori LaValley	*EW vol–Eco Lab*	Timothy Shultz	*Sq Sup–Areas C West & G*
John Lawlor	*Sq Sup–Areas D & G*	Peter Soderman	*Sq Sup–Areas B & F*
Robert M. Little (AU)	*Physical Anthropol*	Marilyn Stickle	*Sq Sup–Areas B & F*
Scott Longacre	*Assist–Area F*	James H. Stirling (LLU)	*Physical Anthropol*
Frank Lounsberry	*Assist–Area F*	Bjørnar Storfjell	*Sq Sup–Areas B & F*
Myra Mare	*Sq Sup–Area C West*	Margit Suring	*Sq Sup–Area A*
W. Harold Mare (CovTS)		Merryanna Swartz	*EW vol–Eco Lab*
	F Sup–Area C West	Marilyn Tanis	*Assist–Area F*
Sissy May	*EW vol–Eco Lab*	Abraham Terian (AU)	*Coins*
Julia Middleton	*EW vol–Eco Lab*	Hester Thomsen (GNYA)	*Pottery Registrar*
Larry Mitchel	*Sq Sup–Areas B & G*	Michael Toplyn	*EW vol–Eco Lab*
Carol Moerman	*Sq Sup–Areas C East & G*	Mitchell Tyner	*Photo Staff*
Julia Neuffer	*Sq Sup–Area A*	Patricia Tyner	*Sup–Eco Lab*
S. Thomas Parker (UCLA)	*F Sup–Area C East*	William Urbrock	*Sq Sup–Area C East*
Sheri Paauw	*Sq Sup–Area G*	Anita Van Elderen	*Architec Draft Staff*
Paul Perkins (Digital Equipment)		Bastiaan Van Elderen (CalTS)	*F Sup–Area A*
	Computer Programmer–Eco Lab	Paul Vance	*EW vol–Eco Lab*
David Piper	*Architec Draft Staff*	Angela von den Driesch (UMun)	
Nabil Qadi	*Sq Sup–Area C West*		*Zooarchaeolgist–Eco Lab*
Douglas Robertson	*Sq Sup–Area C West*	Carl Wheat	*Arch Sur Staff*
Scott Rolston	*Photo Staff*	Donald H. Wimmer	*Sq Sup–Area G*
Mahmoud Rusan	*Rep–Dept of Ant &*	Mary Witt	*Sq Sup–Area C East*
	Sq Sup–Area A & G	Nathaniel Yen	*Sq Sup–Area C East*
Daniel Salzmann	*Architec Draft Staff*	Omar Yunis	*Rep–Dept of Ant &*
Saleh Sari	*Sq Sup–Area C West*		*Sq Sup–Area C East*

Plate C.5   1976 Heshbon Expedition staff

REFERENCES

REFERENCES

Abel, F. M.
1933   *Géographie de la Palestine*, vols. 1 & 2, ed. J. Gabalda. Paris: Librairie Lecoffre.

Abidi, A.
1965   *Jordan: A Political Study, 1948-57*. London: Asia Publishing House.

Abujaber, R. S.
1984   Yadoudeh: The Modern History of its People. Pp. 30-31 in *Madaba Plains Project 1: The 1984 Season at Tell el-'Umeiri and Subsequent Studies*. Berrien Springs, MI: Andrews University Press.

Abu Jaber, K. S.; Gharaibeh, F.; Khasawneh, S.; and Hill, A.
1976   *Socio-Economic Survey of the Badia of Northeastern Jordan*. Amman: University of Jordan.

Adams, R. McC.
1965   *Land Behind Baghdad: A History of Settlement on the Diyala Plains*. Chicago: University of Chicago Press.

1966   *The Evolution of Urban Society: Early Mesopotamia and Prehispanic Mexico*. Chicago: Aldine Publishing Co.

1974   The Mesopotamian Social Landscape: A View from the Frontier. Pp. 1-20 in *Reconstructing Complex Societies*, ed. C. B. Moore. Supplement to the *Bulletin of the American Schools of Oriental Research* No. 20.

1978   Strategies of Maximization, Stability, and Resilience in Mesopotamian Society, Settlement, and Agriculture. *Proceedings of the American Philosophical Society* 22: 329-335.

1981   *Heartland of Cities*. Chicago: University of Chicago Press.

Adams, R. McC., and Nissen, H. J.
1972   *The Uruk Countryside: The Natural Setting of Urban Societies*. Chicago: University of Chicago Press.

Agrar- und Hydrotechnik
1977   *National Water Master Plan of Jordan*, vols. 1-8. Amman: Natural Resources Authority.

Albright, W. F.
1924   The Archaeological Results of an Expedition to Moab and the Dead Sea. *Bulletin of the American Schools of Oriental Research* 14: 2-12.

1932   *The Archaeology of Palestine and the Bible*. New York: Fleming H. Revell Co.

Allison, N. E.
1977   *A Case of Honor: Arab Christians in a Jordanian Town*. Ph.D. dissertation. University of Georgia.

Almagro, A., and Olavarri, E.
1982   A New Umayyad Palace at the Citadel of Amman. Pp. 305-321 in *Studies in the History and Archaeology of Jordan I*, ed. A. Hadidi. Amman: Department of Antiquities.

Alomia, M.
1978   Notes on the Present Avifauna of Hesban. *Andrews University Seminary Studies* 16: 289-303.

Amiran, D. H. K.
1950   A Revised Earthquake-Catalogue of Palestine. *Israel Exploration Journal* 1: 223-246.

Amiran, D. H. K., ed.
1970   *Atlas of Israel: Cartography, Physical Geography, Human and Economic Geography History.* Amsterdam: Elsevier Publishing Co.

Amiran, D. H. K., *et al.*
1952   A Revised Earthquake-Catalogue of Palestine. *Israel Exploration Journal* 2: 48-65.

Ammerman, A. J.
1981   Surveys and Archaeological Research. *Annual Review of Anthropology* 10: 63-88.

Angel, J. L.
1972   Ecology and Population in the Eastern Mediterranean. *World Archaeology* 4: 88-105.

Angress, S., and Reed, C. A.
1962   *An Annotated Bibliography on the Origin and Descent of Domestic Mammals, 1900-1995.* Chicago: Natural History Museum.

Antoun, R.
1968   The Social Significance of Ramadan in an Arab Village. *Muslim World* 58: 36-104.

1972   *Arab Village: A Social Structural Study of a Trans-Jordanian Peasant Community.* Bloomington: Indiana University Press.

1979   *Low-Key Politics: Local Level Leadership and Change in the Middle East.* Albany: New York State University Press.

Applebaum, S.
1971   Decapolis. Cols. 1449-50 in vol. 5 of *Encyclopædia Judaica*, ed. C. Roth. Jerusalem: MacMillan Co.

Applebaum, S.; Dar, S.; and Safrai, Z.
1977   The Towers of Samaria. *Palestine Exploration Quarterly* 109-110: 91-100.

Aresvik, O.
1976   *The Agricultural Development of Jordan.* New York: Praeger Publishers.

Arnold, D. E.
1985   *Ceramic Theory and Cultural Process.* New York: Cambridge University Press.

Aruri, N. H.
1972   *Jordan: A Study in Political Development (1921-1965).* The Hague, Netherlands: Martinus Nijhoff.

Asad, T.
1973   The Bedouin as a Military Force: Notes on Some Aspects of Power Relations Between Nomads and Sedentaries in Historical Perspective. Pp. 61-73 in *The Desert and the Sown*, ed. C. Nelson. Berkeley, CA: University of California Institute of International Studies.

Ashtor, E.
1981   Levantine Sugar Industry in the Late Middle Ages: A Case of Technological Decline. Pp. 91-132 in *The Islamic Middle East, 700-1900.* A.L. Udovitch, ed. Princeton: The Darwin Press, Inc.

Avi-Yonah, M.
1950   The Development of the Roman Road System in Palestine. *Israel Exploration Journal* 1: 54-60.

1958   The Economics of Byzantine Palestine. *Israel Exploration Journal* 8: 39-51.

1977   *The Holy Land—From the Persian to the Arab Conquests (536 B.C.-A.D. 640): A Historical Geography.* Rev. ed. Grand Rapids: Baker.

Avi-Yonah, M., and Stern, E., eds.
1979   Rabbath-Ammon. Cols. 987-93 in vol. 4 of *Encyclopedia of Archaeological Excavations in the Holy Land.* Englewood Cliffs, NJ: Prentice-Hall, Inc.

Awad, M.
1970 Living Conditions of Nomadic, Semi-Nomadic and Settled Tribal Groups. Pp. 133-148 in *Readings in Arab Middle Eastern Societies and Cultures*, eds. A. B. Lutfiyya and C. W. Churchill. The Hague, Netherlands: Mouton & Co.

Baedeker, K., ed.
1876 *Palestine and Syria: Handbook for Travelers*. London: Dulau and Co.

Al-Bakhit, M. A.
1982 Jordan in Perspective: The Mamluk-Ottoman Period. Pp. 361-362 in *Studies in the History and Archaeology of Jordan I*, ed. A. Hadidi. Amman: Department of Antiquities.

Baldwin, M. W.
1987 The Crusades. Pp. 880-892 in vol. 16 of *The New Encyclopædia Britannica*.

Baly, D.
1957 *The Geography of the Bible*. New York: Harper & Row.

Banning, E. B.
1986 Peasants, Pastoralists and *Pax Romana*: Mutualism in the Southern Highlands of Jordan. *Bulletin of the American Schools of Oriental Research* 261:25-50.

Banning, T., and Köhler-Rollefson, I. K.
1986 Ethnoarchaeological Survey in the *Beda* Area, Southern Jordan. *Sonderdruck aus Zeitschrift des Deutschen Palästina-Vereins* 102: 152-170.

Barker, P.
1977 *Techniques of Archaeological Excavation*. New York: Universe Books.

Barlett, P. F.
1980 Adaptive Strategies in Peasant Agricultural Production. *Annual Review of Anthropology* 9: 545-573.

Barnett, H. G.
1953 *Innovation: The Basis Of Cultural Change*. New York: McGraw-Hill.

Barth, F.
1961 *Nomads of South Persia*. Boston: Little, Brown, and Co.

1973 A General Perspective on Nomad-Sedentary Relations in the Middle East. Pp. 11-21 in *The Desert and the Sown: Nomads in the Wider Society*, ed. C. Nelson. Berkeley, CA: University of California Institute of International Studies.

Bates, D., and Rassam, A.
1983 *Peoples and Cultures of the Middle East*. Englewood Cliffs, NJ: Prentice-Hall, Inc.

Bayer, B.
1971 Hasmoneans. Cols. 1455-59 in vol. 7 of *Encyclopædia Judaica*, ed. C. Roth. Jerusalem: MacMillan Co.

Beaumont, P.; Blake, G. H.; and Wagstaff, J. M.
1976 *The Middle East: A Geographical Study*. New York: John Wiley & Sons.

Beisheh, G.
1973 Roman Period. Pp. 45-49 in *The Archaeological Heritage of Jordan*, ed. G. Barakat. Jordan: Department of Antiquities.

Bell, L. G.
1927 *The Letters of Gertrude Bell*, vol. 1. New York: Boni and Liveright.

Ben-Arieh, Y.
1983 *The Rediscovery of the Holy Land in the Nineteenth Century*. 2nd ed. Jerusalem: Magnes Press.

Benham, H.
1981 *Man's Struggle for Food*. New York: University Press of America.

Bennett, C.-M.
1982 Neo-Assyrian Influence in Transjordan. Pp. 181-187 in *Studies in the History and Archaeology of Jordan I*, ed. A. Hadidi. Amman: Department of Antiquities.

Bennett, J. W.
1976   *The Ecological Transition: Cultural Anthropology and Human Adaptation.* New York: Pergamon Press Inc.

Binford, L. R.
1962   Archaeology as Anthropology. *American Antiquity* 28: 217-225.

1964   A Consideration of Archaeological Research Design. *American Antiquity* 29: 425-441.

1965   Archaeological Systematics and the Study of Culture Process. *American Antiquity* 31: 203-210.

1968   Some Comments on Historical versus Processual Archaeology. *Southwestern Journal of Anthropology* 24: 267-275.

1983   *In Pursuit of the Past.* New York: Thames and Hudson Inc.

Bird, P. A.
1969   Heshbon 1968: Area D. *Andrews University Seminary Studies* 7.2: 165-217.

Bishop, R.; Rands, R.; and Holley, G.
1982   Ceramic Compositional Analysis in Archaeological Perspective. Pp. 275-330 in *Advances in Archaeological Method and Theory*, vol. 5, ed. M. B. Schiffer. New York: Academic Press.

Boas, F.
1940   *Race, Language and Culture.* New York: Free Press.

Bocco, R.
1984a Nomadismo pastorale e società beduina in Giordania: un orientamento bibliografico. *Studi per l'Ecologia del Quaternario* 6: 129-134.

1984b I Bani Sakhr: cenni storici su una tria beduina della Giordania. *Studi per l'Ecologia del Quaternario* 6: 93-102.

1984c The Bedouin of Jordan: A People Without History? Paper presented at the symposium "Anthropology in Jordan: State of the Art." Amman.

Bodley, J. H.
1976   *Anthropology and Contemporary Human Problems.* California: Cummings Publishing Co., Inc.

Boessneck, J.
forth- Bird Bones. In *Faunal Remains: Tapho-*
coming *nomical and Zooarchaeological Studies of the Animal Remains from Tell Hesban and Vicinity. Hesban 13.* Berrien Springs, MI: Andrews University Press.

Boessneck, J., and von den Driesch, A.
1978a Preliminary Analysis of the Animal Bones from Tell Hesban. *Andrews University Seminary Studies* 16: 259-287.

1978b The Significance of Measuring Animal Bones from Archeological Sites. *Approaches to Faunal Analysis in the Middle East.* Edited by R. H. Meadow and M. A. Zeder. Peabody Museum Bulletin 2.

1981   Erste Ergebnisse unserer Bestimmungsargbeit an den Tierknochenfunden vom Tell Hesban, Jordanien. *Sonderdruck aus Archäologie und Naturwissenschaften.* 2: 55-72.

Bokonyi, S.
1971   The Development and History of Domestic Animals in Hungary: The Neolithic Through the Middle Ages. *American Anthropologist* 73: 640-674.

Boneh, D.
1983   *Facing the Uncertainty: The Social Consequences of Forced Sedentarization Among the Jaraween Bedouin, Negev, Israel.* Ann Arbor, MI: University Microfilms International.

Boraas, R. S., and Geraty, L. T.
1976   The Fourth Campaign at Tell Hesban. *Andrews University Seminary Studies* 14 (entire journal).

1978   The Fifth Campaign at Tell Hesban. *Andrews University Seminary Studies* 16 (entire journal).

Boraas, R. S., and Horn, S. H.
1969   The First Campaign at Tell Hesban. *Andrews University Seminary Studies* 7 (entire journal).

1973   The Second Campaign at Tell Hesban. *Andrews University Seminary Studies* 11 (entire journal).

1975   The Third Campaign at Tell Hesban. *Andrews University Seminary Studies* 13 (entire journal).

Boserup, E.
1965   *The Conditions of Agricultural Growth.* Chicago: Aldine Publishing Co.

1983   The Impact of Scarcity and Plenty on Development. *Journal of Interdisciplinary History* 14: 383-407.

Boughey, A. S.
1973   *Ecology of Populations.* New York: Macmillan Co.

Bowersock, G. W.
1983   *Roman Arabia.* Cambridge: Harvard University Press.

Braidwood, R. J.
1964   *Prehistoric Men.* Glenview, IL: Scott, Foresman and Co.

Braudel, F.
1967   *Capitalism and Material Life 1400-1800.* New York: Harper and Row.

Brothwell, D., and Brothwell, P.
1969   *Food in Antiquity: A Survey of the Diet of Early Peoples.* Ancient Peoples and Places 66. London: Thames and Hudson.

Brown, R. M.
1978   Heshbon 1976: Area G.11, 16, 17, 18. *Andrews University Seminary Studies* 16: 167-182.

Brunnow, R. E., and Domaszewski, A. V.
1904   *Die Provincia Arabia.* Strassburg: Verlag von Karl J. Trubner.

Buckingham, J. S.
1825   *Travels in Syria and the Holy Land.* London: Longman, Hurst, Ress, Orme, Brown, and Green.

Bullard, R. G.
1972   Geological Study of the Heshbon Area. *Andrews University Seminary Studies* 10: 129-141.

Bulliet, R. W.
1975   *The Camel and the Wheel.* Cambridge: Harvard University Press.

Burckhardt, J. S.
1822   *Travels in Syria and the Holy Land.* London: John Murray.

1831   *Notes on the Bedouins and Wahabys,* vols. 1 & 2. London: Henry Colburn and Richard Bentley.

Burton, I.; Kates, R. W.; and White, G., eds.
1978   *The Environment as Hazard.* New York: Oxford University Press.

Butzer, K. W.
1976   *Early Hydraulic Civilization in Egypt.* Chicago: University of Chicago Press.

1982   *Archaeology as Human Ecology.* London: Cambridge University Press.

Campbell, D. J.
1984   Response to Drought Among Farmers and Herders in Southern Kajiado District, Kenya. *Human Ecology* 12: 35-64.

Canaan, T.
1933   The Palestinian Arab House: Its Architecture and Folklore. Jerusalem: Syrian Orphanage Press.

Caskel, W.
1959   The Bedouinization of Arabia. *American Anthropologist* 56: 36-46.

Cassel, J.
1974 Psychosocial Processes and Stress: Theoretical Formulation. *International Journal of Health Services* 4: 471-482.

Casteel, R.
1972 Some Biases in the Recovery of Archaeological Faunal Remains. *The Proceedings of the Prehistoric Society* 38: 382-386.

Chang, C.
1982 The Contribution of Ethnoarchaeological Research to the Diachronic Perspectives of Changing Land Use Patterns. Paper presented at the Annual Meeting of the Society for American Archaeology. April 15, Minneapolis.

Chaplin, R. E.
1971 *The Study of Animal Bones from Archaeological Sites.* London: Seminar Press.

Chappell, J. E. Jr.
1970 Climatic Change Reconsidered: Another Look at "The Pulse of Asia." *Geographical Review* 60: 347-373.

Childe, V. G.
1946 *What Happened in History?* New York: Penguin Books.

Chirot, D., and Hall, T. D.
1982 World-System Theory. *Annual Review of Sociology* 8: 81-106.

Clapham, W. B. Jr.
1981 *Human Ecosystems.* New York: Macmillian Publishing Co., Inc.

Clark, G.
1962 *World Prehistory: An Outline.* Cambridge: Cambridge University Press.

Clutton-Brock, J., and Uerpmann, H.-P.
1974 The Sheep of Early Jericho. *Journal of Archaeological Science* 1: 261-274.

Cohen, M. N.
1977 *The Food Crisis in Prehistory: Overpopulation and the Origins of Agriculture.* New Haven, CT: Yale University Press.

Cohen, R., and Dever, W. G.
1981 Preliminary Report of the Third and Final Season of the "Central Negev Highlands Project." *Bulletin of the American Schools of Oriental Research* 243: 57-77.

Cohen R., and Service, E., eds.
1978 *Origins of the State: The Anthropology of Political Evolution.* Philadelphia: Institute for the Study of Human Issues.

Cole, D. P.
1973 The Enmeshment of Nomads in Sa'udi Arabian Society: The Case of Al Murrah. Pp. 113-128 in *The Desert and the Sown: Nomads in the Wider Society,* ed. C. Nelson. Berkeley, CA: University of California Institute of International Studies.

Colson, E.
1979 In Good Years and in Bad: Food Strategies of Self-Reliant Societies. *Journal of Anthropological Research* 35: 18-30.

Conder, C. R.
1889 *The Survey of Eastern Palestine.* London: Palestine Exploration Fund.

1891 *Palestine.* New York: Dodd, Mead.

1892 *Heath and Moab: Explorations in Syria in 1881 and 1882.* London: Watt.

Conrad, L. I.
1981 The Qusur of Medieval Islam. *Al-Abhath* 29: 7-23.

Cook, S. F.
1973 The Significance of Disease in the Extinction of the New England Indians. *Human Biology* 45: 485-508.

Coon, C.
1958 *Caravan: The Story of the Middle East.* New York: Holt, Rinehart and Winston.

Cowgill, G. L.
1975a   Population Pressure as a Non-Explanation. *American Antiquity* 40: 127-131.

1975b   On Causes and Consequences of Ancient and Modern Population Changes. *American Anthropologist* 77: 505-525.

Cox, G. W., and Atkins, M. D.
1979   *Agricultural Ecology: An Analysis of World Food Production Systems*. San Francisco: W. H. Freeman and Co.

Cox, J. J. C.
1976   A Rhodian Potter's Date-Stamp. *Andrews University Seminary Studies* 14: 149-156.

Crawford, P.
1986   Flora of Tell Hesban and Area, Jordan. Pp. 75-98 in *Environmental Foundations. Hesban 2*, eds. Ø. S. LaBianca and L. Lacelle. Berrien Springs, MI: Andrews University Press.

Crawford, P., and LaBianca, Ø.
1976   The Flora of Hesban. *Andrews University Seminary Studies* 14: 177-184.

Crawford, P.; LaBianca, Ø.; and Stewart, R.
1976   The Flotation Remains. *Andrews University Seminary Studies* 14: 185-188.

Crawley, E. A.
1927   *The Mystic Rose: A Study of Primitive Marriage and of Primitive Thought in its Bearing on Marriage*. Revised and greatly enlarged by Theodore Besterman. London.

Crone, P.
1980   *Slaves on Horses: The Evolution of the Islamic Polity*. Cambridge: Cambridge University.

Crosby, A. W.
1972   *The Columbian Exchange: The Biological and Cultural Consequences of 1492*. Westport, CT: Greenwood Publishing Co.

Crowfoot, G. M.
1932   Pots, Ancient and Modern. *Palestine Exploration Quarterly*, (January): 179-187.

Dalman, G.
1964   *Arbeit und Sitte in Palästina. Band III: Von der Ernte zum Mehl: Ernten, Dreschen, Worfeln, Sieben, Verwahren, Mahlen*. Hildesheim: Georg Olms Verlagsbuchhandlung.

Deetz, J.
1967   *Invitation to Archaeology*. Garden City, NY: Natural History Press.

1972   Archaeology as a Social Science. Pp. 108-117 in *Contemporary Archaeology*, ed. M. Leone. Carbondale: Southern Illinois University Press.

De Saulcy, F.
1853   *Journey Round the Dead Sea and in Bible Lands*, vols. 1 & 2. London: Richard Bentley.

Devos, A.
1969   Ecological Conditions Affecting the Production of Wild Herbivorous Mammals on Grasslands. In *Advances in Ecological Research*, vol. 6, ed. J. B. Cragg. London: Academic Press.

De Vries, B.
1986   The Islamic Bath at Tell Hesban. Pp. 223-235 in *The Archaeology of Jordan and Other Studies*, eds. L. T. Geraty and L. G. Herr. Berrien Springs, MI: Andrews University Press.

Dirks, R.
1980   Social Responses During Severe Food Shortages and Famine. *Current Anthropology* 21: 21-44.

Dols, M. W.
1977   *The Black Death in the Middle East*. Princeton, NJ: Princeton University Press.

Donner, F.
1981   *The Early Islamic Conquests*. Princeton: Princeton University Press.

Douglas, M.
1966   *Purity and Danger: An Analysis of Concepts of Pollution and Taboo.* London: Routledge and K. Paul.

1971   Deciphering a Meal. Pp. 61- 81 in *Myth, Symbol and Culture,* ed. C. Geertz. New York.

Douglas, M., and Isherwood, B.
1979   *The World of Goods.* London: Allen Lane.

Dow, M. M.
1985   Agricultural Intensification and Craft Specialization: A Nonrecursive Model. *Ethnology* 24: 137-152.

Duckham, A. N., and Masefield, G. B.
1971   *Farming Systems of the World.* London: Chatto and Windus.

Dyson-Hudson, R., and Dyson-Hudson, N.
1970   The Food Production System of a Semi-Nomadic Society: The Karimojong, Uganda. In *African Food Production Systems,* ed. P. F. M. McLoughlin. Baltimore: Johns Hopkins Press.

Edelstein, G., and Gat, Y.
1980   Terraces Around Jerusalem. *Israel—Land and Nature* 6: 72-78.

Edelstein, G., and Kislev, M.
1981   Mevasseret Yerushalayim: The Ancient Settlement and its Agricultural Terraces. *Biblical Archeologist* 44: 53-56

Eickelman, D.
1981   *The Middle East: An Anthropological Approach.* Englewood Cliffs, NJ: Prentice-Hall, Inc.

Elazary, E., and Porten, B.
1971   Tobiads. Cols. 1178-80 in vol. 15 of *Encyclopædia Judaica,* ed. C. Roth. Jerusalem: MacMillan Co.

Ellison, R.
1984   The Uses of Pottery. *Iraq* 46.1: 63-68.

English, P. W.
1977   *World Regional Geography: A Question of Place.* New York: Harper's College Press.

Eph'al, I.
1982   *The Ancient Arabs: Nomads on the Borders of the Fertile Crescent 9th-5th Centuries B.C.* Jerusalem: Magnes Press.

Epstein, E.
1938   The Bedouin of Transjordan: Their Social and Economic Problems. *Journal of the Royal Central Asian Society* 25: 228-236.

1939   Correspondence: The Economic Situation of the Transjordan Tribes. *Journal of the Royal Central Asian Society* 26: 177-184.

Evans, J. G.
1978   *An Introduction to Environmental Archaeology.* Ithaca, NY: Cornell University Press.

Evenari, M.
1956   Masters of the Desert. *Scientific American* 194,4: 39-45.

Evenari, M.; Shanan, L.; and Tadmor, N.
1971   *The Negev: The Challenge of a Desert.* Cambridge: Harvard University Press.

Feliks, J.
1971   Hyrcanus. Cols. 1146-48 in vol. 8 of *Encyclopædia Judaica,* ed. C. Roth. Jerusalem: MacMillan Co.

Ferguson, K., and Hudson, T.
1986   Climate of Tell Hesban and Area. Pp. 7-22 in *Environmental Foundations. Hesban 2,* eds. Ø. S. LaBianca and L. Lacelle. Berrien Springs, MI: Andrews University Press.

Fikery, M.
1979   The Maqarin Dam and the East Jordan Valley. Unpublished manuscript. Amman: USAID.

Firth, R. W.
1964 *Elements of Social Organization.* Boston: Beacon Press.

Fish, H. C.
1876 *Bible Lands Illustrated: A Pictorial Handbook of the Antiquities and Modern Life of all the Sacred Countries.* Hartford, CT: American Publishing Co.

Fisher, W. B.
1971 *The Middle East.* London: Methuen & Co. Ltd.

Flannery, K. V.
1967 Culture History vs. Cultural Process: A Debate in American Archaeology. *Scientific American* 217: 119-122.

1969 Origins and Ecological Effects of Early Domestication in Iran and the Near East. Pp. 73-100 in *The Domestication and Exploitation of Plants and Animals,* eds. P. J. Ucko, and G. W. Dimbleby. Chicago: Aldine Publishing Co.

1970 The Ecology of Early Food Production in Mesopotamia. Pp. 29-52 in *Peoples and Cultures of the Middle East,* ed. L. E. Sweet. New York: Natural History Press.

1972 The Cultural Evolution of Civilizations. *Annual Review of Ecology and Systematics* 3: 399-426. California: Annual Reviews Inc.

1974 Origins and Ecological Effects of Early Domestication in Iran and the Near East. In *The Rise and Fall of Civilizations,* eds. C. C. Lamberg-Karlovsky and J. A. Sabloff. California: Cummings Publishing Co.

Flannery, K. V., ed.
1976 *The Early Mesoamerican Village.* New York: Academic Press.

1982 *Maya Subsistence: Studies in Memory of Dennis E. Puleston.* New York: Academic Press.

Flannery, K. V., *et al.*
1967 Farming Systems and Political Growth in Ancient Oaxaca, Mexico. *Science* 158: 445-454.

Fohrer, G.
1961 Eisenzeitliche Anlagen im Raume Südlich von Na'ur und die Südwestgrenze von Ammon. *Zeitschrift des Deutschen Paästina-Vereins* 77: 56-71.

Forbes, R. J.
1955 *Studies in Ancient Technology,* vols. 1, 2 & 3. Netherlands: E. J. Brill.

Ford, R. I.
1979 Paleoethnobotany in American Archaeology. In *Advances in Archaeological Method and Theory,* vol. 2, ed. M. B. Schiffer. New York: Academic Press.

Forder, A.
1909 *Ventures Among the Arabs.* New York: Gospel Publishing House.

Frank, A. G.
1966 *The Development of Underdevelopment.* New York: Monthly Review Press.

Franke, R. W., and Chasin, B. H.
1980 *Seeds of Famine: Ecological Destruction and the Development Dilemma in the West African Sahel.* New Jersey: Allanheld, Osmun & Co. Publishers, Inc.

Franken, H. J.
1982 A Technological Study of Iron Age I Pottery from Tell Deir 'Alla. *SHAJ* 1: 141-144.

Frazer, J.
1890 *The Golden Bough.* New York: MacMillan Co.

Fried, M.
1967 *The Evolution of Political Society: An Essay in Political Anthropology.* New York: Random House.

Fuller, N. B., and Fuller, M. J.
1983   Food Production at the Decapolis City of Abila. Paper presented at the Annual Meeting of the American Schools of Oriental Research. December 21, Dallas.

Geertz, C.
1963   *Agricultural Involution.* Berkeley: University of California Press.

Geraty, L. T.
1976   The 1976 Season of Excavations at Tell Hesban. *Annual of the Department of Antiquites of Jordan* 21: 41-53.

Geraty, L. T., and LaBianca, Ø. S.
1985   The Local Environment and Human Food-Procuring Strategies in Jordan: The Case of Tell Hesban and Its Surrounding Region. Pp. 323-330 in *Studies in the History and Archaeology of Jordan II,* ed. A. Hadidi. Amman: Department of Antiquities.

Geraty, L. T., and Willis, L.
1986   The History of Archaeological Research in Transjordan. Pp. 3-72 in *The Archaeology of Jordan and Other Studies,* eds. L. T. Geraty and L. G. Herr. Berrien Springs, MI: Andrews University Press.

Geraty, L. T., *et al.*
1986   Madaba Plains Project: A Preliminary Report of the 1984 Season at Tell El-'Umeiri and Vicinity. Pp. 117-144 in *Preliminary Reports of ASOR-Sponsored Excavations 1980-1984,* ed. W. E. Rast. Supplement to the *Bulletin of the American Schools of Oriental Research* No. 24.

Germer-Durand, J.
1904   Rapport sur l'exploration archéologique en 1903 de la voie romaine entre Amman et Bostra (Arabie). *Bulletin archéologique du comité des travaux historiques et scientifiques* 22: 1-43.

Gese, H.
1958   Ammonitische Grenzfestungen zwischen Wadi es-Sir und Na'ur. *Zeitschrift des Deutschen Palästina-Vereins* 74: 55-64.

Gibbon, E.
n.d.   *The Decline and Fall of the Roman Empire.* New York: Modern Library.

Gilbert, E. H.; Norman, D. W.; and Winch, F. E.
1980   *Farming Systems Research: A Critical Appraisal.* Lansing: Michigan State University Department of Agricultural Economics. MSU Rural Development Paper No. 6.

Gilliland, D. R.
1986   Paleoethnobotany and Paleobotany. Pp. 121-142 in *Environmental Foundations. Hesban 2,* eds. Ø. S. LaBianca and L. Lacelle. Berrien Springs, MI: Andrews University Press.

Glock, A. E.
1985   Tradition and Change in Two Archaeologies. *American Antiquity* 50: 464-477.

Glubb, J. B.
1938   The Economic Situation of the Trans-Jordan Tribes. *Journal of the Royal Central Asian Society* 25: 448-459.

1948   *The Story of the Arab Legion.* London: Hodder and Stoughton, Ltd.

1967   *Syria, Lebanon, Jordan.* New York: Walker and Co.

Glueck, N.
1939   *Explorations in Eastern Palestine, III. Annual of the American Schools of Oriental Research* 18-19. New Haven, CT: American Schools of Oriental Research.

1946   *The River Jordan.* Philadelphia: Westminster.

1959   *Rivers in the Desert.* New York: Farrar, Straus and Cudahy.

Goode, J.; Theophano, J.; and Curtis, K.
1985   A Framework for the Analysis of Continuity and Change in Shared Sociocultural Rules for Food Use: The Italian-American Pattern. Pp. 66-68 in *Foodways*, eds. L. K. Brown, and M. K. Brown. Knoxville: University of Tennessee Press.

Goody, J.
1982   *Cooking, Cuisine and Class.* Cambridge: Cambridge University Press.

Gould, R. A., ed.
1978   *Explorations in Ethnoarchaeology.* Albuquerque: University of New Mexico Press.

Gouldner, A., and Peterson, R. A.
1962   *Notes on Technology and the Moral Order.* Indianapolis: Bobbs-Merrill.

Grabar, O.
1955   Umayyad "Palace" and the 'Abbasid "Revolution." *Studia Islamica* 4: 5-18.

Graf, D. F.
1980   The Hisma Desert in Southern Jordan. Paper presented at the Annual Meeting of the American Schools of Oriental Research. November 8, Dallas.

Green, S. W.
1980   Toward a General Model of Agricultural Systems. Pp. 337-344 in *Advances in Archaeological Method and Theory*, vol. 3, ed. M. B. Schiffer. Academic Press.

Grigg, D. B.
1974   *The Agricultural Systems of the World.* New York: Cambridge University Press.

Gubser, P.
1973   *Politics and Change in Al Karak, Jordan.* Oxford: Oxford University Press.

1983   *Jordan.* Boulder, CO: Westview Press.

Gulick, J.
1971   The Arab Levant. Pp. 79-171 in *The Central Middle East*, ed. L. Sweet. New Haven: HRAF Press.

Haas, J. D., and Harrison, G. G.
1977   Nutritional Anthropology and Biological Adaptation. *Annual Review of Anthropology* 6: 69-101.

Hadidi, A., ed.
1982   *Studies in the History and Archaeology of Jordan I.* Amman: Department of Antiquities.

1985   *Studies in the History and Archaeology of Jordan II.* Amman: Department of Antiquities.

1987   *Studies in the History and Archaeology of Jordan III.* Amman: Department of Antiquities.

Halbaek, H.
1959a   Domestication of Food Plants in the Old World. *Science* 130: 365-371.

1959b   How Farming Began in the Old World. *Archaeology* 12: 183-189.

Hamblin, R. L., and Pitcher, B. L.
1980   The Classic Maya Collapse: Testing Class Conflict Hypotheses. *American Antiquity* 40: 246-267.

Hammond, P. C.
1973   *The Nabataeans—Their History, Culture and Archaeology.* Sweden City: Paul Astroms Forlag.

Hardesty, D. L.
1977   *Ecological Anthropology.* New York: John Wiley & Sons.

Harding, G. L.
1959   *The Antiquities of Jordan.* New York: Crowell.

1960   Amman. Cols. 447-48 in vol. 1 of *The Encyclopædia of Islam.* London: Luzac & Co.

Harner, M. J.
1970   Population Pressure and the Social Evolution of Agriculturists. *Southwestern Journal of Anthropology* 26,1: 67-86.

Harris, M.
1968   *The Rise of Anthropological Theory.* New York: Thomas Y. Crowell Co., Inc.

Hashemite Kingdom of Jordan
1967   *Report on Agricultural Census 1965.* Amman: Department of Statistics Press.

1975   *General Results of the Agricultural Census 1975.* Amman: Department of Statistics Press.

1979   *Agricultural Statistical Yearbook and Agricultural Sample Survey 1979.* Amman: Department of Statistics Press.

Hassan, F.
1983   Earth Resources and Population: An Archeological Perspective. Pp. 191-226 in *How Humans Adapt: A Biocultural Odyssey,* ed. D. J. Ortner. Smithsonian Institution Press.

Hatch, E.
1973   The Growth of Economic, Subsistence, and Ecological Studies in American Anthropology. *Journal of Anthropological Research* 29: 221-243.

Helms, S. W.
1981   *Jawa: Lost City of the Black Desert.* Ithaca, NY: Cornell University Press.

1982   Paleo-Bedouin and Transmigrant Urbanism. Pp. 97-113 in *Studies in the History and Archaeology of Jordan I,* ed. A. Hadidi. Amman: Department of Antiquities.

Henke, O.
1959   Zur Lage von Beth Peor. *Zeitschrift des Deutschen Palästina-Vereins* 75: 155-63.

Henry, D. O.
1980   Paleolithic in Southern Jordan. Paper presented at the Annual Meeting of the American Schools of Oriental Research. November 8, Dallas.

1985   Late Pleistocene Environment and Paleolithic Adaptations in Southern Jordan. Pp. 67-77 in *Studies in the History and Archaeology of Jordan II,* ed. A. Hadidi. Amman: Department of Antiquities.

Hentschke, R.
1960   Ammonitische Grenzfestungen südwestlich von 'Amman. *Zeitschrift des Deutschen Palästina-Vereins* 76: 103-23.

Herr, L. G.
1976   Area G.5. *Andrews University Seminary Studies* 14: 107-108.

1978   *The Scripts of Ancient Northwest Semitic Seals.* Missoula, MT: Scholars Press.

forth-   *Iron Age Strata: A Study of the Stratig-*
coming *raphy of Tell Hesban from the Twelfth through the Fifth Centuries B.C. Hesban 6.* Berrien Springs, MI: Andrews University Press.

Heskel, D. L.
1983   A Model for the Adoption of Metallurgy in the Ancient Middle East. *Current Anthropology* 24: 362-66.

Hess, A. C.
1985   Islamic Civilization and the Legend of Political Failure. *Journal of Near Eastern Studies* 44.1: 27-39.

Hiatt, J. M.
1984   *Between Desert and Town: A Case Study of Encapsulation and Sedentarization among Jordanian Bedouin.* Ann Arbor, MI: University Microfilms International.

Hobhouse, L. T.; Wheeler, G. C.; and Ginsberg, M.
1914   The Material Culture and Social Institutions of the Simpler Peoples: An Essay in Correlation. *Sociological Review* 7: 203-231; 332-368.

Hodder, I.
1982   *The Present Past: An Introduction to Anthropology for Archaeologists.* New York: Pica Press.

Hole, F.
1978   Pastoral Nomadism in Western Iran. Pp. 127-167 in *Explorations in Ethnoarchaeology*, ed. R. Gould. Albuquerque: University of New Mexico Press.

Hole, F.; Flannery, K. V.; and Neely, J.
1969   *Prehistory and Human Ecology of the Deh Luran Plain*. Memoirs of the Museum of Anthropology, University of Michigan, Number 1.

Holling, C. S.
1973   Resilience and Stability of Ecological Systems. *Annual Review of Ecology and Systematics* 4: 1-22.

Hopkins, D. C.
1985   *The Highlands of Canaan*. The Social World of Biblical Antiquity Series 3. Decatur, GA: Almond Press.

Horn, S. H.
1979   *Seventh-Day Adventist Bible Dictionary*. Washington, DC: Review and Herald.

1982   *Heshbon in the Bible and Archaeology*. Occasional Papers of the Horn Archaeological Museum, Andrews University 2. Berrien Springs, MI: Siegfried H. Horn Archaeological Museum.

Hoskins, F. E.
1912   *From the Nile to Nebo*. Philadelphia: Sunday School Times Co.

Hostetler, J. A., and Huntington, G. E.
1980   *The Hutterites in North America*. New York: Holt, Rinehart and Winston.

Hourani, A. H., and Irvine, V. E.
1975   History and Syria and Palestine: From the Islamic Conquest to 1920. Pp. 951-955 in vol. 17 of *The New Encyclopædia Britannica*.

Hunt, R.
1985   The Role of Bureaucracy in the Provisioning of Cities: A Framework for Analysis of the Ancient Near East.

Unpublished manuscript. Brandeis University.

Hunt, R., and Hunt, E.
1976   Canal Irrigation and Local Social Organization. *Current Anthropology* 17: 389-411.

Huntington, E.
1907   *The Pulse of Asia*. New York: Houghton, Mifflin and Co.

Hutteroth, W.
1975   The Pattern of Settlement in Palestine in the Sixteenth Century. Pp. 2-11 in *Studies on Palestine during the Ottoman Period*, ed. M. Ma'oz. Jerusalem: Magnes Press.

Hutteroth, W., and Abdulfattah, K.
1977   *Historical Geography of Palestine, Transjordan and Southern Syria in the Late 16th Century*. Erlangen: Selbstverlag der Frankischen Geographischen Gesellschaft in Kommission bei Palm und Enke.

Ibach, R.
1976   Archaeological Survey of the Hesban Region. *Andrews University Seminary Studies* 14: 119-126.

1978   Expanded Archaeological Survey of the Hesban Region. *Andrews University Seminary Studies* 16: 201-214.

1987   *Archaeological Survey of the Hesban Region*. Hesban 5. Berrien Springs, MI: Andrews University Press.

Irby, C. L., and Mangles, J.
1823   *Travels in Egypt and Nubia, Syria and Asia Minor: During the Years 1817 and 1819*. London: Thomas White and Co.

Jackson, K. P.
1983   *The Ammonite Language of the Iron Age*. Chico, CA: Scholars Press.

Jeffery, A.
1952   The Birthplace of Islamic Civilization. Pp. 84-95 in *Background of the Middle*

East, ed. E. Jackh. New York: Cornell University Press.

Johnson, D. L.
1973   *Jabal al-Akhdar, Cyrenaicia: An Historical Geography of Settlement and Livelihood.* University of Chicago: Department of Geography. Research Paper No. 148.

Jones, A. H. M.
1964   *The Later Roman Empire 284-602,* vols. 1 & 2. Norman, OK: University of Oklahoma Press.

1970   Ancient Empires and the Economy: Rome. Pp. 114-139 in *The Roman Economy: Studies in Ancient Economic and Administrative History,* ed. P. A. Brunt. Oxford: Blackwell.

Joralemon, D.
1982   New World Depopulation and the Case of Disease. *Journal of Anthropological Research* 38: 108-127.

Kates, R. W.; Johnson, D. L.; and Haring, K. J.
1977   Population, Society and Desertification. In *Desertification: Its Causes and Consequences.* New York: Pergamon Press.

Keith, A.
1844   *The Land of Israel According to the Covenant.* New York: Harper and Brothers.

Kenyon, K.
1952   *Beginning in Archaeology.* New York: Frederick A. Praeger.

Khairy, N.
1982   Fine Nabataean Ware with Impressed and Rouletted Decorations. Pp. 275-283 in *Studies in the History and Archaeology of Jordan I,* ed. A. Hadidi. Amman: Department of Antiquities.

Khare, R. S., and Rao, M. S. A., eds.
1986   *Food, Society, and Culture.* Durham, NC: Caroline Academic Press.

Khun, T. S.
1962   *The Structure of Scientific Revolutions.* Chicago: University of Chicago Press.

King, P.
1984   *American Archaeology in the Mideast.* Philadelphia: American Schools of Oriental Research.

Kirk, M. E.
1944   An Outline of the Ancient Cultural History of Transjordan. *Palestine Exploration Quarterly* 76: 180-98.

Kirkbride, A. S.
1945   Changes in Tribal Life in Trans-Jordan. *Man* 22-23: 40-41.

Kitchener, H. H.
1878   Lieutenant Kitchener's Reports, 7th September, 1877. *Palestine Exploration Fund,* pp. 10-15.

Knudson, S. J.
1978   *Culture in Retrospect: An Introduction to Archaeology.* Chicago: Rand McNally College Publishing Co.

Konikoff, A.
1943   *Trans-Jordan: An Economic Survey.* Jerusalem: Economic Research Institute. Jewish Agency for Palestine.

Kraeling, C. H.
1938   *Gerasa: City of the Decapolis.* New Haven, CT: American Schools of Oriental Research.

LaBianca, Ø. S.
1973   Tell Hesban 1971: The Zooarchaeological Remains. *Andrews University Seminary Studies* 11: 133-144.

1974   A Preliminary Research Design for Enthnographic Studies at Hesban in Jordan. Unpublished manuscript. Andrews University Institute of Archaeology.

1976   Tell Hesban 1974: The Village of Hesban, An Ethnographic Preliminary

Report. *Andrews University Seminary Studies* 11: 133-144.

1977 Local Habitat and Modes of Livelihood at Heshbon Through Time: A Summary of Methods and Emerging Conclusions. Prepared for ASOR Symposium on Heshbon. San Francisco: American Schools of Oriental Research.

1978a Man, Animals, and Habitat at Hesban: An Integrated Overview. *Andrews University Seminary Studies* 16: 229-252.

1978b The Logistic and Strategic Aspects of Faunal Analysis in Palestine. *Approaches to Faunal Analysis in the Middle East.* Edited by R. H. Meadow and M. A. Zeder. Peabody Museum Bulletin 2: 3-9.

1980 Taphonomy: The Study of the Processes of Destruction and Deposition of Animal Remains. Paper presented at the American Center of Oriental Research. November 11, Amman.

1984 Objectives, Procedures, and Findings of Ethnoarchaeological Research in the Vicinity of Hesban in Jordan. *Annual of the Department of Antiquities of Jordan* 28: 269-482.

1986 Food System Transitions and Mechanisms of Abatement. Unpublished manuscript. Andrews University Institute of Archaeology.

LaBianca, Ø. S., and LaBianca, A. S.
1975 Tell Hesban 1973: The Anthropological Work. *Andrews University Seminary Studies* 13: 235-247.

1976 Domestic Animals of the Early Roman Period at Tell Hesban. *Andrews University Seminary Studies* 14: 189-200.

LaBianca, Ø. S., and Lacelle, L., eds.
1986 *Environmental Foundations. Hesban 2.* Berrien Springs, MI: Andrews University Press.

Lacelle, L.
1986a Bedrock Geology, Surficial Geology and Soils. Pp. 23-58 in *Environmental Foundations. Hesban 2,* eds. Ø. S. LaBianca and L. Lacelle. Berrien Springs, MI: Andrews University Press.

1986b Surface and Groundwater Resources of Tell Hesban and Area, Jordan. Pp. 59-73 in *Environmental Foundations. Hesban 2,* eds. Ø. S. LaBianca and L. Lacelle. Berrien Springs, MI: Andrews University Press.

1986c Ecology of the Flora of Tell Hesban and area, Jordan. Pp. 99-119 in *Environmental Foundations. Hesban 2,* eds. Ø. S. LaBianca and L. Lacelle. Berrien Springs, MI: Andrews University Press.

Lancaster, W.
1981 *Changing Cultures: The Rwala Bedouin Today.* Cambridge: University Press.

Landels, J. G.
1981 *Engineering in the Ancient World.* Berkeley, CA: University of California Press.

Lappe, F. M., and Collins, J.
1977 *Food First: Beyond the Myth of Scarcity.* Washington, DC: Institute for Food and Development.

1985 Why Can't People Feed Themselves? Pp. 200-204 in *Anthropology 85/86,* ed. E. Angeloni. CT: Dushkin Publishing Group, Inc.

Lawrence, B.
1978 Analysis of Unidentifiable Bone from Cayonu: An Early Village Farming Community. *Approaches to Faunal Analysis in the Middle East.* Edited by R. H. Meadow and M. A. Zeder. Peabody Museum Bulletin 2.

Layne, L.
1984 The Use of Space Amongst the 'Abbad Bedouin of the Jordan Valley. Paper presented at the symposium "Anthro-

pology in Jordan: State of the Art."
February 25-28, Amman.

Leone M. P.
1972   *Contemporary Archaeology: A Guide to Theory and Contributions.* Carbondale: Southern Illinois University Press.

Lepiksaar, J.
forth-   Fish Remains from Tell Hesban, Jordan.
coming   In *Faunal Remains: Taphonomical and Zooarchaeological Studies of the Animal Remains from Tell Hesban and Vicinity. Hesban 13.* Berrien Springs, MI: Andrews University Press.

Le Strange, G.
1886   Ride Through 'Ajlun and the Belka during the Autumn of 1884. Pp. 268-323 in *Across the Jordan,* ed. G. Schumacher. London: Richard Bentley and Sons.

Lewis, N.
1954   The Frontier of Settlement in Syria, 1800-1950. *International Affairs* January: 48-60.

Libbey, W., and Hoskins, F. E.
1905   *The Jordan Valley and Petra.* New York: Putnam's Sons.

Lindner, H.
1979   *Zur Fruhgeschichte Des Haushuhns in Vorderen Orient.* Ph.D. dissertation. Universität München.

Little, R. M.
1969   An Anthropological Preliminary Note on the First Season at Tell Hesban. *Andrews University Seminary Studies* 7: 232-239.

London, B. D.
forth-   The Metallurgy of Archeological Sam-
coming   ples from Tell Hesban. In *Small Finds: Studies of the Bone, Stone, Iron, Glass, and Precious Metal Objects from Tell Hesban and Vicinity.* Berrien Springs, MI: Andrews University Press.

Lugenbeal E. N., and Sauer, J. A.
1972   Seventh-Sixth Century B.C. Pottery from Area B at Heshbon. *Andrews University Seminary Studies* 10: 21-69.

Luke, H. C.
1924   *The Traveler's Handbook for Palestine and Syria.* London: Simpkin, Marshall, Hamilton, Kent and Co.

Luke, H. C., and Keith-Roach, E.
1930   *The Handbook of Palestine and Trans-Jordan.* London: MacMillan and Co.

Lundquist, J. M.
1980   Gilead (Yarmuk and Zerqa). Paper presented at the Annual Meeting of the American Schools of Oriental Research. November 8, Dallas.

Lutfiyya, A. M.
1966   *Baytin: A Jordanian Village.* The Hague: Mouton & Co.

Lyman, R. L.
1982   Archaeofaunas and Subsistence Studies. Pp. 331-393 in *Advances in Archaeological Method and Theory,* vol. 5, ed. M. B. Schiffer. New York: Academic Press.

Lynch, W. F.
1849   *Narrative of the United States' Expedition to the River Jordan and the Dead Sea.* Philadelphia: Lea and Blanchard.

MacDonald, B.
1980   Edom. Paper presented at the Annual Meeting of the American Schools of Oriental Research. November 8, Dallas.

MacNeish, R. S.
1974   Speculation About How and Why Food Production and Village Life Developed in the Tehuacan Valley, Mexico. Pp. 43-55 in *The Rise and Fall of Civilizations,* eds. J. A. Sabloff and C. C. Lamberg-Karlovsky. California: Cummings Publishing Co.

Malinowski, B.
1935   *Coral Gardens and Their Magic.* New York: Dover Publications, Inc.

Malthus, T. R.
1914   *On the Principle of Population*, vol. 1. New York: E. P. Dutton & Co.

Marx, E.
1967   *Bedouin of the Negev*. University of Manchester: University Press.

1977   The Tribe as a Unit of Subsistence: Nomadic Pastoralism in the Middle East. *American Anthropologist* 79: 343-365.

May, J. M.
1961   *The Ecology of Malnutrition in the Far and Near East*. New York: Hafner Publishing Co., Inc.

Mayerson, P.
1962   The Ancient Agricultural Regime of Nessana and the Central Negeb. Pp. 211-269 in *Excavations at Nessana*, ed. H. D. Colt. London: British School of Archaeology in Jerusalem.

Mazar, B.
1957   The Tobiads. *Israel Exploration Journal* 7: 137-145; 229-238.

McCreery, D.
1979   Flotation of the Bab edh-Dhra' and Numeira Plant Remains. Pp. 165-169 in *Annual of the American Schools of Oriental Research* 46. Cambridge, MA: American Schools of Oriental Research.

1980   Paleobotany. *Bulletin of the American Schools of Oriental Research* 240: 52-53.

McGovern, P. E.
1982   Exploring the Burial Caves of the Baqᶜah Valley in Jordan. *Archaeology* 35: 46-57.

1983   The Earliest Steel from Transjordan. *MASCA Journal* 2: 35-39 (with V. Pigott and M. Notis).

1985   Environmental Constraints for Human Settlement in the Baqᶜah Valley. Pp. 144-148 in *Studies in the History and Archaeology of Jordan II*, ed. A. Hadidi. Amman: Department of Antiquities.

1986   *The Late Bronze and Early Iron Ages of Central Transjordan: The Baqᶜah Valley Project, 1977-1981*. University Museum Monograph. Philadelphia: University Museum.

McNeill, W. H.
1963   *The Rise of the West: A History of the Human Community*. Chicago: University of Chicago.

1976   *Plagues and People*. New York: Doubleday.

1979   Historical Patterns of Migration. *Current Anthropology* 20: 95-102.

McNicoll, A., and Walmsley, A.
1982   Pella/Fahl in Jordan during the Early Islamic Period. Pp. 339-345 in *Studies in the History and Archaeology of Jordan I*, A. Hadidi. Amman: Department of Antiquities.

McQuitty, A.
1984   An Ethnographic and Archaeological Study of Bread-Ovens in Jordan. Paper presented at the symposium "Anthropology in Jordan: State of the Art." February 25-28, Amman.

Meadow, R. H.
1978   Effects of Context on the Interpretation of Faunal Remains: A Case Study. Pp. 15-21 in *Approaches to Faunal Analysis in the Middle East*. Edited by R. H. Meadow and M. A. Zeder. Peabody Museum Bulletin 2.

Meadow, R. H., and Zeder, M. A. eds.
1978   *Approaches to Faunal Analysis in the Middle East*. Peabody Museum Bulletin 2. Harvard University: Peabody Museum of Archeology and Ethnology.

Merrill, S.
1877   The American Explorers in Palestine. *Palestine Exploration Fund*, pp. 150-154.

1881 *East of the Jordan: A Record of Travel and Observation in The Countries of Moab, Gilead, and Bashan.* London: Richard Bentley & Son, New Burlington Street.

Merry, D. L.
1969 *The Bedouin of Southeast Jordan.* Ann Arbor, MI: University Microfilms International.

Messer, E.
1984 Anthropological Perspectives on Diet. *Annual Review of Anthropology* 13: 205-249.

Miller, J. M.
1980 Moab. Paper presented at the Annual Meeting of the American Schools of Oriental Research. November 8, Dallas.

1982 Recent Archaeological Developments Relevant to Ancient Moab. Pp. 169-173 in *Studies in the History and Archaeology of Jordan I*, ed. A. Hadidi. Amman: Department of Antiquities.

Mitchel, L.
1980 The Hellenistic and Roman Periods at Tell Hesban, Jordan. Ph.D. dissertation. Andrews University, Berrien Springs, MI.

Mittman, S.
1970 *Beiträge zur Siedlungs- und Territorialgeschichichte des nördlichen Ostjordanlandes.* Wiesbaden: Harrassowitz.

Morris, J.
1959 *The Hashemite Kings.* New York: Pantheon Books, Inc.

Morris, Y.
1961 *Masters of the Desert: 6000 years in the Negev.* New York: G. P. Putnam's Sons.

Mountfort, G.
1964 Disappearing Wildlife and Growing Deserts in Jordan. *Oryx* 7: 229-232.

Muhly, J. D.
1980 The Bronze Age Setting. Pp. 25-67 in *The Coming of the Iron Age*, eds. T. A. Wertime and J. D. Muhly. New Haven: Yale University Press.

1982 How Iron Technology Changed the Ancient World. *Biblical Archaeology Review* 8: 42-54.

Murdock, G. P.
1965 How Culture Changes. Pp. 113-128 in *Culture and Society*. Pittsburg: University of Pittsburg Press.

Murdock, G. P., and Provost, C
1973 Measurement of Cultural Complexity. *Ethnology* 12: 379-392.

Murray, P., and Chang, C.
1980 An Ethnoarchaeological Study of a Contemporary Herder's Site. *Journal of Field Archaeology* 8: 370-382.

Musil, A.
1907 *Arabia Petraea.* Part I. Wein: Kaiserliche Akademie der Wissenschaften.

1926 *The Northern Hegaz: A Topographical Itinerary.* New York: AMS Press, Inc.

1927 *Arabia Deserta.* New York: AMS Press, Inc.

1928 *The Manners and Customs of the Rwala Bedouin.* Oriental Explorations and Studies 6. New York: American Geographical Society.

Naveh, Z., and Dan, J.
1973 The Human Degradation of Mediterranean Landscapes in Israel. Pp. 273-389 in *Ecological Studies of Mediterranean Type Ecosystems*, eds. F. di Castri and H. A. Mooney. Springe-Verlag: Heidelberg.

Newman, J. L.
1970 *The Ecological Basis for Subsistence Change among the Sandawe of Tanza-*

nia. Washington, DC: National Academy of Sciences.

Nyrop, R. F. *et al.*
1974 *Area Handbook for the Hashemite Kingdom of Jordan,* 2nd edition. Washington, DC: American University.

Oded, B.
1971 Moab. In vol. 12 of *Encyclopædia Judaica,* ed. C. Roth. Jerusalem: Macmillan Co.

1979 Neighbors on the East. Pp. 247-275 in *The Age of the Monarchies: Political History,* vol. 4, ed. A. Malamat. Jerusalem: Massada.

Olsen, S. J.
1971 *Zooarchaeology: Animal Bones in Archaeology and Their Interpretation.* Reading, MA: Addison-Wesley Publishing Co., Inc.

Orme, B.
1981 *Anthropology for Archaeologists: An Introduction.* Ithaca, NY: Cornell University Press.

Ortner, D. J.
1983 The Skeletal Biology of an Early Bronze Ib Charnel House at Bab edh-Dhra, Jordan. Pp. 93-95 in *Studies in the History and Archaeology of Jordan I,* ed. A. Hadidi. Amman: Department of Antiquities.

Palmer, E. H.
1872 *The Desert of the Exodus.* Cambridge: Deighton, Bell and Co.

Parker, S. T.
1975 The Decapolis Reviewed. *Journal of Biblical Literature* 94: 437-441.

1976 Archaeological Survey of the Limes Arabicus: A Preliminary Report. *Annual of the Department of Antiquities of Jordan* 21: 19-31.

1982 Preliminary Report on the 1980 Season of the Central *Limes Arabicus* Project.

Bulletin of the American Schools of Oriental Research 247: 1-26.

1986 *Romans and Saracens: A History of the Arabian Frontier.* ASOR Dissertation Series No. 6. Winona Lake, IN: ASOR.

1987 Peasants, Pastoralists, and *Pax Romana*: A Different View. *Bulletin of the American Schools of Oriental Research* 265: 25-51.

Parr, P. J.
1975 History of Syria and Palestine: Syria and Palestine, c. 1550 BC-AD 634. Pp. 934-951 in vol. 17 of *The New Encyclopædia Britannica.*

Patai, R.
1951 Nomadism: Middle Eastern and Central Asian. *Southwest Journal of Anthropology* 7: 400-414.

1958 *The Kingdom of Jordan.* Princeton, NJ: Princeton University Press.

1970 The Middle East As a Culture Area. Pp. 187-204 in *Readings in Arab Middle Eastern Societies and Cultures,* eds. A. M. Lutfiyya and C. W. Churchill. The Hague, Netherlands: Mouton & Co.

Payne, S.
1972 On The Interpretation of Bone Samples from Archaeological Sites. Pp. 65-81 in *Papers in Economic Prehistory,* ed. E. S. Higgs. Cambridge: University Press.

Peake, F. G.
1935 *The History of East Jordan.* Jerusalem.

1958 *A History of Jordan and Its Tribes.* Coral Gables, FL: University of Miami Press.

Pedersen, J. R.
1968 *Food Grain Storage, Marketing, Handling and Transportation in Jordan.* Manhattan: Kansas State University.

Pelto, G. H., and Pelto, P. J.
1983   Diet and Delocalization: Dietary Changes since 1750. *Journal of Interdisciplinary History* 14,2: 507-528.

Perowne, S. H., and Prawer, J.
1987   Jerusalem: History. Pp. 359A-359B in vol. 22 of *The New Encyclopædia Britannica*.

Petrie, W. M.
1904   *Methods and Aims in Archeology*. New York: Benjamin Blom, Inc.

Piccirillo, M.
1985   Rural Settlement in Byzantine Jordan. Pp. 257-261 in *Studies in the History and Archaeology of Jordan II*, ed. A. Hadidi. Amman: Department of Antiquities.

Pimentel, D., and Pimentel, M.
1979   *Food, Energy, and Society*. New York: John Wiley & Sons.

Polk, W. R.
1980   *The Arab World*. 4th ed. Cambridge, MA: Harvard University Press.

Potts, G. R., and Vickerman, G. P.
1974   Studies on the Cereal Ecosystem. Pp. 99-147 in *Advances in Ecological Research*.

Prag, K.
1985   Ancient and Modern Pastoral Migration in the Levant. *Levant* 17: 81-88.

Radcliffe-Brown, A. R.
1922   *The Andaman Islanders*. Cambridge: University Press.

Ragin, C., and Chirot, D.
1984   The World System of Immanual Wallerstein: Sociology and Politics as History. Pp. 276-312 in *Vision and Method in Historical Sociology*, ed. T. Skocpol. New York: Cambridge University Press.

Rappaport, R. A.
1965   Nature, Culture and Ecological Anthropology. Pp. 237-267 in *Man, Culture and Society*, ed. H. L. Shapiro. New York: Oxford University Press.

1967   Ritual Regulation of Environmental Relations Among a New Guinea People. *Ethnology* 6: 17-30.

1968   *Pigs for the Ancestors: Ritual in the Ecology of a New Guinea People*. New Haven: Yale University Press.

1969   Sanctity and Adaptation. Prepared for Wenner-Gren Symposium, "The Moral and Esthetic Structure of Human Adaptation." New York: Wenner-Gren Foundation.

1971   The Flow of Energy in an Agricultural Society. *Scientific American* 224: 116-133.

1977   Ecology, Adaptation and the Ills of Functionalism (Being, Among Other Things, A Response to Jonathan Friedman). Pp. 138-190 in *Michigan Discussions in Anthropology*. Ann Arbor, MI: University of Michigan.

Raschke, M
1976   Roman Trade with the East. *Aufsteig und Niedergang der Römischen Welt* II: 604-1361.

Redford, D. B.
1982   A Bronze Age Itinerary in Transjordan. *Journal for the Society for the Study of Egyptian Archaeology* 12: 55-74.

Redman, C. L.
1973   Multistage Fieldwork and Analytical Techniques. *Archaeological Survey* 38: 60-79.

1976   Anthropological Archaeology in the Near East. Pp. 213-218 in *The Study of the Middle East*, ed. L. Binder. New York: John Wiley & Sons.

1978 *The Rise of Civilization*. San Francisco: W. H. Freeman and Co.

Reed, C. A.
1983 Archeozoological Studies in the Near East: A Short History (1960-1980). Pp. 511-536 in *Prehistoric Archaeology along the Zagros Flanks*, eds. R. J. Braidwood *et al.* Chicago: University of Chicago Press.

Reifenberg, A.
1955 *The Struggle Between the Desert and the Sown*. Jerusalem: Government Press.

Reilly, J.
1981 The Peasantry of Late Ottoman Palestine. *Journal of Palestine Studies* 10: 82-95.

Renfrew, J. M.
1973 *Palaeoethnobotany*. New York: Columbia University Press.

Reventlow, H. G.
1963 Das Ende der ammonitischen Grenzbefestigungskette? *Zeitschrift des Deutschen Palästina-Vereins* 79: 127-37.

Rhindos, D.
1980 Symbiosis, Instability, and the Origins and Spread of Agriculture: A New Model. *Current Anthropology* 21: 751-771.

Rice, P. M.
1981 Evolution of Specialized Pottery Production: A Trial Model. *Current Anthropology* 22: 219-240.

Richards, A.
1939 *Land, Labour and Diet in Northern Rhodesia*. International Institute of African Languages and Cultures. London: Oxford University Press.

Robertshaw, P. T., and Collett, D. P.
1983 The Identification of Pastoral Peoples in the Archaeological Record: An Example from East Africa. *World Archaeology* 15: 67-78.

Rollefson, G. O.
1985 Late Pleistocene Environments and Seasonal Hunting Strategies: A Case Study from Fjaje, Near Shobak, Southern Jordan. Pp. 103-107 in *Studies in the History and Archaeology of Jordan II*, ed. A. Hadidi. Amman: Department of Antiquities.

Rollefson, G. O., and Simmons, A. H.
1986 The Neolithic Village of ʿAin Ghazal, Jordan: Preliminary Report on the 1984 Season. Pp. 145-164 in *Preliminary Reports of ASOR-Sponsored Excavations 1980-1984*, ed. W. E. Rast. Supplement to the *Bulletin of the American Schools of Oriental Research* No. 24.

Rosenfeld, H.
1958 Social Changes in an Arab Village. *New Outlook* 2: 37-42.

1965 The Social Composition of the Military in the Process of State Formation in the Arabian Desert. *Journal of the Royal Anthropological Institute* 95.

Rosner, D.
1976 *The Moabites and Their Relationship with the Kingdoms of Israel and Judah in the Military, Political and Cultural Spheres*. Jerusalem: Makor.

Rostovtzeff, M.
1928a Ptolemaic Egypt. Pp. 109-154 in *The Cambridge Ancient History: Volume VII, The Hellenistic Monarchies and the Rise of Rome*, eds. S. A. Cook, F. E. Adcock, and M. P. Charlesworth. Cambridge: University Press.

1928b Syria and The East. Pp. 155-196 in *The Cambridge Ancient History: Volume VII, The Hellenistic Monarchies and the Rise of Rome*, eds. S. A. Cook, F. E. Adcock, and M. P. Charlesworth. Cambridge: University Press.

1932   *Caravan Cities.* Oxford: At the Clarendon Press.

Rotter, G.
1982   Die Umayyaden und der Zweite Bürgerkrieg (680-692). In *Abhandlungen Für die Kunde des Morgenslandes.* Band XLV.3. Weisbaden: Kommissionsverlag Franz Steiner GMBH.

Rowton, M. B.
1976   Dimorphic Structure and Topology. *Oriens Antiques* 15: 2-31.

Russell, K. W.
1985   The Earthquake Chronology of Palestine and Northwest Arabia from the 2nd through the Mid-8th Century A.D. *Bulletin of the American Schools of Oriental Research* 260: 37-59.

Russell, M. B.
1989   Hesban during the Arab Period: A.D. 635 to the Present. Pp. 25-35 in *Historical Foundations. Hesban 3,* eds. L. T. Geraty and L. G. Running. Berrien Springs, MI: Andrews University Press.

Sabloff, J. A.
1981   When the Rhetoric Fades: A Brief Appraisal of Intellectual Trends in American Archaeology During the Past Two Decades. *Bulletin of the American Schools of Oriental Research* 242: 106.

Sahlins, M.
1972   *Stone Age Economics.* Chicago: Aldine.

1976   *Culture and Practical Reason.* Chicago: University of Chicago Press.

Salibi, K. S.
1977   *Syria Under Islam: Empire on Trial 634-1097.* Delmar, NY: Caravan Books.

Saller, S. J., and Bagatti, B.
1949   *The Town of Nebo (Khirbet El-Mekhayyat) with a Brief Survey of other Ancient Christian Monuments in Transjordan.* Jerusalem: Franciscan Press.

Sanders, W. T.
1973   The Cultural Ecology of the Lowland Maya: A Reevaluation. Pp. 325-365 in *The Classic Maya Collapse,* ed. T. P. Culbert. Albuquerque: University of New Mexico Press.

Sauer, J. A.
1973   Area B. *Andrews University Seminary Studies* 11: 35-71.

1976   Area B and Square D.4. *Andrews University Seminary Studies* 14: 133-168.

1978a   Heshbon 1976: Area B and Square D.4. *Andrews University Seminary Studies* 16: 31-49.

1978b   *Archaeology of Jordan.* Amman: Ministry of Information.

1980   The East Jordan Valley. Paper presented at the Annual Meeting of the American Schools of Oriental Research. November 8, Dallas.

1982   The Pottery of Jordan in the Early Islamic Periods. Pp. 329-337 in *Studies in the History and Archaeology of Jordan I,* ed. A. Hadidi. Amman: Department of Antiquities.

Sawyer, J. F. A. and Clines, D. J. A., eds.
1983   *Midian, Moab and Edom.* Sheffield: JSOT.

Schaub, R. T.
1982   The Origins of the Early Bronze Age Walled Town Culture of Jordan. Pp. 67-75 in *Studies in the History and Archaeology of Jordan I,* ed. A. Hadidi. Amman: Department of Antiquities.

Schiffer, M. B.
1976   *Behavioral Archeology.* New York: Academic Press.

Schiffer, M. B; Sullivan, A.; and Klinger, T.
1978   The Design of Archaeological Surveys. *World Archaeology* 10: 1-28.

Schumacher, G.
1886 *Across the Jordan.* London: Richard Bentley and Son.

Seabrook, W. B.
1927 *Adventures in Arabia.* New York: Harcourt, Brace and Co., Inc.

Seetzen, U.
1813 *A Brief Account of the Countries Adjoining the Lake of Tiberias, the Jordan, and the Dead Sea.* London.

Selye, H.
1956 *The Stress of Life.* London: McGraw-Hill Book Co., Inc.

Service, E.
1975 *Origins of the State and Civilization: The Process of Cultural Evolution.* New York: Norton Press.

Shahid, I.
1984a *Rome and the Arabs: A Prolegomenon to the Study of Byzantium and the Arabs.* Washington, DC: Dumbarton Oaks.

1984b *Byzantium and the Arabs in the Fourth Century.* Washington, DC: Dumbarton Oaks.

Shami, S. K.
1984 *Ethnicity and Leadership: The Circassians in Jordan.* Ann Arbor, MI: University Microfilms International.

Shwadran, B.
1959 *Jordan: A State of Tension.* New York: Council for Middle Eastern Affairs Press.

Sinai, A., and Pollack A., eds.
1977 *The Hashemite Kingdom of Jordan and the West Bank: A Handbook.* New York: American Academic Association for Peace in the Middle East.

Smith, D. F., and Hill, D. M.
1975 Natural and Agricultural Ecosystems. *Journal of Environmental Quality.* 4.2: 143-145.

Smith, P. E.
1976 *Food Production and Its Consequences.* Menlo Park, CA: Cummings Publishing.

Smith, P. E., and Young, T. C. Jr.
1972 The Evolution of Early Agriculture and Culture in Greater Mesopotamia: A Trial Model. Pp. 1-51 in *Population Growth: Anthropological Implications,* ed. B. Spooner. Cambridge: MIT Press.

Smith, W. R.
1889 *Lectures on the Religion of the Semites.* Edinburgh: Adam and Charles Black.

Snow, P.
1972 *Hussein: A Biography.* New York: Robert B. Luce, Inc.

Solomon, D.
1971 Ptolemy. Cols. 1347-49 in vol. 13 of *Encyclopædia Judaica,* ed. C. Roth. Jerusalem: Macmillan Co.

Sperber, D.
1972 Trends in Third Century Palestinian Agriculture. *Journal of the Economic and Social History of the Orient* 15: 237-255.

1974 Drought, Famine and Pestilence in Amoraic Palestine. *Journal of the Economic and Social History of the Orient* 17: 272-298.

1976 Objects of Trade Between Palestine and Egypt in Roman Times. *Journal of the Economic and Social History of the Orient* 19: 113-147.

Spooner, B., ed.
1972 *Population Growth: Anthropological Implications.* Cambridge, MA: MIT Press.

Spuler, B.
1960 *The Muslim World.* Leiden: E. J. Brill.

Stager, L. E.
1976 Farming in the Judean Desert during the Iron Age. *Bulletin of the American*

Schools of Oriental Research 221: 145-58.

1982 The Archaeology of the East Slope of Jerusalem and the Terraces of the Kidron. *Journal of Near Eastern Studies* 41: 11-21.

Steinhart, J. S., and Steinhart, C. E.
1975 Energy Use in the U.S. Food System. In *Food: Politics, Economics, Nutrition and Research*, ed. P. H. Abelson. Washington, DC: American Association for the Advancement of Science.

Sterud, E.; Straus, G.; and Abramovitz, K.
1980 Recent Developments in Old World Archaeology. *American Antiquity* 45.

Steward, J.
1936 The Economic and Social Basis of Primitive Bands. In *Essays in Honor of A. L. Kroeber*. Berkeley: University of California Press.

1937 Ecological Aspects of Southwestern Society. *Anthropos* 32.

1955 *Theory of Culture Change*. Urbana: University of Illinois Press.

Stini, W. A.
1973 Adaptive Strategies of Human Populations under Nutritional Stress. In *Biosocial Interrelations in Population Adaptation*, eds. E. Watts *et al.* Chicago: Aldine.

1975 *Ecology and Human Adaptation*. New York: William Brown Co.

Stoltzfus, V.
1973 Amish Agriculture: Adaptive Strategies for Economic Survival of Community Life. *Rural Sociology* 38: 196-206.

Storfjell, J. B.
1983 *The Stratigraphy of Tell Hesban, Jordan, in the Byzantine Period*. Ph.D. dissertation. Andrews University, Berrien Springs, MI.

Stuart, D. E., and Gauthier, R. P.
1981 *Prehistoric New Mexico: Background for Survey*. New Mexico: Department of Finance and Administration.

Sweet, L. E.
1960 *Tell Ṭoqaan: A Syrian Village*. Ann Arbor, MI: University of Michigan.

Swidler, W. W.
1973 Adaptive Processes Regulating Nomad-Sedentary Interaction in the Middle East. Pp. 23-41 in *The Desert and the Sown: Nomads in the Wider Society*, ed. C. Nelson. University of California, Berkeley: Institute of International Studies.

Tannahill, R.
1973 *Food in History*. New York: Stein and Day.

Taqqu, R.
1979 Internal Labor Migration and the Arab Village Community under the Mandate. Pp. 261-285 in *Palestinian Society and Politics*, ed. J. A. Migdal. Princeton, NJ: Princeton University Press.

Taylor, C. E.
1983 Synergy among Mass Infections, Famines, and Poverty. *Journal of Interdisciplinary History* 14: 483-501.

Tcherikover, V.
1972a The Political Situation from 332 B.C.E. to 175 B.C.E. Pp. 53-86 in *The World History of the Jewish People, vol. 6. The Hellenistic Age*, ed. A. Schalit. New Brunswick: Rutgers University Press.

1972b Social Conditions. Pp. 87-114 in *The World History of the Jewish People, vol. 6. The Hellenistic Age*, ed. A. Schalit. New Brunswick: Rutgers University Press.

Tell, S. K.
1982 Early Islamic Architecture in Jordan. Pp. 323-328 in *Studies in the History and Archaeology of Jordan*, ed. A. Hadid. Amman: Department of Antiquities.

Thomas, R. B.; Winterhalder, B.; and McRae, S. D.
1979   An Anthropological Approach to Human Ecology and Adaptive Dynamics. *Yearbook of Physical Anthropology* 22: 1-46.

Thompson, J. A.
1958   The Economic Significance of Transjordan in Old Testament Times. *Australian Bible Review* 6: 145-168.

Thompson, S. I.
1972   From Functionalism to Cultural Ecology: plus ce change, plus c'est la même chose. Pp. 58-65 in *Steward Anthropological Society Journal.* Urbana, IL.

Thomsen, P.
1917   Die römischen Meilensteine der Provinzen Syria, Arabia und Palästina. *Zeitschrift des Deutschen Palästina-Vereins* 40: 1-103.

Thomson, W. M.
1880   *The Land and the Book,* vol. 3. New York: Harper.

Thorley, J.
1969   The Development of Trade Between the Roman Empire and the East Under Augustus. *Greece and Rome* (2nd Series) 16: 209-223.

Toynbee, J. M. C.
1971   *Death and Burial in the Roman World.* London: Thames and Hudson.

Trigger, B. G.
1968   Major Concepts of Archaeology in Historical Perspective. *Man* 3: 526-541.

1971   Archeology and Ecology. *World Archeology* 2: 321-336.

Tristram, H. B.
1865   *The Land of Israel: A Journal of Travels in Palestine, Undertaken with Special Reference to Its Physical Character.* London: Society for Promoting Christian Knowledge.

1873   *The Land of Moab: Travels and Discoveries on the East Side of the Dead Sea and the Jordan.* New York: Harper & Brothers.

1880   *The Natural History of the Bible.* London: Society for Promoting Christian Knowledge.

Turnbull, C. M.
1972   *The Mountain People.* New York: Simon and Schuster.

Ucko, P. J., and Dimbleby, G. W., eds.
1969   *The Domestication and Exploitation of Plants and Animals.* Chicago: Aldine Publishing Co.

Upham, S.
1984   Adaptive Diversity and Southwestern Abandonment. *Journal of Anthropological Research* 40: 235-256.

Van Elderen, B.
1978   Area A. *Andrews University Seminary Studies* 16: 19-30.

1986   Byzantine Churches and Mosaics in Transjordan. Pp. 237-246 in *The Archaeology of Jordan and Other Studies,* eds. L. T. Geraty and L. G. Herr. Berrien Springs, MI: Andrews University Press.

Van Zyl, A. H.
1960   *The Moabites.* Leiden: Brill.

Vatikiotis, P. J.
1967   *Politics and the Military in Jordan: A Study of the Arab Legion.* New York: Frederick A. Praeger.

Vayda, P., and McCay, J.
1975   New Directions in Ecology and Ecological Anthropology. *Annual Review of Anthropology* 4: 293-306.

Vita-Finzi, C.
1978   *Archaeological Sites in their Setting.* London: Thames and Hudson.

Von den Driesch, A., and Boessneck, J.
forth-   Final Report on the Zooarchaeological
coming Investigation on Animal Bone Finds
         from Tell Hesban, Jordan. In *Faunal
         Remains: Taphonomical and Zooar-
         chaeological Studies of the Animal
         Remains from Tell Hesban and Vicinity.
         Hesban 13.* Berrien Springs, MI:
         Andrews University Press.

Von Oppenheim, M. F.
1943   *Die Beduinen.* Band II. Leipzig: Otto
         Harrassowitz.

Von Thünen, J. H.
1930   *Der Isolierte Staat in Beziehung auf
         Landwirtschaft und Nationalökonomie.*
         Jena, Germany: Fischer.

Waldbaum, J. C.
1980   The First Archaeological Appearance of
         Iron and the Transition to the Iron Age.
         Pp. 69-98 in *The Coming of the Iron
         Age,* eds. T. A. Wertime and J. D.
         Muhly. New Haven: Yale University
         Press.

Wallerstein, I.
1974   *The Modern World System: Capitalist
         Agriculture and the Origins of the
         European World-Economy in the Six-
         teenth Century.* New York: Academic
         Press, Inc.

Walpole, G. F.
1948   Land Problems in Transjordan. *Journal
         of the Royal Central Asian Society* 35.1:
         52-65.

Warren, Captain R. E.
1869   Expedition to East of Jordan, July and
         August, 1867. *Palestine Exploration
         Fund* 1: 284-311, 381-388.

Waterhouse, S. D., and Ibach, R.
1975   The Topographical Survey. *Andrews
         University Seminary Studies* 13: 217-233.

Watson, A. M.
1974   The Arab Agricultural Revolution and
         Its Diffusion, 700-1100. *Journal of
         Economic History* 34.1: 8-33.

1981   A Medieval Green Revolution: New
         Crops and Farming Techniques in the
         Early Islamic World. Pp. 29-58 in *The
         Islamic Middle East, 700-1900,* ed. A. L.
         Udovitch. Princeton: Darwin Press, Inc.

Watson, P. J.
1980   The Theory and Practice of Ethnoarche-
         ology with Special Reference to the
         Near East. *Paleorient* 6: 55-60.

Weightman, G. H.
1970   The Circassians. Pp. 91-98 in *Readings
         in Arab Middle Eastern Societies and
         Cultures,* eds. A. M. Lutfiyya and C. W.
         Churchill. The Hague, Netherlands:
         Mouton & Co.

Weiler, D.
1981   Saeugetierknochenfunde vom Tell
         Hesban in Jordanien. Doctor of
         Veterinary Medicine dissertation.
         Ludwig-Maximilian University, Munich.

Wenke, R. J.
1981   Explaining the Evolution of Cultural
         Complexity: A Review. Pp. 79-127 in
         *Advances in Archaeological Method and
         Theory,* vol. 4, ed. M. B. Schiffer. New
         York: Academic Press, Inc.

White, K. D.
1970   *Roman Farming.* New York: Cornell
         University Press.

White, L. A.
1943   Energy and the Evolution of Culture.
         American Anthropologist 45: 335-56.

1947   Evolutionism in Cultural Anthropology:
         A Rejoinder. *American Anthropologist*
         49: 400-11.

Wimmer, D. H.
1978   Heshbon 1976: Area G.4, 13, 15.
         Andrews University Seminary Studies
         16: 149-166.

Wing, E. S., and Brown, A. B.
1979   *Paleonutrition: Method and Theory in
         Prehistoric Foodways.* New York:
         Academic Press.

Winterhalder, B.
1978   Environmental Analysis in Human Evolution and Adaptation Research. *Human Ecology* 8: 135-170.

Wright, G. E.
1966   *Biblical Archaeology.* Philadelphia: Westminster Press.

1974   The Tell: Basic Unit for Reconstructing Complex Societies in the Near East. Pp. 123-143 in *Reconstructing Complex Societies,* ed. C. B. Moore. Supplement to the *Bulletin of the American Schools of Oriental Research* No. 20.

Yacoub, S.
1969   Sociological Evaluation of a Pilot Project for Bedouin Settlement. *Faculty of Agricultural Sciences, Publication No. 40.* Beirut: American University of Beirut.

Yellen, J. E., and Lee, R. B.
1976   *Kalahari Hunter-Gatherers.* Cambridge: Harvard University Press.

Zayadine, F.
1985   Caravan Routes Between Egypt and Nabataea and the Voyage of Sultan Baibars to Petra in 1276. Pp. 159-174 in *Studies in the History and Archaeology of Jordan II,* ed. A. Hadidi. Amman: Department of Antiquities.

Zenner, W. P.
1972   Aqiili Agha: The Strongman in the Ethnic Relations of the Ottoman Galilee. *CSSH* 14: 169-192.

Ziadeh, N. A.
1953   *Urban life in Syria under the Early Mamluks.* Beirut: American University of Beirut. Oriental Series.

Zohary, M.
1962   *Plant Life of Palestine.* New York: Ronald Press Co.

ARABIC SUMMARY OF VOLUME

Translated by
Adnan Hadidi

حسبـــــــان ١

حضـــــارة وبـــــــداوه

دورات النظام الغذائي في حسبان وضواحيها بشرقي الاردن

بقـــلم اوستن سكالا لبينكـــا

منشورات جامعة اندروز (١٩٨٧)

الموزعون آيزنبراون صب ٢٧٥، وينونا ليك ، انديانا ٤٦٥٩٠ ، الولايات المتحـــــده

معد للتوزيع صيف عام ١٩٨٨.

هذا المجلد هو الاول من ١٤ مجلدا تشمل النتائج النهائيه لمشروع تل حسبان. وفيـــــه سرد للاحداث والنشاطات الحياتيه للسكان الذين عاشوا في حسبان وضواحيها بشرقـــــي الاردن. ويروى المجلد حكاية هؤلاء السكان عبر ثلاثة آلاف وخمسمائة عام أى منذ اواخر العصر البرونزى الى يومنا هذا، وهي حكاية اناس كانت حياتهم تتأرجح بين الولاء لحياة البـداوه وقيمـها والمحافظه عليها أو لحياة الاستقرار والتحضر وقيمها والتمسك بهـــا . ان مجلد حسبــان ١ يصف المكتشفات الاثريه ويسرد لنا متى وكيف ولماذا كان هذا التأرجح بين انماط الحياة البدويه والحضريه من خلال تحليل هذه المكتشفات .

ويتصل بهذا الموضوع اتصالا وثيقا النشاط الفكرى الذى بذله العلماء القائمون علـــــى هذا المشروع خلال عشرين عامـا من البحث والتحليل . ونتعرف من قصة هذا النشاط الفكرى على كيفية تطور الاهداف ووجهات النظر من بداية بسيطة ومحدوده تمثلت في محاولة معرفة طبيعة حدث توراتي معين (احتلال بني اسرائيل للاراضي الكنعانيه) الى ان اصبحـــــت اهدافا واهتمامات واسعة وشامله لتاريخ انماط معيشة السكان وحياتهم اليوميه ودراسة طبيعة التغيرات والتطورات التي طرأت على الثقافه في مناطق وسط الاراضي الاردنيـــه . ان هذا التركيز في البحث بالنسبة لايعني اهمال المسائل التاريخيه والاثريه التقليديه وانما بذل من الاهتمام لفهم حياة الناس ونشاطاتهم المعيشيه في اطار الاحداث السياسيه المؤثـره .

الفصــــــل الاول

المشكله : بين النظرية والواقـــــــــع

يتركز الحديث في الفصل الاول على بيان المنهج الذى اتبعه الباحثون في اعادة تصويـــر النشاطات المعيشيه وتغيراتها ، وهو ما يسمى بمفهوم النظام الغذائي. وبعد استعـــراض جذور هذا النظام الغذائي في الابحاث الانثروبولوجيه البريطانيه والفرنسيه والاميركيه فان ثمة تعريف يقدمه لنا المؤلف وفيه يؤكد الوحده المركبه القائمه بين نشاطــــات الانسان الخاصه بالحصول على الغذاء وتجهيزه وتوزيعه وتحضيره وثم استهلاكه والتخلــــص من فضلاته. لقد استغل الانسان جل وقته في تامين الغذاء والنشاطات المتصله بذلك كمـا ان ما عثر عليه في الحفريات الاثريه من مباني ومنشآت وادواتوبقايا متحجرة لنباتــات وحيوانات ما هي الا شواهد على ان هذا النشاط كان يحتل جزءا كبيرا من حياة البشــــر.

ومن اجل بيان التغيرات التي طرأت على اسلوب الانسان في الحصول على الغذاء خلال الزمن في منطقة معينه ، فان المؤلف يوصي في الفصل الاول هذا بتركيز البحث حول خمس نقـــاط رئيسيه ذات صلة بانظمه الغذاء والتي يمكن توضيحها بالشواهد الاثريه. وبالتحديد فان المؤلف يقترح بان يجرى تحليل الشواهد الفعليه المكتشفه بما يمكن ان يدلنا علـــــى المتغيرات التي طرأت على البيئة الطبيعيه واماكن الاستقرار البشرى واستعمالات الاراضي والاحوال الغذائيه. وبالنسبة للدراسة التي يشمل عليها هذا الكتاب فان المتغيـــرات الخاصه بنظام الغذاء جرى التأكد منها بواسطة تحليل مصادر المعلومات العشر الاتيـــه : وصف الطبقات الاثريه وتصنيف الفخاريات وتسجيل المكتشفات الصغيره وعظام الحيوانــــات والحبوب المتفحمه وما عثر عليه اثناء المسح الاثرى والبيئي والمكتشفات الاثنواركيولوجيه وسجلات الرحاله الاوائل والمصادر الثانويه المدونه.

ومما يلفت النظر هو عدم التوازن الذى نجده في بحوث الانثروبولوجيا بالنسبة لتفسيـــر اسباب تغير نظم الغذاء وكيفية حدوثها. فبينما نجد هذه البحوث تزخر بالتفسيـــرات العلميه الدقيقه بالنسبة لاسباب ازدهار هذه النظم ، فاننا بالمقابل نجدها تقدم لنـا تفسيرات محدوده جدا فيما يتعلقباسباب انحطاط هذه النظم أو تداعيها. ان اهم ما تهدف

اليه هذه الدراسه هو الاسهام في تلافي عدم التوازن هذا٠ ومن اجل ذلــــك فان الفصل الاول يعرض مفهوم التخفيف كوسيلة للوصول الى حل وسط حينما يشتـــد التكثيف من الناحية الثانيه ٠

ولتزويد الباحثين المهتمين بنظام الغذاء وتغيراته باسباب او بتطورات توئخـــذ بعين الاعتبار لتفسير مراحل اشتداد الكثافه الغذائيه وتخفيفها، فان الفصـــل الاول يحتوى على نظرة شموليه لامكانية تغير الوسائل ، التى جميعها مأخوذ مـــن مراجعة للمصادر الثانويه المناسبه٠ ويدور البحث حول ثماني وسائل او تقنيات توئدى الى تكثيف نظام الغذاء- ويشمل ذلك الابتكار ونمو السكان والمركزيه لارتفاع تكلفــه النقل والفرص الجديده والتخصص في الحرف ونشوء الدول والبيروقراطيه وتغيير اماكـــن الغذاء - وكذلك سبع وسائل توئدى الى نقص نظام الغذاء - ويشمل ذلك مخاطر التخزيـــن وضياع الفرص وفرط الالتحام وسوء التخطيط والتخلف والمجاعات والاوئبئه ٠

الفصـــــــل الثانـــــــي
الحضـــــــارة والبـــــداوة

يعرض الفصل الثاني المحور الاخر الذى يدور حوله البحث ٠ ويتألف ذلك من نقــاش يرتكز على المصادر الثانويه ، لبعض الاسباب المؤديه الى مرونة الوحدات الاجتماعيــه في الشرق الاوسط٠ فمثلا هنالك جدل انه بينما ان الاخطار الطبيعيه وخصوصا نقــص المياه قد ادت من ناحية تقليديه الى ضرورة انتشار المخاطره من خلال عدة امكانيات للاعتماد على الحيوانات والمحاصيل الموسميه في انتاج الغذاء فان الانظمه الاجتماعيـه كاحترام الاب او كبار السن والتمسك بالشرف وواجبات الضيافه والتي تعتبر من المثــل التي تملأ الثغرات او الفوارق الناجمه عن عدم تواصل او انتظام وسائل المعيشــــه ٠ وعلاوه على ذلك فانه بينما ان التغيرات البيئية والسياسيه والاجتماعيه جعلت الانتقا ل في حالات فرديه في اماكن وازمان مختلفه - من حالة البداوه الى حالة التحضـــــر والاستقرار او العكس ضرورة ملحه ، نجد ان الايمان بمفاهيم مشتركه قد سهل كثيرا هذه التحولات او التغيرات ٠ ان النتائج التاريخيه لهذا الوضع في الشرق الاوسط خــــلا ل

القرون أو الاف السنين الماضيه هو اننا نجد انماط أو اشكال التحضر والبداوه مرتبطه ارتباطا وثيقا بانماط أو سائل تكثيف النظام الغذائي أو نقصه. ويجد القارىء امثله على ذلك في بحوث روبرت الدامز عن انماط الاستقرار البشرى في بلاد ما بين النهرين وفي دراسة دوغلاس جونسون حول موضوع الاستقرار ووسائل المعيشه في الجبل الاخضر في مقاطعة سيرنيه في ليبيا.

الفصــــل الثالـــــث

النظام الغذائي في حسبان خلال الماضي القريب

يدور اطار البحث الثالث فيهذا المجلد حول الابحاث الاثنواركيولوجيه التي اجريت في هذه المنطقه لتحديد مراجع اختباريه لكل عنصر من العناصر الخمس المتعلقه بالنظام الغذائي التي سبق ذكرها في الفصل الاول. وبالاضافه الى ذلك ، فان هذا البحث الذى يعالج الماضي القريب واحواله ضمن المشروع الدراسي يهئ لنا الفرصه للفحص عن كثب تلك التغيرات الحديثه التي طرات على مجتمع حسبان ومعرفه مدى ارتباطها بتغير الغذاء ؛ ومدى ارتباط تغير استعمالات الاراضي بالتغيرات التي حدثت في مجال الاداره وهلم جـرا .

وسنجد بنهاية هذا البحث انه يمكن التعرف على ثلاث مراحل أو مستويات من كثافة النظام الغذائي وهي : مرحله ضعيفه كان الاعتماد فيها على الرعي الموسمي ومرحلة متوسطه تميزت بانتاج الحبوب حول القرى وثم مرحلة اشتد فيها الانتاج الغذائي نتيجة الاستقرار الحضرى والزراعة المنظمه. ومن ناحية تاريخيه فقد سادت المرحله الاول خلال الفتره الاخيره من العصر العثماني والثانيه خلال اوائل العصر الحديث واما الثالثة فكانت خلال العصر الحديث من تاريخ شرقي الاردن . وتساعدنا هذه النتائج على الاكتشاف بانفسنا المتغيرات وبالنشاطات المرتبطه بالنظام الغذائي الذى يمكننا من الاستمرار بالبحث لمعرفه التغييرات التي حدثت في الماضي وذلك بالاسترشاد بالمعلومات التي يزودنا بها علم الاثار.

الفصــــــل الرابــــــع

الاستدلال على طرق الانظمه الغذائيه من المعلومات الاثريه

لقد كان من نتائج التعرف على طرق الانظمه الغذائيه على اثر الانتهاء من البحــــث
الاثرى الميداني (عام ١٩٧٨) هو تلك الفجوه بين المعلومات الاثريه المكتشفه مـــن
جهة وبين ما كان الباحثون يتوقعون العثور عليه من جهة ثانيه حسب هذا المنهج العلمي
الجديد، ان ابرز هذه الفجوات مثلا هو ان الحفرية الاثريه في تل حسبان والمسح الاثــرى
للمنطقة المحيطه به كانا يتركزان على " التل الاثرى، نفسه، وكان هذا يعنى بالطبـــع
ان البحث يتركز على اكتشاف معلومات اثريه عن اناس يعيشون في حسبان هم في الاصـــل
من السكان المتحضرين ، علما بان من اهداف المشروع الاثرى اصلا هو دراسة اوضــــاع
السكان الذين يعيشون حياة البداوه (وان ذلك كان من الاهتمامات الرئيسيه للفريــــق
المختص بعلم الاثنواركيولوجي) .

وبعد ان يستعرض المولف في الفصل الرابع الاطار العلمي الذى يحدد مسار مشروع حسبان
وطريقة تنفيذه ،ينتقل الى توضيح الاجراءات التي ابتعت في شرح البراهين المتعلقــــه
بالتغيرات بالنسبة للابعاد الخمسة الخاصه بالنظام الغذائي . كما يشرح استعمال هذه
البراهين للدلالة على التغيرات التي ادت الى التحول من حياة التحضر الى حياة البداوة
ومن اجل ذلك يستعمل المولف ثلاث فرضيات بسيطه لتلخيص ما سبق الاستفادة منه من البحث
الاثنواركيولوجي الوارد شرحه في الفصل الثالث ، وتشتمل على اشكال فيها عناصـــر
مختلفه بالنسبة للنظام الغذائي في حسبان وضواحيها وتتفاعل هذه العناصر بقوة متفاوته
تبعا لشدة الاحوال الملازمه :

الاشكال الغذائيه ذات الكثافة الضعيفه وتتميز بتنوع كبير من النباتات وانــــواع
الحيوانات ،واختلاف في المواسم المحليه وكثافة سكانيه ناجمه عن الهجرات الداخليـه ،
وانتشار النشاط الرعوى وقلة الزراعه وعدم تواصل المعرفة بالفنون الزراعيه وشيـــوع
اسلوب الاعتماد في الغذاء على ما يمكن ان تنتجه الحيوانات او ما تعطيه الارض مـــن
حبوب وفاكهه موسميه وعلى الصيد وجمع الثمار البريه .

اشكال الكثافه الغذائيه المتوسطه وتتميز بتنوع معتدل لانتشار النباتات وانواع الحيوانات ، وتغيرات موسميه معتدله ايضا في الاماكن والكثافه السكانيه الناجمه عن ازدياد اعداد الاسر المستقره ، وانتشار العنايه بالمحاصيل الزراعيه والمحافظه على التربه في السهول الخصبه والوديان ، وانتشار تقنيات العنايه بمصادر المياه وتوزيعها ، وشيوع تأسيس المزارع أو القرى الحصينه واستعمال الماشيه للحراثه ، وشيوع الاعتماد في الغذاء على مشتقات الانتاج الزراعي مدعوما بزراعة الحدائق الخاصه والبساتين وتربية الخراف والماعز والدجاج والطيور.

اشكال الكثافه الغذائيه العاليه وتتميز بتنوع منخفض لانتشار انواع النباتات والحيوانات ، ومحدودية الاختلاف الموسمي في الاماكن وفي الكثافه السكانيه لازدياد اعداد الاسر المستقره ، وشيوع الاعتماد على المحاصيل الزراعيه من الحقول والحدائق والبساتين وخصوصا في المرتفعات ، انتشار المعرفه التقنيه بالمحافظه على مصادر المياه وتوزيعها ، والصناعات الغذائيه ووسائل النقل والتسويق في المدن والقرى وانتشار استعمال البغال والخيل للحراثه ، وشيوع استعمال الفواكه والخضار المستورده في المدن وبعض الارياف نتيجه ازدهار التجاره الخارجيه.

الفصل الخامس

اشكال النظام الغذائي في عصر الحديد حوالي ١٢٠٠ ــ ٥٠٠ قبل الميلاد

اذا جمعنا خيوط البراهيين المتوفره عن الالف عام التي امتد عبرها عصر الحديد في حسبان وضواحيها ، فان الصوره المتوفره هي لشعب تتأرجح حياته بين حياة البداوه والحضاره نتيجه تفاعله مع رياح الاحداث او التقلبات السياسيه. وكانت المجتمعات الرعويه خلال هذا الالف عام من هذا العصر تنقلب باستمرار بين الحياة الزراعيه والحياه الرعويه. وبين القرن الثاني عشر والقرن السادس قبل الميلاد نجد معدل نسبة السكان الزراعيين تزيد عن نسبة البدو الرحل مما ادى الى نشوء القرى وتعاظم استعمالات الاراضي التي

ان بلغ شكل الكثافه الحضريه اقصاه في القرن السابع قبل الميلاد.

ان اثار هذه الفتره المتميزه بكثافة الانتاج الغذائي تشمل بقايا المزارع الحصينه والابراج والابيار والخزان الكبير للمياه في تل حسبان. بالاضافه الى المحاصيل الوفيره من الفواكه والخضار والحبوب وتربية قطعان الماشيه والاغنام. كما واكتشف عدد كبير من الاختام والرموز التي تدل على السلطه مما يشير الى ان نخبة متحضره وثريه كانت تسيطر على الانتاج الزراعي وتوزيعه آنذاك. وكانت عودة المجتمعات الرعويه بنهاية الفترة الثانيه من عصر الحديد الى الظهور قد ادت الى هجر هذه المنشآت الزراعيه ثم نجدها تعود الى الازدهار مره ثانيه في القرن الخامس قبل الميلاد واستمرت احوال البداوه هذه في الانتشار الى ان ظهر شكل ضعيف من النظام الغذائي في القرن الرابع قبل الميلاد. ويبدو ان هذا الشكل من حياة البداوه استمر في الانتشار خلال القرن الثالث والثاني قبل الميلاد لتقلص عدد المواقع الزراعيه خلال هذه القرون.

الفصل السادس
النظام الغذائي خلال الالف عام من العصر الاغريقي ـ الروماني
٣٣٣ ق . م . ـ ٦٣٠ م .

اصبحت حسبان في العصر الهلينستي منطقة قرويه وحولها سكان رعويون يمتلكون قطعان الجمال تغلب عليهم صفات الحياة البدويه. وكان تل حسبان نفسه أو أسبوس خاليا من السكان حتى اواخر العصر الهلينستي ، حين اخذت جماعات من الناس الاستقرار فيه وكانت ادواتهم وطريقة حياتهم اغريقيه لان تل حسبان اتخذ طابع القلعه في هذه الفتره واغلب سكانه كانوا من الجنود المزارعين وكانوا يزرعون الحقول بنشاط كبير وتنوعت محاصيلهم لتشمل القمح والشعير والذره والحمص والعدس والفاصوليا. كان هؤلاء السكان يعملون على نشر الافكار الحضاريه الاغريقيه الى جانب سعيهم لادخال الوسائل الزراعيه الحضريه.

وفي العصر الروماني المبكر استمرت اسبوس قلعة حصينه تمارس حولها انواع من الزراعة المحدوده ويقيم في مناطقها جماعات من الرعاه ٠ وفي أواخر العصر الروماني تسارع النشاط الحضرى في اسبوس واشتد استعمال الاراضي في الاماكن المرتفعه والجبليه ومما زاد في هذا النشاط الحضرى والزراعي ان اسبوس تحولت الى محطة تجاريه على الطريق المعروف باسم طريق اسبوس ـ ليفياس كما ارتبطت المدينه بالطريق الملكي الذى اصبح اسمه في العصر الروماني : طريق تراجان (فيا نوفا ترايانا) وهو الطريق الرئيسي الشهير الممتد من شمال الاردن الى جنوبها ٠ ورافق هذا التوسع الحضرى والازدهار الاقتصادى انتشار زراعة الاشجار المثمرة في المنطقة الواقعة بين حسبان جنوبا الى عمان ـ فيلادلفيا شمالا ٠ وهنالك براهين اثريه تشير الى ان بعض الناس اخذوا يهجرون مزارعهم في المرتفعات الشماليه وفي سهول حسبان ٠ وهكذا برز الى حيز الوجود نوع من الاستقطاب الاجتماعي والزراعي في اواخر العصر الروماني ٠ فبينما ان جماعات من سكان الارياف اخذوا يهاجرون الى المدن والقرى نجد ان آخرين بدأوا يقودون الى حياة المجتمعات الرعويه بدليل اكتشاف عدد كبير من عظام الجمال والماشيه في الطبقات الاثريه من اواخر العصر الروماني ٠ وبلغت حسبان ذروة النشاط الزراعي والغذائي خلال العصر البيزنطي٠ واكتشفت بقايا كثيره لوسائل الرى الشبيهة بالاسلوب النبطي والتقنيات النبطيه بالاضافه الى الخزانات المائيه بالاسلوب الروماني وكذلك طواحين الماء المستخدمه في هذا العصر٠ وفي هذا الزمن ازداد عدد القرى والمدن٠ ومن ناحية ثانيه تقلص عدد المجتمعات الروعويه وقلت اعداد الجمال التي كان يرعاها البدو الرحل وذلك لانتشار الزراعه الحضريه ، واشتداد الحاجه الى استعمال الاراضي للفلاحه والزراعه ٠ وقد ادى ابعاد رعاة الجمال عن المناطق المأهوله والزراعيه في شرقي الاردن ومناطق اخرى في الامبراطوريه البيزنطيه الى ازدياد عدد القبائل البدويه في الصحارى والقفار ، وبمرور الزمن انضمت هذه القبائل الى صفوف الجيوش العربيه التي استولت على العالم الاغريقي ـ الروماني القديم تحت راية الاسلام٠

الفصـــل الســـابع

النظام الغذائي في العصر الاسلامـــــــــــــي ٦٣٠ - ١٩٠٠م.

لقد انتشر في الشرق الاوسط خلال عدة قرون منذ نهاية العصر الروماني الــــي يومنا هذا تمازج حضاري تلاقت خلاله المصالح المشتركه للقبائل الريفيه وسكــان المدن المثقفين في اطار التعاليم الاسلاميه التي بشر بها النبي محمد صلــــى الله عليه وسلـــم. لقد كان تاريخ حسبان خلال العصر الاسلامي يتميز بالمرونـــه التي ابداها السكان امام رياح التغييرات السياسيه او الاقتصاديه المتقلبـــه خلال مئات السنين. وتنعكس هذه الظاهره التاريخيه في ما عثر عليه من آثــار ماديه في منطقة حسبان وباستعمالات الاراضي. وتشير هذه المكتشفات الى ان نظام غذائي متوسط الكثافه واحيانا ضعيف الكثافه كان هو النمط المألوف في هــــذا العصر نتيجة الاضطرابات السياسيه المتلاحقه وتبدل الاحوال الاقتصاديه.

ويعرض المؤلف في الفصل السابع عدة نماذج جديده من الانظمه الغذائية فــي شرقي الاردن خلال العصر الاسلامي ، فنهالك على سبيل المثال تحليل لاثر الثـــوره الزراعيه العربيه في انتاج الغذاء في منطقة حسبان وضواحيها وخصوصا الممارسا ت الزراعيه في العصرين الايوبي والمملوكي . كما يشرح المؤلف الدور المميــــز لمفهوم "القصر" أو المزرعة الحصينه في ايام القلاقل والحروب أو الاضطرابـــات السياسيه والتي كانت تتيح للبدو أو رجال القبائل الريفيه التحرك نحو المناطق الزراعيه واماكن الاستقرار الحضرى. كما يعالج في هذا الفصل دور الكهوف التـي كانت تستعمل اماكن اقامة موءقته للزراع أو الفلاحين خلال العصر العثماني.

الفصـــل الثامـــــن

غزارة الانتاج الغذائي وقلتـــــــه

ان هذا الفصل الاخير من مجلد حسبان ١ يعطينا صورة اجماليه عن التغييرات فـي الانتاج الغذائي وانماط المعيشه في حسبان وضواحيها منذ اواخر العصر البرونزى

وفيه مقترحات عن الاسباب التى ادت الى حدوث دورات متعاقبه من ازدياد الانتاج الغذائي احيانا ونقصانه احيانا اخرى · فالموءلف يعتقد مثلا ان الزراعه كانت اصعب في الجبال الاردنيه منها في جبال الضفة الغربيه · والسبب في رأيه هـو قرب الجبال الاردنيه من الصحراء ، مما يقلل من الرطوبه اللازمه لنمو النباتات والاشجار ولحياة البشر اجمالا · كما ان القبائل البدويه القاطنه في الصحراء كانت تشكل خطرا في معظم الاحيان على المحاصيل الزراعيه · وهكذا فان الروتين الاداري للتنظيم الاجتماعي الذى تتميزبه اشكال الانظمه الغذائيه لم يلاقي قبولا في شرقي الاردن نظرا لتأصل القبليه وعاداتها بين السكان· ويختـم الموءلف الفصل بالحديث عن امكانات الاستفاده من هذا البحث في مشروعات تطويـر انظمه الانتاج الغذائي في الاردن·

نبذه عن الموءلـــــف

عمل اوستين ساكالا لابيانكا في مشروع حفريات ودراسة تل حسبان باشراف الاساتـــذه سيغفريد ه · هورن ولورنس ت · جيراتي وروجر س· بوراس منذ عام ١٩٧٠ · وكانـــت مهماته بصفته عالم انشروبولوجيا مسوءول في المشروع تشمل تحليل بقايا الحيونات والنباتات في الميدان وذلك بالتعاون مع المشرفين عن المسوحات الاثنواركيولوجيه والجيولوجيه · وكان ايضا قد قام بنفس الواجبات في مشروع وادى تميلات باشــراف الاستاذ جون س· هولندى وذلك في مصر· كما يساعد الدكتور لورنس ت· جيراتي في نشر النتائج النهائيه لمشروع حسبان منذ عام ١٩٧٦· وقد امضى جل وقته حينما كان دارسا في المركز الاميركي للابحاث الشرقيه في عمان بعد حصوله على منحة فولبرايت لمدة سبعة شهور في جمع المعلومات وتحليلها ودراستها تمهيدا لنشر هذا المجلد الاول من سلسلة مجلدات حسبان· وعلى اثر عودته الى جامعة اندروز عام ١٩٨١ شارك في تأسيس معهد الاثار فيها· والموءلف يعمل حاليا مديرا مشاركـا في مشروع سهول مادبا الاثرى الاثنواركيولوجي ،مسوءولا عن المختبر الميداني لدراسة البيئه· وهو يعمل ايضا استاذا مشاركا في جامعة اندروز لتدريس علم الانشروبولوجيا ورئيسا لدائرة العلوم المسلكيه·

ولابيانكا حاصل على درجة الدكتوراه في علم الانثروبولوجيا من جامعة براندايـــس
(١٩٨٧) وهو متزوج من آستا ساكالا لابيانكا التي ساعدته في اعداد بحوثـــــــه .
ولهم من الاولاد ثلاثه هم آريك وآرين وايفان .

AUTHOR INDEX

Author Index

GENERAL INDEX

General Index

329